THE AGE OF ENTERPRISE

*the text of this book is printed
on 100% recycled paper*

THE AGE OF ENTERPRISE

A Social History of Industrial America

REVISED EDITION

by *Thomas C. Cochran*
and *William Miller*

HARPER TORCHBOOKS
Harper & Row, Publishers
New York, Hagerstown, San Francisco, London

CONTENTS

PREFACE TO THE TORCHBOOK EDITION ix
PREFACE TO THE FIRST EDITION xiii

I. INTRODUCTION I

II. THE OLD AND THE NEW 3
How Transportation Built Markets 6
False Starts in Manufacturing 8
Conditions for Success 12
The Industrial Workers 18
Decline of the Crafts 23
The Metamorphosis of Society 27

III. THE INTENSIVE FRONTIER 30
The Captive South 32
Settling the West 36
The Panic of 1837 43
England Learns a Lesson 47
The Agrarian Revolt 49

IV. THE EARLY RAILROAD AGE 52
Enterprise Moves West 53
Paced by Machines 56
The Pressures of Overhead Costs 59
The Worker in the Town 63
The Corporation and the Nation's Business 67
Business and the State 77
The Panic of 1857 81
Optimism and Protest 86

PAGE

V. TRIAL BY BATTLE   90
   The House Divided   92
   The Road to War   98
   First Things First 104
   Preparing for "Progress" 111
   Profits for Whom? 117

VI. A PHILOSOPHY FOR INDUSTRIAL
     PROGRESS 119
   Patterns of Heresy 120
   The Magnificent Exegesis 121
   Herbert Spencer: Apostle to the Americans 124

VII. THE TRIUMPH OF INDUSTRIAL
     ENTERPRISE 129
   Railroad Imperialism 130
   The Industrial Scene 135
   Pools, Trusts, and Corporations 140
   Other People's Money 146
   Industrial Society 150

VIII. THE BUSINESS OF POLITICS 154
   "Nothing Counts Except to Win" 156
   The End of the Spoilsmen 160
   Elections Without Issues 164
   The Defense of National Business 168
   The High Priests 177

IX. THE RISE OF FINANCE CAPITALISM 181
   A Technological Revolution 183
   The Consolidation of Business Government 188
   The "Money Trust" 192
   Beyond Continental Frontiers 202

X. COMMERCIAL FARMERS IN AN
     INDUSTRIAL AGE 211
   Planning and Planting 213
   Marketing and Credit 215

X. COMMERCIAL FARMERS IN AN
      INDUSTRIAL AGE (*Continued*)
   Politics and Self-Help 219
   The Misuse of Prosperity, 1897–1920 222
   The End of an Era 225

XI. INDUSTRY AND LABOR 228
   The Broadening Gulf 230
   Labor's Welfare Campaigns 233
   The Prophets of Radical Change 236
   The Employers' Campaign of Resistance 238
   Welfare Capitalism 243

XII. INDUSTRY AND THE CITY 249
   The Façade of Business Culture 251
   Prosperity of the "Upper Half" 256
   How the Other Half Lived 261
   Why the Cities Were Misgoverned 265
   The Imperialism of Urban Culture 268

XIII. PRESSURE POLITICS IN AN AGE OF
       REFORM 273
   The Progressives Organize 276
   Meeting Business Resistance in the States 281
   The National Theater 284
   The "New Freedom" 291
   Farewell to Reform 295

XIV. THE CLIMAX OF FINANCE CAPITALISM . 298
   The First World War 300
   A Revolution in Business Techniques 303
   The Search for New Opportunities 309
   The Fabulous Boom of the Twenties 315
   The End of Prosperity 321

XV. THE LEADERSHIP OF BUSINESS 323
   The Decline of Individualism 326
   Directing Corporate Society 331

CONTENTS

PAGE

XV. THE LEADERSHIP OF BUSINESS
 (*Continued*)
  Politics During the Boom 342
  The Promise of the Arts 348

XVI. EPILOGUE 354

 BOOKS FOR READING AND REFERENCE 359

 INDEX 369

PREFACE TO THE
TORCHBOOK EDITION

When *The Age of Enterprise* was first written, the American economy, stimulated by war orders from Europe and what were then called "defense" orders at home, had just begun to emerge from the cataclysmic depression of the 1930's. Since then the United States has engaged in World War II, the Korean War, and the continuing Cold War with Communism; and "defense" has continued to play a large part in American economic activity. At the same time, the so-called stabilizers built into the economic system by the New Deal—federal unemployment insurance, social security for the aged, housing subsidies, and farm price supports—helped significantly to soften the occasional slumps and recessions of the 1950's. The reforming surge of the early Roosevelt administrations had been spent even before F.D.R. had ventured, unprecedentedly, to run for a third term in 1940. So far as the economy itself is concerned, there has been little occasion for a renewal of the reform spirit, partly, of course, because the state has assumed a seemingly permanent role in business affairs and a seemingly permanent responsibility for the general welfare.

In the closing paragraph of the first edition of this book, we wrote: "In a broad sense the Age of Enterprise may still be young. The 'union of business and government' . . . may yet result in even greater opportunities, greater freedom, greater wealth for the multitude than did the hustling, optimistic economy based exclusively upon private initiative." We believe we may now change "may yet result," to "did result," without doing violence to the last two decades of American economic history. If there remain some who continue to deplore the "interference" of government with the freedom of "private enterprise" in the United States, most Americans would now relegate such viewers with alarm to the diminishing heap of die-hards. There can be no return to the economy examined in detail in *The Age of Enterprise*. Yet much of the American spirit that enlivened that economy remains vigorous still, and many more Americans, perhaps, now share it.

Economic problems, of course, remain; and not least among them are the maintenance of continued high employment and continued economic growth. Yet even more, perhaps, than American revolutionary traditions and American ideas of liberty, it is the high American standard of living that is now the goad to world-wide unrest and the goal of world-wide ambition. The American standard of living has grown strikingly in the two decades since we first wrote. But its standing as a primary American "value" was firmly established during what we have called The Age of Enterprise. In that sense, we feel, our book remains not untimely, and we have, except for some small corrections and alterations here and there, left it alone.

The Age of Enterprise was written only five or six years after John Maynard Keynes published his seminal book, *The General Theory of Employment, Interest and Money*. *The Age of Enterprise* was itself first published only a year after the National Bureau of Economic Research issued Simon Kuznets's monumental study, *National Income and Its Composition, 1919–1938*. The concept of GNP, Gross National Product, had not yet come into use as a measure of general economic activity and of over-all economic growth or decline. The serious study of the history of individual business companies and even of different industries was still in its infancy. The vocabulary of social science had not yet been enriched, nor encumbered, by such terms as "role-sets," "dependency ratios," or "social overhead capital." It was part of our original purpose to write history without jargon. It would, of course, have been foolhardy for us to undertake to revise *The Age of Enterprise* to accommodate currently fashionable terminology. Most likely we could not have done it. We feel also that, without resorting to transient modes of expression, some of them, of course, illuminating, we have perhaps conveyed in our original language much of the meaning of the latest modes of thought.

In this new edition we have revised the Bibliography of *The Age of Enterprise* to bring to the attention of the reader significant new work in American economic history and related subjects. Otherwise, *The Age of Enterprise* is presented here very largely as it was first written. We are, of course, deeply gratified that our book has been so well received by professors, students, and the general public for so many years. And we are grateful to Harper & Brothers, the publishers of Torchbooks, for making it available now to what we hope will be a large new audience at a price all can afford.

Thomas C. Cochran
UNIVERSITY OF PENNSYLVANIA

William Miller
RIDGEFIELD, CONN.

May 1, 1961

PREFACE TO THE
FIRST EDITION

The Age of Enterprise is a new interpretation of the history of the United States based upon the existing monographic material in American history, economics, and related social subjects. It is not a book of original research though the authors themselves have published a few of the articles from which material has been drawn. The quotations from contemporary sources which run through the book have not been used as evidence or proof but as illustrations of conditions or opinion at any given time. Most of these quotations have been selected from secondary works with which professional historians are familiar. Our purpose has been simply to make the non-professional reader acquainted with what we believe to be at once the most useful and most easily available books and magazines which bear upon our subject. Our bibliography consists only of such books and magazines and makes no pretense of being complete. A complete bibliography of the broad fields covered in this volume would require a book as large again as this one. Such a book would be a worth-while contribution to scholarship, but we have made no effort to supply it here.

The authors, entering an unexplored field in American history, have felt peculiarly dependent upon their friends for advice and criticism. Above all, they want to thank Richard Hofstadter and Felice Swados Hofstadter for unfailing encouragement and assistance at every step in the development of the manuscript. For continuous help and many invaluable suggestions they wish also to acknowledge the contributions of Kenneth Burke; Rosamond Beebe Cochran and James Putnam of The Macmillan Company; Merle E. Curti of Columbia University; William Charvat and James O. Wettereau of New York University.

Howard K. Beale of the University of North Carolina, Henry Steele Commager of Columbia University, Paul W. Gates of Cornell University, E. A. J. Johnson and James D. Magee of New York University, Henrietta Larson of Harvard University, and Matthew Josephson have read parts of the manuscript or the proofs; and for many acute criticisms the authors wish to express their gratitude.

For secretarial work of the most efficient and good-natured kind the authors wish to thank Miss Maret Beckman and Miss Pauline Chytalo of the History Department of Washington Square College, New York University.

They feel a special debt to Mulford Martin and Virginia Lee Bliss of the Library of the School of Commerce, Accounts, and Finance of New York University for their continuous aid, but especially for their extraordinary patience over long periods during which the authors practically monopolized large portions of that library's excellent collection.

The authors, of course, are solely responsible for all errors that may occur in the book and for all opinions expressed in it.

THE AGE OF ENTERPRISE

I

INTRODUCTION

ALMOST from the start of their national experience Americans were presented with a vast continent, irrigated by numberless rivers sweeping down the sides of mountains fabulously rich in precious metals and inexhaustible supplies of fuel. America's soil was the richest in the world, her forests thick and varied. Deep harbors indented her coasts; her rivers and lakes beckoned trade. Freed from Britain when British industry was casting off the fetters of mercantilism, Americans were at liberty to develop their land, to improve their magnificent heritage, to make it yield every ounce of wealth stored for countless centuries for them to claim. To this task they gave their waking hours, and while they slept they dreamt of it.

Men's lives are determined chiefly by habits formed in daily activities. In the United States each year after 1800 more and more men spent their days in factories and mines, on canals and railroads, tending machines, locomotives, and steamboats, keeping accounts, selling commodities, digging coal, copper, lead, and iron, drilling oil and natural gas. As time passed they spent their profits, wages, and commissions on goods announced for sale in newspapers supported by business advertisements and friendly to business objectives. Their literature was issued by publishers engaged in business enterprises. Their amusements were not spontaneous street dances but spectacles staged for profit. Their colleges, founded in many cases to prepare young men for the ministry of God, became devoted to science, and their scientists became servants of business. Their public architecture concerned itself with banks, insurance offices, grand hotels for commercial travelers. Their mature philosophy discarded metaphysics—or so its practitioners claimed, describing their speculation felicitously for our pecuniary culture as the quest for the "cash value" of ideas. To get attention in industrial America, a school, a mechanical invention, a cure or a game had to be presented, as Veblen said, as a "business proposition." No one explained industrial America better than Richard Croker of Tammany Hall when he cried to Lincoln Steffens: [1]

Ever heard that business is business? Well, so is politics business, and reporting—journalism, doctoring—all professions, arts, sports—everything is business.

America has been settled mainly by enterprising immigrants seeking economic opportunities and economic freedom. That this quest has been most powerful in determining the nature of our culture, historians acknowledge when they write *economic* interpretations of our politics, our literature, our philosophy, our religion. They fail to do it justice when they make these and not business itself the kernel of their discussions. We have not been a people essentially political, literary, metaphysical, or religious. Our habits and folkways have not been formed only by voting, reading, logic-chopping or prayer. Our manners are not simply those of conventions, lyceums, schools, or churches. We have been primarily a business people, and business has been most important in our lives. Abstracting colorful aspects of our culture, historians have interpreted them naïvely in terms of the "profit motive." In doing so they have ignored the most dramatic story in our history, the story of business enterprise itself, the story of its institutions and their impact upon American society. Many aspects of this story cannot yet be told. Enormous amounts of research yet remain to be done in the relation of business to religion, education, ethics, and creative arts in the United States, as well as to other fields like charity and philosophy. It is time, however, that an attempt was made, however inadequate it may turn out, to synthesize what has already been learned, to try to chart the course of our history from a business point of view, to try also, by the mistakes that will be made, by the omissions, exaggerations, and oversimplifications that will occur, to indicate where the most profitable investigations might immediately be undertaken. These are the purposes of this book.

---

[1] Steffens, *Autobiography*, vol. I, p. 237.

THE OLD AND THE NEW

IN 1800 five million Americans were scattered over an enormous country that reached from the St. Lawrence valley to the borders of Spanish Florida, from the seacoast to the Mississippi. Not one in ten among them lived in a town of a thousand inhabitants, and all but a handful outside these towns were farmers. They grew food for their own tables and staples like wheat and corn in the North, tobacco, rice, and cotton in the South. They made their own clothes, blankets, candles, soap, furniture, rum, and cider. They cut their own logs, built their own fences, erected their own barns and houses. Only infrequently did they visit local merchants whose general stores carried sugar, coffee, salt, paint, guns, gunpowder, hardware, china, glass, and finer textiles than could be woven at home.[1] More often they dealt with blacksmiths and brickmakers, with cobblers, coopers, dyers, and tanners, each of whom in his own village had a virtual monopoly of the services required by rural communities and their household industries.

American provincialism was intense at the beginning of the nineteenth century. Communication among the larger cities was slight, and among towns and villages it was even more limited. Roads were few and in abominable condition. Turnpikes and canals were just beginning to be built. There were no railroads, telegraphs, or telephones, and the post office in 1800 handled altogether three million letters, much less than one per person per year. News traveled very slowly, and information once acquired about prices and credit in other villages could be used only with enormous difficulty and expense. No wonder then that

---

[1] Jones, *Middlemen*, p. 44.

3

competition, outside the great seaports, was dormant, that enterprise was stifled, that the Nation for all its political independence was still a colony looking to the mother country for manufactured goods and markets for commercial crops.

Even before the new government was established in 1789, men like Alexander Hamilton and Tench Coxe had been urging Americans to surrender local self-sufficiency for specialization and the national exchange of commodities. A little later Albert Gallatin, Matthew Carey and Henry Clay took up the old arguments, urging their fellow citizens to diversify their economy, to separate manufacturing from agriculture, to remove the factory from the home. Among most Americans with capital, however, manufacturing evoked little enthusiasm, and the failure of industrial enterprises actually undertaken by Hamilton and others only strengthened the aversion to new lines. England and France had gone to war in 1793, and Americans were capturing more and more of the world's carrying trade and making great fortunes in ocean commerce. Many other fortunes were being made in land speculation as American population grew rapidly and the demand for new farms increased. There seemed little reason, therefore, for American capitalists to divert their funds to manufacturing, in which nearly all of them were utterly inexperienced and in which most of them were profoundly convinced of their inability to compete with the English.

The very increase in American foreign trade, however, and the very growth of American population that seemed to prejudice American capitalists against manufacturing, gradually began to have an opposite effect. Imported factory products, landed in quantity at coastal ports, were sold more and more to country merchants, thus creating a desire for factory goods among farmers who had been making almost everything at home. As the number of farmers increased through immigration and natural reproduction, the demand for factory goods grew steadily. Local merchants began to seek new sources of supply, and new roads and canals to give them access to important distributing points. Farmers began to seek new markets for commercial crops so that they might get cash to buy "store" goods. Transportation was steadily improved. The circle of trade widened. Household industries became fewer, and village monopolies began to yield to competition from towns and cities. Manufacturing took on a brighter aspect as markets thus became available for the products of big textile and shoe factories, hardware and munitions plants, iron mills, leather establishments, and distilleries.

These changes did not come in a day or in a decade. They were already in progress, however, when America's relations with England reached the boiling point around 1806, when the embargo of 1807 and the non-intercourse acts of 1810 checked the flow of British goods into American ports. Such measures not only gave established American manufacturers a monopoly of the American market but, wrecking the shipping trade, they set the capitalists in that trade to looking for new investments. The War of 1812 and its preliminaries did not create overnight an American manufacturing industry. But it made great opportunities available, and it stimulated enthusiasm for investments in new factories. Business depressions and British competition between 1816 and 1820 wiped out many of the new enterprises, proving that the wartime expansion had been too rapid and America was still industrially immature. After 1820, however, the weak beginnings made before and during the war were definitely in the past. The spectacular growth of American population guaranteed constantly expanding markets. The great burst of turnpike, canal, and railroad building promised to make those markets accessible at every season of the year. The high rate of profit for successful firms drew more and more capitalists into factory enterprises and made it easier to finance rapid plant expansion.

In the early decades of the nineteenth century a new society thus was emerging in America out of the colonial, agricultural past. Rivers were being dammed, factory towns were springing up, farm families were being disrupted as sons and daughters sought the excitement and wages of factory work. Rigid class boundaries were disintegrating; groups long static in personnel and interests were admitting strangers with new ideas. An urban proletariat was slowly forming, and new technicians, factory managers, and white-collar office workers were being trained and put to work. America was beginning that gigantic exploitation of unparalleled resources that by the end of the century was to make her by far the richest country in the world.

HOW TRANSPORTATION BUILT MARKETS

Nature had provided well for internal and coastal trade in America. The Delaware and the Hudson were majestic rivers, each navigable for more than a hundred miles. The Raritan, Connecticut, Potomac, Susquehanna, Savannah, James, and Rappahannock were all deep enough for big ships to enter and long enough for flatboats to embark on many days' journeys from the hinterlands. To the east was the Atlantic, to the north the Great Lakes, to the south the Gulf of Mexico, to the west the Ohio and Mississippi, all traversing magnificent distances and deep enough for steamboats.

Traffic became increasingly heavy on these waterways during the colonial period, but only after 1807 when Robert Fulton made practical the commercial steamboat did they really hum with activity. By 1820 Albany, Hartford, Harrisburg, and Pittsburgh were busy commercial centers. By 1830 Cincinnati, Louisville, and St. Louis were thriving ports. By 1840 businessmen in Rochester, Buffalo, and Cleveland were getting rich from lake traffic in grain, hides, iron ore, lead, and lumber. New Orleans throughout this period was the commercial center of the West and South—a magic city at the mouth of the Mississippi, French and Catholic in law and custom, slave mart and cotton depot, surpassed only by New York and Philadelphia in volume of trade.

Settlers moving inland and outward beyond the river valleys, however, were soon past the reach of steamboats plying natural waterways. To send their produce to market, to get manufactures from eastern ports and factories, these settlers required overland connections. After the Lancaster road of 1792, therefore, until 1830, turnpikes were built extensively in every section of the land while post roads, as early as 1840, connected with the eastern seaboard the regions of Minnesota, Kansas, and Oklahoma long before any of these were states. North to Sault Ste. Marie, south to Tampa Bay, they ran, knitting into a pattern with smaller cities and rural areas the business life of Savannah and Boston, Lexington and St. Louis, Norfolk and Pittsburgh, New York and Cleveland, Philadelphia and Natchez.[2]

Following turnpikes came canals, though it was only after 1825 that the latter became important. In that year the Erie Canal was opened in New York State, reducing freight rates between Albany and Buffalo by 85 per cent. The great boom in land values along the path of the Erie and the immense profits it returned in tolls encouraged the projection of similar waterways throughout the North and West. The Erie Canal brought factory products past the Appalachians and lake commerce to the coast. Other canals promised manufacturers immense markets in the hinterlands. The Panic of 1837[3] momentarily postponed the completion of many new projects, but by 1850 the Pennsylvania System was carrying Pittsburgh coal and iron to Philadelphia and manufactures to the West. The Lehigh Coal & Navigation Company canal joined Coalport and Easton; the Morris Canal connected Easton with the sea by way of Jersey City. The Wabash joined Toledo and Evansville; the Miami, Toledo and Cincinnati; the Ohio, Cleveland and Portsmouth— all bringing coastward the produce of lake and river regions, taking to the banks of the Ohio the products of the port of New York.[4]

Travel over turnpikes was slow and expensive, costing at least 15 cents a ton-mile for freight. Water transportation was much cheaper, but four months in the year northern routes were frozen. It remained for the steam railroad, therefore, to free industry from the shackles of the weather and the snail pace of horses and wagons. In 1812 it took six days to go from Philadelphia to Pittsburgh by stagecoach and at least sixteen days for freight.[5] By 1854 the railroad covered the distance in fifteen hours.

The first railroads in the United States were the Baltimore & Ohio, the Mohawk & Hudson, the Charleston & Hamburg,

---

[2] Paullin, *Atlas,* plate 138k.
[3] See chap. III, pp. 43 ff.
[4] Harper's *Encyclopedia,* vol. VII, p. 49.
[5] Foulke, *Sinews of Commerce,* p. 109.

all opened in 1830. Soon after, the Erie in New York, the Western in Massachusetts and at least a score of others were under
construction. By 1850 the eastern seaboard was latticed with
double bars of iron reaching out toward Buffalo, Pittsburgh, and
Cleveland, while even in the deep South the Western & Atlantic, passing through Chattanooga, Tennessee, was striving
to wrest from the North the grain trade of Kentucky, Ohio,
Indiana, and Illinois.

With typical folk wisdom a wagon driver's ballad hinted at
the railroad's later grip:[6]

> Now all you jolly wagoners, who have got good wives,
> Go home to your farms and there spend your lives.
> When your corn is all cribbed and your grain is good,
> You will have nothing to do but curse the railroad.

In the thirties and forties, however, the railroads' chief function
seemed to be to consume capital, wood, and iron and to encourage
speculation in stocks and land. Rivers, canals, and turnpikes remained the chief avenues of internal trade.

FALSE STARTS IN MANUFACTURING

Transportation built markets in America, but first to benefit
besides western settlers were British industrialists. English goods
were attractive to a people who for two hundred years had been
using English china, linen, wool, and iron, who read English
books and papers, who dealt in foreign currency and calculated
their gains in pounds, shillings, and pence. Besides, English goods
generally were cheaper than American manufactures. Labor was
scarce in early American factory centers, and wages were high,
especially for skilled mechanics who had to be imported secretly
from abroad. American machinery was not as good as British,
American workmanship was inferior. In addition, British agents
and rich American importers and jobbers selling through the
auction markets could offer more and longer credit than pioneer
manufacturers who were usually pressed for cash.

---

[6] Dunbar, *Travel in America,* p. 769.

Competing with the products of American factories were also domestic household manufactures. Merchant capitalists who imported British goods often hired American artisans to work at home or in sweatshops making shoes, coarser textiles, and other commodities which they would sell in the expanding national market. Reminiscing of the Reed brothers whose shoe business in Weymouth, Massachusetts, was conducted in this way in the 1820's, Quincy Reed said:[7]

Sales were made in the cities of the United States between Boston and New Orleans. Branch houses were established in Richmond and New Orleans, where business up the Mississippi River was immense. . . . Mr. Harvey Reed was a man of remarkable ability. He had the care of the outside business of the firm, attending to its larger interests in the South and elsewhere. I think he was one of the original promoters of the Union Bank of Weymouth and Braintree, and of the Weymouth Savings Bank.

The artisans who worked for merchant capitalists had once been "master workers" or journeymen who had owned their own tools, processed their own raw materials, and sold their own finished products at wholesale and retail in restricted vicinities in the larger towns. As new markets were opened, however, and merchants began to get orders from outside their neighborhoods, they hired masters or journeymen to produce goods exclusively for the new trade. From an independent employer, therefore, the master was gradually reduced to a wage earner supplying goods for the merchant capitalist. Isaac Felch, a veteran of the Natick, Massachusetts, shoe industry, describes its methods:[8]

The shoes were put out to be bottomed in little shops all over the community. The quarters were to be bound, the uppers closed, and the stock for it was carted to these workmen. My Uncle Asa was the first man in Natick to make shoes to sell for the Boston market. It was in 1836 or 1837. I have heard father tell of the Boston merchants coming out to meet Uncle Asa at the toll gates of the Worcester Turnpike, to secure his shoes. The first time they failed to meet him, he thought the bottom had fallen out of the business.

Good wages were paid for this kind of skilled work as long as

---

[7] Hazard, *Boot and Shoe Industry,* p. 50.
[8] Hazard, *Boot and Shoe Industry,* p. 53.

factory production remained in its infancy. Soon after 1815, however, long hours and poor pay became the rule. Under such conditions household manufactures could compete favorably with machine-made products, and until after the panic of 1837 more manufacturing was done in American homes and sweatshops than in the new mills.

Besides struggling for markets with British agents, American importers and merchant capitalists, early American industrialists had to compete for capital with agriculture, ocean commerce, domestic transportation, and speculation in land and securities. That "agriculture is the most beneficial and productive object of human industry" was a common American belief, inculcated by colonial propagandists, reiterated by agrarians like Thomas Jefferson, George Logan, and Thomas Cooper. Time and again they expressed in strong language their fears of manufacturing, industrial cities and factory workers. "I consider the class of artificers as the panders of vice and the instruments by which the liberties of a country are generally overturned," wrote Jefferson in the *Notes on Virginia.* "I view great cities as pestilential to the morals, the health and the liberties of man," he added in 1800.[9] Hamilton, Coxe, and Carey attacked these prejudices, arguing, writing, debating indefatigably, setting forth in detail the advantages of the factory system. In the very year of the Constitutional Convention they helped form the Pennsylvania Society for the Encouragement of Manufactures and Useful Arts in the capital of the new nation. Similar associations were formed in other cities and states, while newspapers were established in some towns simply to create a favorable public attitude toward manufacturing. Before 1806, however, these efforts brought small reward. Farmers who would purchase stock in turnpikes, bridges, and canals, continued to fear factories. Bankers continued to finance only familiar enterprises. Speculators continued to invest only in land, ships, and public securities. European rentiers who poured lamented millions into American transportation and land schemes, continued to ignore American industrial corporations.

---

[9] Jefferson, *Writings,* vol. IV, p. 88, and vol. VII, p. 459.

After 1806 the outlook became more favorable. The non-importation laws and the impending war with Britain or France or both, stimulated the adoption of policies to encourage manufacturing. Bounties and premiums were offered for fine goods and for technological improvements. Fairs and festivals were held where these goods and improvements could be displayed and studied. To raise funds lotteries were conducted in many cities while some cities themselves invested directly in factories. At a Philadelphia dinner in 1808, Colonel David Humphreys offered a toast: "The Best Mode of Warfare for our Country— the artillery of carding and spinning machinery, and the musketry of shuttles and sledges." [10] Patriotism was enlisted on every possible occasion, even Jefferson and Madison conceding the need for domestic manufactures in the country's emergency. Encouraged by such support, American capitalists in the next decade built a diversified industrial plant and captured the markets abandoned by the British. Cotton and woolen factories, machine shops, iron forges, and flour mills were scattered through New England, New York, Pennsylvania, Kentucky, and Ohio, joining the few similar establishments erected before 1806. Many millions of dollars were invested in these enterprises, chiefly in machines and buildings, and thousands of girls and men found employment in them.

As soon as the War of 1812 was over, however, and England no longer consumed her energies in military and naval conflict, American industrialists felt once again the impact of foreign competition. And it was not long before most of the money invested in the new factories and most of the jobs which these enterprises afforded were lost. While discussing industrial policy in the British Parliament in April, 1816, Henry Brougham, Esq., declared: [11]

It was well worth while to incur a loss upon the first exportation, in order, by the glut, to stifle in the cradle, those rising manufactures in the United States, which the war has forced into existence, contrary to the natural course of things.

---

[10] Reznick, in *Journal of Economic and Business History,* vol. IV, p. 801.
[11] Clark, *Manufactures.* vol. I, p. 240.

Whether losses actually were incurred is difficult to say. Great shipments of English goods, however, were made, and the effect was as anticipated. American factories shut down; American workers returned home to the farms or became public charges in the cities. In a few years the panic of 1819 and the ensuing depression completed the destruction. In June, 1819, Joshua Gilpin wrote: [12]

Nearly all the manufacturing establishments of the country were broken up, their owners ruined, and their property sold at enormous sacrifices; it may be said, indeed, that nearly the whole of these establishments changed owners, and were taken up at successive abandonments and reductions of capital, all which, however, proved but successive steps to ruin.

In April, 1820, protectionist Henry Clay told Congress: [13]

In passing along the highway one frequently sees large and spacious buildings, with the glass broken out of the windows, the shutters hanging in ruinous disorder, without any appearance of activity and enveloped in solitary gloom. Upon inquiry what they are, you are almost always informed that they were some cotton or other factory, which their proprietors could no longer keep in motion against the overwhelming pressure of foreign competition.

CONDITIONS FOR SUCCESS

American industrialists, inexperienced in organization and management, assailed by agrarian publicists and bankrupted by foreign and domestic competition, nevertheless were not discouraged by these early failures. Instead of mourning over the ruins of lost enterprises, they re-formed their ranks, sought aid from the government, capital and credit from private sources, and markets in every accessible region. Business and financial difficulties immediately following the war had weeded out the weaker factories and left only the most efficient. As the latter continued to profit, attracting the attention of capitalists looking for new opportunities, other factors combined to brighten the dismal scenes of collapse and raise the hopes of industrial entrepreneurs.

Perhaps most important among the new factors, aside from

---

[12] Clark, *Manufactures,* vol. I, p. 380.
[13] Clark, *Manufactures,* vol. I, p. 380.

improved transportation facilities, was the great increase in American population. The number of people in the United States almost doubled between 1820 and 1840. A favorable economic environment stimulated reproduction, while land speculators and canal and railroad builders brought in boatloads of foreigners. Ohio, Indiana, western New York, and Pennsylvania were filling up with farmers careless of beauty or handwork, demanding ever greater quantities of cheap textiles, boots and shoes, farm implements, glass, nails. But the growth in population did more than broaden the market for factory goods. It increased the available supply of factory labor. Many foreigners, as soon as they landed in our ports, sought and found work in the new enterprises. Perhaps even more important, new western farmers began to ship East greater and greater quantities of corn and wheat to compete with the produce of New England farms. This forced depressed eastern farmers to send their children in increasing numbers to work in the mills—the daughters in order to raise their own marriage dowries, and both sons and daughters in order to support themselves and thus reduce the strain on farm family budgets.

This increase in available customers and workers was accompanied by the appearance of new sources of capital. By the middle twenties falling prices in America were reducing sharply the value of Atlantic cargoes. At the same time the markets for oriental finery were becoming saturated, while supplies of American furs and Hawaiian sandalwood—both used in exchange for far eastern goods—were diminishing and threatening the China trade with extinction. Faced with such conditions, between 1826 and 1830 John Jacob Astor liquidated his investments in ocean commerce, John P. Cushing returned for good from China, shippers Bryant and Sturgis, and Perkins & Company retired from business. Of the capital thus released, manufacturing attracted its share. The "Boston Associates" began to concentrate on the production of textiles rather than on shipping.[14] Astor, investing in land, transportation, and insurance, also, in 1834 loaned $60,000 to Philip Hone's Matteawan Company to expand its textile mills.[15]

---

[14] See chap. IV, pp. 71–74.
[15] Porter, *Astor*, vol. II, p. 1015.

Faced with a growing army of steady customers and with funds seeking investment, American industrialists in the 1820's and 1830's had the opportunity to mechanize their plants at a rapid rate. They took advantage of this opportunity, plowing profits and loans into new buildings and new machines. Between 1820 and 1840 investments in American factories rose from $50,000,000 to $250,000,000. Cotton spindles in American factories in the same period jumped from 220,000 to 2,250,000. Woolen spindles multiplied with equal speed. The result was a sharp decrease in the cost of commodity production, hence a more favorable basis upon which to compete for the domestic market.

So interested were Americans in new machines, and so eager were they to put new devices into operation that, under our lax laws, they became the victims of a regular racket in "phony patents." In the decade 1820–1830 patents for the United States averaged about 535 annually against 145 for Great Britain, the greatest industrial nation in the world. The difference was mainly in scruples; the number of patents was no clue to the number of new inventions. Before 1836 America allowed every "inventor" a patent without requiring any proof of originality— he had but to convince the Patent Office his device was not harmful to the community. In such circumstances early American racketeers received monopolies on devices already in use and fleeced their credulous countrymen by demanding money under threat of suit for infringement. After 1836 the law was made much more strict, however, and a witness before a British Parliamentary committee, investigating the possibility of the repeal of laws prohibiting the export of machinery, declared: [16]

I apprehend that the chief part, or a majority, at all events, of the really new inventions, that is, of new ideas altogether, in the carrying out of a certain process by new machinery, or in a new mode, have originated abroad, especially in America.

In 1844, Devyr, the land reformer, wrote in the *Working Man's Advocate*: [17]

[16] Clark, *Manufactures*, vol. I, p. 435.
[17] Commons, *Labour*, vol. I, p. 491.

Machinery has taken almost entire possession of the manufacture of cloth; it is making steady—we might say rapid—advance upon all branches of iron manufacture; the newly invented machine saws, working in curves as well as straight lines, the planing and grooving machines, and the tenon and mortise machine, clearly admonish us that its empire is destined to extend itself over all our manufactures of wood; while some of our handicrafts are already extinct, there is not one of them but has foretasted the overwhelming competition of this occult power.

While the casual patent policy of an agrarian-commercial government failed to impede the progress of American invention and the mechanization of American industry, other governmental policies assisted more directly the growth of American manufacturing. The Federal Supreme Court in the Dartmouth College case in 1819 declared corporation charters contracts, protecting them, as it thought, from unilateral changes by state legislatures.[18] This gave new security to corporate enterprise in all lines. In 1824, in *Gibbons* v. *Ogden,* the court denied the right of the Livingston-Fulton group to monopolize Hudson and Mississippi steamboat traffic. This gave additional protection against state restrictions on interstate commerce. Three years later, in *Brown* v. *Maryland,* the Court declared unconstitutional a Maryland license tax on goods imported into that state, insisting in strong language upon the *exclusive* right of Congress to control interstate and foreign trade.

While the Court thus was guaranteeing a free national market, Congress and the states were aiding internal improvements to make that market accessible. Perhaps most stimulating to young industry among government policies, however, was the protective tariff.

In 1816, American manufacturers were but a corporal's guard in a nation of farmers and shippers but they had helped to win a war. That point never escaped the attention of Henry Clay, Matthew Carey, and lesser trumpeters for protection. The War of 1812 was an agrarian war fought by an agrarian nation. But without the aid of bold industrialists it could not have ended as

---

[18] After 1819, the states circumvented this decision by placing in most subsequent charters, with the enforced consent of the petitioner, a clause admitting the right of the legislature to alter the "contract" when it saw fit without consulting the corporation.

successfully as it did. Were manufacturers to be rewarded? "No," cried John Randolph of Roanoke, in Congress, in 1816:[19]

No, I will buy where I can get manufactures cheapest, I will not agree to lay a duty on the cultivator of the soil to encourage exotic manufactures; because, after all, we should only get much worse things at a higher price.

Spokesman for a majority in the South, Randolph fought a losing fight in the Nation. Clay and Calhoun, by appealing to farmers in terms of the "home market"—markets in great factories for cotton, hemp, flax, and wool, markets in landless industrial cities, for wheat, corn, and barley—won enough votes in the West and South to defeat the shippers of Webster's Massachusetts and the conservative cotton planters. Arguing in terms of national self-sufficiency, recalling with irresistible rhetoric the difficulties of the past war, they carried the day for protection. The tariff act of 1816 raised the duties on cotton, woolen, and iron goods.

For four years, however, this seemed but a token victory. The act failed to protect. Where the duties were levied on the *value* of imports and not specifically on *weight* or *quantity,* it was simple for the British to underestimate their goods to get them past our customs inspectors at low rates. Fraud and graft also marked the administration of the act and simplified the problem of evasion. After 1820, however, when cotton production grew rapidly and cotton prices tumbled, the 1816 duties began to afford sufficient protection for manufacturers of coarser textiles.[20]

By the 1820's, also, manufacturers had learned to help themselves in political affairs. Falling cotton prices had alienated southern planters from any tariffs that would raise the cost of essential manufactures, while New England shippers remained adamant against threats to reduce the volume of trade. Together therefore they defeated high-tariff bills in 1820, 1821, and 1823. But in 1824, with Clay back in Congress, the home-market argument cemented unity between the middle states and the wool and hemp states of the West, the combination that year enacting higher duties. Aiding in the victory were new associations in New York, Connecticut, and Philadelphia, formed simply to agitate for

19 Hicks, *American Nation,* vol. I, p. 337.
20 Clark, *Manufactures,* vol. I, p. 307.

protection. In 1820 these came under the leadership of the National Institution for the Promotion of Industry, which had among its members Peter Colt, E. I. du Pont, P. H. Schenk and the veteran protectionist, Matthew Carey. Its first step was to publish the *Patron of Industry,* a paper devoted entirely to high-tariff propaganda.[21]

Business was learning the sweet security of tariff walls and the strategy to keep them high. After the failure of a special woolen tariff in the Senate in 1827, the Pennsylvania Society for the Promotion of Manufactures and Mechanic Arts held a convention in Harrisburg the next summer. To it came aroused manufacturers "together with a sprinkling of newspaper men, enthusiastic pamphleteers, and interested politicians, all friends of the American system." They outlined a comprehensive program for enhanced duties, prefaced it with an eloquent plea for protection, shipped one copy as a memorial to Congress, another to eager journals in the form of an address to the people.[22]

The tariff of 1828 did not result simply from such agitations, but its enactment convinced politicians that their attitude toward manufactures had become crucial to presidential aspirations. Industry had assumed its place beside commerce and agriculture, capturing the leaders of New England, making most of the allegiance of the West. Against the demands of the Harrisburg Convention, Dr. Thomas Cooper, president of the College of South Carolina, cried out:[23]

We thought it hard enough to combat the tariff in favor of the cotton manufacturer, the woolen manufacturer, the iron manufacturer; but now there is not a petty manufacturer in the Union, from the owner of a spinning factory to the maker of a hobnail, who is not pressing forward to the plunder; who may not be expected to worry Congress for *permission* to put his hand into the planter's pocket . . . this is a combined attack of the whole manufacturing interest. The avowed object is to tax us for their own emolument; to force us to cease to buy of our most valuable customers; to force on us a system which will sacrifice the South to the North, which will convert us into colonies and tributaries.

---

[21] Reszneck, in *Journal of Economic and Business History,* vol. IV, p. 800.
[22] Carman, *Social and Economic History,* vol. II, p. 36.
[23] Carman, *Social and Economic History,* vol. II, pp. 36–37.

Such cries failed altogether to impress representatives of northern factories and western farms, who proceeded to enact the "abominable tariff." "Its enemies," said Webster of the act of 1828, "spiced it with whatever they thought would render it distasteful; its friends took it, drugged as it was." For the first time, Webster listed himself among the "friends." In Pennsylvania, Matthew Carey was toasted as a "pillar of adamant to the American system; a hedge of thorns to British agents." [24]

The tariff act of 1832 removed the worst features of its predecessor, but left high duties on iron and textile manufactures. That was the last high-tariff act until 1861. Under the leadership of nullifying South Carolina, agrarians had at last mustered their national majority, and in 1833 Congress began to reduce the rates. By then, however, industry had enjoyed a dozen years of high protection. At least partly because of the tariffs factories had prospered and manufacturers were able to adapt themselves to the change. American industry had outgrown its infancy. False starts were well in the past.

THE INDUSTRIAL WORKERS

When textile factories first were constructed in America, our great cities were mainly ports, our rural areas were devoted to farming. We had no facilities to accommodate new armies of workers. Rooming houses were scarce in the towns; in farming areas, where swift rivers affording power to run machines made it likely that factories would be located, there were few vacant rooms, no stores, schools, or churches to accommodate new people. Thus many of the earliest factory enterprises—in Waltham, Chicopee, Lowell, Nashua—had to develop company towns from the start. Workers began to live in company houses, to purchase in some cases in company stores, to attend company churches and schools. Their employers generally became absentee owners whose interests extended beyond manufacturing to real estate, transportation, water-power development, finance.

Such conditions were typical of the New England textile

---

[24] Gabriel, *American Democratic Thought*, p. 82.

industry but were not found in flour-milling regions or in the iron industry in New Jersey and Pennsylvania. The iron industry was organized on a feudal rather than a corporate basis. Great barons on huge tracts of mineral lands bound in almost complete servility hundreds of families, all of whose members worked in the mines and mills. While textile companies supplied houses and other accommodations, they paid money wages and did not force operatives to buy in company stores when others were available. In western Pennsylvania, wages rarely were seen, employees being always in debt to the barons. Corporations entered the industry after 1830, and conditions gradually were improved; but as late as 1858 one partnership, with a capital of $1,000,000, still housed and employed 508 families.[25]

We know little more about the condition of the ironworkers. For textile operatives information is better but not plentiful. Yankee girls made up the great majority. They were first brought to the factories from neighboring farms by agents touring the countryside in wagons and emphasizing the moral and educational advantages of factory work. Railroads early in the thirties extended the area of search, and, as new sources of labor were opened each year, wages gradually fell. By 1834, a Dover girls' "workers' committee" announced after a series of pay cuts:[26]

We think our wages already low enough, when the peculiar circumstances of our situation are considered, that we are many of us far from our homes, parents and friends, and that it is only by strict economy and untiring industry that any of us have been able to lay up anything.

Though they came from families which could no longer support them at home or which required contributions from their earnings, most of the girls had some education. Taught at least to read and write, they improved their scant leisure time in such pursuits. One operative, from a particularly poor family, tells literately enough how she came to work in a factory and how she acquired literary habits:[27]

---

[25] Shannon, *Economic History*, p. 262.
[26] Shlakman, *Factory Town*, p. 60.
[27] Shlakman, *Factory Town*, p. 59.

It so happens that I was born in New Hampshire, where my mother still resides, with a large family of young children, dependent on her for support, and hard does she have to struggle to gain a livelihood for herself and offspring; and but for the charity of several kind friends and neighbors, she would have to put them out before they knew the first rudiments taught in our common schools. Sensible that she had a weight upon her heavy to be borne, to lighten the load, I left home and came to Cabotville. When I came here, I could not read, except by spelling out the words like a child of very few years. I had not commenced learning to write, and all the learning I now have has been gained without instruction, having obtained it alone, and that too, after I had labored in the mill twelve hours a day on the average through the year.

In Massachusetts, the working day consisted of twelve and one-half or thirteen and one-half hours. The weekly wage for female workers was about $2.50. A bed in a company house was given free, and about $1.25 was deducted each week for board. "The company will not employ any one who is habitually absent from public worship on the Sabbath, or known to be guilty of immorality," said an announcement of the Boston Associates. Matrons of working girls' dormitories were responsible for enforcing a ten o'clock curfew and keeping their homes puritanically in order. Apparently they were successful. M. Chevalier, the French traveler, reaching Lowell in 1835, declared that "Lowell is not amusing, but Lowell is clean and decent, peaceful and sober."

As we might expect, the new factory towns lacked adequate living facilities; and the same was true of company houses. An old mill hand who knew early conditions, described them some years later: [28]

The chief problem was overcrowding. . . . Six girls often slept in one room, in three double beds. . . . They ate together at long tables and were fed plain and hearty food. Among the appurtenances of the back yard of the Chicopee tenements was a conventional line of pig pens operated by each boarding-house in the interests of economy. Near these were the wells. When the ground became properly saturated during the early forties, there was an epidemic of typhoid fever that was a record breaker. This resulted in the securing of a water supply from the hill above the town, and gradually the pig pens were abolished.

[28] Shlakman, *Factory Town*, pp. 53–54.

Massachusetts factories were owned by Appletons, Lowells, Dwights, Jacksons, Cabots, each nurtured in the Puritan tradition. Their early emphasis upon moral and educational advantages in factory work certainly was not hypocritical, not designed merely to entice Puritan girls into the mills. In Rhode Island there was no mention of libraries and schools. Yet there was no special difficulty in acquiring suitable operatives at reasonable wages, though the supply probably was less plentiful than in Massachusetts. The Boston Associates talked in earnest though only in a few model factories did they actually supply the promised educational facilities.

The real obstacles to the fulfillment of ideal promises were falling prices, business depressions, and periodic declines in profits. The growth of the ten-hour-day movement among the girls also alienated the early industrialists, and paternalism gradually gave way to indifference. In 1842 a petition to the Massachusetts legislature declared that "the population of manufacturing places are now, in great measure, dependent for the means of physical, intellectual and moral culture, upon the will of their employers." [29] An observer in Lowell in 1846, described the factory regimen at that date: [30]

The operatives work thirteen hours a day in the summer time, and from daylight to darkness in the winter. At half past four in the morning the factory bell rings, and at five girls must be in the mills. A clerk placed as a watch, observes those who are a few minutes behind the time, and effectual means are taken to stimulate punctuality. This is the morning commencement of the industrial discipline (should we not rather say industrial tyranny?) which is established in these Associations of this moral and Christian community. At seven the girls are allowed thirty minutes for breakfast, and at noon thirty minutes more for dinner, except during the first quarter of the year, when the time is extended to forty-five minutes.

Puritan girls just removed from New England farms were no material for a militant labor movement, especially when they were hired by contract and threatened with blacklisting for misconduct. In New Jersey and Pennsylvania, however, men worked

---

[29] Adams, *Epic of America,* p. 181.
[30] Faulkner, *Economic History,* p. 291.

the mules and industrial organization appeared during the boom of the thirties. In 1833 a federation of locals from "some nine villages . . . in the vicinity of Philadelphia" organized "The Trades' Union of Pennsylvania." In 1835, preparing to strike, workers in a Paterson plant formed the "Paterson Association for the Protection of the Labouring Classes, operatives of cotton mills, etc." But these were feeble and temporary organizations that soon petered out. Strikes were few, almost always defensive, aimed against wage cuts. Rarely were they successful. In Manayunk, a manufacturing town near Philadelphia, there was a strike in 1828 against a 25 per cent reduction in pay. "Even at the old prices, it was said, a spinner could make only 'from $7.50 to $8.50 per week for himself by working the full period of twelve hours daily, and in doing this he actually earned for his employers from 40 to 50 dollars per week.'"[31] Three strikers were brought before the Philadelphia county court charged with disturbing the peace by threatening strike breakers, and convicted. Ultimately the strike was lost, though somehow it was formally maintained for three months.

In Lowell, even without organization, factory girls rebelled against a 15 per cent cut in February, 1834:[32]

Some 800 to 2,000 of them not only went on strike but were persuaded by one of their leaders to "'make a run' on the Lowel Bank and the Savings Bank." "We are told," said the Boston *Transcript*, "that one of the leaders mounted a pump, and made a flaming Mary Wollstoncraft speech on the rights of women and the iniquities of the 'monied aristocracy' which produced a powerful effect on her auditors, and they determined to have their own way, if they died for it."

They didn't persist very long. "In a few days all except the ringleaders, who were 'refused entrance into the mills,' went back to work at the reduced wages." A few other female "turn-outs" ended similarly.

Though early factory strikes were poorly managed and generally unsuccessful, and weak unions either fell with defeat or died in the long depression after the panic of 1837, operatives

---

[31] Commons, *Labour*, vol. I, p. 418.
[32] Commons, *Labour*, vol. I, p. 423.

in the thirties were becoming distinctly class-conscious. Entering factories with the notion of accumulating a dot or storing up insurance against a rainy day, they were soon disabused of such ideas by the very low wages they received. Embarking on a temporary industrial excursion, they soon found there was no road back. By 1840, Orestes Brownson commented on the Lowell factory girls:[33]

The great mass wear out their health, spirits and morals without becoming one whit better off than when they commenced labor. The bills of mortality in these factory villages are not striking, we admit, for the poor girls when they can toil no longer go home to die.

Becoming aware of their predicament in an age of abolitionism, the girls began bitterly to complain of their own "slavery." "We view this attempt to reduce our wages," wrote the Dover girls in 1834, "as part of a general plan of the proprietors of the different manufacturing establishments to reduce the Females in their employ to that state of dependence on them in which they openly, as they do now secretly, abuse and insult them by calling them their 'slaves.'"[34] A poem recounting the death of a factory operative from overwork ended with this stanza:[35]

> That night a chariot passed her,
> While on the ground she lay;
> The daughters of her master
> An evening visit to pay—
> Their tender hearts were sighing
> As negroes' woes were told;
> While the white slave was dying
> Who gained their father's gold.

DECLINE OF THE CRAFTS

The success of infant factories in America was hindered by an inadequate supply of skilled labor, but production rarely was blocked by labor troubles. Factory operatives were comparatively few, mainly women and children, not yet systematically organized. They were beyond the reach of union leaders who

[33] Commons, *Labour*, vol. I, p. 495.
[34] Shlakman, *Factory Town*, pp. 60–61.
[35] Shlakman *Factory Town*, p. 61.

flourished among depressed handicrafters especially in the half-decade before the panic of 1837.

The earliest trade unions in America probably were composed of masters and journeymen organized to "stand out" against price-haggling merchant capitalists who brought them orders. When master workers began to yield to the merchants and to use cheap goods and inferior workmen, journeymen alone assumed union leadership. At first they fought mainly against the employment of "learners, runaway apprentices and half-way journeymen" as well as foreigners—"miserable botches," complained the New York Typographical Society in 1811, who "will work for what they can get." As division of labor in the handicrafts reduced emphasis upon special skills, however, and highly trained artisans were forced to work beside beginners doing monotonous tasks at work desks, wage and hour agitation came to dominate union activity. By the early thirties journeymen had lost their special status and could but strive to make a living wage at whatever jobs were available.

From the start, trade unions encountered the hostility of American courts, which had adopted the common-law doctrine that combinations of workers were conspiracies against the state. First to feel the force of this doctrine were the cordwainers of Philadelphia, in 1806; but it was applied with zeal throughout the nineteenth century. A New York court in 1809 anticipated the famous decision in *Commonwealth* v. *Hunt* (Massachusetts, 1842) denying that the formation of unions was conspiracy, emphasizing only that it was "the means they used" that were crucial, for these might be [36]

of a nature too arbitrary and coercive, and [if indulged in would] deprive their fellow citizens of rights as precious as any they contended for.

This proved a distinction without a difference, the New York court itself demonstrating the loopholes in its dictum: It was easy to call combinations a "means" and thereby block the workers.

Labor movements are as sensitive to the fluctuations of the

[36] Commons, *Labour*, vol. I, p. 143.

business cycle as the most speculative security. When business is good and order logs are full, strikes are effective; in depressions they are usually suicidal. It is in depressions, however, that labor is most in need of aid and the failure of strikes, for judicial or economic reasons, leaves the choice only between legislation and revolution. For the latter there was no basis whatever in Jackson's United States. Politics, however, was still untried, and the workers had a program. In the short depression of 1828–1829, therefore, craftsmen organized the first American Working Men's Party in Philadelphia. New York artisans soon followed. Their platforms demanded abolition of imprisonment for debt, abolition of chartered "monopolies," of public lotteries, and of compulsory militia service. In addition they demand the ten-hour day, mechanic lien laws to protect workers' tools, and, above all, free public education. That, they said, was "the first and most important . . . object for which they were contending." A workingmen's circular issued in Philadelphia in 1830 declared: [37]

All history corroborates the melancholy fact, that in proportion as the mass of the people becomes ignorant, misrule and anarchy ensue—their liberties are subverted, and tyrannic ambition has never failed to take advantage of their helpless condition. . . . Let the productive classes, then, unite, for the preservation of their free institutions, and by procuring for all the children in the Commonwealth Republican Education, preserve our liberties from the dangers of foreign invasion or domestic infringement.

On such platforms Working Men's parties ran candidates for local, state and Federal offices, endorsing also nominees of other parties who subscribed to their demands. Some of their candidates and some of their endorsees won office, but the movement itself failed. In the twenties skilled craftsmen were too few in number, too poor, too ignorant of politics. Like all third parties theirs had no victorious tradition, no skilled leadership, no spoils of office with which to win the lasting allegiance of an army of party workers. At the polls their candidates had to depend for support upon other groups. When they won office, older interests by bribery, chicanery, or false promises turned them into

---

[37] Commons, *Labour,* vol. I, p. 227.

their own political pawns. That is what happened in Philadelphia, where trade unions were strongest and the Working Men's Party began. In New York City, where leaders committed the party to a radical program and where labor had the support of such middle-class liberals as Robert Dale Owen and Fanny Wright, the movement was swallowed up by the voracious Tammany machine.

Returning prosperity early in the thirties revived the hopes of labor, and unionization between 1834 and 1837 proceeded at a rate unequaled again in America until the twentieth century. Union membership increased from 26,000 in 1834 to 300,000 in 1837, the latter figure representing about half the urban skilled workers in the country. From Louisville to Boston recruits joined the movement. Aided by improved communication in the larger cities, they organized central councils to unify action. In Philadelphia, in 1835, we had our first general strike. For the allied crafts in that city it won the coveted ten-hour day. In the same year and the next, in every metropolis, organized workers struck for the same goal. Everywhere but in Boston they were successful.

Then came depression. Labor's defense against lockouts and blacklists had been the great boom in all lines of business during which workers were badly needed. "With the first descent of the panic of 1837," however, "the labour movement was crushed out of existence. The local societies, the city assemblies, the national federation of assemblies and locals, and the national trade unions disappeared. With them went their official organs, the newspapers they had started for purposes of agitation and for carrying news of interest to their members." [38]

Wages were cut, jobs disappeared. In New York City alone, said the *Public Ledger* on April 15, 1837, "6,000 masons and carpenters and other workmen connected with building have been discharged." "Forty whale ships are lying at the wharves," reported New Bedford, "but nothing doing to fit them out for sea." Haverhill, Massachusetts, announced "the almost entire failure of the shoe business in this vicinity. . . . It was the re-

---

[38] Commons, *Labour*, vol. I, p. 456.

source of almost every family, men, women and children were engaged, and many have no other means of obtaining their daily bread. Should the present state of things continue long, it must produce many cases of extreme suffering." [39]

Their unions wrecked, skilled workers turned again to politics. But they were no more successful than before, and soon fell prey to all kinds of utopian schemes. Factories had no room for them, nor would they have tended machines if they could. Instead, some joined cooperative associations and communities marked by religious zeal and mystic rituals. A few of these were notably successful, but most failed almost as soon as they began, finding no place in an expanding industrial economy.

THE METAMORPHOSIS OF SOCIETY

Simple distinctions between seaboard and piedmont, agriculture and commerce, did not disappear from American society between 1800 and 1837; but they were complicated by new elements. Conflicts engendered by the new manufacturing interest sharpened the differences between city and country, producer and seller, employer and employee. More subtle class cleavages could be discerned, caused by new ramifications in American business.

The growth of the country, the extension and improvement of transportation facilities, were making distribution the master key to profits. By producing goods beyond the needs of their immediate communities, factories were destroying local industrial monopolies in many villages, leaving farmers dependent upon outside sources for goods and services. By drawing thousands of young men and women into the new manufacturing cities, factories were also making new workers dependent upon outside sources for food. A landless population was gathering in many new towns and older cities, and gradually there were appearing an urban proletariat and urban paupers. Such groups were insignificant in America in the eighteenth century. By the time of the panic of 1837, however, they presented grave problems to young municipalities. In addition American cities were harassed

[39] Commons, *Labour*, vol. I, p. 457.

by new problems in housing, sanitation, water supply, police and fire protection. The spectacular fire that gutted New York in 1835 impressed metropolitan leaders there and elsewhere with the deficiencies of our antiquated set-up. Toward correcting such deficiencies, however, they did little. Cooperative municipal life, like cooperative economic life, was yet in its infancy in individualistic America.

"Commerce and agriculture must intrench themselves against the manufacturers," exclaimed Judge Van Ness in the New York Constitutional Convention of 1821. He feared the new class that was arising, clamoring for power: a landless class of artisans, mechanics, teamsters, factory operatives, and—perhaps more important—bookkeepers, salesmen, clerks, tellers, mercantile and steamship agents. Quick and regular communication with distant markets had led to the shortening of credit terms and more rapid turnover of capital and goods. More complex business techniques and much larger office staffs had become necessary to maintain the new pace of American industry. Thus there appeared, for the first time in American society in sufficient numbers to be influential, the urban white-collar worker. As early as 1820 the New York Chamber of Commerce formed an association of such workers, giving them new cohesion and improved morale.[40] And Judge Van Ness's fears thus were well founded that such workers might align themselves with factory operatives and factory owners to rout the landed aristocracy that for so long had ruled the state. When the Convention in 1821 adopted universal manhood suffrage, the Judge's fears were put on the road to realization.

Dressed in drab alpaca, hunched over a high desk, this new worker credited and debited, indexed and filed, wrote and stamped invoices, acceptances, bills of lading, receipts. Adequately paid, he had some extra money and leisure time. He patronized sporting events and theaters, saving banks and insurance companies. He read Day's *New York Sun* or Bennett's *Herald*—the "penny press" supported by advertising, filled with police reports, crime stories, etiquette advice for the rising bourgeoisie. In

---

[40] Albion, *New York Port*, p. 252.

a world of six-cent contemporaries, these one-centers were spectacular successes, the *Sun* by 1837 selling thirty thousand copies daily, the *Herald* frequently surpassing it. Exploring *Godey's Lady's Book* for patterns, patronizing the new industries for materials, Mrs. Clerk began to compete with the boss's wife in dress and fashion.

In the higher brackets of society also, economic distinctions were becoming blurred. Expanding opportunities for profit in young America encouraged businessmen to undertake heterogeneous activities that conflicted sometimes one with another. Thus New England factory owners who feared the development of the West, lest it drain off their labor supply, speculated nevertheless in western lands and western railroads from which profits could be secured only if the West were developed. Boston commercial magnates, fearing the loss of political power to new industrialists, attempted to check the progress of industry by fighting protective tariffs, only in the end to be themselves won over to manufacturing. On the other hand, shippers in Philadelphia, threatened by the canal and packet lines of New York, encouraged local industry from the start, anticipating vigorous trade in the raw materials and finished goods of thriving factories. Business corporations attained prominence in this period, permitting through the separation of ownership and management, these side investments by businessmen whose major energies were occupied elsewhere.

While American business in the early decades of the nineteenth century was thus becoming more complex, complicating American society at the same time, it was developing also a unity of personnel and interest within itself that boded ill for politically dominant agrarians and the diminishing number of unadaptable shippers who remained the political allies of great planters.

III

THE INTENSIVE FRONTIER

WHILE textile and other factories in New England and the Middle States were absorbing into their mechanized routine a new class of factory operatives, the agricultural West was being transformed by a great influx of immigrants from Europe and farmers from the East. The virgin wilderness across the Appalachians, each year in these early national decades, was echoing with swishing axes, crashing timber, the steady tapping of ten thousand hammers building homes. The Indian frontier, always on the edge of civilization, was pushed each year nearer the Pacific. And restless pioneers, always in the van of permanent settlers, were opening more and more new areas for the surging westward movement.

Historians seeking the quintessence of American life have made much of this moving frontier and its effects upon the development of American character and American habits of thought. In emphasizing the role of new geographic conditions, however, and the role only of the primitive environment, historians have neglected the great reservoirs of older traits that settlers brought with them across the mountains. In casting their eyes only westward, away from the Atlantic, away from eastern towns and cities, away from turnpikes, canals, and railroads which were bringing the culture of the East to frontier settlers, historians have neglected also the impact of changing conditions in older regions upon the settlers of the new. Pushing west with American farmers and alien immigrants were salesmen, lawyers, bankers, speculators, teachers, preachers, writers, mechanics. As nomadic pioneers moved always farther west, so these steadier Americans followed, buying cabins and clearings, building shops, schools, churches, factories, boats. As white woodsmen advanced upon Indian territory exterminating or subjecting the redmen, eastern businessmen, eastern intellectuals, and eastern workers advanced upon the occupied West, winning settlers to the manners and morals, the security and creature comforts of a familiar culture. They directed the new settlers not westward to escape once again engulfing civilization, but eastward for the means to build new communities patterned after those they had left behind. Easterners softened the difficulties of frontier life. They tempered the violence of frontier justice and the stark simplicity of frontier thought in politics, religion, and art.

In 1910 Frederick Jackson Turner, the greatest of the "frontier" historians, declared that "world-wide forces of reorganization incident to the age of steam production and large scale industry" were writing a "wonderful chapter" in American life. Later he regretted that he could not "start all over and investigate more in detail the eastern aspects of American culture." [1] In 1800 these aspects certainly were most important in the United States, and they were beginning to exert a stronger and stronger influence in all spheres of American activity. The extensive frontier has become a legend to all Americans; superficially it affected millions of settlers; in its pure form it touched very few. It has left its stamp upon American culture, but it has not been the only stamp. It has given indigenous aspects to developments America has shared with the world, but these developments themselves have probably been more important in shaping American society. The industrial revolution in the eighteenth and nineteenth centuries radically changed the history of England, Europe, and the rest of the earth. It revolutionized the history of the United States, and its locus here was in the eastern cities. It is in these cities, then, and not only on the frontier that we must seek the new forces in America and the sources of change in American life. It is to these cities and not so much to the West that we must turn to find the impulses behind the changes in western history itself.

While eastern business was beginning its conquest of infant western communities, it was bringing within its pale also

---

[1] Craven, *Jernegan Essays,* p. 263.

the cotton South. Unlike the West, this was a settled region.
Southern peculiarities were becoming each year more clearly defined. Southern institutions and southern culture were becoming
more hotly defended. By capturing the trade of the South, however, and by forcing domestic manufactures upon southern
planters, eastern businessmen levied a heavy toll upon the southern economy and ruled it from afar. The cultural conquest of
the South never was complete, not even after the Civil War.
Unlike the Ohio valley or the region of the Lakes, the South
never became accustomed to modern industrialism. Since the
earliest decades of the nineteenth century, however, it has paid
an increasingly heavy debt to eastern and northern business.

THE CAPTIVE SOUTH

Once in the cherished past Virginia's exports had been four
times New York's; South Carolina's, twice those of New York
and Pennsylvania combined. Richmond and Norfolk had been
great tobacco ports shipping the golden leaf all over the world
and receiving in exchange European and oriental finery. Charleston, dealing in rice and indigo and African slaves, had had its
own humming trade. By 1820, however, Virginia's tobacco kingdom had been declining for more than a decade, and cotton had
replaced rice and indigo as the leading staple of the deep South.
In one sense southern prosperity was just beginning, for the
voracious textile factories of England and New England were
demanding more and more raw cotton and southern agriculture
boomed. But from another point of view the travails of the cotton South had also just begun. In 1790 the six original states
below the Mason-Dixon line contained almost half the American people. By 1830 they had less than one-fifth. The enervating
climate, the competition of slave labor, and the peculiarities of
cotton cultivation had kept European immigrants away from the
southern states, while soil exhaustion, erosion, and rising prices
for land and slaves had forced many planters into new regions.
Southern markets for European manufactures became much smaller than northern markets. Southern interest in domestic manufacturing declined. So great was the initial profit from cotton

cultivation in new areas that capital could no longer be attracted to other enterprises, and southern shipping, southern banking, southern merchandising languished. The South began to look to the North and West for food, to the East for credit, to New York for ships and warehouses. Trying to arouse his neighbors to their new predicament, William Gregg of South Carolina wrote:[2]

> An exclusively agricultural people in the present age of the world will always be poor. They want a home market. They want cities and towns. They want diversity of employment.

But the South refused to listen. "Cotton is King!" cried the great planters, and King Cotton would see them through any possible emergency.

While southerners thus were tying all their prospects to the production of cotton, energetic New Yorkers were working out the program that was to give them hegemony over southern trade. After the War of 1812, New York shippers were the first in America to reestablish commercial connections with British manufacturers and to draw into their magnificent harbor British textiles and ironware. In 1817, New York merchants insured their supremacy over Philadelphia, Boston, Baltimore, or Charleston by attracting to their piers the Black Ball Line, the first packet company to run ocean liners *on a regular schedule* between America and Europe. In that year also, the Erie Canal was begun. Opened to traffic in 1825, it gave New York the first direct route to the booming West, capturing for the Empire City much of the trade that once could go nowhere but down the Ohio and Mississippi to New Orleans. It took nerve for Black Ball promoters to pledge the sailing of their ships "full or not full," to expose them to winter crossings of the North Atlantic regardless of weather and lack of freight. But New York shippers took these risks and outdistanced all their rivals. The first eastbound packet, the *James Monroe,* left in a snowstorm as scheduled on January 5, 1818, though a snowstorm "would have been regarded as a valid excuse for delay by any regular trader" and

---

[2] Mitchell, *Gregg,* p. 15.

skeptics had predicted postponement.[3] Adherence to the "principle of punctuality" was one of the things the Black Ball promoters depended upon to attract cargoes to their holds, and their success in maintaining their schedules won good publicity for them. The following appeared in the New York *Commercial Advertiser* of April 2, 1818:[4]

REMARKABLE EXPEDITION—The packet ship *Pacific,* Captain Williams, arrived at this port from Liverpool on the evening of the 25th of March and commenced discharging the next day. She has discharged her cargo and reloaded in the short space of *six* days. We understand that she was completely ready for sea at 11 o'clock. She will sail at the appointed time, Sunday, the 5th of April.

All that New York shippers lacked was cargo for the journey eastward across the Atlantic. Their enterprise had gained them access to the greatest American markets, and they had organized ocean and inland shipping to bring to those markets the manufactures and luxuries of the world. But what to export to pay for these manufactures and these luxuries? Cotton supplied the answer. With rich banks to extend commercial credit, large warehouses to store up raw materials, and a great merchant fleet to carry these materials to established and growing markets, New York merchants began their invasion of southern cotton depots in a strong competitive position. And as southerners came more and more to despise trade, to hate moneychangers, to spend their profits in Charleston in the "season," or to invest them only in more cotton lands and more slaves, they made the task of the northerners easier. By 1830, so successful were northern merchants engaged in the cotton trade that forty cents of every dollar paid for the planter's staple went North. This was distributed over interest, commissions, freight tolls, and insurance, and all who shared in this distribution were added to the ranks of southern "enemies" already thick with northern manufacturers who had placed high tariffs on finished commodities that the agricultural South refused to produce for itself.

As a triangular trade thus developed among the cotton South,

[3] Albion, *New York Port*, p. 42; Albion, *Square Riggers*, p. 22.
[4] Gras and Larson, *Casebook*, p. 350.

commercial New York, and industrial England, southern planters fell deeper and deeper into debt. The more cotton they produced, the more they contributed to the treasuries of northern shippers and northern bankers. Soon they were producing so much cotton that prices began to fall, and when the panic of 1837 checked the expansion of industry and trade the world over, southerners suffered severely.[5] All their eggs had been in one basket, and the bottom of that basket had fallen out. As early as 1830, Charlestonian Maria Pinckney exclaimed that the South was "now in vassalage to the North, East and West."[6] In 1832 South Carolina had shown the temper of its region when it nullified the high tariff imposed by northern manufacturers. In 1837 one of the earliest conventions for the revival of direct trade between the South and Europe addressed southern planters as follows:[7]

You hold the element from which [the New York merchant] draws his strength and you have only to withdraw it to make him as subservient to you as you now are to him. You have but to speak the word, and his empire is transferred to your own soil, and his sovereignty to the sons of that soil.

But they did not "speak the word," and two years later another trade convention, this time meeting in Charleston, described the plight of the South:[8]

The direct trade, which was her own [the South's] by every law of commerce and nature, and which should have grown and increased every year, grew less and less until it almost disappeared, . . . transferred to the northern ports and people. . . . The importing merchants of the South became an almost extinct race, and her direct trade, once so great, flourishing and rich, dwindled down to insignificance.

Perhaps in the end it was better that too much faith was not placed in the revival of direct trade, for by 1837 it would have been quixotic for southerners to try to compete with New York. Their banks could not approach those of the great metropolis in credit facilities. Their ports could not match those of the

5 Robbins, *Landed Heritage*, pp. 60–61; Shannon, *Economic History*, p. 314.

6 Carpenter, *The South as a Conscious Minority*, p. 27.

7 Russel, *Southern Sectionalism*, p. 21.

8 Albion, *New York Port*, p. 120.

North in wharves, piers, or warehouses. Their markets for imported manufactured goods were comparatively insignificant. Besides, after 1833 northern capitalists had yielded on the protective tariff. Graciously they bore part of the cost of southern education, welcoming southern students to Harvard, Yale, and Princeton, supplying Charleston, Norfolk, Savannah, Richmond with teachers and ministers trained in the North. More than this, they had chased Garrison from the market place lest his abolition doctrine unbalance the sensitive scales of domestic finance. By 1833 northern businessmen had yielded the scepter of politics to the more graceful lords of the South, but while Capitol Hill echoed with southern oratory cotton dollars continued to cheer countinghouses in the North.

SETTLING THE WEST

In the Northwest of the 1830's, two great fingers of population marked the limits of the occupied frontier. One followed the Ohio valley, crooking its lowest joint up the Mississippi beyond St. Louis. The other, bending along the American shore of Lake Erie touched with its tip modern Sandusky and Toledo. The valley was southern, its people coming from below the Mason-Dixon line through Virginia and Kentucky. The Lake region was cosmopolitan, absorbing through the Erie Canal a rich stream of northeasterners and Europeans. Settling the upper counties of Ohio, Indiana, and Illinois, the latter were bound to the North by transportation and culture and were soon to fight their slave-holding downstate neighbors as New York fought South Carolina and Massachusetts fought the whole "black belt." It is well to remember that Cairo, Illinois, is farther south than Richmond, that Cincinnati is farther south than Baltimore, that plantations in southern Indiana and Illinois were cultivated partly by Negroes.

The story of the influence of this western frontier on democratic culture in America became popular long ago. But like all popular stories it is only partly true and that part is but a sequel to another story that scarcely has been told. The East did not export only goods. It sent West people and patterns of life.

Settlers in the Ohio valley and along the Lakes did not appear there miraculously with the wind and the rain, the rivers and the trees. They came from older sections, North and South, clung to whatever they could of their early lives, accommodated themselves only reluctantly to the strange environment across the mountains. Chiefly for western consumption in these decades there streamed from the presses of "etiquette publishers" in Boston and Philadelphia *The Young Man's Own Book* (1832), *A Manual of Politeness for Both Sexes* (1837), *The Laws of Etiquette* (1839), *A Manual of Good Manners* (1844), Maberley's *Art of Conversation* (1844). In religion and art also, the East was shown only in higher relief in the design of western culture, and eastern businessmen determined from the start to control western education. Edward Everett, nationally famous politician from Massachusetts, exclaimed in 1833:[9]

Let no Boston capitalist, then, let no man, who has a large stake in New England, and who is called upon to aid this [educational] institution in the center of Ohio, think that he is called upon to exercise his liberality at a distance, toward those in whom he has no concern. . . . They ask you to contribute to give security to your own property, by diffusing the means of light and truth throughout the region, where so much of the power to preserve or to shake it resides.

In another plea Everett declared:

The learning, religion, and the living ministry bestowed on the great West by these Colleges, unite in special benefit to mercantile morality and hence to the safety and value of business engagements there formed. Eastern merchants have an especial and increasing concern in the commercial integrity of this immense market for Eastern industry. . . . These colleges thus plead to every enlightened merchant, his own self-preservation.

Business standards also were defined for the West by eastern preceptors. "We shall be pleased," wrote Amos Lawrence, Boston manufacturer, in 1836,[10]

to see the best buyers of the large places west and southwest at old Boston to buy our domestic fabrics. . . . They will find it for their interest to come and to get thoroughly acquainted with our dealers. *At present we do*

---

[9] Curti, *American Educators*, pp. 69-70.
[10] Ware, *Textile Industry*, p. 187. Unless otherwise noted, all italics are author's.

*not want to see any but the first class buyer; a year or two hence, we shall
be glad to see the second class as we can fix the prices to correspond to the
risks.*

The leathered pioneer, with his sack, his ax and his flintlock
gun, is a colorful figure in the American epic and a legitimate one.
Epitomized by Daniel Boone, etched unforgettably by Cooper
and Theodore Roosevelt, he and his humor contributed the only
folk culture to come out of the West. He blazed the trail, ex-
plored the wilderness, helped to pacify or destroy the Indian.
These were important preparations for settlement, but in the
larger story of American growth the pioneer looms small beside
the eastern "squatter" and the speculator in western lands.

Trail blazers went singly and settled nowhere. They staked out
little land and improved less. They were adventurers not farmers,
fur trappers not husbandmen. Coming rapidly in their wake,
the "squatters" spread into the woodlands and over the prairies
until they pressed upon the borders of Indian territory. Careless of the fact that such distant land had not been opened for
sale, that no legal title, therefore, could be acquired, they cleared
the timber, built their cabins, broke the sod and planted their
first crops.

Even while "squatters" were taking their land free of charge
the government was opening large areas to public sale at auctions,
and the "squatter" himself—especially if he held good land that
was in demand—had to compete at such sales with speculators
and other purchasers. Since he so often proved he could not compete, the government eventually passed a series of preemption
laws and in 1841 a general preemption law was enacted, granting
the "squatter" on improved land the right to purchase that land
at the minimum price of $1.25 per acre before it was placed on
the open market. These laws only helped to protect the "squatters" from the speculators;[11] they did not greatly impede the

---

[11] The squatters had already developed means to protect themselves. These
were organizations of their own like "honor associations" and "claim clubs" as well
as the more amorphous but equally strong pressure of western public opinion. An
editorial in the Chicago *Democrat*, June 3, 1835, warned the speculator: "Public
opinion is stronger than law, and we trust that a stranger who comes among us,
and especially our own citizens, will not attempt to commit so gross an act of
injustice as to interfere with the purchase of the quarter sections on which the
settler has made improvements." (Robbins, *Landed Heritage*, p. 68).

latter's total operations, and huge quantities of land eventually were purchased for resale by eastern capitalists and land companies. The natural rise in the auction price of good government land was checked by these speculators through collusive bidding among themselves, by taking advantage of convenient loopholes in the laws regulating payments, or by bribing government land agents. Thus enterprising easterners got their western acreage at or near the minimum price and were ready to round up in Europe and the eastern states thousands of farmers interested in going to the West to settle.[12]

A great new stimulus thus was given to the westward movement by eastern speculators. In addition to "squatters" and the customers of the speculators, many farmers who could raise money by selling their eastern lands or who had funds from inherited estates or savings from successful farming in the East, also began to purchase government land directly, their independent action increasing still more the population of the trans-Allegheny. The Green Bay land office in Wisconsin, for example, estimated that of the total of 13,000,000 acres of government land sold in 1835, no more than 8,000,000 went to speculators, leaving at least 5,000,000 acres that were purchased by independent moneyed settlers.[13]

Coming from the East with tools, animals, and food, those who participated in the westward movement were draining the older sections of capital. And losing, for the time being, contact with organized trade, commerce, and production, they were able to send back no products to replace the supplies they had taken with them. So great was this movement to newer and newer areas that the country seemed to be growing poorer because of it. One estimator has held that between 1809 and 1829, America's per capita real income fell 20 per cent.[14] Eastern businessmen quickly became alarmed at the drain on their resources, and in 1827 Secretary of the Treasury Richard Rush warned that something had better be done to check it. He said:[15]

---

12 Hibbard, *Land Policies*, p. 103.
13 Robbins, *Landed Heritage*, p. 62.
14 National Industrial Conference Board, *Studies*, p. 79.
15 Robbins, *Landed Heritage*, p. 42.

The manner in which the remote lands of the United States are selling and settling, whilst it may tend to increase more the population of the country, . . . does not increase capital in the same proportion. It is a proposition too plain to require elucidation, that the creation of capital is retarded, rather than accelerated, by the diffusion of a thin population over a great surface of soil. Anything that may serve to hold back this tendency to diffusion from running too far and too long into an extreme can scarcely prove otherwise than salutary.

Despite Rush's plea, nothing was done by the government to stem this westward tide; but even as he spoke, the most important effects of the movement were being rectified by the coming of transportation. The great increase in the cultivated area of the West had created a strong demand for turnpikes, bridges, canals, and railroads to open markets for new farm produce and to bring to the West the imports and manufactures of the East. This in turn helped to bring to an early end the isolation of western settlers, whether "squatters" or original purchasers. It stimulated the creation of banks and factories to service and supply the new areas. It helped in the early restitution to the East of capital drained away—restitution in the form of goods to pay interest on commercial loans and mortgages that were to keep the West constantly in debt to eastern credit institutions. As early as 1820 Thomas H. Benton of Missouri could cry out against the Bank of the United States in Philadelphia: [16]

All the flourishing cities of the West are mortgaged to this money power. They may be devoured by it at any moment. They are in the jaws of the monster!

While population continued to be scattered all over the West, increasing numbers of western settlers soon were reestablishing their contacts with the regions they left behind. And as reports from the rich river valleys of Ohio, Indiana, and Illinois flowed back to struggling farmers on the rock-ribbed terrain of New England or the exhausted soil farther south, the movement west of those farmers or their younger sons soon became so strong that land prices soared. So persistent was this movement and so spectacular was this rise in land prices that many farmers

---

[16] Turner, *New West*, p. 137.

1832, the price was $100; in 1834, $3,500. In 1836 the state legislature at last approved the canal connecting Chicago with La Salle, giving the lake city its first hope of Mississippi traffic. In that year a lot along the canal route cost $21,400. This was the climax of the boom that swept the country from Back Bay Boston to the Mississippi, from the Gulf to the Lakes. Nowhere was it as intense as in the old Northwest, but always it followed the western pattern. Even Philadelphia and Baltimore were caught up in it, and lots in New York City tripled in value between 1830 and 1837.[20]

Encouraging this boom were the eastern and English bankers and the note-issuing western banks which looked to them for ultimate support. Between 1829 and 1837 the number of banks in the United States grew from 329 to 788, most of the increase taking place in the West. Their circulation increased from $48,-000,000 to $149,000,000; their loans, from $137,000,000 to $525,000,000. The bankers who ran these institutions knew little of business cycles, cared nothing for liquidity. In the whirlwind of prosperity, when would it be necessary to liquidate? Surely not before the farmers could pay off their new mortgages, not before canals and railroads could amortize their costs. Giving still another stimulus to speculation was the removal in 1832 of the government's funds from the Bank of the United States and their subsequent deposit in Jackson's "pet banks." The removal of the funds ended the efforts of the Bank of the United States to keep a centralized check on inflation while their deposit in less sound institutions broadened the base upon which such institutions could make speculative loans.

THE PANIC OF 1837

A hundred years ago, as today, pet hobbies were ridden to death by interested apologists for panics and depressions. In 1837 many blamed the *Specie Circular;*[21] others pointed to the misuse of surplus government funds. Failure to recharter the Second

---

[20] Sakolski, *Land Bubble*, pp. 232–254.

[21] By the *Specie Circular*, President Jackson ordered receivers of public money and deposit banks to accept in payment for public land sold after Aug. 15, 1836, only gold, silver, or Virginia land scrip.

Bank was an attractive explanation to hundreds. The tardy action of the Bank of England to check excessive capital exportation, caught the fancy of sophisticates. Hopefully, a New York bankers' convention, in 1838, summed up all these explanations, declaring: [22]

> Such a coincidence of extraordinary and unfortunate incidents, as produced the catastrophe, must be rare, and may never again occur.

Needless to say, none of these explanations is sufficient; nor do all together adequately explain why the panic came in 1837, the depression not until 1839. They describe only accidents of the specific occasion, symptoms, not causes.

Booms feed upon the pervasive and growing expectation that continued expansion will produce larger and larger profits, whether it be from quicker turnover of land, or accelerated construction of railroads. As expanding business uses more and more capital and labor, however, interest rates, wages, and other costs rise, following the curve of prosperity, and profits soon become jeopardized. In industrial society the first men to respond to the possibility of declining profits are the buyers of capital goods like machines or railroad track. These buyers must consider needs eighteen months and two years in the future, for it makes a crucial difference to the long-run profits of competitive companies whether new railroad equipment or new machines are purchased in markets that are high or low in relation to average prices over long periods of years. When purchasers of such equipment become wary, therefore, depressions are foreshadowed. And when their orders fall off, the consequent slackening of the rate of production of capital goods puts men out of work, reduces purchasing power, sets up sympathetic movements in other lines, and shakes the confidence of businessmen. The wiser ones begin to liquidate their investments or stabilize their production many months before the whole business community is affected. This speeds the decline, prompts hopeless efforts to check it, ends in panic.

That is the recurring pattern of prosperity and depression in

---

[22] Miller, *Banking Theories*, p. 188.

nineteenth century industrial society. In 1837 America, while not yet a mature industrial state, was already so involved in the construction of new transportation facilities that the continuance of these enterprises had by then become crucial to her economy. And when in 1836, for instance, only 175 miles of railroad track were built as against 465 miles the previous year a depression was apparently on the way. The effect of this decline in canal and railroad building was aggravated by the huge sums invested in western lands and urban real estate. When these investments, like those in new transportation, failed to return profits quickly, and succeeded only in tying up capital required to maintain the rate of expansion in other lines, the boom collapsed.

First to feel the pinch in the money market were the famed three W's—the English bankers Timothy Wiggin, Thomas Wilson, George Wilde. Theirs were not the most important English banking houses, but they were the three houses most deeply involved in American trade. Between January 1, 1834, and January 1, 1837, their American acceptances, mostly for cotton, jumped from £2,354,000 to £5,573,000. Between February and March, 1837, however, cotton prices in the English market fell 25 per cent. Alarmed by this and by the *Specie Circular,* the Bank of England announced for July and August a high rediscount rate of 5 per cent, and made it clear that at no price would it handle more cotton paper. The three houses were marooned. Thrice they appealed to the Bank of England for aid sufficient only to finance day-to-day activities. Twice this aid was granted. The third time, it was denied; and on June 2, 1837, all three houses shut down.

These failures sealed the market for the cotton acceptances eastern bankers had piled into their vaults as security for commercial and speculative loans. Themselves in difficulties, these bankers called upon their western correspondents. But the latter were even worse off. The *Specie Circular* had produced a run on the gold reserves of western banks and these banks in addition had issued paper money and extended credit to speculators far above the amount legally permitted by their remaining meager specie. The slight liquidity in their inflated business had depended entirely upon eastern credit. When this failed, western banks failed, bringing down their eastern correspondents and the clients who depended upon them.

In England, however, where speculation ran not so high, and where credit resources were not so tenuous, hope lingered. The crash in America caused a great flurry among traders in American securities and carried some English failures in its wake. But the London money market, with resources on the Continent and in the Empire, did not break in 1837. Nicholas Biddle saw in this an opportunity to save American banks.

If English bankers now abhorred American cotton acceptances, they still credited the short-term notes of leading eastern banks. These twelve- to eighteen-month obligations Biddle collected and discounted in London. With the receipts he cornered the American cotton export, kept up the price of cotton, and insured, for as long as he could maintain his corner, the stability of southern banks. This eased their calls on metropolitan correspondents in the North and enabled the latter to support some western banks and endure the failure of others. By renewing these bankers' notes or exchanging them for new state bonds Biddle kept his system in operation until 1839 and managed to absorb into the United States additional millions of British pounds sterling. In effect these were used to get American bankers out of the West while the British shouldered the heavy load of dead canals, railroads, state bonds, and mortgages on deflated land.

Obviously, the English, blinded by the glitter of western publicity and enticed by high interest rates on American loans, did not know how shaky were American finances between 1830 and 1837. By 1839, however, they realized the extent of their credulity. The suspension of the Bank of Belgium late in 1838 added to difficulties over American investments, and the European liquidations following that failure made the ensuing panic worldwide. Biddle's pool collapsed, and Britain, America, France, Germany, and Belgium all began to suffer for excessive speculation. Work stopped on railroads, canals and public buildings, and laborers engaged on them joined the mobs of unemployed released by the shutting down of industry. Prices fell. In the cities the poor rioted for bread and flour, while farmers resisted with arms efforts to foreclose their land. Thomas Benton in 1840 described the situation in the West: [23]

The goods are worn out, the paper money has returned to the place from whence it came; the operation is over, and nothing remains to the transactions but the 170 millions of debt, its devouring interest, and the banks, canals and roads which represent it. The whole of these banks have failed once, and most of them twice, in two years; the greater part of the roads and canals are unfinished, and of those finished, several are unproductive.

ENGLAND LEARNS A LESSON

It cannot be said too often that the construction of railroads, canals, turnpikes, and steamboats gave the greatest stimulus to the development of American industry. Such construction used men, lumber, iron, land. It opened markets for finished goods and gave access to raw materials. Of separate sections marked off by formidable natural boundaries, it made a united nation.

For much of this accomplishment the United States depended upon foreign capital.

We have seen how British investments accelerated the transportation and land booms in the West. These booms collapsed when foreign funds stopped coming. Had there been no British investments in the United States, we should, of course, still have had railroads and canals in Ohio, Indiana, or Mississippi, we should have had steamboats on the Hudson and the lakes and a boom in western farms. But how slow these developments would have been, we learned in the forties, when the flow of foreign capital became a mere trickle in the gorge worn by the earlier activity.

The world depression of the "Hungry Forties" prevented the accumulation of much investment capital anywhere in the western world. The flow of British funds to the United States in that decade, however, fell off much more sharply than was warranted by the depression alone.[24] Excess credulity bred excess care and once-gullible British investors, even when they had the

---

[23] Myers, *Money Market*, p. 31.
[24] Hidy, in *Tasks of Economic History*, pp. 61, 64.

money, refused to consider investments in American state bonds. Such investors of course had reason and experience on their side. When Biddle's corner collapsed in 1839 about $200,000,000 in American securities were owned in England. By 1841, $120,-000,000 of these were in jeopardy. The next year, Illinois, Indiana, Michigan, Pennsylvania, Alabama, Maryland, Louisiana, Mississippi, and Florida either defaulted on interest or repudiated altogether. It was bad enough for the West to go down. Even the British thought western bonds slightly speculative. But what of the $35,000,000 in Pennsylvania? Were they not as sound as the Bank of England? Clearly, they were not; but it took experience rather than research to show their weakness. And experience bred bitterness as well.

Englishmen agitated to have the federal government assume the obligations of the bankrupt states. When this agitation came to naught, invective scorched the pages of British journals. Sydney Smith, founder and editor of the *Edinburgh Review*, said he never met a citizen of Pennsylvania at a London dinner [25]

without feeling a disposition to seize and divide him—to allot his beaver to one sufferer and his coat to another—to appropriate his pocket handkerchief to the orphan, and to comfort the widow with his silver watch, Broadway rings, and the London Guide which he always carries in his pockets. How such a man can set himself down at an English table without feeling that he owes two or three pounds to every man in the company, I am at a loss to conceive. He has no more right to eat with honest men than a leper has to eat with clean.

Even the federal government, seeking a loan in Europe in 1842 to replenish the national Treasury, was rebuffed unceremoniously. "The people of the United States may be fully persuaded," thundered the *Times* of London, "that there is a certain class of securities to which no abundance of money, however great, can give value; and that in this class their own securities stand preeminent." [26] "You may tell your government," said the Paris Rothschild to Duff Green, the American agent, "that you have seen the man who is at the head of the finances of Europe, and

[25] McGrane, *State Debts*, p. 59.
[26] Jenks, *British Capital*, p. 106.

that he has told you that they cannot borrow a dollar, not a dollar." [27]

THE AGRARIAN REVOLT

We have seen how young industry, vigorously organized into cohesive pressure groups in the Northeast between 1816 and 1832, had wrested from indecisive agrarians favorable tariff and banking laws and encouraging decisions in the federal courts. During these years of prosperity, clouded only temporarily by the panic and depression of 1817–1822, and the decline of 1828–1829, northern industry flourished. Profits were large, and surpluses were nursed partly for reinvestment in the businesses that produced them, partly for investment directly or through eastern banks, in the triangular cotton trade or western state bonds and mortgages. These investments paid good dividends to the financial interests in the Northeast—so good, indeed, that agrarian leaders in many parts of the West and the South began at last to marshal their followers in order to challenge northern and eastern business for political leadership in the nation.

It is true that there were many in the agricultural West who had their own mills and forges and thus were generally in favor of protective tariffs. It is also true that many western farmers who grew flax and hemp wanted protection against European and far eastern competition, while many wheat farmers also were not averse to the high-tariff policy of their industrial customers in New England. In addition, South Carolina, opposed to protection of any sort, numbered among its citizens owners of stock in the second Bank of the United States. Thus, like the tariff, the Bank also escaped attack in a region where it might well have expected it.

These local conditions, however, were exceptions to the general situation in the United States, and by 1828 the feast that industry was enjoying, as far as political favors were concerned, was practically over. Agrarian leaders had been successful in their organizing efforts and were ready at last to assert the power their superiority in numbers gave them. Their first step, of course,

---

[27] Jenks, *British Capital*, p. 106.

was to elect Jackson, though it is possible that they did not quite know what to expect of the military hero from the Southwest. Jackson's campaign did not enlighten them, for he so obscured his views on the tariff, internal improvements, and the Bank that many industrialists were also won to his support despite his agricultural background. It was not long, however, before Jackson and his party embarked on a course that was to alienate his industrial supporters in the North.

Ostensibly for the construction of a national road, the Maysville bill was introduced into the Senate in 1830. Many claimed that the real purpose of the bill was to draw out the oracular Jackson on federal aid to roads and canals. If that alone was its purpose it succeeded, for Jackson vetoed the bill. It had had the support of northern financiers, northern industrialists, and speculators in western lands, but Jackson hoped for more from his southern followers and he was not to be disappointed.

Next in order was the Bank. Designed again to catch the President in a political snare, the bill to recharter the Bank of the United States was introduced four years early. Jackson vetoed the bill, called down upon his head vitriol and invective, but saw the "monster" end its official career as a national bank in 1836. Farmers and jealous local bankers were highly pleased, but industry and commerce were thoroughly shaken during the next few years of speculation and dispute.

Finally there was the tariff, a more spectacular issue as it turned out than the Bank. By 1832, South Carolina had become tired of having to sell her high-cost crop in a world market, and of having to purchase her manufactures in a protected one. Her response to the tariff of that year was the threat of nullification. When her leaders prepared to resist customs collection with the state militia, Jackson replied with the Force Act. Incipient rebellion was quelled without violence, however, by Clay's compromise tariff of 1833. This was a real victory for the agrarians, for it assured declining duties until 1842. In that year an effort was made to raise tariff rates in some schedules, and while increases in duties were enacted for revenue, even these increases were reduced again four years later.

These victories were the measure of agrarian strength, though there was no unity among the farmers in all the political contests. The South congratulated itself on the Maysville veto; the West championed the defeat of the Bank; but neither section had the united support of the other in its victory, and both victories offended the eastern financial interests and brought economic havoc in their wake. Though the Maysville bill obviously was hatched for political purposes, its veto cast the whole burden of internal improvements upon the states. They could not bear it. What the speculative bubble might have been had the national government instead of the states undertaken the financing of western improvements, we can only conjecture. This much, however, it is safe to say: there would have been no repudiation by state governments, England would not have been alienated, and construction might have been conducted at a more even pace with a better transportation system operating in the end. Even the pervasive emphasis upon states' rights and intense localism, however, did not reduce by much the impact of eastern business, its money, its credit, its practices and principles upon the South and the constantly changing West.

IV

THE EARLY RAILROAD AGE

THE year 1837 was one of panic in the United States, 1857 was another. Between were two decades that, whatever their seasonal and cyclical ups and downs, produced more wealth, more waste, more hope and disillusion than any previous twenty years in the country's history. During this period the United States reached the Pacific, her railroads crossed the Mississippi, her money crops more than doubled, yet her manufactures passed them in value. Wrought into an economic unit by bands of iron, by locomotives roaring through the river valleys and across the mountains, America simultaneously was torn asunder by political, religious, and financial problems. The conflict between the North and the South became more acute each year of these decades, and the threat of civil war hung heavily over the nation. At the same time other conflicts began to be felt, conflicts in the North itself between native and alien workers, between Protestants and Catholic immigrants and, most important as far as the future was concerned, conflicts between the owners of American industry and the rising bankers, between the stockholders of new corporations and the financiers who managed them.

Once organized by entrepreneurs who sought profits simply through economies in production and shrewdness in competition, northern industry in the 1840's and 1850's was beginning to be run by businessmen who kept one eye on the stock exchange and sought profits through cooperation in marketing and manipulation of securities. The seminal development of the period was the spread of corporate stocks and bonds among a larger and larger investing public. Related to this development was the growth of private banking houses. Investment capital began to flow confidently to the eastern money markets, and through these banking houses such capital was finding its way to the new securities of railroad construction companies, textile and iron factories, ship-building corporations, commercial banks, and insurance compa-nies. Increased speculation in stocks and bonds symbolized the change that was coming over American business, and the develop-ment of stock exchanges in key cities speeded this change.

All the new institutions through which American business was conducted were concentrated in northern cities, and the rapid growth of these cities began to create new problems in American urban life, began to change social and economic relations between rich and poor, employers and workers, bankers and investors. Dealing more in liquid *rights to property*—in paper currency, mortgages, land warrants, stocks and bonds—than in real prop-erty itself, these institutions made the North more money-con-scious than ever before. They gave a fillip to speculation in all fields where exchange could be consummated by negotiable paper, and they put a premium upon money wealth rather than landed wealth. In the forties and fifties the growth of privately endowed universities, libraries, and museums showed the impact of new business fortunes upon American society, just as grandiose car-riages, fine clothes, liveried servants, fancy-dress balls and elab-orate theater parties revealed the growth of a leisure class living in great cities, drawing its wealth from every part of the industrial and commercial world. In politics too, the new condi-tions were felt, the "monopolies" exercising new weight through lobbying and liberal contributions to party chests.

Prosperous and pushing, northern business by 1860 thus had developed a new society, intricately tied to the economy of the South but profoundly at odds with the feudal mores of planta-tion culture.

ENTERPRISE MOVES WEST

The hope of Jefferson in the eighteenth century, the American West in 1840 still enchanted easterners like Emerson, Thoreau, Whitman, and Melville. "America begins with the Alleghenies" —that was their belief, deprived as they were of their native agrarian environment by the factories and railroads that dammed the rivers and broke the silence of the countryside. "God has predestined, mankind expects great things from our race and great things we feel in our souls," wrote Melville in 1850. "The rest of the nations must soon be in our rear. We are the pioneers of the world; the advance guard, sent on through the wilderness of untried things, to break a new path in the New World that is ours. In our youth is our strength; in our inexperience our wisdom." [1] To New England farmers, southern youths, and the poor peasants of Europe, the West was the promised land. The panic of 1837 had left, as legacy, bankruptcies, debts, high taxes, fine crops and low prices, the mockery of unfinished railroads and canals. But the panic was over, the depression past by 1845. Ours "is a country of beginnings, of projects, of vast designs and expectations," wrote Emerson. "It has no past: all has an onward and prospective look." [2]

Symbolic of the tremendous growth of the next twelve years was the vision of Asa Whitney, China merchant of New York. Accustomed by his business to great distances, Whitney cast his eye over the western plains, over the barrier of the Rockies, on to the Pacific where he saw a railroad joining that ocean with the Atlantic. "Sail to the West and the East will be found"— that was the paradox of Columbus. In 1845 the East still beckoned, and Whitney petitioned Congress to bring it nearer. That was before the Mexican War, before the Oregon Treaty, before the discovery of gold in California. So sanguine had Americans become, they would straddle the continent before it was theirs. They would join the two oceans with bands of iron before railheads had reached the Mississippi—but one-third the distance from east coast to west.

Such was the spirit of the nation in the two decades before the Civil War, and the West justified this optimism by the rapidity of its growth, the fertility of its soil, the wealth of its mines and forests. More than twenty years passed before Whitney's dream came true. It took a foreign war to capture the path of the first transcontinental railroad and a fratricidal war to dissolve the political obstacles in its way. By 1866, however, the Union Pacific

[1] Mumford, *Golden Day*, p. 89.
[2] Mumford, *Golden Day*, p. 89.

and the Central Pacific were under construction over land wrested from Mexico, along a route the South had long opposed. In the intervening years the West had grown tremendously, and men less visionary than Whitney had knit a pattern of smaller railroads in the older sections of the land.

In nineteenth century society, large savings and a leisure class were necessary for the flowering of art, and neither was found in the West where the Cary sisters wrote anemic poetry and McGuffey sold his Readers. The West was intent only on breaking ground, building railroads and steamboats, sowing, reaping, harvesting crops, feeding southern plantations and eastern cities. Unaccustomed to stability or security, the westerner when he became rich refused to rest on his wealth and adorn his society. Each prosperous year in these prosperous decades, he produced a greater money crop, but each year he only plowed more cash and credit back into the land, often mortgaging his holdings with eastern banks as he sought greater and greater eastern and southern markets.

During the forties, but six thousand miles of railroad track were laid in the United States—most of them in the eastern area out of Boston, New York, Philadelphia, and Baltimore. In the next decade American railroad mileage increased by 21,000 miles, most of them in the new West. The railroad net by 1860 captured Milwaukee, St. Louis, Memphis, New Orleans. Chicago then had "fifteen lines and well over a hundred trains." In 1851 the fabulous Erie opened the first trunk line to the West, from Piermont on the Hudson to Dunkirk on Lake Erie. By 1854, the New York Central ran to Buffalo, the Pennsylvania to Pittsburgh, the Baltimore & Ohio to Wheeling. All four by 1860 had direct rail connection with the "Windy City," tying to Atlantic ports the rich valleys of the Ohio and Mississippi. Beyond the great river the iron horse was finding passage in Missouri, Iowa, Arkansas, and Texas. Land grants, city and state bonds were reviving the speculative fever of the thirties as the newer and newer West thus responded to the optimism of the nation over western prospects.

In the 1840's the West was at last becoming permanently settled by farmers, merchants, manufacturers. It was visited regularly by land agents, lawyers, salesmen, surveyors. A St. Louis Business Directory in 1854 listed forty-eight insurance agents or companies.[3] According to the Census of 1850, Ohio had 2,028 lawyers, ranking in this respect third only to New York and Pennsylvania. Illinois reported thirty-one brokers, concentrated mainly in real estate in Chicago, while Missouri counted 2,879 clerks in all lines of trade. Between 1840 and 1860, Ohio, Illinois, Indiana, Michigan, and Wisconsin doubled their population, tripled the production of their fields. No wonder the West tuned the nation to its optimistic key, attracting still more settlers and capital and justifying the hopes of both.

PACED BY MACHINES

Men and oxen, horses and mules are plodders compared with machines. Had the United States to depend upon animal power, it would have developed at a medieval pace. The factories of the East would have choked on their goods without railroads to rush them to market. Eastern banks would have slept on their credit without the express and telegraph. The West grew a wheat crop large enough to feed the nation in 1860, but that crop would have rotted in the fields had there been no machines to harvest it. It would have overflowed the warehouses had it depended upon old-fashioned wagons and flatboats for distribution.

In 1840, by rivers, canals, or turnpikes, through the Gulf or up the coast, it took almost a week to go from New York to Cleveland, Cincinnati, or Louisville; two weeks to New Orleans, St. Louis, or Detroit; three weeks to Chicago or Milwaukee.[4] By 1860 weeks had been reduced to days: St. Louis was seventy-two hours from New York; Detroit and Chicago, forty-eight; Cleveland, less than twenty-four. As early as 1851, J. D. B. De Bow declared that northern enterprise had "rolled back the mighty tide of the Mississippi and its ten thousand tributary streams until their mouth, practically and commercially, is more

---

[3] Gras and Larson, *Casebook*, p. 392.
[4] Paullin, *Atlas*, plate 138B (slightly adjusted for change in date).

at New York and Boston than at New Orleans." [5] Canals aided in this manipulation of nature, but railroads completed the job. Speedier, unimpeded by frost or low water, railroads by 1860 had joined the western granary to eastern and western factories, had joined markets to the new machines, the country to the town. Communication, not production, was the key to industrialism in the United States. Settled haphazardly to suit real estate speculators rather than farmers or manufacturers, America was made up of separate economic areas, gratuitously dispersed, needlessly distant from markets or raw materials until knit by railroad and telegraph into a cohesive Union. By 1860, east of the Mississippi this cohesion had been achieved.

Before turnpikes, canals, or railroads were extended into new areas, the western farmer like his eastern forebear of an earlier period ground his own flour and made his own clothes. He sowed his seed broadcast, reaped with scythe and sickle, harvested with his hands, and threshed with his flail. He produced for his table and his neighbor just as the household worker in the East had spun cotton and wool, made shoes, coats, and furniture for the area around his home and shop. By the late thirties, however, as machines grew in number and regional specialization increased, this local self-sufficiency was passing; by the time of the Civil War it had virtually disappeared. As early as 1838, William Buckminster of Massachusetts wrote: [6]

The times are changed and we must change with them. We cannot now, as formerly, raise much grain for the market. The virgin soils of the West and the increasing facilities of intercourse with that region render it probable that much of our grain will be imported thence; and when no obstacles are thrown in the way of commerce, this is no evil. We purchase, not because we cannot produce the same commodity, but because we can produce others to more profit. Let them supply our cities with grain. We will manufacture their cloth and their shoes.

By 1860 Buckminster's probabilities had materialized. Early transportation facilities had made the factory possible and every subsequent advance in speed of communication and accessibility

[5] Carman, *Social and Economic History*, vol. II, p. 142.
[6] Carman, *Social and Economic History*, vol. II, pp. 275, 276.

of cities had increased the "circle of the market" for manufactured goods. At the outbreak of the Civil War northern farmers had very largely abandoned household industry and had begun to concentrate on money crops while in limited specialized areas industrial production was carried on for the whole nation. The South, overladen with slaves and satisfied with the glacial pace of feudal agriculture, could not so easily adapt itself to the changes going on all about it. In the East and West, however, farm and factory grew steadily in size, enlisted more and more men and machines, speeded operations many times, and by 1865 had proved the supremacy of industrial culture.

In 1830 De Tocqueville wrote:[7]

If the democratic principle does not on the one hand induce men to cultivate science for its own sake, on the other, it does enormously increase the number of those who do cultivate it. . . . Permanent inequality of conditions leads men to confine themselves to the arrogant and sterile researches of abstract truths, whilst the social condition and institutions of democracy prepare them to seek the immediate and useful practical results of the sciences. The tendency is natural and inevitable.

In expanding America there was a premium on new devices, new gadgets, and 5,942 new patents were issued in the 1840's; 23,140, in the 1850's. Mechanical drills and saws, steam engines, carders, water wheels, pumps—all were being improved while our new agricultural machinery was winning world supremacy. At the Paris exhibition in 1854, six men were pitted against four different threshers for half an hour. Their respective labors yielded:[8]

Six men with flails	60 liters of wheat
Belgian thresher	150
French thresher	250
English thresher	410
American thresher	*740*

In another test, an Algerian reaper cut an acre of oats in seventy-two minutes, an English reaper in sixty-six, an American in twenty-two. The job would have taken the best hand worker

---

[7] Beard, *Rise of American Civilization*, vol. I, p. 741.
[8] Bogart, *Economic History*, p. 278.

three times as long as the slowest machine.[9] At the same time, water turbines were increasing factory efficiency 50 per cent. Sewing machines in carpet factories were doing the work of eight or ten men; in the boot and shoe industry and the manufacture of ready-to-wear clothes, sewing machines worked a revolution in speed and costs of production. Rapid express service after 1840 and uniform postage rates a decade later speeded and cheapened exchange. In communication of orders, in the settlement of bank balances, in determining the state of distant markets, the telegraph was like a favorable wind. Stimulated by these improvements American manufactures in 1850 passed the billion dollar mark in value. By 1860 this figure was almost doubled.

THE PRESSURES OF OVERHEAD COSTS

Tireless, efficient, often requiring but the cheapest unskilled labor to tend it, the machine was the creator of industrial wealth. In a country expanding as rapidly as the United States in mid-century, its use could be extended almost without limit to supply the needs of a rich and voracious market. Yet under a system of free competition, in an atmosphere of incorrigible optimism, there were dangers in mechanization so great that periodically the capital of producers was consumed, turning lively enterprises into failures almost overnight, turning competition into cutthroat channels, and encouraging the growth of monopolies.

Like the factories that house them, expensive machines are often purchased with borrowed money and thus come burdened with fixed interest charges that have to be met each year. In addition, against the time when they have to be replaced a fund for depreciation should be maintained. Thus machines are generally purchased only when the market outlook *seems* favorable for a long period, when the horizon is clear of apparent obstacles and customers seem to be growing in number and wealth. Only by working to full capacity will machines yield maximum returns on their original cost. Only when it seems that their maximum production can profitably be sold, therefore, will they be installed.

---

[9] Rogin, *Farm Machinery*, p. 126.

In a freely competitive society, however, such as America had in the middle of the nineteenth century, an expanding market is open to everyone. It can be exploited by anyone with capital without asking permission from government or gild. Thus when attractive opportunities appear, each enterprising factory manager, each railroad operator, each shipbuilder, enlarges his plant, buys new machines, rents new land for new buildings. From other lines come new investors, each repeating the process, each bitten by the bug of optimism, assuming constant expansion of the market, constant consumption of all the goods he can produce or deliver.

In optimistic America, these rash assumptions, on the slightest provocation, flourished like green bay trees in investors' minds, and while for long periods these capitalists seemed justified in their appraisals of market conditions, every so often they were proved wrong. Somewhere there was always an end to the rainbow; its graceful arch started at the bottom, and eventually it always returned there. As the unsatiated market drew producers to satisfy it, competition among these producers quickly turned opportunities to ashes. Soon there were too many railroads, soon there was too much cotton cloth or too much salt or flour or packed meat; too much, that is, to yield a profitable return. Free enterprise allowed free expansion in any line, and free expansion periodically unbalanced the market.

In such situations workers could be discharged, orders for raw materials could be withdrawn, salaries could be cut. But the machine was untouchable. Interest charges continued even if sales did not. To collect some money to pay these charges, therefore, businessmen often slashed prices, even selling at appreciable losses to attract new buyers into the market or to gobble up a competitor's share of it.

Under such pressure, weak producers always surrender. Unable long to sell at a loss, they soon go out of business. They either close their plants or sell them to salvage what they can for investment in some more promising venture. To the perseverance even of the most economical producers, however, continued losses and depletions of capital also set a limit. And when, from the gossip of the trade, they learn that their competitors would also like to put a stop to ruinous below-cost sales, they meet to seek ways and means to end cutthroat practices. Competition is thus curtailed or abandoned. Price agreements replace price wars. Markets are divided among former competitors. Trade associations are formed to enforce fair-trade practices, to see that parties to the new agreements do not break the rules. Many companies merge with their competitors on the threat of annihilation or, in more equitable cases, to save duplications in costs, hoping thus the better to dominate the remaining firms in the industry and prevent the reappearance of price wars.

That is the recurrent pattern of nineteenth century business. The machine, an instrument of competition, tended always to become mother to monopoly.

In a community expanding as rapidly as America in the two decades before the Civil War, competition was usually preserved and monopoly avoided by the sheer elasticity of the market. By the fifties, however, there were indications that the burdens of overhead costs were beginning to take their toll. The capital of cotton factories almost doubled between 1840 and 1860, the value of their product almost tripled, while the number of spindles operated in them increased more than 100 per cent. The number of factories, however, fell from 1,240 to 1,091. Machine production was making it difficult for the inefficient man to stay in business, just as the pressure of great trunk lines was making it hard for the inefficient railroad. Mergers were frequent in the fifties, the most important being the formation of the New York Central Railroad in 1853. In the same year, the American Brass Association was formed "to meet ruinous competition." In 1854, the Hampton County Cotton Spinners Association was organized to control price policies. For the same purpose in 1855, was formed the American Iron Association. In 1857,[10]

a railroad convention . . . in New York City urged the abolition of expensive fast trains, free passes, and the ruinous system of seeking business by hand bills, runners, and freight solicitors, and the substitution of a uniform and increased freight tariff.

In 1849, the Pittsburgh *Morning Post* revealed a movement

---

[10] McMaster, *History,* vol. VIII, pp. 292, 293.

among iron men "to break up the small establishments." " 'The big fish are going to swallow up the little ones,' " declared a member of one of the firms involved. The editor commented: [11]

> The wealthy monopolists are anxious to crush those who are doing a small business, and get them out of the way, in order that they may fix prices to suit themselves!

In 1851, the *Cincinnati Gazette* reported: [12]

> About four years ago, the salt manufacturers of the Kanawha River, finding that their capacity to manufacture salt, was larger than the demand for consumption; and it having consequently went down to a ruinous price, formed themselves into an association, for the purpose of protecting their interests, by fixing the price of the article, and limiting the amount manufactured to the actual wants of the west.

Apparently this association was inadequate for the purpose, for in 1851 a new plan was evolved. A joint-stock company was organized, composed only of salt manufacturers, based upon a compact some of the provisions of which were reported by the *Gazette:*

> . . . one to prevent the transfer of stock, so that it cannot get into the hands of speculators; one to regulate the quantity of salt manufactured at any time, so that while it will be ample to supply the regular demand it shall not exceed it; one to regulate the price of the article so that foreign salt cannot under any circumstances be brought into competition. The present rate is fixed at twenty-five cents per bushel; but they will not bring any into the market, until all outside lots now in the hands of speculators have been disposed of.

These were but a few of the early efforts to escape the penalties of overexpansion. How well they worked may be surmised from the words of a speaker at a convention of New England railroad executives in January, 1851: [13]

> We make solemn bargains with each other to be governed by certain principles and rules, and violate them the same day, by a secret bargain with an individual, to obtain a small pittance of freight from another road. . . .

---

[11] Hunter, *Studies,* p. 78.
[12] Hunter, *Studies,* p. 59.
[13] Meyers and MacGill, *Transportation,* p. 567.

The people seeing this, lose all respect for us, as we seem to have none for ourselves, and they approach us to dicker with us like jockeys, without even thinking that we may deem it an insult. In this way we have already sunk our characters so low that the term "railroad man" is one of reproach and at once jeopardizes his rights and those of his corporation, even in our courts of justice.

THE WORKER IN THE TOWN

Besides intensifying competition in some lines to the point where it had to be abandoned or pursued *sub rosa,* the mechanization of American industry led to the rapid growth of American cities. Machine production drew thousands of industrial workers into the new factory towns and into new industrial suburbs in the metropolises. Machine production of large quantities of goods in specialized areas also created great distribution centers in which were mobilized indispensable banking, retail, and transportation facilities. Ever more prominent on the map, therefore, Chicago, Cincinnati, Buffalo, St. Louis, New York, Baltimore, Boston, and Philadelphia grew constantly richer, more populous, and stronger in political and economic power. They centralized control of production and communication and made agrarian markets and industrial workers accessible to the businessmen.

Machines called to American factories the native poor, the impoverished and ignorant of Europe. Herded into factory towns or into the slums of great cities, housed in jerry-built structures eight and ten to the room, these workers created typical municipal problems in the fields of sanitation, education, and recreation, and in the protection of property from brigandage and fire. Anxious to start production as soon as possible, absentee landlords of Holyoke or Chicopee, Manayunk or Conshohocken, brought workers to their factories before they supplied the towns with streets, sewers, or schools. In the older cities landlords moved to new sections, leasing the old to factory workers at premiums of 15 to 50 per cent. Production once under way, absentee owners saw no need to rush costly improvements in places where neither they nor their families lived.

A large amount of cheap labor often stimulates business enterprise, especially in a country where natural resources are awaiting development, where agriculture is expanding and manufacturers do not have to depend upon their workers for a market. In America of the fifties, all these conditions were present, and they contributed to the greatest prosperity in the nation's history up to that time as well as the lowest degradation of American labor. To the contrast many shut their eyes, pretending to see only the flower, forgetting that it had roots in factory towns and slums. Had they visited Holyoke in the 1850's, however, they would have seen the condition in which factory workers lived. That town's Board of Health reported in 1856:[14]

Many families were huddled into low, damp and filthy cellars, and others in attics which were but little if any better, with scarcely a particle of what might be called air to sustain life. And it is only a wonder (to say nothing of health) that life can dwell in such apartments.

Conditions were no better even in the great metropolis of New York. Concerning that city the New York Association for the Improvement of the Condition of the Poor reported in 1853:[15]

In Oliver Street, Fourth Ward, for example, is a miserable rear dwelling, 6 feet by 30, two stories and garret, three rooms on each of the first and second floors, and four in the attic—in all, ten small apartments, which contain *fourteen families*. The entrance is through a narrow, dirty alley, and the yard and appendages of the filthiest kind. . . . In Cherry Street, a "tenement house," on two lots, extending back from the street about 150 feet, five stories above the basement, so arranged as to contain 120 families, or more than 500 persons. A small room and bedroom are allowed each family in this building, which is of the better class; but the direful consequences of imperfect ventilation and overcrowding are severely felt. . . . Sub-letting is common in this Ward, which increases rents about 25 per cent.

Between 1840 and 1855 many Irish and some German immigrants began to replace American labor in the factories of New England and in railroad and canal construction work in the West. Accustomed to poverty, ignorant and strange, they were willing to work for next to nothing, to sleep in crowded hovels,

---

[14] Green, *Holyoke,* p. 43.
[15] Commons, *Labour,* vol. I, p. 491.

to wear out their lives digging ditches, tending machines, doing the menial tasks of industrial society. In 1850, in Chicago and St. Louis there were more foreigners than natives. By 1859 Massachusetts' mill population was at least 60 per cent Irish. Under such conditions, of course, there were no funds to finance labor organizations in the factories, no leaders to develop an *esprit de corps* among factory workers. Even in the fifties, when skilled artisans were reviving their trade unions, factory operatives, alien, ignorant, poor, and unskilled, were left to shift for themselves.

Laboring twelve, fourteen, and sixteen hours a day, such workers were too busy to play or show themselves on city streets. But if they were hidden from respectable travelers, their presence was felt by native artisans who were impoverished by machine competition. Their presence was felt also by the politicians who organized city voters. As early as 1840 a "nativist" paper wrote: [16]

Our laboring men, native and naturalized, are met at every turn and every avenue of employment, with recently imported workmen from the low wage countries of the old world. Our public improvements, railroads and canals are thronged with foreigners. They fill our large cities, reduce the wages of labor, and increase the hardships of the old settler.

Organized by Tammany politicians and their equivalents outside New York, the Irish especially were disliked by all classes in American society. Quarrelsome and Catholic, they aroused "respectability" to a "Protestant Crusade." So profound was the fear of their foreign culture, so deep the revulsion against their low condition in the 1840's and 1850's, that strong third parties appeared in our politics depending solely on appeals to nativism and antipopery and sponsored legislation to exclude from our shores alien communicants of the Vatican. In 1855 under the name of the Know-Nothings or Native Americans such parties elected governors in New Hampshire, Rhode Island, Connecticut, Massachusetts, California, and Kentucky. This marked the high point of the movement that threatened permanently to divide

---

[16] Billington, *Protestant Crusade*, p. 200.

American labor on nationalistic lines. Caused in part by the mechanization of industry, by the crowding of alien workers into industrial cities, the movement, paradoxically enough, flourished also because it opened an avenue of escape for politicians frightened by the new problems of this very machine culture. Perhaps the most important of these problems was the rising conflict between northern industrialists and the vassals of "King Cotton." Between 1856 and 1860 this sectional conflict at last became too intense to be any longer ignored. At the same time, because of business depression, the number of immigrants fell sharply. Both tendencies helped push the nativist movement temporarily into the background.

While foreign workers thus were attacked on the economic as well as the political front, the return of prosperity in the late forties was encouraging skilled American printers, stonecutters, hat finishers, molders, machinists, and blacksmiths to form national unions and to fight for the ten-hour day. These workers, however, were few compared to industrial laborers. In the factories operatives got nowhere bargaining with employers who were already combining successfully to resist their workers' demands. Speeding up communication in decades when labor was depressed, the railroad, telegraph, and improved mail service made employer organizations more effective in combating labor unions. In the middle thirties, skilled workers organized faster than blacklists could be circulated. In the forties and fifties, however, forced by cutthroat competition into trade associations, employers began to use these new organizations to exchange labor information and adopt integrated policies. "Cooperative action was also taken," writes B. H. Meyers, of the Convention of the New England Association of Railway Superintendents of 1848, "in the matter of discharging employees and employing persons discharged by other companies, and the association adopted a form of certificate of discharge covering the occupation, time on road, and cause of discharge, which came into general use." [17] Many years were to pass before industrial workers could organize effectively against their richer and stronger employers.

---

[17] Meyer and MacGill, *Transportation*, pp. 565, 566.

THE CORPORATION AND THE NATION'S BUSINESS

Industry is concerned with the production and movement of goods. Business is concerned with the making of profits. We tend to identify the two, assuming pecuniary gain to be the only incentive to economic activity. That there is no complete identification of the first type of activity with the second, however, is clear from the experiences of railroad engineers like John B. Jervis of the Delaware & Hudson, Jonathan Knight of the Baltimore & Ohio, Roswell B. Mason of the Illinois Central. These technicians, eager to build the best railroads with good beds, good grades, and durable rails, often came into conflict with the financiers, who showed interest in traffic conditions only as they affected the movements of securities. Using exorbitant construction and maintenance charges to line their own pockets, many of these financiers supplied their roads with the cheapest materials and services and catered to the needs of industrial society only sufficiently to insure themselves maximum profits from minimum facilities. That Daniel Drew, Edward Crane, or Robert Schuyler was hailed a railroad pioneer in his time was not the reward for his contributions to American progress but simply the reflection of America's love of success. Railroad securities, not transportation service, were their main stock in trade. To get control of our industrial plant they depended upon business, not technical, skill. Their instrument was the modern corporation.

The corporate device was used originally in America chiefly as a means to accumulate capital for large enterprises. In the 1840's and 1850's, however, the corporation was already tending to control great fortunes with little personal risk for the directors. Modern devices like non-voting stock and management shares were yet unknown, but diffuse stockholding already was inevitably separating ownership from control. As in many other aspects of American economy, railroad corporations showed the way in this development.

The railroad in the two decades before the Civil War was beginning to dominate not only transportation in the United

States, but the whole of American life. It gave tone to American industrial business which was tempering American agrarian society. William Ellery Channing felt this as early as 1841 when he exclaimed: [18]

The opening of vast prospects of wealth to the multitude of men has stirred up a fierce competition, a wild spirit of speculation, a feverish, insatiable cupidity, under which fraud, bankruptcy, distrust, distress are fearfully multiplied, so that the name American has become a by-word beyond the ocean.

Emerson experienced a similar reaction when he wrote: [19]

The rapid wealth which hundreds in the community acquire in trade enchants the eyes of all the rest, the luck of one is the hope of thousands, and the whole generation is discontented with the tardy rate of growth which contents every European community.

More than anyone else, the railroad promoter attracted the savings of American widows, doctors, poets, merchants, manufacturers, bankers, and shippers and tied the nation to his fortune. Accumulator of great capital, he gave big orders for wood, coal, iron, land. Chasing the Indian from the white man's country, opening the West for easterner and European, he materialized the ideal of "Manifest Destiny." Builder of track which by 1860 cost more than a billion and a half dollars, he represented the greatest investment in the land. No wonder businessmen in other lines went to school to the railroad promoter, and politicians catered to his needs.

The corporation was as essential to railroad construction as the track was to railroad operation. Huge fortunes were required, far beyond the means of any single man or any small group. In 1845 probably no American besides John Jacob and William B. Astor, Peter G. Stuyvesant, or Cornelius Vanderbilt was worth more than a million or two million dollars. On the other hand, to build the Baltimore & Ohio cost about $15,000,000; the New York Central cost about $30,000,000, the Erie about $25,000,000. How impossible to finance construction without

---

appealing to the public's purse directly or through the state!
What opportunities to play fast and loose with "other people's
money"!

As early as 1838 the Western Railroad in Massachusetts had
2,331 stockholders.[20] The New York Central in 1853 had 2,445.[21]
The Pennsylvania, financed almost entirely by house to house
sales of stock, had over 2,600.[22] According to the charters of
these companies, subscribers could vote at stockholders' meetings
or by proxies. But where was the hall that could accommodate
so many thousands of stockholders? Who would pay their passage from farm to city, from Buffalo to New York, from Pittsburgh to Philadelphia, from Wheeling to Baltimore? Could a
farmer leave his crop to vote his share, a storekeeper his shop,
a miller his mill? Commenting on the free passes that deluged
his line, President Wilkinson of the Syracuse & Utica wrote, "It
snowed like fury all day." But only editors, judges, preachers,
and legislators rode free, not stockholders.[23]

"No individual or combination of individuals had a controlling
monetary influence," writes Stevens of the New York Central,
consolidated in 1853. "Such control as there was arose wholly
from the character and standing of the men possessing it and
confidence felt in their ability, judgment and integrity." [24] The
management of the New York Central earned this confidence.
Could the same be said of Erie when Daniel Drew got hold of it?
Yet it took a Vanderbilt to run him out, not an army of little
stockholders.

Dispersed over the territory of the roads, unorganized, ignorant of high finance, the railroad "owners" were shut off
from information, from company funds or company press—em-
bossed stationery, imposing signatures, free postage. They could
map no strategy to implement their theoretical power. In a proxy
election in 1854, the Erie management defeated a stockholders'
ticket 35,000 to 9,000. The management had withheld until

---

[20] Kistler, *Rise of Railroads*, p. 84.
[21] Stevens, *New York Central*, p. 352.
[22] Cleveland and Powell, *Railroad Promotion*, p. 187.
[23] Stevens, *New York Central*, p. 159.
[24] Stevens, *New York Central*, p. 352.

after the vote the report of an investigation into company affairs. This investigation had disclosed falsified treasurer's reports, crooked manipulation of the "construction account." Bonds had been issued to maintain the road; the receipts had found their way into the management's pockets. Erie had become a plaything of Wall Street; plant and equipment had been allowed to decay while insiders had drained the treasury. In the election the manipulators were returned to power; the "owners" returned to paying.[25]

In 1860 the managers of the Baltimore & Ohio tried to escape the fetters of government ownership of some of its stock. Opponents of their effort described President Garrett of the road as "by far the most powerful individual in the Commonwealth." "The removal of state and municipal supervision," they claimed, "would place the road in the hands of a small group of Baltimore capitalists who would build up 'an oligarchy as dangerous, odious and irresistible as any that ever ruled or ruined a people.' "[26]

"In a former age," wrote Emerson in 1834, "men of might were men of will; now they are men of wealth." If this seemed a prophecy in its time, by the 1850's it was fact; and it was made so by the corporation. Nearly half of all the business corporations chartered in America between 1800 and 1860 were chartered in the decade of the fifties. Of the 1,448 transportation charters granted in Pennsylvania in those sixty years, 637 were issued after 1849.[27] General incorporation acts had begun to stimulate the demand for charters in nearly all the states. But the growth in number of corporations was least portentous. Businessmen's new power came from the opportunities created by the corporation for the concentration of the nation's wealth, for interlocking directorates and absentee ownership. These opportunities were most frequently embraced by railroad men. In other lines, however, financiers also were using the new methods to acquire wealth and influence. And the most successful of these financiers were the so-called "Boston Associates."

---

25 Mott, *Erie,* p. 116.
26 Summers, *Baltimore and Ohio,* pp. 38, 232.
27 Miller, in *Quarterly Journal of Economics,* vol. LV, pp. 154–159.

Since Massachusetts was the first industrial state in the United States, technologically the most advanced and productive, it was no accident that by 1860 the possibilities latent in "corporateness" were most highly developed there, with Boston the center of activities. By 1850, fifteen Boston families—the "Associates"—controlled 20 per cent of the nation's cotton spindleage, 30 per cent of Massachusetts railroad mileage, 39 per cent of Massachusetts insurance capital, 40 per cent of Boston banking resources.[28] Their first big industrial enterprise had been the Boston Manufacturing Company, founded in 1813. In 1818 they organized the Massachusetts Hospital Life Insurance Company, their first venture in that field.[29] After that they added steadily to their power in business and politics until in mid-century they were among the greatest of the new type of American businessman. Tightly knit, their organization had power far beyond what the simple figures show. They controlled water power on the Connecticut and Merrimack rivers and levied water rates on their textile manufacturing competitors who depended upon those waters. They held patents on many important machines, and for their use they collected royalties. Builders of canals and key railroads, they owned important transportation facilities in their state and section. They financed their interprises through their own credit institutions, which also numbered among their debtors many other businessmen and business corporations. They insured their factories and other holdings through their own companies and sold life and fire policies to businessmen throughout the nation. They influenced state and local politics and sent Daniel Webster to the United States Senate. Lawrences, Lowells, Appletons, Cabots, Dwights, Eliots, Lymans, Searses, Jacksons—in a sense *they* were Massachusetts, dominating its conservative press and pulpit, its schools and platforms, charities and philanthropies, supporting the Boston Brahmins and their cultural renaissance.

These were the "Boston Associates," the Morgans, Bakers, and Stillmans of their day, the modern men who made Holyoke a typical company town, Chicopee an industrial suburb, Lowell a

---

[28] Shlakman, *Factory Town*, pp. 37–45.
[29] Stalson, *Life Insurance*, p. 70.

great manufacturing city, and spread their empire of factories, railroads and canals, water power, real estate and insurance, to Dover, Nashua, Manchester, Somersworth in New Hampshire; Biddeford and Saco in Maine.[30] Through their banks they speculated in western lands; their insurance companies bought railroad bonds in Missouri, Illinois, and Minnesota. One Iowa promoter indicated the range of their influence when in 1842 he

expressed entire confidence (based upon letters from some of the leading Boston capitalists) that if a liberal charter should be granted by the legislature, a large portion of the capital necessary to construct the road, would be at once subscribed in Boston.[31]

Living sumptuously on Beacon Hill, admired by their neighbors for their philanthropy and their patronage of art and culture, these men traded in State Street while overseers ran their factories, managers directed their railroads, agents sold their water power and real estate. They were absentee landlords in the most complete sense. Uncontaminated by the diseases of the factory town, they were also protected from hearing the complaints of their workers or suffering mental depression from dismal and squalid surroundings. In the metropolis, art, literature, education, science flowered in the Golden Day; in the industrial towns children went to work with their fathers and mothers, schools and doctors were only promises, a bed of one's own was a rare luxury.

The corporation permitted ambitious financiers to diversify their holdings, to give their energy, insight, and daring to multifarious ventures. With the bulk of their personal property protected by limited liability, they could speculate with small risk and take great chances with other people's money. Under lax laws, their banks and insurance companies could invest in almost any type of speculative securities: in stocks and bonds of other banks and railroads, in land warrants, mortgages, and foreign consols. Unfettered by publicity, corporation directors could manipulate accounts, cancel great losses with great successes, pay dividends out of debts. They could speculate with

---

[20] Shlakman, *Factory Town,* pp. 39–42.
[31] Turner, *1830–1850,* p. 314.

a free hand and fail with impunity. Such license gave an impetus to American development that was completely lacking under the older system of individual or partnership enterprise, but it also left scars on many unwary sufferers. A saddened stockholder in "Associate" enterprises expressed the feelings of thousands with these words: [32]

The physician must watch his patient with care and skill, . . . the merchant, tradesman, or proprietor of property must assiduously guard his interests; the politician must serve his constituents. . . . Only the managers of our Manufacturing Corporations can outrage right and common decency, and then with impunity defy their employees, owners, and all the world.

The "Boston Associates" probably capitalized corporate advantages more thoroughly than any others in their times. But they were unique only in the range of their activities. Erastus Corning of New York, for instance, was also active on a great many economic and social fronts. So were Abram Hewitt and many others. Corning was a director of the Michigan Central and Hudson River railroads and the St. Mary's Ship Canal Company. He was interested in hardware and rolling-mill companies. He had been mayor of Albany and state senator. For four years during his presidency of the New York Central Railroad he was a Representative in the United States Congress. Abram Hewitt, ironmaster, was drawn into mines, railroads, telegraphs, land. Son-in-law to Peter Cooper, he shared the latter's business and philanthropic activities. His concern with iron tariffs involved him in politics. Alumnus of Columbia College, he gave it much of his time. A similar diversity of interests marked the "prominent shipping magnates" who often were presidents and directors of marine insurance companies. "A secretary handled the routine work; while a retired captain served as inspector" for these companies, according to Professor Albion. Their "stocks were traded on Wall Street, with frequent fluctuations." [33]

Through corporations men could invest in diverse ventures with moderate risk. Through stock markets they could withdraw

---

[32] Kirkland, *Economic Life,* p. 331.
[33] Albion, *New York Port,* p. 270.

almost at will. Organized security exchanges guaranteed liquidity for corporate paper and attracted small investors to great enterprises without forever tying up their savings. That such investors thus became prey for bulls and bears in Wall Street and·State Street, many learned after hard experience, but the stimulation their funds gave to the development of the continent was great.

Organized for the buying and selling of securities, New York, Boston, and Philadelphia exchanges were already the money markets of the nation when corporations became the most active users of capital. By the 1850's they had drawn funds from almost every group in the land. Writing about the years just before the panic of 1857, James K. Medbery declared:[34]

The entire country was in stocks. The farmer, the country lawyer, jobbers, heavy domestic dealers, the whole foreign trade, were more or less holders of shares, bonds, county, city or State paper. These they used as capital, drew therefrom dividends or interest, raised money for immediate needs by hypothecation, and, in a word, based their business movements upon the belief that this property could always be converted into coin or employed as collaterals.

Making their debut on the exchanges in 1830 when Mohawk & Hudson bonds were first offered to the brokers, "Rails" became most active after 1834. The "Boston Associates" sold shares in their enterprises through the Boston and New York exchanges, but smaller industrialists found few takers among the investing and speculating public. Railroads required more capital than any other enterprises and promised highest dividends. Their securities fluctuated most spectacularly yet offered apparent security. By 1850, they dominated the transactions on the New York Exchange and elsewhere.

With capital so liquid, temptations to manipulate and defraud the market were magnified. "The men of those days [the thirties] knew everything," wrote Medbery. Not as famous as the plungers of a later day, the Jacob Littles, Nat Primes, John Wards, and Jacob Barkers of the thirties worked "corners," "wash sales," bull and bear stampedes. In the fifties, with the

---

[34] Medbery, *Wall Street*, p. 319.

growth of corporations, speculation in the ups and downs of stocks became the respectable avenue to great fortunes, the occupation of leaders of society. Stocks were "bulled" with dividend announcements or rumors of government largesse, after insiders had purchased in low markets; or "beared" with horrendous gossip which sent prices tumbling and short sellers buying. Often the dividends were paid out of capital, the gossip manufactured in the "Street." Out of the fluctuations they set in motion the great financiers got rich, the little margin traders got fleeced.

Such activities generally were accepted in the spirit of roulette or faro. A game among plungers, "Playing the Market" gave spice to drab mercantile existence, attracted little Daniels to the lions' den. More important to the business community were the frauds perpetrated through the market. Uninspected at issue, fake stocks encountered no barriers if the company in whose name they were issued was listed. Thus Robert Schuyler, President of the New York and New Haven Railroad, could sell at par for his own benefit, in 1854, 20,000 unauthorized shares of stock—$2,000,000 worth—in his own company. In the same year, Alexander Kyle of the Harlem Railroad issued forged stock to the tune of $300,000 for his own purse, Parker Vein Coal Company officials flooded the market with five times as many shares as their charter authorized while President Edward Crane of the Vermont Central Railroad for his own profit scattered 10,000 illegitimate shares so widely that they were irretrievable, forcing the legislature to increase the authorized capitalization of his road to save his victims from being fleeced.[35]

These operations, when discovered, created a financial panic in 1854. They depressed prices, made the investing public wary, and temporarily frightened capital away from private corporations. Only the most flagrant offenders, however, were punished. The rest were soon excused. Business, the art of making money, had by the fifties "ceased to be a mere occupation which must be carried on in accordance with the moral code. It had itself become part of that code. Money-making having become a virtue,

---

[35] Medbery, *Wall Street*, p. 309; Kistler, *Rise of Railroads*, p. 225.

it was no longer controlled by the virtues, but ranked *with* them, and could be weighed against them when any conflict occurred." [36]

If growing corporations benefited from the accumulation of large amounts of security capital in the great money markets of the country, they had the private bankers to thank for making this capital available to corporate enterprises. Most chartered banks in the United States had capsized after the panic of 1837, and many states refused to charter any new ones. As corporation promoters began to seek more and more funds with the return of prosperity in the middle forties, therefore, they had to come to great private financiers. Connected with leading European houses like Rothschilds or Barings, with headquarters in New York, Philadelphia, Baltimore or Boston and branches in the hinterlands, such firms as E. W. Clark & Co., Brown Brothers, Drexel & Co., Chubb & Schenck, August Belmont, and Lee, Higginson thus began to expand their business. On the exchanges of the nation they began to arrange flotations of railroad securities, as well as federal, state, and municipal bonds. Dealing also in short-term commercial notes, acceptances, currency exchange, and land warrants, they had made an important part of their business by the 1850's the handling of long-term corporate securities. Still other private bankers were engaging in investment banking on a smaller scale, these bankers concentrating mainly on commercial short-term paper. In 1854, according to the *Bankers' Magazine,* there were eighteen private bankers in New York, ten in Boston, twenty in Philadelphia. St. Louis had fifteen and Chicago as many as twenty-five.

Like insurance companies and savings banks, these private bankers grew in wealth and number, the leaders among them gradually gaining access to the most important sources of American and European capital. As governments and private promoters came to them for funds, they extended their influence in American business and American politics. Starting modestly in the 1830's, they had become the greatest powers in the land by 1900.

---

[36] Adams, *Epic of America,* p. 191.

BUSINESS AND THE STATE

Between 1840 and 1860 American businessmen constructed an industrial plant and developed the financial machinery to control it from key points. Still only a small minority of the population, however, these businessmen had always to contend with a political state dominantly agrarian in attitude. They had, as well, to deal with political tensions within the competitive world of business itself. Labor was making "extravagant" demands for a ten-hour day, and American workers were trying to restrict the importation of immigrants who built the railroads for meager pay and tended machines for less. Railroad companies were competing with other railroad, canal, and turnpike companies for traffic monopolies, bounties, and subsidies while ironmasters were fighting railroads for tariff favors, and manufacturers and merchants were battling over protection or free trade. There was little unity of purpose, little concentration of forces among businessmen in their relations with the politicians of their day. Perhaps there was little they needed besides being left alone, little they hoped to get from a government dominated by landed aristocrats.

The closing of the Second Bank of the United States was a blow to industrial business. The independent treasury was an expensive experiment. Wildcat banking was a road to panic and depression. Business failed to get Pacific railroads. It escaped homestead laws only because southern and western agrarians split on the issue. It failed notably in the fight to keep import duties high on manufactured goods.

Only the railroads got what they wanted from the politicians in this period—sometimes at the expense of other interests, almost always at the expense of the public. For the railroads were still the hope of the farmers; in the fifties, the railroads still had the sympathy of the agricultural West, and the political support that went with it. The battles in Congress and state legislatures over railroad legislation were most frequently among railroad representatives themselves fighting over the spoils. Banking privileges, monopoly charters, great gifts of land and loans of money were readily bestowed upon the strongest of them. The farmers rebelled only when their representatives, gilded by railroad lobbies, became altogether too lavish with gifts from the state, altogether too blind to railroad excesses.

Lobbies are as old as organized governments. They were sent by American colonies to Parliament in London, by bank, turnpike, canal, and steamboat promoters to American Congresses and state capitals. They caught the spotlight in the early railroad age because they had more money to spend than ever before, greater interests at stake, stronger opponents to advertise their seeming offenses. Railroad lobbyists were often dishonest according to the lights of their age, and their opponents, poorer and out-maneuvered, made much of their derelictions. But railroad men knew what the people wanted, boldly played interest against morality and won. As James Buchanan said to Congress in 1843:[37]

If you defeat them [the railway companies] at this session, they will be here in greater force than ever at the commencement of the next. Their importunity will never cease whilst the least hope of success shall remain, and we have learned from our experience that they have both the ability and the will to select shrewd and skillful agents to accomplish their purposes before Congress.

Filling political portfolios with railroad stock, stuffing wallets with free passes, handing out inside tips on market movements, railroad lobbyists found it easy to convince Congressmen and Senators in Washington and state capitals that it was to the "general welfare of the United States" to build railroads over public lands, that they were "cooperating to the public good" even while satisfying their own "insatiable avarice and ambition." Prominent participants in railroad favors were Senators Stephen A. Douglas of Illinois, Lewis Cass of Michigan, Thomas H. Benton of Missouri, each an investor in western lands, a speculator in railroad securities. Between 1850 and 1857 they helped the railroads to 25,000,000 acres of public land, free beyond the cost of their own unofficial services. From willing states and cities lesser politicians got enormous railroad loans.

---

[37] Haney, *Railroads to 1850*, p. 417.

From Congress they won, in addition, low tariffs on British rails.

Ironmasters alone protested regularly against these railroad aggressions, but in doing so they had themselves to adopt railroad practices. Led by Abram Hewitt of New Jersey, they petitioned Congress in 1849 for protection of domestic rails. They argued for high tariffs in Bryant's *New York Evening Post,* and they hired the professional lobbyist John L. Hayes to represent them in Washington. The only result of their activity, however, was a lesson in democracy. Hayes "early learned," writes Allan Nevins, "that if the ironmasters wished results, they must show they had political strength. If they could prove that they controlled 60,000 votes in New York, New Jersey, and Pennsylvania, they would be treated respectfully." " 'I can name a dozen politicians,' " wrote Hewitt to his colleagues in 1851, " 'who can do us more good than one thousand ironmasters, but they must be paid. Last year we were deficient in means, and this year we will fail beyond a doubt unless every man send in his quota.' " In 1852, after a visit to Washington, Hewitt wrote: " '(1) No tariff bill can be passed without Southern and Western votes; (2) These votes cannot be secured unless a concession is made on railroad iron.' " [38]

Until after 1860, most of the rails used on American railroads were imported from England at prices American producers could not match. So discouraged were they that as late as 1857, "Pittsburgh did not have a single mill engaged in the manufacture" of rails.

State and local legislatures were eager to extend every privilege to the railroads in order to get the roads to pass through their towns, to make their villages railroad terminals. They were susceptible to every evidence of railroad favor, eager to grant any rights promoters might require. Monopoly of traffic between terminals was often sought and, in the early days, was frequently bestowed. [39] Always contested by shippers and by other types of transportation companies, such monopolies often were retained by bribery and wit. Thus the Camden & Amboy in 1831, presented

[38] Nevins, *Hewitt,* pp. 154, 155.
[39] Cleveland and Powell, *Railroad Promotion,* p. 165.

to the state of New Jersey 1,000 shares of stock. The string attached to the gift was the provision that these must be surrendered "if . . . any other railroad should be constructed between New York and Philadelphia." "The purpose of this act," writes Doctor Lane, "was admittedly to insure a monopoly of traffic through the reluctance of any future legislature to forfeit an asset with a nominal value of $100,000." [40]

Second only to monopoly, were banking privileges: the right to finance construction by the issuance of bank notes the only security for which was the *proposed* railroad. This privilege proved so fascinating that many companies ignored altogether their initial purpose to live richly off the printing press. According to the historian of banking in Mississippi: [41]

From December 20, 1831, when banking privileges were conferred on the West Feliciana and Woodville Railroad, until the crash came in 1837, Mississippi was gridironed with imaginary railroads, and beridden with railroad banks. In these enterprises there was more watered stock sold than cross-ties laid; reckless speculation brooked nothing as prosaic as the actual construction of railroads, on the successful operation of which it was supposed fabulous dividends would be declared.

So pernicious had these banking privileges become that, between 1835 and 1850, South Carolina, Georgia, Illinois, Wisconsin, Michigan, Florida, Pennsylvania, and Alabama prohibited them. In 1857, Kansas and Nebraska followed suit.

Where monopoly and banking powers failed to attract railroads to states or municipalities, loans and land grants succeeded. In the forties, while the states were still trying to extricate themselves from their earlier misadventures in railroad finance, the cities were the most generous grantors of their credit. By 1853, Wheeling's railroad debt was $55 per capita; Baltimore's was $43; Pittsburgh's, $34; St. Louis', $30; Louisville's, $25; New Orleans', $23; Philadelphia's, $20—making a total of about $21,000,000 for these cities alone. [42]

After 1850, the states once again interested railroad men,

---

[40] Lane, *Indian Trail to Iron Horse*, p. 324.
[41] Cleveland and Powell, *Railroad Promotion*, p. 171.
[42] Cleveland and Powell, *Railroad Promotion*, p. 206.

and their lobbies once more invaded legislative halls. Across the Mississippi were new states that had not been in the Union during the boom of the thirties, and older ones that had not then gone overboard on railroad bonds. In the fifties, these states repeated the mistakes of the more experienced ones, with the same consequences after 1857.

Easy prey to railroad promises, Minnesota and Missouri, between 1850 and the panic, used their credit to buy railroad bonds amounting to more than $22,000,000. In addition, they gave away a fortune in timber and agricultural land. Like other western states, they had become trustees of undistributed federal lands within their borders, with power to give such lands to the railroads. The scramble among the roads for these lands in Wisconsin in 1856 was typical. There the La Crosse & Milwaukee railroad company won the prize of a million acres by distributing about nine hundred thousand dollars in securities to the right people: "to 59 members of the Assembly, $355,000 worth; to 13 Senators, $175,000; to Governor Coles Bashford, $50,000; to other state officials, including one judge of the Supreme Court, $50,000; and to the governor's private secretary, $5,000." The rest was distributed among the lobbyists and their assistants who had worked to such good purpose in the legislative halls in Madison. By 1858 the road had gone bankrupt and the bribed got nothing but opprobrium for their greed. Only the governor had had the good sense to turn his $50,000 bonds into $15,000 cash. He spent the rest of his days in Arizona after a legislative inquiry revealed the corruption.[43]

The "Gilded Age" in American politics obviously began with the railroads, not with the Civil War and Reconstruction.

THE PANIC OF 1857

Westward, ever westward, ran the railroad promoter, the railroad lobbyist, the hopes of eastern financiers. A cloud in 1851, a squall in 1854, hardly checked their speculative flight. The storm gathering in New York, the shadows it was casting over the money markets in Boston and Philadelphia caused little ap-

---

[43] Raney, *Wisconsin*, pp. 182, 183.

prehension—until in 1857 the lightning struck. In a trice paper collateral was burned away and thunder echoed the crash of banks, railroads, factories, and canals.

The panic of 1857 was not as severe as that of 1837. The earlier boom had been a land boom based upon premature expectations from the unbroken soil; the later one, a railroad boom, was based more reasonably upon the hope of traffic from cultivated farms and busy factories in new cities. Expectations still outran reality by a wide margin, but not quite as widely as before. There was real value in the roads actually constructed, there were great quantities of goods to exchange, new city populations to feed, new plantations that were turning to the East and West for food and clothing, for the necessities and luxuries of life. These changes gave reasonable grounds for the expectation of profits, built legitimate foundations for optimism. But optimism always feeds upon itself, blows itself up beyond reason. In the middle fifties, it had soared to the stratosphere of fancy, ready to disappear.

By 1850, the vestiges of the long depression after the panic of 1837 had vanished. Victory in the Mexican War, the flow of California gold, the rapid growth of population and its steady movement to the rich and virgin West created a new tide of confidence. In the next four years every line of business boomed; commodity prices started their ascent, and profits kept the pace. In response, often with railroad stock as collateral, manufacturers borrowed to expand their plants, merchants borrowed to allow their western debtors longer credits. Both were joined by doctors, lawyers, teachers, writers, in gambling on precarious margins in Wall Street or State Street or through brokers' offices in the hinterlands connected by telegraph with the great exchanges in the East. To meet these new and continuing demands upon their resources, the banks of the country, besides issuing notes, created new instruments of credit in the form of call loans and deposits. Between 1848 and 1854, these three items—notes, loans, deposits —jumped from $538,000,000 to $950,000,000. By 1856, they had soared to $1,042,000,000. Collateral consisted chiefly of personal paper not acceptances, railroad stock not gold.

Between 1850 and 1857, 2,300 miles of track were constructed annually in the United States at an average cost of $60,000,000. Funds from every walk of life, from every section of the land, were pouring into eastern money markets and out again to western railroads to push construction of the Illinois Central, the Rock Island, the Hannibal & St. Joseph, the Pacific Railroad of Missouri; to extend the Pennsylvania, the Erie, the Michigan Central and scores of other lines in the North, East, South, and West. By 1860, $1,500,000,000 was invested in American railroads, more than 25 per cent of the total active capital in the country. No wonder the financial structure collapsed when railroad profits proved smaller or slower than expected.

According to *Hunt's Merchant's Magazine,* there was increasing difficulty, in August, 1853,[44]

in introducing new enterprises requiring financial aid from either domestic or foreign capitalists, and the limit to the issue of this class of bonds would appear to be nearly reached. The works of internal improvement now in progress will, most of them, be completed, and a few connecting links may yet be undertaken; but we do not think the market, either here or abroad, will sustain any material outlay for new schemes.

The magazine was correct in its analysis, though mistaken in its prediction. It had not allowed for the momentum of speculation, for its inability to reverse its direction despite sharp warnings of danger ahead. Steady immigration had kept industrial labor costs low, but raw materials for manufacturing, and ties, rails, cinders, and gravel for railroad construction, were rising steadily in price. Transportation charges and interest rates followed suit, and costs thus began their usual upward course, gradually threatening the continuation of profits and beginning to frighten capital from the market. By 1854 businessmen were already feeling uncertain about the future. In that year the outbreak of the Crimean War and the revelation of gigantic stock frauds in England and America caused widespread liquidation and created a minor panic. Depression might well have set in then, had it not been for California gold which permitted continued expansion of American bank credit, and the timely boost given American shipping by the Crimean War, and two acts of

---

[44] *Hunt's Merchant's Magazine,* vol. 29, p. 205.

Congress which gave new stimulus to land and railroad speculation.

These two acts were the Graduation Act and the Kansas-Nebraska Act. The first, reducing the price of unclaimed land in some cases to twelve and one-half cents an acre, led to huge speculative purchases. Land sales, that since 1840 had averaged less than $2,000,000 a year, jumped for the three years 1854–1856 to a total of $29,673,983. How much of this was actually taken up for settlement is, of course, impossible to tell, but the febrile activity gave a great impetus to investment in struggling railroads and to the promotion of many new ones despite the prevalent tightness of money.

In opening up great territories to settlement by slaveholders and free farmers alike, the Kansas-Nebraska Act unloosed in a compact area all the pent-up feeling between North and South. Zealots from each section stormed the region, hotly competing for control. Since dominance would go to the side with the largest number of supporters, immigrant societies in the North and great planters in the South sent settlers West, promising them all expenses provided they would stay on the land. By 1860, the combined population of both territories was 136,047. The speed and size of the migration created a local land boom of great proportions and influenced speculation throughout the country. With so many people streaming West after 1854, there was little chance to check accounts, no time for panic.

Their hopes heightened by these new developments, speculators could afford to ignore for a while the constant scarcity of money, the usurious rates demanded for loans. Money was tight after 1853, and tight it remained until 1858. Interest rates on all types of commercial paper were higher than in twenty years, call loan rates rose steadily, but speculation did not let up. Prices on railroad stock fluctuated sharply between 1853 and 1857, and the general trend was down. Yet the turnover increased steadily, many still playing for the rise, hoping for the completion of their favorite roads and for golden streams of dividends.

As time went by and dividends failed to appear, hope turned to uncertainty, uncertainty to fear. The Crimean War had drained British and French funds from the American market, thus pushing stock prices down faster than before. The decline was further accelerated by the 15 per cent rise in American commodity prices between 1856 and 1857, and by the difficulties this promised for the continuation of railroad construction. By the summer of 1857, railroad stocks had fallen 45 per cent from the peak of 1853.[45] Nearly every bank in the land had loaned on such collateral; now all were jittery. The failure of the Ohio Life Insurance & Trust Company in August, 1857, brought collapse. The weakest link in a weak chain, the Ohio company was one of the first to have to sell railroad stock to meet depositors' demands. Its holdings by summer were so greatly depreciated that its New York branch had to suspend payment. The panic was on.

In the absence of a national bank, New York, after 1840, had become the reserve city of the nation. Western banks, country banks, great banks in other cities, deposited their surplus funds there for note redemption. New York's less stable institutions paid interest on these deposits, thus attracting them from sounder banks to use them for their own profit. The result was the great growth in call loans and their employment in speculation on the New York Stock Exchange. Here was the most liquid market in the country, hence the safest place for funds that might be called for at any instant. This gave a great boost to stock speculation, and created grave danger in time of panic.

When the Ohio Company failed, western banks began to demand their funds from New York. This only aggravated the seasonal withdrawal which had forced contraction in 1851 and 1854. The banks should have been prepared but were not. Thus they had suddenly to call in their loans, forcing speculators to sell stocks at any price to turn them into cash. In a week thirteen leading issues dropped 40 per cent; the best bonds, 10 per cent. In six weeks, Reading, Erie, Illinois Central, and Michigan Central failed. The market had collapsed, and the banks with it, for they had depended upon railroad securities for their own collateral.

---

[45] Smith and Cole, *Fluctuations in Business,* p. 184.

During September, Philadelphia and Baltimore financial houses closed. In the West, but for the Bank of the State of Indiana, every bank shut down. In New York on October 13, eighteen small and medium-sized banks whose directors had speculated in western funds, closed their doors while the rest rushed to suspend specie payment. By mid-October, deposits in New York had fallen from sixty-nine to forty-three million dollars, loans from one hundred twenty to ninety-seven million.[46] This marked the end of deflation.

In the next few months, gold poured in from California to be kept in New York, indeed in such quantities that a loan from the Rothschilds through August Belmont could be returned immediately. Down to eight million on October 17, specie in New York banks at the end of the year was at twenty-eight million, and specie payments were resumed on December 14. The panic was over.

The panic of 1857 was an international panic, affecting all the industrial countries of Western Europe. It might well have started in London in June had not the activity of the Rothschilds in underpinning shaky banks in England and on the Continent delayed it for a time. Late in 1857, however, after the Ohio Company collapse, depression was rife in the old world. For us perhaps most important was the effect this had on the South. Having weathered the domestic panic better than any other section of the land, the South felt a justification of its economy in comparison with that of the North and West. Even the English collapse affected the cotton market only slightly, thus making more confident than·ever the devoted subjects of "King Cotton."

OPTIMISM AND PROTEST

Hardly checked by the panic, unabashed by the immensity of the task, northern businessmen, by 1860, were ready once again to resume their conquest of the continent. They were ready once more to bind to older regions each new city and each new farming area. They were ready to make mine, forest, river, and field

---

[46] Myers, *Money Market*, pp. 142, 143.

yield richer and richer tribute to new machines. Work, scheme, bargain, sell!—that was the new circle of northern life. Land of a thousand newspapers, each with recipes for begetting wealth! Land of churches, schools and lyceums, telegraphs and cables, each singing paeans to the power of money! Offended by the materialism of changing America, Emerson described his country in 1844:[47]

In America, out of doors, all seems a market, in doors, an air-tight stove of conventionalism. Everybody who comes into our houses savours of these habits; the men, of the market; the women, of the custom. I find no expression in our state papers or legislative debate, in our lyceums or churches, specially in our newspapers, of a high national feeling, no lofty counsels, that rightfully stir the blood. I speak of those organs which can be presumed to speak a popular sense. They recommend conventional virtues, whatever will earn and preserve property; always the capitalist; the college, the church, the hospital, the theatre, the hotel, the road, the ship, of the capitalist—whatever goes to secure, adorn, enlarge these, is good, whatever jeopardizes any of these is damnable.

Webster was the hero of the North—not Emerson, Parker, Garrison, or Phillips; Webster the tariff man, the land speculator, the corporation lawyer, politician for the Boston Associates, inheritor of Hamilton's coronet. "The great object of government," said he, "is the protection of property at home, and respect and renown abroad." For these he preached union; for these he surrendered the fugitive slave.

America had been the hope of the oppressed. Founded as an asylum, conceived in liberty, dedicated to the soul of man—or so it seemed to radicals in the fifties—it had in their eyes become instead a land of greed and oppression. Agricultural simplicity had been left far behind, they said, and agrarian individualism had been curtailed by the growth of factories and industrial cities, by the urban movement of population, by the emergence of a landless proletariat. Some, like Dr. Oliver Wendell Holmes, found new hope in these changes and described a great and glowing future for industrial America. Holmes wrote:[48]

---

[47] Emerson, *English Traits etc.*, pp. 370, 371.
[48] Parrington, *American Thought*, vol. II, pp. 455, 456.

I tell you Boston has opened and kept open more turnpikes that lead straight to free thought and free speech and deeds than any other city of live men or dead men—I don't care how broad their streets are, nor how high their steeples.

And on the same theme he expressed himself again:

A new nursery, Sir, with Lake Superior and Huron and all the rest of 'em for washbasins! A new race, and a whole new world for new-born souls to work in! And Boston is the brain of it, and has been any time these hundred years! That's all I claim for Boston—that it is the thinking center of the continent, and therefore of the planet.

But the *radicals* of New England thought they knew better. Emerson complained: [49]

In Boston is no company for a fine wit. There is a certain *poor-smell* in all the streets, in Beacon Street and Mount Vernon, as well as in the lawyers' offices, and the wharves, and the same meanness and sterility, and leave-all-hope-behind, as one finds in a boot manufacturer's premises.

In a wilderness of stocks and bonds, cutthroat competition and growing monopoly, optimism seemed quite fatuous. Foolish to hope for the spirit in the world of the flesh! "Money is this day the strongest power of the nation," cried Parker, and in his "Sermon on Merchants" he expressed for all time his burning hatred of the new society to whose spiritual needs it was his duty to attend. He told his Boston Congregation: [50]

The bad merchant still lives. He cheats in his trade; sometimes against the law, commonly with it. His truth is never wholly true nor his lie wholly false. . . . He is the stone in the lame man's shoe. He is the poor man's devil. The Hebrew devil that so worried Job is gone, so is the brutal devil that awed our fathers. But the devil of the nineteenth century is still extant. He has gone into trade and advertises in the papers. He makes money; the world is poorer by his wealth. He can build a Church out of his gains, to have his morality, his Christianity, preached in it, and call that the gospel. He sends rum and missionaries to the same barbarians, the one to damn, the other to save, both for his own advantage, for his patron saint is Judas, the first saint who made money out of Christ. He is not forecasting to dis-

---

[49] Parrington, *American Thought*, vol. II, p. 398.
[50] Commager, *Parker*, p. 182.

cern effects in causes, nor skillful to create new wealth, only spry in the scramble for what others have made. In politics he wants a Government that will ensure his dividends; so asks what is good for him, but ill for the rest. He knows no right only power; no man but self; no God but his calf of gold.

The factories that made the businessman rich populated the cities with alert minds. The machines that depressed the workers cut as well the cost of printing and gave these new minds food. It was to them that Emerson, Phillips, Garrison and Parker, Bryant, Leggett, Owen, and Greeley spoke. Under their leadership, in the forties and fifties, especially in New England but in the middle states as well, there was a great intellectual and religious awakening, driven by the new exploitations of the times into humanitarian channels. Prohibitionists, Abolitionists, Feminists, Public Educationists, Communists, Fourierists, Owenites, Millerites, Mormons, Evangelists, Prison, Diet, and Dress Reformers—all wrote letters, essays, books; held meetings, conventions, debates. Nightly, crowded lyceums heard propagandists as varied as the languages of Babel, each with a plan to change the world or to save its denizens in a novel way. For a time, they made a great noise, caused a great tumult. The Civil War stilled them. They had not altered the course of northern business; they did not slow its conquest of the land, the people, the press, or the church. In the end they had only accelerated its conquest of the South.

V

TRIAL BY BATTLE

THE decade ending with the panic of 1857 was one of unprecedented prosperity in the United States. Western farms, southern plantations, northern factories had grown constantly in size and number, had brought forth ever greater quantities of goods. Each section of the country had begun to specialize in its own most profitable enterprises: the West producing food for the nation; the South, cotton for northern and English factories; the North, manufactures for every corner of the land and transportation facilities to deliver them. This was a decade of rapid intercourse, of increasing dependence of one section upon another. It was a decade of constant expansion and yet of growing unity. The telegraph in an instant conquered a thousand miles with the messages of a business culture, the railroads sped to far-flung regions goods, men, books and magazines. Yet over all, casting a dark and sinister shadow, hung the cloud of secession, of disunion, the threat to sunder the nation into slave states and free.

New York and Boston capitalists, in this decade, had supplied most of the funds for the construction of factories, railroads, ships, and canals, for the mortgaging of farms and plantations. And they had, therefore, gathered up the greatest profits. On the other hand, the old South had managed desperately to cling to national political leadership despite the severe limitations of its single-staple, slave economy. As more and more southern wealth went to enrich northern industrialists, bankers, and shippers, southern leaders were more and more deeply offended with northern affluence, and when in 1860 their political supremacy seemed also about to be captured by the North, they decided to break up the nation. On more than one earlier occasion South Carolina had tried to organize her neighbors in the Cotton

Kingdom, only to fail because of lack of public support. By 1861, however, her leaders had finally lined up most of the other states below the Mason-Dixon line and marched with them out of the Union. The threatening secession cloud had burst.

Coming so soon after the panic of 1857, this forceful severance of relations with the South plunged northern business into a new decline. Huge debts became uncollectible, ships and factories were made idle by the unavailability of cotton, while war threatened to bring new taxes, new regulation, new government interference with the normal functioning of trade. Northern businessmen made no secret of their opposition to war with the South. But they could offer no plan to avoid it, and by April, 1861, hostilities had begun.

If northern businessmen opposed war with the South before such a war had opened, once it was under way they knew precisely how to make the most of it, and by 1863 a war boom was in progress. The South had broken up the Union when northern votes had conquered the planter aristocracy and captured control of the federal government. During the war the spoils of that conquest were bestowed lavishly upon many manufacturers in the form of lucrative contracts, cheap labor, high tariffs; railroad men and land speculators got huge grants from the public domain; bankers received war securities to market at handsome premiums; trade was facilitated by nationalization of the currency, by the creation through government loans of a great reserve of credit for business purposes. The opportunities presented to advantageously situated entrepreneurs by the spoils of political victory dissolved the gloom that had settled over American business in 1861. By the middle of the war, northern farms, factories, railroads, and canals were paying dividends as high as 40 and 50 per cent. Emphasis on war production retarded the expansion and modernization of essentially civilian industries. But this did not impede businessmen, capable of filling every order of the army and navy, from catering successfully at the same time to the extravagant tastes of the new "sybarites of shoddy" who had begun to appear in America— men who had made great fortunes by selling to the government the cheapest kinds of clothing, blankets, munitions, and food. At the end of the war the South was exhausted, prostrate, her economy shattered, many of her people homeless and impoverished. In the North there was a stronger concentration of capital and a sharper incentive to industrial enterprise than had ever been found there before.

THE HOUSE DIVIDED

Until 1845 southern Ohio, Indiana, and Iilinois had dominated the American West. Tied to the South by the great rivers that carried their produce to market, by settlers who had come from Virginia, Kentucky, and Tennessee, by slavery that had filtered in unmolested though prohibited by law in the Northwest Territory, these regions had frequently united with the slave power to check the surge of northern industry. They had helped the South kill the national bank. They had helped diminish the protection afforded to eastern manufacturers. They had helped augment the agricultural area of "King Cotton." In politics, therefore, as well as in sentiment, they were essential portions of the "Cotton Kingdom," and after 1845 as southern supremacy in western states was threatened by the more northerly sections around the Lakes, the planters had to find new ways to keep the West in line. Above all else the South feared high tariffs on manufactured goods. And above all else the northern part of the West wanted cheap land, Pacific railroads, and federal river and harbor improvements. In exchange for votes against high-tariff bills, therefore, the planters began to promise all these things to western politicians. This was a shrewd game as played by the South and, for a time, a successful one. In the end, however, it was doomed to failure. The South could not grant the West free homesteads without sacrificing southern political hegemony. She could not grant a Pacific railroad through Chicago without further enriching the hated North. She dared not sanction river and harbor bills for which the South would have to pay while the Lake region got the benefit. The South could promise, but she dared not deliver. Her strength lay in using the West, not in gratifying it. And as early as 1847 the West had begun to rebel. After the veto of the rivers and harbors bill that year, the Chicago *Daily Journal* exclaimed:[1]

The North can no longer be hoodwinked. If no measures of protection and improvement of anything North or West are to be suffered by our Southern masters, if we are to be downtrodden and all our cherished interests crushed by them, a signal revolution will eventually arise.

And the Cleveland *Plain Dealer,* severing its relations with the southern Democracy on the same occasion, cried, "We do not belong to the blubbering party." This paper "threatened a combination of the East and West to check the South and called upon freemen from the North to rally under the cry of 'let the boundaries of slavery be set.' "[2]

A new climate thus had begun to permeate the West by the late 1840's, a northern climate dedicated to progress and freedom. In the turbulent decades before the Civil War, New York, New England, and Pennsylvania had gathered up the funds of the nation, had developed financial techniques to manipulate them and mastered the arts of credit expansion. With these they had invaded the West. They had bought up western land, gridironed it with canals and railroads, settled it with northerners and Europeans, sold them manufactures and taken their produce in return. By 1857, northern capitalists had completed their trunk lines to the Mississippi; New York had supplanted New Orleans as the entrepôt for western exports; Chicago, Cleveland, Buffalo were ready to challenge Cincinnati and St. Louis for western municipal leadership. Just as the South by 1830 had become a minority in the nation and had to rely on the West for her strength, so by 1860 the southern parts of the old Northwest had become minorities in their respective states and southern strength was gone.

The South was not friendless in the North. In New York, James Gordon Bennett attacked the vilifiers of slavery, asking:[3]

What business have all the religious lunatics of the free states to gather in this commercial city for purposes which, if carried into effect, would

---

[1] Craven, in *Journal of Southern History,* vol. II, p. 316.
[2] Hubbart, *Middle West,* p. 26.
[3] Parrington, *American Thought,* vol. II, p. 357.

ruin and destroy its prosperity? . . . Public opinion should be regulated. These abolitionists should not be allowed to misrepresent New York. . . . On the question of the usefulness to the public of the packed, organized meetings of these abolitionists, socialists, Sabbath-breakers, and anarchists, there can be but one result arrived at by prudence and patriotism. They are dangerous assemblies—calculated for mischief, and treasonable in their character and purposes. . . . That half a dozen madmen should manufacture opinion for the whole community, is not to be tolerated.

In Massachusetts, Caleb Cushing cried for defense of the South against abolitionist fury. Virginia must be protected from Ohio raiders, he warned.[4]

If not, then are the days of the great Union numbered, and they ought to be numbered. If not, then I say it is the right, nay it is the duty, of the southern states to separate from the northern states, and to form a confederation of their own.

President Pierce had been friendly to the great planters though he was a New Englander. Buchanan himself was a Pennsylvanian. Northerners like the Belmonts, Vanderbilts, and Astors in 1860 had given time, money, and the benefit of their prestige to defeat Lincoln. New York and Philadelphia had refused to vote for the Republican candidate though his party won control of most of Pennsylvania and the Empire State.

For thirty years, however, the South had been exploited by her northern friends, flayed by northern abolitionists. Through lyceum, press and pulpit, Garrison, Parker, Phillips, and Weld, Beecher, Birney, Giddings, and Stowe, had kept up a steady fire, while in Congress Sumner, Seward, Chase, and Wade added official fuel to the flame, attacking in turn southern slavery, southern culture, southern leaders, southern domination of the federal government. "The cause of civilization and human improvement would lose nothing by their annihilation," said Birney of the slave states in 1844. "The South is full of mulattoes," cried Theodore Parker; "its 'best blood flows in the veins of slaves.'" Garrison shouted in 1845:[5]

The SLAVE POWER must be attacked and vanquished openly as such, and no quarter given to it either in gross or in part. . . . There is but one

---

4 Sandburg, *Prairie Years,* vol. II, p. 208.
5 Garrison, *Life,* vol. III, p. 142.

mode and one alternative presented to the people of the free states, and that is to have NO RELIGIOUS, NO POLITICAL UNION WITH SLAVE HOLDERS.

And again he said: [6]

We would sooner trust the honor of the country . . . in the hands of inmates of our penitentiaries and prisons than in their hands. . . . They are the meanest of the thieves and the worst of the robbers. . . . We do not acknowledge them to be within the pale of Christianity, of republicanism, of humanity.

The more wealth the South had contributed to northern manufacturers, northern bankers, northern shippers, and northern brokers as the prewar decades unfolded, the fairer game she seemed for northern agitators crying out against the slave foundation of her culture.

Southerners, of course, had jumped to the immediate defense of their section. Calhoun and Stephens, Yancey and Rhett, Harper, Hammond, and Professor Dew had evolved a "Pro-Slavery Argument" to justify before a hostile world every facet of their "peculiar institution." As early as 1839 Calhoun had set the key for this defense when he said: [7]

We now believe it [slavery] has been a great blessing to both of the races—the European and African, which, by a mysterious Providence, have been brought together in the Southern section of this Union. The one has greatly improved, and the other has not deteriorated; while, in a political point of view, it has been the great stay of the Union and our free institutions, and one of the main sources of the unbounded prosperity of the whole.

Another tack was to carry the fight directly to the North. Hammond cried, in 1858: [8]

Your slaves are white, of your own race. You are brothers of one blood. They are your equals in natural endowment of intellect and character; they feel galled by their degradation. Our slaves do not vote. We give them no political power. Yours do vote; and being in the majority they are the depositories of all your political power. If they knew the secret that the ballot box is stronger than an army with bayonets, and could combine, where would you be? Your society would be reconstructed, your government

---

[6] Craven, *Repressible Conflict*, p. 84.

[7] Van Deusen, *Clay*, pp. 80-81.

[8] Schlüter, *Lincoln and Labor*, pp. 115-116.

overthrown, your property divided, not as they have mistakenly attempted to initiate such proceedings in parks, with arms in their hands, but by the quiet process of the ballot box. You have been making war on us to our very hearthstones. How would you like us to send lecturers or agitators North to teach the people this, to aid and assist in combining and to lead them?

Often these southerners spoke of secession, often they threatened. "The South can do nothing to redress her wrongs as long as she stays in the Union," wrote John Townshend of Charleston in 1850. "It is the highest duty of patriotism," exclaimed the Savannah *Georgian* in 1851, "to wage an undying hostility to this Union."

As long as the South had been dominant in the councils of the nation, however, as long as she had been able to count on western support to check the industrial North, most of her leaders had opposed secession. While northern abolitionists belabored them, to the discomfiture of the great capitalists in both sections, southern politicians had won Texas, the Fugitive Slave Law, the repeal of the Missouri Compromise, the Dred Scott case, the low tariff of 1857. In addition, they had obstructed federal aid to internal improvements, protective tariffs for northern manufacturers, a national bank, ship subsidies, homestead laws. "The real cause of this Southern disposition to listen to the appeals of the Palmetto nullifiers," wrote George Weston in 1858, "was Southern discontent at the prosperity of the North." [9] And as long as the South had had the power to rein that prosperity, to postpone the political ascent of "business," to trammel up the "tradesmen" whom she affected to despise, she had been ready to endure abuse and Union both. Starting in 1850, South Carolina had devoted herself to organizing a southern confederacy, to trying to get Virginia to take the lead in secession, to get Georgia and Mississippi, Alabama and Louisiana, Texas and Florida, North Carolina and Arkansas to follow. But she had never succeeded. So persistent had been her efforts, so frequently were they failures, that by 1860 James Russell Lowell could sneer at her threats as "the old Mumbo Jumbo." [10] Seward could deride them as "a feeble and muttering voice." Thurlow Weed could write: "Dissolving the

[9] Russel, *Southern Sectionalism,* p. 197.
[10] Milton, *Eve of Conflict,* p. 484.

Union is a game for the presidency. It is nothing but a game." [11]

By 1860, however, times had changed at last in South Carolina's favor. The whole South had now lost political power, and secession thus had ceased to be simply a South Carolinian threat, simply a "game." As early as May 20, 1859, a rural South Carolina editor crystallized the feelings of the South: [12]

> That the North sectionalized will acquire possession of this government at no distant day we look upon as no longer a matter of doubt. . . . It is inevitable. The South—the whole South even—cannot avert it. We may determine to fight the battle with our foes within the Union. . . . But we will fight only to be defeated. The Union of the South is indeed of great moment—not however for successful resistance in this Union, but for going out of it under the circumstances the most favorable to the speedy formation of a separate and independent government.

At the same time, Governor Brown of South Carolina warned: [13]

> So soon as the Government shall have passed into Black Republican hands a portion of our citizens must, if possible, be bribed into treachery to their own section, by the allurements of office; or a hungry swarm of abolition emissaries must be imported among us as officeholders, to eat out our substance, insult us with their arrogance, corrupt our slaves, and engender discontent among them, while they flood the country with inflammatory abolition documents, and do all in their power to create in the South, a state of things which must ultimately terminate in a war of extermination between the white and the black race.

Three decades of harassing debate, of vitriolic charges and countercharges, bitter accusations and replies had whipped up an emotional surge that for years had been licking at the dam, brimming over from time to time in the Kansas-Nebraska border war, in Brooks's attack upon Sumner in the Senate, in John Brown's raid on Virginia, in abolitionist riots in Ohio and Massachusetts. But as long as the South, vilified and exploited, had control of federal politics she felt safe enough. As soon as she lost her political grip, however, she dared not linger in the Union. Robert Toombs cried from Washington in December, 1860: [14]

---

[11] Storey, *Sumner*, p. 179.
[12] Phillips, in *American Historical Review*, vol. XXXIV, p. 36.
[13] Fish, *Civil War*, p. 44.
[14] Fish, *Civil War*, p. 42.

Secession by the fourth of March next should be thundered from the ballot box by the unanimous voice of Georgia . . . such a voice will be your best guarantee for liberty, tranquillity and glory.

If the voice of Georgia thundered and the voice of the other cotton states thundered, the rest of the South was less demonstrative. But by May 20, 1861, the eleven commonwealths of the new Confederacy had made their memorable decisions. None of these decisions had been unanimous, and the Confederacy was to be plagued during its entire existence by bitter internal strife.

THE ROAD TO WAR

Northern business took advantage of the Civil War once it began and after it was over, but that does not prove that business wanted the war; it does not prove, certainly, that business started the war. Northern and western businessmen were bound to the South by ties which they deemed strongest—ties of profit. Secession strained these almost to the breaking point; war would shatter them altogether. New England cotton factories depended upon the South for raw materials; boot and shoe factories found their markets there, northern shippers their cargoes. All but the shippers could hope to preserve these ties with the South in or out of the Union, and the shippers certainly wanted no war. Commerce feeds on peace: no one knew it better than they.

From every section of the industrial North, from many types of industry, had come business spokesmen for peace. On December 19, 1860, August Belmont reported a meeting of "our leading men . . . composed of such names as Astor, Aspinwall, Moses H. Grinnell, Hamilton Fish, R. M. Blatchford, &c. They were unanimous for reconciliation, and that the first steps have to be taken by the North." [15] From New Jersey came the voice of Abram Hewitt, who had suffered as much as any one from southern tariff and railroad policies but who in November, 1860, was "using every effort to induce the public mind to give up the idea of coercion, and to take that of peaceable separation." [16]

---

[15] Foner, *Business and Slavery*, p. 238.
[16] Nevins, *Hewitt*, p. 190.

As late as March 1, 1861, George Lyman, Boston Associate, wrote hopefully of news "that an arrangement will be made in Washington satisfactory to the business men of the country if not to other persons, and that peace will prevail among the people." [17] As late as April, 1861, the *New York Journal of Commerce* and the *New York Observer* were still clamoring for peace; and on the 9th of the month, but three days before Fort Sumter, the *New York Herald* had declared: [18]

Far better that the Union should be dismembered forever than that fraternal hands should be turned against one another to disfigure the land by slaughter and carnage.

With the South out of the Union, no one could deny northern business its tariffs, Pacific railroads, national banks, and free land. The opposition was removed: why fight to bring it back? The South in turn wanted independence, not conflict. Robert Hunter of Virginia wrote in December, 1860: [19]

We already hear threats of coercing the seceding states by force. But if, unfortunately, such an experiment should ever be tried, even the stronger section would find the remedy worse than the disease. . . . I hold coercion by force to be almost impossible. It would fail if attempted, and would never be attempted, unless madness ruled the hour and passion raged where reason ought to govern.

The South knew it could win only freedom, not supremacy; that it could but escape the North, not conquer it. The South wanted to depart from the Union in peace; in the North, sentiment acquiesced in secession. The country's most influential editor, Horace Greeley, in November, 1860, declared in his *Tribune:* [20]

If the cotton states shall decide that they can do better out of the Union than in it, we insist on letting them go in peace. The right to secede may be a revolutionary one but it exists nevertheless.

---

[17] Green, *Holyoke*, p. 70.
[18] Fish, *Civil War*, p. 104.
[19] Ambler, *Hunter Letters*, pp. 339–340.
[20] Beard, *Rise of American Civilization*, vol. II, p. 63.

Equally powerful in the pulpit, his *Independent* was almost as important as the *Tribune,* Henry Ward Beecher a little later announced his attitude: [21]

> The time has come when the public mind must take some position and make some expression. I for one, do not believe in Union for the sake of it. . . . There is but' one question: . . . "Do you think the South will secede?" My answer is: "I don't think they will; and I don't care if they do."

To be sure, there was war sentiment on both sides; there were shortsighted manufacturers looking for war profits, debt-ridden planters seeking excuses for repudiation of debts owed in the North, young fire-eaters clamoring for combat, professional military men eager to practice their trade. In the West, there was a strong faction that cried insistently for war. Governor Yates of Illinois asked in his inaugural address on January 14, 1861: [22]

> Can it for a moment be supposed that the people of the valley of the Mississippi will ever consent that the great river shall flow hundreds of miles through a foreign jurisdiction, and they be compelled, if not to fight their way in the face of forts frowning upon its banks, to submit to the imposition and annoyance of arbitrary taxes and exorbitant duties to be levied upon their commerce? . . . I know I speak for Illinois and I believe for the Northwest, when I declare them a unit in the unalterable determination of her millions, occupying the great basin drained by the Mississippi, to permit no portion of that stream to be controlled by a foreign jurisdiction.

The *Illinois State Journal* seconded this declaration: [23]

> The great Northwest will wage war with the Slave States bordering on that river [the Mississippi] as long as she has a man or a dollar, but what she will enjoy the right of free and unobstructed navigation of the natural southern outlet.

In January, 1861, however, these were but the war cries of extremists. After the secession convention of February, 1861, the federal post office collected and delivered mail in the South;

[21] Hibben, *Beecher,* p. 178.
[22] Coulter, in *Mississippi Valley Historical Review,* vol. III, pp. 278–279.
[23] Coulter, in *Mississippi Valley Historical Review,* vol. III, p. 279.

federal customs men collected duties in southern ports; railroads ran unmolested across the borders of slave states and free; telegraph messages flew North and South; New Orleans handled southern and northern goods on equal terms. The instruments of peace, at least, seemed able to transcend new boundaries.

As days and weeks went by, however, and people watched developments, the crisis did not abate; neither side could satisfactorily adjust itself to the new arrangement. South Carolina's demand of federal forts in Charleston harbor went unheeded. The "Crittenden Compromise" failed, the Virginia Peace Convention failed, the attempt to reenforce Fort Sumter in January failed. Meanwhile, the Confederacy was taking form. Her constitution was published, her president elected, her government set up in Montgomery. While the North looked on with indecision, the South had become a sovereign nation, a foreign government on the borders of the United States, claiming federal territory within her limits, finally taking military measures to assert her independence.

Incident followed incident as the crisis worked on frayed nerves and the newspapers administered stimulants. So contagious, indeed, was the excitement the newspapers stirred up, that sometimes they fell prey to their own enthusiasm. By December 11, 1860, the pacific Greeley had discovered a dangerous paradox in the situation. A state could not "make herself really independent" without seizing all forts within her borders; and such seizure would render it incumbent upon the President "to repel force with force." Three weeks later, Greeley declared:

Though we acknowledge prayer to be indispensable for the saving of individuals and nations, we nevertheless consider powder a good thing.

By April 3, 1861, he demanded that the "intolerable suspense and uncertainty give way to the alternative of war." [24]

The publisher's business is to sell papers. Regardless of his own attitudes or the philosophy of his editorial page, he must compete with the field for patronage. Thus he seeks always to build up suspense, to enhance excitement even if he is opposed

[24] Fahrney, *Greeley and The Tribune*, pp. 54, 55, 73.

to the trend his headlines encourage. Secession made good copy. Every one was concerned with it, with all its aspects, with every incident created by the friction of the new arrangement. The newspapers, those for peace and those for war alike, could not afford to play down secession.

Three months of such agitation had led to a swelling cry in the North for decision. And while limp Buchanan, pledged to defend the Union but pledged as well to his southern Democratic colleagues, wavered between the two, there came from the West another cry that was to give direction to any decision that might be made.

Illinois, Indiana, Ohio, Michigan, Iowa, Wisconsin, Minnesota—none of these knew the time when they had been *sovereign* states. They had been brought into existence by the federal Congress; great numbers of their people had been naturalized by the federal government, had purchased their rich land from federal agents. "You cannot sever this Union," cried Stephen Douglas of Illinois in 1860, "without severing every hope and prospect that a Western man has on this earth." And he exclaimed to the farmers of the Ohio Valley in April, 1861 : [25]

[Your] very existence depends upon maintaining inviolate and forever that great right secured by the Constitution, of freedom of trade, of transit, and of commerce, from the center of the continent to the ocean that surrounds it. [The question was not only one of Union or disunion but] of order, of the stability of the government; of the peace of communities. The whole social system is threatened with destruction.

Meanwhile, Lincoln had been inaugurated. Born in Kentucky, bred in Indiana and Illinois, he needed no instruction in western feeling, no mentor to guide him along the path chosen by his section. He would discuss anything with the South, but Union must be the basis for discussion. Seward, to remove the spotlight from domestic strife, devised fantastic schemes to conquer the world. Seward demanded time for southern tempers to cool, for the South to learn that independence was a hazardous if not foolhardy venture. Seward urged the President to surrender federal forts to the South. But Lincoln was adamant.

[25] Milton, *Eve of Conflict,* p. 564.

The Union must be preserved. No concessions could be made, no wedge allowed for severance. In reply to Bennett's insistent demand for peace, throughout the month of April, he declared: [26]

> I will suffer death before I will consent or advise my friends to consent to any concession or compromise which looks like buying the privilege of taking possession of the Government to which we have a constitutional right.

War, of course, is the business of armies; defense of the nation, their sworn duty. Sumter must be provisioned; Sumter was a northern fort. In southern territory? And the South was now sovereign in her own domain? Let her prove it. The instruments of peace may transcend new boundaries, the instruments of war must contest them. The North must provision her forts; the South must defend her sovereignty. For nations on edge, these were challenges. To refuse them was to admit weakness, to invite contempt; to accept them meant war.

In a last effort Lincoln appealed to the "leaderless people" of the South to cast off the yoke of the "slave profiteers" and return to the national fold. But in the South, too, publicists had been at work. The South had become a nation, proudly conscious of her new status. On the abolitionists' anvil her leaders had forged a unified people dedicated to white supremacy and impressed with the power such supremacy seemed to afford. As early as 1856, Robert J. Walker wrote: [27]

> In all the slave states, there is a large majority of voters who are non-slaveholders; but they are devoted to the institutions of the South—they would defend them with their lives and on this question the South are a united people. The class, composed of many small farmers, of merchants, professional men, mechanics, overseers, and other industrial classes, constitute mainly the patrol of the South, and cheerfully unite in carrying out those laws essential to preserve the institution of slavery.

"In fact," said Rives of Virginia in 1861, to the Peace Convention called by his state, "it is not a question of slavery at all. It is a question of race." [28]

---

[26] Sandburg, *War Years*, vol. I, p. 12.
[27] Phillips, in *American Historical Review*, vol. XXXIV, p. 33.
[28] Carpenter, *South As a Conscious Minority*, p. 11.

In November, 1860, war could not have started. By April, 1861, it could scarcely have been avoided. The sides had been drawn, and as peace efforts one by one came to naught each side had gradually clarified its position and convinced its people of the righteousness of its cause. When Lincoln insisted at last on provisioning Fort Sumter, as an unmistakable token of northern determination, the South, if it was to succeed in what it had started, could not allow the act to pass unchallenged. After the firing of cannon, there was no turning back. On April 21, 1861, George Ticknor wrote:[29]

The heather is on fire. I never knew before what popular excitement can be. Holiday enthusiasm I have seen often enough, and anxious crowds I remember during the War of 1812, but never anything like this. Indeed, here at the North, at least, there was never anything like it; for if the feeling were as deep and stern in 1775, it was by no means so intelligent and unanimous; and then the masses to be moved were as a handful compared to our dense poulation now. The whole people, in fact, have come to a perception that the question is whether we shall have anarchy or no.

And on April 28 he explained how such unanimity had come about:

Through the whole of the last six months, you see the working of our own political institutions most strikingly. The people were the practical sovereigns, and until the people had been appealed to, and had *moved,* the Administration, whether of Buchanan or of Lincoln, could act with little efficiency. We drifted. Now the rudder is felt.

FIRST THINGS FIRST

For the first time in almost fifty years, the crash of cannon was heard in the United States on April 12, 1861. War! Very few among the people knew what war meant. Very few of their leaders knew what was expected of them. Lincoln hoped the "insurrection" would be quelled in three months; it was five before hostilities seriously got under way. In either section there was practically no army, no machinery for organizing one or financing it when it would be ready. The North had railroads, factories, money, men. But it took two years to rig them into a

---

[29] Fish, *Civil War,* p. 124.

war machine. The South, by comparison, had nothing—except generals. The South had to create, not adapt.

While military men were muddling their unaccustomed tasks, however, veteran northern politicians swung immediately into action. The Republican platform of 1860 had been a blunt appeal to businessmen—to manufacturers, railroad promoters, land speculators, bankers. It had promised protective tariffs, homesteads, Pacific railroads, easy admission for foreign laborers, federal appropriations for river and harbor improvements. Even before southern congressmen had fled the Capital, this program was being enacted.

Satisfied with the tariff of 1857, some New England manufacturers feared higher rates.[30] Rice of Massachusetts said in 1860:[31]

> The manufacturer asks no additional protection. He has learned among other things, that the greatest evil, next to ruinous competition from foreign sources, is an excessive protection, which stimulates a like ruinous and irresponsible competition at home.

To entice to the Republican banner iron manufacturers in Pennsylvania and woolgrowers in the West, however, the Morrill Tariff Act was passed by the House in 1860. At the next session, in February, 1861, the Union Senate approved it. Simply a political measure, this act was supplemented in August and December, 1861, by the first war tariffs.

Like all subsequent levies, these proved insufficient to meet rising costs of government; and as the conflict continued beyond its allotted ninety days, beyond six months, beyond a year with no sign of abatement, no sign of northern victory, new and drastic steps had to be taken. To avoid bankruptcy early in 1862, the government began to print huge quantities of "greenbacks," declaring them legal tender for all debts. By the middle of the year even these proved inadequate, and the government's position was further complicated by the refusal of many bankers who were opposed to the Treasury's regulations to market government bonds. To augment federal income, therefore, and to show good

---

[30] Hofstadter, in *American Historical Review*, vol. XLIV, p. 50.
[31] Taussig, *Tariff*, pp. 159–160 note.

faith to the bankers, new taxes had to be levied. Among them were sales taxes on manufactured goods, income taxes on railroad, steamboat, and express companies. Novel measures, these duties encouraged tariff politicians to make novel demands. Tariffs for revenue had become traditional in America; tariffs for protection from foreign competition constantly had been sought. After the enactment of these internal excises in July, 1862, however, tariff men developed a new rationale. If manufacturers' costs were raised by excise and income taxes, they said, should not the old margin of protection be maintained? Under the whip of Morrill and Stevens, Congress agreed that it should. Camouflaged as "compensation," the tariff act of July 14, 1862, raised the rates to their highest level in thirty years—much higher, in many cases, than the new excise taxes warranted.

As war expenditures increased, internal taxes and "compensatory" duties increased with them until by 1864 tariff rates were higher than they had ever been. The tariff act of that year, says Taussig, "was in many ways crude and ill-considered; it contained flagrant abuses, in the shape of duties whose chief effect was to bring money into the pockets of private individuals."

When the war ended internal taxes were speedily repealed, but not import duties. Manufacturers, like railroad men before them, had grown rich through government aid. Now they were determined to retain control of the sources of such aid, come what might. In 1870, Morrill himself exclaimed: "It is a mistake of the friends of a sound tariff to insist on the extreme rates imposed during the war." [32] In the ensuing years, he was heeded only to the extent that rates were reduced on articles America could not produce. The protective features stuck.

While Congress was erecting these almost insurmountable tariff walls, the army was decimating the ranks of labor, strikes were spreading, and employers complained. Friendly legislators tried to satisfy them with the Contract Labor Law, signed July 4, 1864. Besides validating contracts made abroad, Congress "took pains formally to declare" that no laborer imported under the terms of this law would be drafted for military

---

[32] Taussig, *Tariff*, p. 173 note.

service. Quickly, a group of industrialists formed the American Emigrant Company capitalized at $1,000,000. To every country in Europe they sent agents, and in all our large cities they opened branch offices where employers could make known their needs with the knowledge that cheap and docile hands promptly would be found for them.[33] The contract with the laborer did not involve his person—it avoided any taint of "slavery" or "involuntary servitude." Under its terms the emigrant had but to pledge his wages for twelve months as compensation to the employer for the costs of emigration. Before its repeal in 1868 this act supplied business and agriculture with thousands of men, many of them serving effectively as strikebreakers.

While the Republican party was financed mainly by urban industrialists and promoters, its victory was won with the votes of western farmers hungry for free land. An Iowan wrote to the New York *World* in 1860:[34]

The people of the West have been deeply mortified by the failure of Congress to pass a proper homestead law. The question will enter largely into the political canvass, and will determine many votes against the Democratic party.

When westerners went to the polls this prediction was fulfilled, and when victorious Republicans organized Congress they seemed eager to satisfy their constituents. In 1860 New England and the Middle States had joined the West in voting almost unanimously for free homesteads only to have the successful act vetoed by Buchanan. In 1862 Buchanan and his followers were no longer in power and a homestead bill easily became law.

The West was jubilant; but not for long. The act granted 160 acres of unoccupied land in the public domain to any one who would cultivate it for five consecutive years. The act provided also, however, that within six months the "cultivator" could purchase his land at $1.25 an acre. The first part of the law was an invitation to any one who had money for the western trek; the second part was an Open sesame to land speculators. Their dummy "settlers" appeared in new areas almost always ahead

[33] Fite, *Industrial Conditions*, p. 191.
[34] Stephenson, *Public Lands*, p. 231.

of genuine farmers. They staked out quarter-sections there, recorded claims, and exercised options to purchase, until most of the best homesteads were gone. When authentic homesteaders came, their only choice was between buying at high prices and moving beyond civilization.

By the very act that offered "land to the landless poor," Congress thus had nullified its apparent gift. Subsequently it adopted other measures that confirmed its seeming sympathy with speculators rather than settlers, businessmen rather than farmers. To aid the Union, Central, and Northern Pacific railroads, chartered between 1862 and 1864, Congress gave them a potential 70,000,000 acres of the public domain. In 1862 Congress enacted the Morrill Act, granting to the states 30,000 acres for each of their senators and representatives, the income from the sale of this land to be used to endow and maintain in each state at least one college for instruction "in agriculture and mechanic arts." To the landless eastern states this act granted scrip to 7,500,000 western acres to be sold for the same purpose. Besides, as western territories became states they were given additional land totaling 140,000,000 acres, which thus became unavailable for free homesteads. For one reason or another, the federal government held out for sale, instead of distributing freely, another 100,000,000 acres, while the removal of the Indians to reservations added 175,000,000 acres more which were to be disposed of to the highest bidders and were closed to homesteaders.[35]

Thus while 50,000,000 homestead acres were distributed in twenty years after 1862, many of them to speculators, almost half a billion acres of the public domain were reserved for businessmen or opened to farmers only at considerable cost. Most of this was the best land in the West. To encourage the colleges, the beneficiaries of the Morrill Act received land which would sell for the highest prices. The same was true of railroad companies which also profited handsomely by promising transportation facilities near their lands. Indian lands in many areas already were improved, making them much more desirable than the un-

---

[35] Gates, in *American Historical Review*, vol. XLI, pp. 661–664.

broken prairie. While the land held for sale by the national government was mainly timber and mineral land, it also included surveyed arable land in favorable locations.

Thus the land policies of the war government, like its tariff and labor legislation, had prepared a feast for eastern businessmen. The railroad grants were making "the whole Northwest and the whole West but little more than a province of New York," complained Senator Howe of Wisconsin, as early as 1864.[36] "Perhaps the largest purchasers of land in Nebraska," writes Paul Wallace Gates, "were a group of Providence, Rhode Island, speculators consisting of Robert H. Ives, John Carter Brown, Charlotte R. and Moses B. J. Goddard." "With Agricultural College scrip of New York," Ezra Cornell located nearly 500,000 acres in Wisconsin, Minnesota, and Kansas. "A group of New York magnates, Thomas F. Mason, George B. Satterlee and William E. Dodge, entered 232,799 acres in the Marquette, Michigan, district, 10,850 acres elsewhere in that state, and 10,359 acres in Wausau, Wisconsin." "John C. Work and Rufus Hatch of New York, and John J. Blair of New Jersey, entered in western Iowa, in 1869 and 1870, 12,200, 28,671, 20,970, acres respectively." Amos Lawrence, Boston Associate, promoter, with others, of the Emigrant Aid Company, "located 58,360 acres in Kansas in 1866 with Agricultural College scrip," while the Emigrant Aid Company itself, "through transactions not always legitimate," purchased 800,000 acres of Cherokee lands at a dollar an acre, the settlers already on the land having no opportunity to claim their cultivated tracts.[37] Soon, selling land became more important to this company than serving emigrants, and in its advertisements it gave publicity to the ills that befell independent farmers who were unaware that free homesteads were overgrown with thorns. Under the homestead law, according to one of its pamphlets,[38]

the settler must, in order to get a good location, go far out into the wild and unsettled districts, and for many years be deprived of school privileges, churches, mills, bridges, and in fact all the advantages of society.

[36] Cole, *Irrepressible Conflict*, p. 359.
[37] Gates, in *American Historical Review*, vol. XLI, pp. 665–673.
[38] Gates, in *American Historical Review*, vol. XLI, p. 663.

The government created these conditions in the West; speculators capitalized them. In Kansas, between 1868 and 1872, for instance, they successfully advertised for sale, up to $15 an acre, land that had once been free public domain. The State Agricultural College offered 90,000 acres of "the choicest land in the state." The Central Branch of the Union Pacific offered 1,200,000 acres, the Kansas Pacific Railroad, 5,000,000 acres. Competing with them were the Kansas & Neosho Valley Railroad, the Capital Land Agency of Topeka, Van Doren and Havens, Hendry and Noyes, T. H. Walker, and not least, the United States Government, offering 6,000 acres of Sac and Fox Indian lands. Such were the benefits of the homestead law.[39]

The Republican party was a Union party, expressly opposed to states' rights. Perhaps as important as any of its specific measures was its rapid transfer of power from the states to the national government. The Union Pacific's was the first federal charter issued since 1816; its land grant was probably the first made by the federal government to a private corporation. The national banking acts virtually eliminated state bank notes from circulation and relegated state banks to a secondary position in the country. The tariff, of course, always was a national matter, but its new protective features greatly extended federal control over the fate of business.

These changes combined to make the federal government stronger than it had ever been. Perhaps as important, they brought upon Washington rather than the state capitals a new army of lobbyists richly laden with gifts. By 1864 the railroads, already experienced in such devices, played for much higher stakes than ever before, and their handouts were commensurate. When the Union Pacific, in that year, had its charter revised, doubling its land grant, increasing its capital and relegating the government's lien to a second mortgage, it obtained these new benefits by spending almost half a million dollars in the nation's capital. J. B. Stewart, a company lawyer, alone dispensed $200,000 to smooth the way for the new bill.[40] By 1865 representatives in Congress had become associated with the notorious Credit

---

[39] Gates, in *American Historical Review*, vol. XLI, p. 663.
[40] Riegel, *Western Railroads*, pp. 73–74.

Mobilier, the Union Pacific's construction company which built a very poor railroad with money gotten from private investors, while its directors distributed among themselves and other insiders the proceeds of the government's lavish contributions.

Neither secession nor Civil War had called industrial businessmen to national leadership; both events only marked their ascension. When the southern states seceded from the Union they left with the conviction that the reign of agrarianism was over. That conviction proved correct. Businessmen had developed their plants, refined their techniques in the fifties. In 1860, aided by northwestern farmers, they had captured political power. By 1865 they had strengthened their control beyond agrarian recall.

PREPARING FOR "PROGRESS"

Northern politicians knew little about conducting a war, but they had few fears over the war's result. During the conflict, therefore, they concentrated not only on war emergencies but also on the future when the war would be over and the country their own. Their acts initiated new policies which, except for contract labor, continued in force long after 1865. While Congress was distributing the spoils of conquest, however, industrial businessmen were also making great strides in self-help, concentrating capital, organizing trade associations, extending factories, applying machinery to industry and agriculture. This program did not get under way immediately after 1861, but when the war was over and businessmen could devote themselves single-mindedly once again to peacetime enterprises, they found that their war activities had prepared the way for rapid forward strides.

Like many wars in modern society, the Civil War started during a business depression, and throughout the conflict many industries remained in the doldrums. The volume of American ocean shipping fell more than 60 per cent between 1860 and 1864. Railroad building, in the fifties more extensive in the United States than in all the countries of Europe combined, virtually ceased during the war. The cotton textile industry, its supply of raw materials cut off, was severely depressed. While factory construction boomed in some industries and some areas,

general construction steadily declined. Even those industries supplying indispensable war goods were slow in getting out of the
rut. At the start of the war $300,000,000 of uncollectible southern
debts dislocated northern credit activity, and optimistic government predictions of quick victory made businessmen wary of
overexpansion to meet emergency needs. As the war continued,
the government's haphazard fiscal policies disturbed businessmen
still more, while the early series of northern defeats and Britain's
undecided attitude toward the belligerents also sapped business
confidence. As late as August, 1862, therefore, the *New York
Tribune* could still complain of "our paralyzed industry, obstructed commerce, our over-laden finances, and our mangled
railroads." [41]

The summer of 1862, however, marked the nadir of depression.
Jay Cooke's hectic door-to-door sale of the "five-twenties" had
rescued the government from bankruptcy. The greenbacks had
helped raise commodity prices. The chartering of the Pacific
railroads and the great opportunities they promised for speculation in western lands had revived business confidence, and the
imposing victories at Vicksburg, Gettysburg, and Chattanooga,
following Farragut's success at New Orleans and McClellan's
at Antietam, seemed to assure in the end a northern victory
and kept business confidence high. In addition the national banking laws were soon to rationalize the crazy state bank-note
currency system. They were to create also a great market for
government securities and, through these securities, a huge
reservoir of credit for private business. When the government,
therefore, its treasury now replenished and its armies triumphant,
began to place orders for huge quantities of shoes, hats, blankets,
uniforms, munitions, flour, corned beef, pork, businessmen showed
a new eagerness to fill these orders. Protected against foreign
competition by high tariffs, and presented with a steadily growing
demand for uniform goods, manufacturers no longer hesitated
to extend and mechanize their plants. The money market became active, employment began to increase, and wartime
prosperity thus began to brighten many sections of the land.

---

[41] Carman, *Social and Economic History,* vol. II, p. 563.

During the war two thousand new sets of woolen cards were erected. In the boot and shoe industry, sewing machines became so widely used that the inventor McKay received annual royalties of $750,000. "Operatives are pouring in as fast as room can be made for them," declared the *Lynn Reporter*, "buildings for shoe factories are going up in every direction; the hum of machinery is heard on every hand." [42] Until 1863, soldiers' uniforms had still to be imported from abroad. After that date, the domestic industry, concentrated in Boston, New York, Philadelphia, and Cincinnati, began to supply all the requirements of an enlarged army. At the start of hostilities, North and South alike had to import munitions. By 1863 the North was able to supply itself, and by the end of the war its light-gun industry was filling orders from Europe as well as Washington. American farms also used more machines to replace the labor lost to the army. In 1862, 35,000 mowers were produced; in 1864, 70,000. In July, 1863, the editor of the *Scientific American* declared: [43]

In conversation a few days since with a most intelligent Western farmer he told us that manual labor was so scarce last autumn that but for horse rakes, mowers, and reaping machines one-half of the crops would have been left standing in the fields. This year the demand for reapers has been so great the manufacturers will not be able to fill their orders.

From much of this prosperity, however, small industrialists were shut out. Mechanization was expensive, and small manufacturers had neither the surplus cash nor the credit to expand their plants. Neither did they have access to friendly ears at Washington where orders were dispensed. Besides, sales taxes on manufactured goods in all stages of production put a premium on integration, and the independent spinning factory, for instance, could not compete in bids for government contracts with corporations handling all stages of the manufacture of blankets or soldiers' uniforms. The result was the concentration of manufacturing capital in fewer hands than before, the construction of larger plants, and the appearance of a new class of

---

[42] Fite, *Industrial Conditions*, p. 91.
[43] Fite, *Industrial Conditions*, p. 7.

war millionaires. The New York *Independent,* during the war, declared that in New York alone there were already "several hundred men worth $1,000,000 and some worth $20,000,000 while twenty years back there had not been five men in the whole United States worth as much as $5,000,000 and not twenty worth over $1,000,000." [44]

While business reorganized for war production, it did not neglect its pressure groups. Trade associations had been formed in the fifties chiefly to control prices and combat labor unions. To these functions during the war were added tax and tariff lobbying. Many new associations were formed, organized on a national basis in sympathy with the shift of power from the states to the federal government. Among those starting or extending their activities between 1861 and 1865, were the California Wine Growers' Association, the Cap and Hat Manufacturers Association of New York, the National Association of Wool Manufacturers, the National Woolgrowers Association, and the American Iron and Steel Association.

The goods that farms and factories produced had, of course, to be shipped to armies, ports, towns, and villages. Though little railroad track was laid between 1861 and 1865, railroad traffic was enormous and some eastern roads paid dividends for the first time. Cutting into profits, however, was cutthroat competition among different roads and between railroad and water transportation companies. Manufacturers and farmers benefited from this competition and joined with a public afraid of great monopolies to resist efforts at transportation rate agreements or consolidations. In many cases this resistance was successful. The New York Central tried to combine with the Harlem, the Hudson River, and the Lake Shore railroads, but failed. Five lines along Lake Erie, between Buffalo and Chicago, tried futilely to come to an agreement. The Boston & Worcester and the Western in Massachusetts tried to form a through line between Boston and Albany but could not come to terms. As businessmen who shipped long distances and army officials who waited anxiously for goods coming from far away became increasingly annoyed during the

---

[44] Fite, *Industrial Conditions,* pp. 166–167.

war by lack of uniformity in railroad operation, however, they demanded more and more consolidation of transportation companies, more and more pooling of facilities and centralizing of management. And their demands did not go entirely unheeded. As in manufacturing, therefore, the war accelerated the growth of large transportation enterprises. Perhaps the most important combination made between 1861 and 1865 was the acquisition by the Pennsylvania of the Pittsburgh, Fort Wayne & Chicago Railroad, completing the first trunk line between Lake Michigan and the Atlantic coast. The Erie purchased several small roads to extend its western terminal from Dunkirk to Buffalo. Seven local lines combined to run from Boston to Ogdensburg, New York, while four western roads between Quincy, Illinois, and Toledo, Ohio, were brought under one management. The Chicago & North Western, among other acquisitions, absorbed the Peninsular line, uniting the lake city with the new iron and copper mines in northern Michigan.[45]

Almost unanimously desired and therefore much more popular was the concentration of telegraph capital into the Western Union monopoly. Combination started in this infant industry when Western Union, organized in 1851, began to gobble up smaller lines in the Middle West. By 1863 it shared the entire country with the American Telegraph Company, though innumerable local independent companies were scattered outside their net. Some of these companies in New England and New York were linked to terminals in Buffalo, Pittsburgh, Cleveland, Chicago, St. Louis, and Milwaukee by the United States Telegraph Company, which invaded the industry during the war. This company, or those from which it had been formed, constructed between 1861 and 1865 about 13,000 miles of line, creating a veritable "telegraph fever" and projecting a new giant into the business.

Telegraph profits were huge during the war though competition was acute in many areas and cooperation among the companies was subject to all the hazards of business rivalry. As use of the systems increased, these hazards became more obstructive

---

[45] Fite, *Industrial Conditions*, pp. 159–160; Shannon, *Economic History*, p. 391.

and businessmen and government officials urged the companies
to unite. By 1865, Western Union had built or acquired 50,000
miles of line, twice as much as its two rivals combined. It was
best able, therefore, to press for consolidation. Its efforts were
successful in 1866. Business had become accustomed, in a short
time, to instantaneous communication between distant offices and
factories. The telegraph monopoly made this service available
uniformly throughout the nation. Under one management it
united 75,000 miles of line, serving 2,250 offices in every region.
Business celebrated the achievement.

Consolidations also were made in the salt and paper industries
while Rockefeller's petroleum empire was beginning to take form.
During the war, the first combination of five refineries was completed. The cause leading to its formation, Rockefeller declared,[46]

was the desire to unite our skill and capital in order to carry on a business
of some magnitude and importance in place of the small business that each
separately had theretofore carried on.

The demands of war and economics thus were combining during the military struggle to enlarge the typical American industrial
plant and concentrate American capital. By 1866 the editor of
the *Commercial and Financial Chronicle* could observe: [47]

There is an increasing tendency in our capital to move in larger masses
than formerly. Small business firms compete at more disadvantage with
richer houses, and are gradually being absorbed into them. Thus we have
more men worth one hundred thousand dollars in some of our large commercial cities than were reputed five years ago to be worth fifty thousand
dollars. No doubt much of this reputed capital is fictitious. But the power
accumulating in the moneyed classes from the concentration of capital in
large masses is attracting the attention of the close observers of the money
market. It is one of the signs of the time and will probably exert no small
influence over the future growth of our industrial and commercial enterprise.

---

[46] Fite, *Industrial Conditions*, p. 164.
[47] Fite, *Industrial Conditions*, p. 165.

PROFITS FOR WHOM?

In his first annual message, President Lincoln declared:

Labor is prior to and independent of capital. Capital is only the fruit of labor and could never have existed if labor had not first existed. Labor is the superior of capital and deserves much the higher consideration.

Northern industrialists probably were pleased that Lincoln was so occupied with other things he could not try to enact these principles. Even so, Lincoln probably stayed the hand of some of his less liberal colleagues when strikes during the early years of the war hindered preparations for conflict.

In February, 1861, the national convention of workmen, meeting regularly after 1858 under the leadership of William Sylvis of the Moulders, had resolved: [48]

That our Government never can be sustained by bloodshed, but must live in the affections of the people; we are, therefore, utterly opposed to any measures that will evoke civil war.

When fighting began, however, Sylvis and other labor leaders actively supported the government. Labor shortages between 1861 and 1865 stimulated unionization and encouraged strikes, most of them successful. Lincoln's administration tolerated these activities until 1864; then the army insisted that they be brought to a halt. In that year and the next, Union Order No. 65 was enforced in St. Louis, Louisville, and other large industrial cities supplying army needs.[49] This order forbade striking and picketing and authorized the protection of strikebreakers.

While skilled trades were successful in organizing during the war, labor as a whole failed to win wage increases at a rate commensurate with the skyrocketing cost of living. Industrial businessmen used the conflict to wrest political leadership from agriculture and commerce, bankers used it to make fortunes speculating in gold and marketing government bonds, manufacturers used it to make extraordinary profits from government

---

[48] Commons, *Labour,* vol. II, p. 11.
[49] Allen, *Reconstruction,* p. 147.

contracts, speculators in railroads and western lands used it to
prepare a great future for themselves; and speculators in contraband used it, in effect, to ruin the morale of the army. But
through all the war years industrial workers suffered privations
because of rising commodity prices, and white-collar workers and
salaried professionals, their incomes less elastic even than those
of organized industrial workers, often fell into dire need. Some
businessmen made legitimate profits, while others secretly
grasped opportunities for fraud. "Bribery and corruption seem
to go into every branch of service," complained General Hurl-
but.[50] General Butler complained that smugglers of contraband
and southern cotton were so successful his soldiers at New
Orleans were anxious to go home, "not wishing to risk their
lives to make fortunes for others." [51] In or out of the army,
the majority of the people found it increasingly difficult to make
ends meet while more and more of their liberties were curtailed.
Not only were strikes forbidden during the last years of the war
but newspapers were gagged, objectors were cast into jail without
trial, and martial law was imposed in many areas.

The Civil War began when a northern party captured the
federal government. During the war that conquest was made
more secure. Men friendly to industrial business were elected
to office. Others were absorbed into the civil service; still others
consolidated their positions in local government. Founded as a
party of protesting western farmers, the Republican party soon
became the instrument of Big Business. Those farmers who escaped the call to the colors profited during the war, but agriculture lost its previous political power. Southern planters, their
wealth destroyed, and western farmers, their party captured,
could do no more than complain about eastern exploitation.

---

[50] Randall, *Civil War*, p. 632.
[51] Randall, *Civil War*, p. 632.

VI

A PHILOSOPHY FOR INDUSTRIAL PROGRESS

AMERICAN industrialists in the half-century after 1812 were hated by southern planters, vilified by New England radicals, despised by landed gentry and Quaker merchants. Attending strictly to business, however, they had by the end of the Civil War passed farming in the production of wealth, ocean shipping in the employment of capital. Aided by new machines, new techniques in industrial organization and finance, they emerged from the war better equipped than ever to develop the resources of the land; and carrying leadership proudly on their shoulders they prescribed their manners and customs to the nation, and their philosophy of progress to the ambitious North.

Worked out most thoroughly by the Englishman Herbert Spencer, this philosophy won America as no philosophy had ever won a nation before. To a generation singularly engrossed in the competitive pursuit of industrial wealth it gave cosmic sanction to free competition. In an age of science, it "scientifically" justified ceaseless exploitation. Precisely attuned to the aspirations of American businessmen, it afforded them a guide to faith and thought perfectly in keeping with the pattern of their workaday lives. When they were hopeful, it was infinitely optimistic; when they were harsh, it "proved" that harshness was the only road to progress; when they had doubts, it allayed these with a show of evidence that apparently was irrefutable. Their cupidity, it defended as part of the universal struggle for existence; their wealth, it hallowed as the sign of the "fittest." Business America in the Gilded Age had supreme faith in itself; no wonder it embraced Spencer's philosophy, which sanctified business activities.

Honored in the United States as no philosopher ever was in

Greece, no artist in Renaissance Italy, no scientist anywhere in his own day, Spencer left an impression on America that was much more profound than his work. He supplied a rationale and a vocabulary that American businessmen were reluctant to abandon even when business practices made Spencerianism obsolete. For this rather than for any contribution to knowledge, Spencer is important to us. From the Civil War to the New Deal, businessmen explained themselves to the "public" in his terms; and during the decade of the 1930's his thought, or textbook variations upon it, formed the basis for conservative attacks upon the reforms of Franklin Roosevelt.

PATTERNS OF HERESY

American industrialists before the Civil War, unlike their English competitors after the struggle with Napoleon, were only a subordinate group in a society dominated by farmers and merchants. Thus they could scarcely be held accountable for social conditions. Unlike English classicists, therefore, American industrial economists in this early period had no need for metaphysical systems seeking in terms of some heavenly plan to justify social distress. Little need they scruple to break "natural laws" as long as they could promise economic gain. Little need they fear logical inconsistencies as long as their maxims justified business practices. Thus they could applaud the benefits of the division of labor and reject Smith's free trade. They could adopt Ricardo's "iron law of wages" and reject his doctrine of rent. They could accept Senior's "abstinence" theory of value and reject other aspects of his thought. They could live by free competition and apotheosize it as the basis for the distribution of wealth, yet they need not, therefore, be as lugubrious as Malthus, as democratic as John Stuart Mill.

Like the English classicists, early American economists agreed that enlightened self-interest was the best guarantee for the greatest good of the greatest number. The Americans, however, thought that this goal could be more quickly attained if businessmen took the initiative themselves and did not depend simply on the beneficent working of natural law. Thus American economists

sympathetic to industrial business simulta
tariff men and sternly antiunion; they coul
patents, subsidies, bounties, loans, while conten
breath that free competition was the life of trad
approve tax remissions to encourage new businesses w
ing as destructive interference with the operation of
economic laws" factory acts regulating conditions of labor.

Before the Civil War, of course, the recommendations of o
industrial economists generally were heeded only to be attacked.
The ascendant American minority was a states' rights minority
cast into a heroic column by Jefferson and John Taylor, Calhoun
and Stephens, Taney and Cooper. Armed with arguments seemingly irresistible, these leaders dedicated themselves to fight to
the finish the proliferating machine culture of northern industry.
And their followers, impassioned by the rhetoric of southern fire-
eaters and the latter's mercantile allies in New England and New
York, for three decades met and persistently defeated bills for
high tariffs, national banks, Pacific railroads, rational currency
and federal bonds for internal improvements.

Without agrarian aid, however, American industry in the fifties
had come of age. Drawing few recruits from the organized ranks
of its enemies, it had enlisted a new army of its own, created
prodigious wealth, stimulated reproduction and immigration to
absorb, to use, to augment it. When civil war broke out, the
leaders of this army already had become the leaders of the nation. By 1865, they had subdued their agrarian adversaries.

In the saddle at last, industrialists had now to bear responsibility for social hardships. They had to account for their
stewardship, to explain away apparent errors. The time for
opportunism had passed.

THE MAGNIFICENT EXEGESIS

Fortunate beyond other people in their natural heritage,
American businessmen were doubly fortunate in developing it
at the very moment when Darwin stunned a theological age
with his *Origin of Species* (1859) and Herbert Spencer was
popularizing "laws" of evolution in his many-faceted picture of

lthus, Darwin successfully ap-
ons the Victorian "struggle for
e the natural process by which
ed themselves to a changing en-
ne source of inspiration, Spencer
o the study of society almost ten
his epochal work. What Darwin
a new point of view, but a scien-
n worked in nature. What Spencer
erica, and in a lesser degree to
industrial Eng...,   ntific" description of how "nature"
worked in society.

Darwin went to flora and fauna, parasites and pigeons for evidence; Spencer went to them for analogies. Imbued from childhood with anarchic ideas about the state, he early translated physical laws of conservation of energy into a natural "equilibration of mechanisms," thus finding a basis in popular science for political *laissez faire*. Like American industrialists, however, Spencer was intolerant of pessimism, and he could not, therefore, follow Malthus or Ricardo in accepting *laissez faire* without giving it direction toward some scientific heaven. Thus, just as he had translated physics into politics, so Spencer, prompted now by Darwin (and Lamarck) was quick to confuse biology and sociology. Freely he transposed Darwin's physical organism into a social organism; casually he applied to the latter the laws of the first. Thus, just as in their primitive struggle for existence the "fittest" among the species of sea and forest adapted themselves to their environment, so for Spencer those competitors who had best adapted themselves to nineteenth century society, became the "fittest" among men. And just as nature worked untrammeled in "selecting" her elite, so that society was headed quickest to perfection which allowed its elite free play.

It was not long before Spencer's conception of the ideal state was at odds with the practices of leading American industrialists, and as the wheels of free competition gradually were clogged by monopoly the differences between theory and practice broadened. It is striking that Spencer's earliest works were published when trade associations and price pools first were being formed by American businessmen, that Spencer had his greatest vogue simultaneously with Protection. Before Spencer's philosophy was outmoded, however, it had given businessmen a rationale which served to justify even to the businessmen themselves their own monopolistic tendencies. Spencer did not write in economic terms, but his words had economic implications. And if trusts and combines were the natural results of free competition worshipers of competition could not logically oppose them.

Like every ruling class, American industrialists, when they came to power, felt the need of a philosophy, of fixed principles to justify, for the long run, activities that appeared at the moment costly or corrupt; they naturally wished to make the lesser seem the greater good, the private seem the national profit. Lured into strange paths by undeniable opportunities, drawn as if by a magnet from the circle of traditional experience in democratic America, they had to find the words to make their tangential excursions seem but extended arcs that soon would return to the habitual course of American life. They had to pay obeisance to the old gods of competition while pursuing new ones; they had to worship publicly at the people's temples while engaging in new rites outside. With the aid of Darwin and Spencer, they found the words; protected by Darwin and Spencer, they themselves could ignore them.

Thus free competition became the keystone of the triumphal arch of American business philosophy, while monopolistic tendencies were ignored; science and mechanization became the grand avenues of progress while patent pools and social regimentation were obscured; thrift remained the first commandment in the decalogue of the new business society though conspicuous consumption was its sign of grace.

To be sure, many activities of industrial *leaders* or their political spokesmen were similar to those of their lesser followers, the privates in the army of business. These activities needed no vindication. They served rather to prove that the departures from tradition were not as cataclysmic as they seemed; they helped to convince those oppressed by monopoly that their hardships were divine visitations, trials sent by the Lord who first made the laws, not by the men who obeyed them. Thus those who were crushed by competition, regimented by machines, too poorly paid to keep up with the Joneses, were invited to find solace in the fact that their sacrifices were essential to national welfare, that without victims there could be no struggle for existence, that without a struggle for existence there could be no progress, that without progress there could be no hope for perfection.

HERBERT SPENCER: APOSTLE TO THE AMERICANS

Herbert Spencer was rejected by professional philosophers as superficial and by professional scientists as ignorant, but his ideas for many years supplied the catchwords for the American middle class. Agnostic himself, Spencer gave the theological mind of America a grander view of divine creation than ever was revealed before. Upon skeptical materialists his seemingly absolute dependence upon the data of biology, geology, zoology, made a profound impression. In his political writings Spencer never deigned to study the history of man but applied to human society popular generalizations from physics and natural science. Americans, however, knew well what they wanted in social theory and eagerly grasped his analogies, just as they knew what they wanted in a President and eagerly elected the hero of Appomattox. "The progress of evolution from President Washington to President Grant," wrote Henry Adams, "was alone evidence enough to upset Darwin." [1] But America was ready to believe otherwise, just as it was prepared to believe that the laws of flora and fauna on land and sea were the laws of human society and that all would grow perfect together.

When Andrew Carnegie first read Spencer, he exclaimed: "Light came as in a flood and all was clear." [2] And Henry Holt wrote: [3]

Probably no other philosopher ever had such a vogue as Spencer had from about 1870 to 1890. Most preceding philosophers had presumably

---

[1] Adams, *Education,* p. 266.
[2] Macpherson, *Spencer,* p. 64.
[3] Holt, in *Unpopular Review,* vol. VIII, p. 345.

been mainly restricted to readers habitually given to the study of philosophy, but not only was Spencer considerably read and generally talked about by the whole intelligent world in England and America, but that world was wider than any that preceded it. . . . When he visited New York in 1873 he was given a great public dinner. Some earlier philosophers may have had such an experience, but if so, knowledge of it never crossed our limited horizon.

When E. L. Youmans got Appleton's to publish Spencer's works and John Fiske, in his efforts to reconcile evolution and theology, acquainted Americans with their contents, Spencer's conquest was assured. No saint ever had more devoted disciples than Spencer had in Fiske and Youmans, and their tireless propaganda helped to sell in America, in less than forty years, more than 300,000 copies of Spencer's works.

One of the most endearing features of Spencer's philosophy was the way it could be used against any reform movement. The master himself was agreeable to some social reforms, claiming against John Stuart Mill, for instance, precedence in the fight for women's rights. He also approved private charities, for while they might tend to prolong the life of the unfit and thus were evil, they helped also to raise "the moral culture" of the elite and in the end speeded "progress." Spencer contended, however, "that there shall not be a *forcible* burdening of the superior for the support of the inferior." [4] And from this his American disciples reasoned that voluntary gifts to churches, hospitals or schools were good, but graduated taxes were bad; that the promptings of public relations men could be followed with impunity, but the regulatory acts of legislatures could be obeyed only at great cost. The indefatigable Youmans had learned this lesson well: [5]

Social forces cannot be created by enactment [he said], and when dealing with the production, distributing, and commercial activities of the community, legislation can do little more than interfere with their natural courses.

More forcefully, the industrialist Hewitt announced: "The invasion of government into the domain of industry must be met with

---

[4] Spencer, *Principles of Biology*, vol. II, p. 533.
[5] Youmans, *Correlation of Forces*, Preface.

uncompromising opposition." [6] At Columbia, Nicholas Murray Butler proved himself a willing disciple when he wrote: [7]

Nature's cure for most social and political diseases is better than man's, and without the strongest reasons the government should withhold its hand from everything that is not, by substantially common consent, a matter of governmental action.

When Wilson and Roosevelt in 1912 won "substantially common consent" for government regulation of Big Business and Wilson began after his election to concern himself with the affairs of industry, Butler was among the distinguished company that reasserted their faith in Spencer and with suitable comments hurled into the teeth of *The New Freedom* Spencer's *Man Versus the State*. Joining Butler was Senator Henry Cabot Lodge, who warned that "no one perhaps has pointed out the ultimate truths involved in the expansion of governmental functions better than Herbert Spencer." [8] Also contributing was Charles W. Eliot, President of Harvard. Accepting the words of the master equally without reserve, he said: [9]

Spencer maintains without reserve that the spontaneous co-operation of men in pursuit of personal benefits will adequately work out the general good, if the state should discharge its plain duties simply of enforcing the sanctity of contracts and preventing cheating, and of securing to each citizen the enjoyment of what he obtains by labor without trenching upon his neighbor's ability to enjoy.

Through a system every one could understand, Spencer gave cosmic values to experiences shared by almost every one in America. The office boy hurrying to be at work at eight in the morning was not just a three-dollar-a-week clerk; according to Spencer, by his speed and diligence he was in some inscrutable way contributing to the progress of mankind. The employer working his men and women too hard could be praised for eliminating the unfit. The monopolist operating in "restraint of trade"

---

[6] Nevins, *Writings of Hewitt*, p. 134.
[7] Butler, in *Forum*, vol. LV, pp. 83–84.
[8] Beale, *Man Versus the State*, p. 31.
[9] Eliot, in *Forum*, vol. LV, p. 712.

could be made a hero for ignoring legislative interference with *natural* law. As the *Outlook* said in 1903, Spencer "expressed the *Zeitgeist* and in expressing it he has helped to develop it, mainly in the direction of a saner, more reverent thinking." [10] "Now every newspaper," said Henry Holt as late as 1923, "is full of little dabs of it [the evolution philosophy] and has hardly a paragraph without some of its terminology—most of it unrealized by those who write it and those who read it." [11]

So profoundly were Spencer's views the products of his times that even his severest critics could not avoid them. Among the most outspoken and influential anti-Spencerians was W. T. Harris, a Hegelian who believed in "progress" but hated Spencer's materialism. Harris, later United States Commissioner of Education, tried to attack Spencer first in the *Atlantic Monthly*, then in the *North American Review*. Both times he was rebuffed by the editors, yet so eager was he to oppose the master that he started his own magazine partly for that purpose.[12] Still it was Harris who later said, "Through private property and free competition 'society gains constantly at the least expense.'" [13] It was Harris who said: [14]

Help the poor and unfortunate *to help themselves,* and elevate them towards human perfection and the divine ideal. . . . [But] adopt all the cunning devices that social science has invented, and you cannot be sure that direct or indirect help of the poor does not undermine their self-respect and weaken their independence.

It was Harris, who, matching Spencer's interest in enterprising women, held up to them as models those corporation officers who studied law only the better to evade it, so that "progress" might not be obstructed. Without a trace of irony, he told these women: [15]

Captains of industry depend on higher education to keep themselves out of jail, for great business *combinations* involve collisions of all kinds with

---

[10] "Herbert Spencer" (editorial), *Outlook,* vol. LXXV, p. 932.
[11] Holt, *Octogenarian Editor,* p. 47.
[12] Curti, *American Educators,* p. 312.
[13] Curti, *American Educators,* p. 323.
[14] Curti, *American Educators,* p. 325.
[15] Curti, *American Educators,* p. 322.

other interests and must adopt legal precautions to avoid civil and criminal liabilities.

In books, pamphlets, lectures, and reports Harris unwittingly preached Spencer, while his disciples in thousands of schoolrooms throughout the country echoed his words. In institutions of higher learning, Spencer's influence was no less great. Eliot and Fiske at Harvard, Butler at Columbia, the magnificent William Graham Sumner at Yale, all impressed upon the minds of young industrialists, preachers, writers, teachers, the precepts of this self-taught Englishman. It was Spencer who gave currency to the study of sociology and supplied the first textbooks. It was he who showed how the "economic man" of economic abstractionists could become the universal man of social scientists. He reduced *homo sapiens* to the level of the machine, and so well adapted was his mechanistic philosophy to the culture of his age that he was warmly embraced as the master theoretician of his time.

The vitality of Spencer's philosophy, the neatness with which it had fitted American experience and merged with American ideals was attested as late as 1936. Then, when its scientific substructure was all but demolished, when it had been mortally attacked by Veblen and partially supplanted by the ameliorative philosophy of the New Deal, it remained the starting point for conservative attacks upon the reformers of the new depression.[16] Even American industrialists themselves, at that late date, admitted that the old system of individual enterprise had collapsed. Many of them still clung, however, to the philosophy of the old system, to the tenets first set forth by Herbert Spencer almost a hundred years before. This philosophy had served American industrialists well in the late decades of the nineteenth century; so well indeed, that they had been able to learn no other despite changing conditions, so well that they were very reluctant to surrender it even when its application to the life around them had become obscure.

---

[16] Cochran, in *Frontiers of Democracy*, vol. VI, p. 19.

VII

THE TRIUMPH OF INDUSTRIAL ENTERPRISE

FOR half a century before 1860, American industrialists had been altering the course of American history. Their corporations had affected property relations, their machines had revolutionized conditions of labor, their locomotives and telegraphs had speeded the pace of American life, their railroads had begun to draw outlying rural areas into the orbits of great cities. At every stage these changes had been resisted by sovereign planters and their commercial allies, until, at last, on the battlefield, their ranks were broken, their influence destroyed. Times had changed in America and in the world since 1800, mainly because of the impact of *industrial enterprise*. It was not strange, therefore, when the revolution came that industrialists should carry the mace of authority.

Traditional language had no words to describe the business activities of the new leaders after the Civil War, no words to define the functions of their institutions. Traditional politics could not cope with their demands, nor could traditional law harness them to social welfare. In place of the old canons, they imposed the rule of the jungle upon a willing people who worshiped at the altar of "Progress." Remorselessly they exploited precious resources, stripping incomparable forests, leaving gaping holes in mountain sides to mark exhausted mines, dotting with abandoned derricks oil fields drained of petroleum and natural gas. In reckless haste, they constructed railroads through the wilderness, and immense factories to supply the needs of millions yet unborn. They promoted many similar projects simply to mulct a nation of speculators for the private benefit of the "Fittest."

With magnificent optimism these industrial leaders plunged forward for thirty years in Olympian combat among themselves

for the spoils of the land and the people. Gradually, however, a
new order began to emerge out of the chaos of brutal competition. Entrepreneurs were learning the profitable lessons of specialized and standardized production, of geographical concentration of plants, of centralized management. Corporations at war
were learning that combination was a surer way to wealth and
power. Above all, a small number of investment bankers were
acquiring interests in great properties against which they had
loaned large fortunes only to see them dissipated by wildcat
managements, or to which they had extended liberal credit on
condition that they participate in control. The nerve centers of
the proliferating system, by the early 1890's, thus were becoming fewer and more complex, the instruments of control more
centralized, the managers a select class of professional corporation directors. In the struggle for survival, competition had
yielded to cooperation, individualism to combination. Corporations, in an age of gigantic personalities, had become super-
persons, as incorporeal as angels and as little amenable to punish-
ment, in mysterious ways directing the life of the new society,
but seemingly outside its laws.

RAILROAD IMPERIALISM

As industrial capitalism spread over Europe in the late nineteenth century and even across the world to Japan, Frenchmen,
Germans, Belgians, Dutch, Italians, Russians, and Orientals
joined the English who had preceded them in seeking raw materials, cheap labor, free markets in Asia, Africa, and the un-
charted islands of the seas. American industrialists, however,
blessed with a fabulously rich continent of their own, a political
system fashioned to their order, a legend irresistibly attractive
to impoverished aliens eager to work for the meanest subsistence
only to breathe the free air of the United States, did not have
to venture so far afield. In America, obstacles were fewer, opportunities infinitely greater, than elsewhere in the world. Need we
seek other explanations for the extraordinary vitality of our
industrialism?

First to operate on a grand scale in the new atmosphere of business enterprise were American railroad men, and they made the greatest fortunes. Vigorous, violent, and corrupt, they showed by their accumulations of wealth that their business methods were best suited to the conditions of their time and place. Their contributions to the Gilded Age, however, were not limited to techniques of exploitation. Though they chased the Indian from western valleys and fertile plateaus, they peopled his territories with Europeans, orientals, and emigrants from eastern states, with farmers and cattlemen who improved the land and laborers who helped them in their tasks. To eastern imperialists they opened mines in Colorado, Nevada, Idaho, Montana, timberlands in Minnesota, Washington, Oregon, and California where nature for countless millennia had stored prodigious wealth. On river shores and crossroads in the wilderness, they laid the cornerstones of future cities. From the Missouri, the Mississippi, and the Great Lakes, over the Rockies, Sierras, and Cascades, they joined in indissoluble union with older commonwealths the Pacific tier of states, ending the threat of other powers to our "continental destiny."

Between 1867 and 1873, more than 30,000 miles of new track were opened to traffic in the United States; and by 1893, though more than eight years of depression intervened, 150,000 miles had been laid since the war. Capital invested in American railroads jumped in this period from two to nearly ten billion dollars.[1] Though most of this mileage and most of this capital went to complete old trunk lines and their links to new centers in the valleys of the Ohio, Mississippi, and Missouri, the most spectacular of all the roads and perhaps the most important were the transcontinentals. These really blazed the trail of American industry in the Gilded Age, gave great impetus to lesser western railroad building, set the fashion in methods of construction and finance. These gave the nation its heroes, its Stanfords, Huntingtons, Hills, and Cookes, as well as its villains in the Crédit Mobilier and other construction companies. These were the gov-

---

[1] Miller, *Inland Transportation*, p. 101.

ernments within governments, the owners of executives, legislators, and judges, the leviers of taxes, the arbiters of the destiny
of cities, counties, states, industries, and farms.

We need seek no further for the key to the power of American
railroad men when we realize that in an age of corruption they
knew best how to use their opportunities; that in a country of
tremendous distances they were gaining a monopoly of long-haul
transportation; that in regions where wealth was mainly land
they were cornering the best of it. The promoters of the transcontinentals as well as lesser railroads spent millions in Washington, state capitals, county seats, and city halls to get land
grants, loans and subsidies, and then spent millions more to
maintain their grants inviolate. The Union Pacific, for instance,
between 1866 and 1872 handed out $400,000 in graft; the
Central Pacific, as late as the decade between 1875 and 1885,
distributed $500,000 annually.[2] Part of this went to fight water
competition, to win rich mail contracts, to riddle with restrictions
and objections bills for river and harbor improvements. Most
of it, however, went to make private capital out of the public
domain. When the fury of competitive building had run its course
in the West and depression shrouded the countryside after 1893,
it was found that railroads had been granted one-fourth of the
whole area of Minnesota and Washington; one-fifth of Wisconsin, Iowa, Kansas, North Dakota, and Montana, one-seventh of
Nebraska, one-eighth of California, one-ninth of Louisiana.[3] It
was found that in 1872, to meet the demands of the Southern
Pacific, Los Angeles County had donated the equivalent of a $100
tax on each of its six thousand inhabitants; that Superior, Minnesota, in 1880, had granted one-third of its "lands, premises and
real estate" as well as a right of way to get the Northern Pacific
to run through it; that between 1867 and 1892 forty-three
sparsely settled Nebraska counties had voted almost $5,000,000
to railroad companies, some of which never built a mile of track.[4]

All told, Congress, in twenty-one grants between 1862 and

---

[2] Josephson, *Politicos,* p. 105; Daggett, *Southern Pacific,* p. 213.
[3] Cleveland and Powell, *Railroad Promotion,* p. 251.
[4] Daggett, *Southern Pacific,* p. 129; Cleveland and Powell, *Railroad Promotion,*
p. 203; and Miller, *Inland Transportation,* p. 95.

1872, chartered to the railroads 200,000,000 acres of land, of which, for one reason or another, slightly more than half actually came into their possession. In addition, federal loans to railroads totaled $64,623,512, the bulk of which went to the Union and Central Pacific. The aggregate of state land grants and state loans was also great and certain cities and counties which had not repudiated their liabilities remained in debt even in the twentieth century for railroad bonds issued in the seventies and eighties.[5] These subsidies and loans supplied hardly enough capital to build the roads to which they were granted and to yield as well an acceptable profit to the promoters. By using such grants to guarantee private loans, however, the promoters were able to supplement public gifts with private capital. Even so, they had their difficulties in raising money. Americans enriched by the war were finding other investments more attractive than transcontinentals that took seven to sixteen years to build, more attractive than shorter lines that traversed as yet untenanted western deserts. On the other hand, foreign rentiers who were eager to invest in booming America demanded higher interest rates than promoters generally cared to offer. Thus even with the support of public grants, the promoters were forced to sell their securities well below par, the Union Pacific, for instance, issuing $111,000,000 worth of bonds for $74,000,000 in cash.[6]

Such practices burdened the roads with excessive capitalizations, forced them to charge high rates to service their debts, left them vulnerable to complaints of shippers at monopoly points and to cutthroat competition in shared territories from lines less speculative in conception and more economically constructed.

Though they encountered many difficulties in raising capital, *promoters* of the transcontinentals and other land-grant railroads, once having accumulated it, had little difficulty in making money. Many great American fortunes have been accumulated not by producing goods or supplying services but by manipulating securities and diverting to personal uses the *capital* these securities nominally represent. We have seen how Drew milked into his

---

[5] Cleveland and Powell, *Railroad Promotion,* pp. 250–257.
[6] Ripley, *Railroads,* vol. II, p. 35.

own bucket the construction funds of the Erie. Of that company's stock, Jay Gould testified before a court in 1869:[7]

There is no intrinsic value to it, probably; it has speculative value; people buy and sell it, and sometimes they get a little too much.

Another time, he said: "The Erie won't be a dividend-paying road for a long time on its common stock."[8] Yet out of Erie, dilapidated and bankrupt as it frequently was, Gould and Fisk made their first millions. By similar methods, the promoters of the transcontinentals and other railroads compensated themselves for their public services. Instead of taking competitive bids, they formed themselves into construction companies and voted themselves the contracts for construction work and equipment. As directors of construction companies they billed their railroads at exorbitant rates; as directors of railroad companies, they gladly paid what was asked. Thus railroad capital was turned into construction profits, public money into private fortunes. Besides cash they paid themselves millions in stock for which there was no immediate market. As building steadily progressed, however, and buyers for such stock were found in Wall Street and on exchanges in other great cities in the East and Middle West, these tokens for speculation netted their holders hundreds of millions of dollars.

Since the government granted lands and loans only as mileage was completed, it put a premium upon speed in construction and length of track. The result was that almost all of the land-grant railroads were poorly built along the most tortuous paths. Within fifteen years after they were completed almost all of them had to be rebuilt to eliminate needless curves, shifting roadbeds, splintering "sleepers" and spreading rails too light to bear the weight of the engines.[9] Thus besides supplying the land and the cash with which the roads were built, and paying rates based on notoriously high capitalizations and taxes to service railroad bonds issued by their governments, the people were soon burdened with new charges to make their roads usable even at mini-

---

[7] Andrews, *Vanderbilt,* p. 141.
[8] Hicks, *High Finance,* p. 97 note.
[9] See Ripley, *Railroads,* vol. II, pp. 45-52.

mum efficiency. Those roads that could not attract new capital after their promoters had diverted the original construction funds to their personal use, were left to rot. President Ingalls of the Chesapeake & Ohio wrote in 1898:[10]

> When the day of reckoning came, as it was bound to, the public found themselves the owners of bonds upon which interest could not be paid; the communities found themselves with a poor railway in which they had no direct pecuniary interest; they saw the contractors with enormous fortunes, and they concluded that they had been robbed.

If the promoters of the land-grant roads were corrupt or crooked according to the moralists of their age, it was mainly because, in an age of private enterprise and the competitive pursuit of profit, they could not otherwise have completed their tasks. If private corporations had to build the western railroads, they could hardly have been expected to do so without making a profit. Since there was little traffic while the roads were being built, profits had to be found from other sources. Through the construction companies, they were taken out of capital. Because that capital had been supplied by public agencies, or by private investors only with public grants as collateral, a hue and cry was raised when this practice was revealed. The crime of the railroad profiteers, however—if crime it may be called—was not that they, as great speculators, milked an army of little speculators either directly or through venal politicians. Their crime was that they built poor roads. It was not so much that their construction work sometimes cost 100 per cent more than was warranted by expenses for labor, materials, and reasonable dividends; it was that for all this expense the nation got a very extensive but very shaky railroad system.

THE INDUSTRIAL SCENE

Though the new railroads were attracting swarms of cheap labor to the United States, opening up vast markets and incredible resources in mines and forests, they were also causing competitive havoc in other industries by their policies of rebates,

---

[10] Cleveland and Powell, *Railroad Promotion,* p. 141.

"midnight tariffs," drawbacks, and special concessions. Such favoritism and secrecy, said the Cullom Senate committee in 1886, "introduce an element of uncertainty into legitimate business that greatly retards the development of our industries and commerce." [11] And speaking of the period before 1887, Carnegie himself declared: "Railway officials, free from restrictions, could make or unmake mining and manufacturing concerns in those days." [12]

Despite their subjection to such practices, however, American industrialists soon outstripped all rivals. By 1893, New England alone was producing manufactured goods more valuable per capita than those of any country in the world. In the manufacture of timber and steel, the refinement of crude oil, the packing of meat, the extraction of gold, silver, coal, and iron, the United States surpassed all competitors. America had more telephones, more incandescent lighting and electric traction, more miles of telegraph wires than any other nation. In specialties like hardware, machine tools, arms, and ammunition, she retained the leadership assumed before the Civil War, while her pianos as well as her locomotives had become the best in the world.

In any age, this would have been a towering performance; in an age wedded to "bigness," it made an impression so profound that, even in the doldrums of the middle seventies, few cared to question the right of the industrial businessmen to leadership. Americans had much to complain of in this early age of industrial enterprise, and their most frequent complaint was of hard times. Yet there was no questioning of the "system," no lessening of faith in entrepreneurial leadership. This was an age of consistently falling prices, a period shaken by three financial panics and a severe depression of seven lean years. It closed on the precipice of another. Yet industrialists were certain that Civilization was safe in their hands, that their methods were those of God and Nature and were in the end as infallible. With their record of physical achievement to boast of and the unassailable authority of Spencer to support them, they had little difficulty convincing the nation they were right.

---

[11] Tarbell, *Nationalizing of Business*, p. 93.
[12] Carnegie, *Empire of Business* (in *Master Workers' Book*, 1916), p. 376.

In the nineteenth century, depressions were viewed simply as the results of errors of judgment that would not be repeated. They were regarded merely as periods of penance for economic sins, and recovery was expected as soon as rituals of liquidation and reorganization could be performed. Thus, instead of destroying hope, depressions paid dividends for faith. They presented opportunities to expand and modernize plants at the lowest cost, to corner raw materials at bottom prices, to capture customers with attractive schedules of rates and deliveries. It was in the seventies that Carnegie built his first steel plant, that Rockefeller organized his oil monopoly, that Armour and Morris built their meat-packing empires, that the Comstock Lode was exploited and Boston capitalists began to finance Bell's telephone.

Of all the undeveloped regions in the world claiming the capital of English and European rentiers, the United States in the late nineteenth century remained the most attractive, not least because of this resiliency of her leaders after shocks of war, bankruptcies, repudiations, and bursting bubbles. In 1871 alone, $110,000,000 of American securities were marketed in London; and though American failures in the depression of the seventies cost Europeans about $600,000,000, by 1893, when a new debacle was impending, we owed abroad some $3,000,000,000.[13] Most of this, to be sure, was in government, railroad, and mining securities, but it released proportionate amounts of American capital for use in industry and agriculture. It allowed Carnegie, for instance, to pour his savings back into steel with the assurance that he would have coal with which to make it and railroads to deliver it. It allowed Rockefeller to devote his energies to petroleum refining and Armour his capital to dressing and packing beef and pork, certain as they were that others would furnish transportation for them.

Perhaps even more important was the stimulus this great debt gave to American enterprise. As our borrowings increased, interest upon them grew proportionately. To meet annual payments, we had to export more and more goods. Just as our tremendously expanding economy was attracting European funds,

---

[13] Clark, *Manufactures*, vol. II, p. 61. National Industrial Conference Board, *International Financial Position*, p. 33.

so service charges for the use of these funds were further stimulating expansion. Since farm products composed most of our exports, it was agriculture that grew fastest under this pressure. To industry, however, it meant greater orders for iron and steel to manufacture farm machinery, to build and maintain railroads in expanding farm areas. It meant extravagant demands for coal and timber for fuel and construction. Starting in these basic industries, it stimulated expansion in every other kind of commodity production. It created in confident America an overwhelming faith in perpetual growth, leaving us at the same time ever more intricately involved in international finance.

Just as we were beckoning capital from abroad, so were we inviting foreign ideas in science and invention and cheap labor to put these ideas to work. International capitalism was creating a world-wide exchange of patents and processes stimulated by expositions, fairs, new trade and technical journals, and foreign travel by businessmen of all nations. The *Commercial and Financial Chronicle* published its first number in 1865. The American Iron and Steel Association *Bulletin* first appeared in 1867. Early in the seventies, Pillsbury and other northwestern millers went to Europe and brought back from Hungary the roller process for making grain. At the same time Carnegie went to England and was converted to Bessemer's method for making steel. In 1867 the United States sent commissioners and exhibitions to the Paris International Exposition and captured many prizes. Nine years later, in the midst of the depression, we held our Centennial in Philadelphia, where the industrial and commercial exhibits were the greatest ever seen.

For all its tremendous records of physical growth and technical innovations, however, for all its magnetic attractiveness to capital and eager receptivity to new ideas, this iron age of American culture was marked from the start by gross inefficiency and waste. Its catalogue of great inventions fails to disclose any social Bessemer system to blow out the impurities of competition or any blue print for scientific management to harness the potentialities of monopoly. To contemporaries, these deficiencies seemed but the results of partial adaptation to the new industrial environment. It is clear now that the costliness of competitive *laissez faire* was a defect of its qualities, and not simply the result of temporary conditions that would ultimately disappear.

In the three decades after the Civil War, as confident entrepreneurs raced to take advantage of every ephemeral rise in prices, of every advance in tariff schedules, of every new market opened by the railroads and puffed up by immigration, they recklessly expanded and mechanized their plants, each seeking the greatest share of the new melon. The more successful they were in capturing such shares and the more efficient they were in promptly satisfying the market, however, the greater was the number of buildings and machines left idle when the new market approached the saturation point and the rate of expansion declined. The result was that all the competitors were left with the problem of amortizing their new buildings and machines precisely at the time when the operation of those new buildings and machines was unable any longer to produce a profit. They were left with great plants, the symbols of great ambitions and with great silences in those plants to mourn their most recent failures. That was true of the whisky industry in which stills overbuilt in moments of prosperity were operated generally at no more than 40 per cent capacity. It was true of the iron industry in which, as the *Bulletin* of the American Iron and Steel Association said in 1884, "Indeed it might almost be rated the exception for half the works in condition to make iron to be in operation simultaneously." [14] It was true in the manufacture of stoves, as the president of the National Association of Stove Manufacturers complained in 1888. "It is a chronic case," he said, "of too many stoves, and not enough people to buy them." [15] And it was true even of the manufacture of bread, as the vice president of the National Millers Association also in 1888 informed his members. "Large output, quick sales, keen competition, and small profits are characteristic of modern trade," he declared. And he continued: [16]

We have the advantage in our business of always being in fashion; the world requires so much bread every day, a quantity which can be ascer-

14 American Iron and Steel Association, *Bulletin,* vol. XVIII, p. 226.
15 Lloyd, *Wealth Against Commonwealth,* p. 10.
16 Wells, *Economic Changes,* pp. 79–80.

tained with almost mathematical accuracy. . . . But our ambition has overreached our discretion and judgment. We have all participated in the general steeplechase for pre-eminence; the thousand-barrel mill of our competitor had to be put in the shade by a two-thousand-barrel mill of our own construction; the commercial triumph of former seasons had to be surpassed by still more dazzling figures. As our glory increased our profits became smaller, until now the question is not how to surpass the record, but how to maintain our position and how to secure what we have in our possession . . . In the general scramble we have gradually lost sight of the inexorable laws of supply and demand. We have been guilty of drifting away from sound trade regulations until our business has not only ceased to be profitable but carries with it undue commercial hazard.

POOLS, TRUSTS, AND CORPORATIONS

Far from being "the life of trade," competition by the last decades of the nineteenth century had reduced efficiency in business, had encouraged colossal waste of natural resources, plant capacity, capital. It had not only destroyed many companies but had decimated the incomes even of those powerful enough to weather from time to time the periodic unbalancing of freely competitive markets. As conditions for such firms in any industry went from bad to worse and even the most liquid among them came to be threatened with destruction, their managers naturally sought some escape from the perils of cutthroat competition. Somehow, order had to be maintained among the anarchists of industry or imposed upon them from outside. Since businessmen feared government regulation even more than they had come to fear competition, their lobbyists, in the popular name of *laissez faire,* neatly eliminated the state as a possible peacemaker. Left to themselves, however, industrialists managed only to devise new schemes to devour one another. It was not until the 1890's, when large corporations had become as prominent in manufacturing as they had been for half a century in railroading, and private bankers thus could impose order in exchange for essential credit, that umpires of adequate stature were found to regulate industrial strife. Until that time, trade agreements, associations, and pools were made and remade only in the end to be broken.

Pools, or pooling agreements administered by trade associations, attempted to limit competition in many ways—by controlling output, by dividing the market among member firms, by establishing consolidated selling agencies, and later by controlling patents. Their object was artificially to keep prices at a profitable level. Their ultimate effect, because of constant breakdowns and reorganizations, was to increase the severity of price movements, thus dislocating business more than stabilizing it.[17]

Unlike the cartels in Germany, where the government itself participated in the agreements, the pools in America, as in England, had no standing in common or statute law. They were obviously in restraint of trade, as restraint was interpreted by classical economists and Spencerian philosophers, and thus had to depend upon the good will of the members to attain their objectives. In a competitive society, this proved to be a precarious foundation. As we saw in the case of the New England Railroad Association of 1851, gentlemen's agreements only put a strain upon the integrity of the gentlemen who made them, tempting them secretly to evade their commitments the better to make profits. "A starving man will usually get bread if it is to be had," said James J. Hill, "and a starving railway will not maintain rates."[18] In a similar vein the president of the Whiskey pool said in 1885:[19]

Distillers, when they have an accumulation of goods on hand, will not hesitate to cut prices *one cent* a gallon to make a sale, when they will hesitate to pay one-half cent a gallon to make cutting *unnecessary,* even if double the amount is placed in their hands.

He continued as follows:

I am well convinced there is cutting going on secretly now, and unless provision is made at once to arrest it, it will be done openly, until there is nothing left of the market. Situated as we are, the question is no longer as to making a great amount of money, but to prevent our suffering great losses.

Pools were a natural refuge for individuals who fought to keep as much of their independence as possible in situations calling desperately for cooperation. They began to disintegrate

---

[17] Ripley, *Trusts*, pp. 42–43. See also Seager and Gulick, *Trust Problems*, ch. VI.
[18] Gras and Larson, *Casebook*, p. 409.
[19] Ripley, *Trusts*, p. 29.

as soon as emergencies seemed to have passed, but, as in the whisky industry, such recurrent lapses into free competition brought also the recurrence of its evils, ultimately forcing businessmen to seek a more stable form of cooperative enterprise. It was in such situations that industrial trusts were formed.

The trust was a device through which the stock of many competing corporations was assigned to a group of trustees in exchange for trustee certificates, ownership remaining in the same hands as before, management now being concentrated in a single board of directors. Trusts could appear only in a society in which the corporation had become the dominant type of business organization, in which property rights were represented not by land or other physical assets, but by negotiable paper easily convertible into other types of negotiable paper. As a business organization the trust was really identical with a large corporation though it was created by different legal contrivances and functioned under somewhat different laws. The Standard Oil Company set the trust pattern in 1879, and so effectively did it operate under this new type of business enterprise that in the next decade appeared the Cottonseed Oil Trust, the Linseed Oil Trust, the Salt Trust, the Lead Trust, the Leather Trust, the Cordage Trust, the Sugar Trust, until by the 1890's the term "trust" was applied invidiously to every seeming monopoly. In 1894, Henry Demarest Lloyd could write: [20]

In an incredible number of the necessaries and luxuries of life, from meat to tombstones, some inner circle of the "fittest" has sought, and very often obtained, the sweet power which Judge Barrett found the sugar trust had: It "can close every refinery at will, close some and open others, limit the purchases of raw material (thus jeopardizing, and in a considerable degree controlling, its production) artificially limit the production of refined sugar, enhance the price to enrich themselves and their associates at the public expense, and depress the price when necessary to crush out and impoverish a foolhardy rival.

In whisky, salt, vegetable oil, leather, and other commodities, trusts were evaded as long as possible. In a few lines like petroleum refining, meat packing, and steel, however, where strong leaders had the perspicacity to see the trend of the times before

---

[20] Lloyd, *Wealth Against Commonwealth*, pp. 3–4.

it bludgeoned them into submission and where they had the vigor
and unscrupulousness to apply their foresight, trusts and giant
corporations were forcibly imposed upon lesser competitors despite their stubborn resistance. John D. Rockefeller was easily
the most outstanding among these leaders. Of the trend toward
consolidation he said: [21]

> This movement was the origin of the whole system of modern economic
> administration. It has revolutionized the way of doing business all over
> the world. The time was ripe for it. It had to come, though all we saw
> at the moment was the need to save ourselves from wasteful conditions.
> . . . The day of combination is here to stay. Individualism has gone, never
> to return.

Rockefeller had little use for half measures. When he went
into oil, he gave up his other interests. When he set out to
organize Cleveland refiners, he tackled "the largest concerns
first." [22] When dependence upon railroads became too trouble-
some and expensive, he built his own pipe lines. When producers
of crude oil combined against him, they found that he had cornered transportation facilities. When he embarked upon retail
distribution, he undersold great wholesalers and little grocers
until they either became his agents or collapsed. When he extended his empire beyond the borders of the United States, he
employed in competition with alien companies the same rigorous
price policies that had proved so profitable at home.

Rockefeller abhorred waste. Having first eliminated it from
every nook and cranny of his own business, mainly by vertical integration and complete utilization of by-products, he was ready to
attack it in the entire oil refining industry and thus give scope
to his imperial ambitions. Aided by the panic of 1873 and the
ensuing long depression, by 1879 he had accomplished his objective.

As early as 1867, Rockefeller had become the greatest refiner
in Cleveland and had extracted his first rebate from the Lake
Shore & Michigan Southern Railroad.[23] With this club he

---

[21] Nevins, *Rockefeller*, vol. I, p. 622.
[22] Flynn, *God's Gold*, p. 140.
[23] Nevins, *Rockefeller*, vol. I, p. 256.

pounded into submission his Ohio competitors, and by 1872 he
was ready to battle refiners in New York, Pittsburgh, and Philadelphia. Before the panic of 1873 they resisted him; but once the
debacle came they were less unwilling to join the Standard or
abdicate in its favor. Rockefeller's managerial genius had prepared his firm to weather any financial storm, and the strength
of his position enabled him to demand from the railroads the
greatest rebates on his own freight payments, and drawbacks
from the rates paid by other refiners. No company could long
resist an opponent so well armed, and by 1879 Rockefeller controlled about 90 per cent of America's refining industry.[24] By
1877, with the aid of the New York Central and Erie railroads,
he had crushed the efforts of Tom Scott of the Pennsylvania to
enter the refining business; and in 1884, by building his own pipe
lines, he forced into submission the Tidewater Pipeline Company,
the last of his competitors.

Expansion meant economy, said Rockefeller, and in pursuit of
economy he was relentless. He was hated by his contemporaries
for his methods, but it was chiefly because he was more adept than
they at using means that lay to his hand. By 1879, he said,[25]

we had taken steps of progress that our rivals could not take. They had
not the means to build pipe lines, bulk ships, tank wagons; they couldn't
have their agents all over the country; couldn't manufacture their own
acid, bungs, wicks, lamps, do their own cooperage—so many other things;
it ramified indefinitely. They couldn't have their own purchasing agents
as we did, taking advantage of large buying.

In a society which strove to apply the laws of individualism to
the activities of corporations, Rockefeller found plenty of company among the successful seekers after loopholes and evasions.
As always, business conditions in the Gilded Age were changing
faster than the legal system; and, being ever in the van among
businessmen, Rockefeller was generally more than two jumps
ahead of the law. Testifying about him and his colleagues before
the Hepburn Committee in 1879, William Vanderbilt expressed
the popular opinion of his time:[26]

[24] Nevins, *Rockefeller*, vol. I, p. 486.
[25] Nevins, *Rockefeller*, vol. I, pp. 434–35.
[26] Montague, *Standard Oil*, pp. 43–44.

Yes, they are very shrewd men. I don't believe that by any legislative enactment or anything else, through any of the States or all of the States, you can keep such men down. You can't do it! They will be on top all the time. You see if they are not.

Much more ebullient than Rockefeller was Andrew Carnegie, and it was quite in character that while the oil nabob's genius was management Carnegie's was salesmanship. Nevertheless, they often used similar methods to achieve like results. Both were wonderfully astute in selecting the right men for the right jobs and pushing them to the limit of their capacities. Both abhorred pools, being the best competitors in their lines and needing no protection. And both believed in the justice of monopoly. "Pullman monopolized everything," wrote Carnegie after he had successfully merged the Woodruff and Pullman sleeping-car companies in 1869. "It was well that it should be so. The man had arisen who could manage and the tools belonged to him." [27] In pressing their pursuit of order and organization both scrupled little over methods, making the ends justify rebates, drawbacks, and, if occasion required, violence. And in achieving their ends, both were materially aided by the panic of 1873. In the depression that followed, Carnegie said afterward,[28]

so many of my friends needed money, that they begged me to repay them. I did so and bought out five or six of them. That was what gave me my leading interest in this steel business.

When other iron moguls were waiting for the depression to run its course, Carnegie was erecting his model rail factory at Braddock's Field, and just as Rockefeller was capturing the refining business from his less efficient rivals, so Carnegie was capturing the market for steel from under the noses of his competitors. On terms of perfect intimacy with Gould, Vanderbilt, Huntington, and Sidney Dillon, he "went out," as he said, "and persuaded them to give us orders."

By 1890, Carnegie had "obtained almost absolute control of the steel-rail business in the Pittsburgh district." [29] In 1892, all

---

[27] Hendrick, *Carnegie,* vol. I, p. 183.
[28] Hendrick, *Carnegie,* vol. I, p. 215.
[29] Clark, *Manufactures,* vol. II, p. 235.

his holdings were consolidated into the Carnegie Steel Company, capitalized at $25,000,000 and composed of the former Edgar Thomson Steel Works, the Duquesne Steel Works, the Homestead Steel Works, the Union Mills, the Beaver Falls Mills, the Lucy Furnaces, and the Keystone Bridge Company. In addition the new corporation owned coal and iron mines and coke ovens. The British Iron Trade Commission said in 1892:[30]

Modern iron making in America began . . . in 1881. . . . It became firmly established when Andrew Carnegie was the first to recognize and act on the necessity for the successful iron producer to control his own material, and it gained international importance when this wonderful man joined to plants and mines the possession of railroads and ships.

Besides the Carnegie Company, by 1892 three other great corporations had organized regional monopolies in the steel industry, preparing the stage for the gigantic consolidations of the twentieth century. In the South was the Tennessee Coal & Iron Company, which in 1892 absorbed its largest competitor and emerged with a capitalization of $18,000,000. In the mountain region was the Colorado Fuel & Iron Company, capitalized at $13,000,000. In the Middle West was the Illinois Steel Company, formed in 1889, a giant equal in capitalization to Carnegie's firm and "believed to have a larger output than any other steel company in the world."[31]

Outside steel and oil, similar combinations were being pushed to completion by Armour and Swift in meat packing, Pillsbury in flour milling, Havemeyer in sugar, Weyerhaeuser in lumber. By 1893 all had become leaders of great corporations composed in part of shoestring competitors that had fallen in every financial storm.

OTHER PEOPLE'S MONEY

The first general use of the "modern" corporation in America was for the construction of railroads which required more capital than any single person could subscribe. As manufacturing

---

[30] Clark, *Manufactures,* vol. II, p. 254.
[31] Clark, *Manufactures,* vol. II, p. 237.

expanded and became more and more mechanized, however, it also began to require large funds, and its managers used the corporate device to raise them. Gradually, therefore, a market was created for industrial stocks as well as for railroad securities and government bonds. As the property represented by such certificates seemed to yield attractive dividends, a greater part of American savings was drawn to them, and competition among investors was creating speculative fluctuations in many issues. To Americans inured to risky enterprises these fluctuations only enhanced the appeal of common stocks, and the stock market in the decades after the Civil War came to play each year a more important role in the breath-taking development of the country. Since the greatest stock exchange was located in New York, that city strengthened its position as the real capital of the nation. From every section the savings of millions flowed there, and with these savings came the sharpest minds bidding for their use.

As new institutions appear or old ones develop new functions, old controls grow obsolete before new ones are perfected. In the interim, adventurers improve the opportunities for profit. In the case of the stock exchange, no one illustrated this better than Jay Gould. Cornelius Vanderbilt unified his railroads while making large speculative profits on the side and Morgan sold securities to fund his mergers and reorganizations, but Gould "played the market" for itself alone. He knew his instrument like a virtuoso, knew every permutation and combination of its possibilities, knew how to exploit them till he hovered again and again on the very brink of failure but never once fell over. "I did not care at that time about the mere making of money," he said with reference to his Missouri Pacific exploits. "It was more to show that I could make a combination and make it a success." [32] Careless of social approval, he was unscrupulous in flouting the unwritten standards of business. The exclusive New York Yacht Club refused him admittance, and Mrs. Astor never invited his family to her quadrilles. With nothing to lose in that direction he was yet freer to fleece high society. By his raids and ripostes in the market he made enemies who did not hesitate to

---

[32] Josephson, *Robber Barons*, p. 194.

reply with violence; and though he was protected day and night by a detachment of plain-clothes men he suffered physical beatings. His retaliation was invariably to arrange a neat transaction that would cost his assailant dearly.

While his contemporaries among manufacturers, therefore, were competing in commodity markets and organizing industrial trusts, and his railroad contemporaries were unifying their systems and making and breaking transportation pools, Gould was also following the monopolistic trend, using the stock market as his lever to force combinations. He learned early that, as long as people could be persuaded to advance money, there was more profit to be made by wrecking concerns than by building them up, that there was more to gain from reorganization proceedings than from management that made such proceedings unnecessary. Having learned this, he became expert in attracting investors, clairvoyant in determining when they had reached the limit of tolerance. Through the New York *World*, of which he became owner in 1879, and Western Union, which he dominated after 1881, he blasted at the credit of companies in which he was interested. Thus getting bear raids under way, he purchased stock in such companies at the nadir of their decline. Gaining control of their resources, he then told his readers how strong his companies had suddenly become, proved his contentions by paying liberal dividends out of capital, and then sold out at the zenith of the speculative course of their securities. Between times, he milked the assets of his companies until they became in fact the carcasses he had claimed they were when he started his bearish machinations.

Gould improvised many variations on this favorite theme of profits through destruction. In one of his earliest ventures in Erie, he, Fisk and Drew merely converted construction bonds into $7,000,000 worth of unauthorized stock, sold these to Vanderbilt who was seeking control of Erie, and then bribed the New Jersey legislature to legalize the transaction. Getting out of Erie in a strong cash position on the eve of the panic of 1873, he was ready to attack the Union Pacific. Running down its stock with ingenious bearish tactics, he bought a controlling interest for very little and then forced the directors to purchase from him the Denver Pacific and Kansas Pacific, both of which he had acquired for a song. Clearing $10,000,000 in this transaction, he made about $10,000,000 more by successively damning and praising Union Pacific and trading its stock accordingly. By 1879 he abandoned it, still keeping control of various western roads which gave him a trunk line of his own to the Pacific. To a Senate commission in 1887 he innocently explained his withdrawal:[33]

> I thought it was better to bow to public opinion, so I took an opportunity, when I could, to place the stock in the hands of investors. In the course of a very few months instead of owning the road I was entirely out of it. . . . Instead of being thirty or forty stockholders there were between 6,000 and 7,000 representing the savings of widows and orphans . . . also a great many lady stockholders.

Gould's next venture was in Western Union, which he forced into submission by typical bear raids. When he got control he increased the capitalization of the company 25 per cent, using part of the funds for his private purposes. Turning next to the New York Elevated Railway, he slashed its stock by advertising that the state Attorney General (one of his men) was going to sue for revocation of the company's charter. In control, he again increased capital and imposed a ten-cent fare, thus making the general public as well as investors his dupes.

Though Gould was the master trader of his time he was not alone in exploiting the new capital that was drawn to the great stock market in New York. Every merger that was consummated, every trust whose stock was offered to the public in the decades after the Civil War, was capitalized at a higher figure than was warranted by the actual physical assets involved. Promoters hoped that the elimination of competition would insure profits sufficient to pay higher fixed charges on new bonds and regular dividends on common stocks, or else they counted on making *managerial* profits simply out of the new money they attracted.[34] In most cases their calculations proved incorrect, and when the panic of 1893 once again rocked the business world the burden of these additional capital charges proved too great.

---

[33] Josephson, *Robber Barons,* pp. 196–97.
[34] Dewing, *Corporate Promotions,* pp. 546–549.

The attractiveness of the stock market had made industrial financing in America much more speculative than ever before, and the collapse was proportionately severe.

As we shall see, this situation prepared the stage for the dramatic entrance of the investment banker as the director of the business life of the nation. Just as competition had made businessmen prey to their own contrivances, so the ceaseless pursuit of speculative profits brought their combinations to the edge of disaster. From competitive anarchy within single industries they had sought to escape through combination. Because they overcapitalized the resulting giants, they had to appeal for succor to the investment banker. That his price was high was due mainly to their own desperate condition, and though they argued and bargained and made a brave show of independence, they knew they must concede his demands in the end. Until 1893 Morgan was the leader in financing corporate reorganizations, and his work was limited mainly to railroads. After the panic his interests spread to other lines, and other private bankers entered the field. In most cases their price was the same: a large fee for services, and participation in the management of the reorganized company. Here was the nursery of the interlocking directorates and imperial holding companies that concentrated the management of American industrial enterprise in the few strong hands of the bankers. They dealt not in steel or meat or salt or coal, they supplied no essential industrial services. They controlled only the avenues to the savings of a maturing industrial society, and thus they controlled its life.

INDUSTRIAL SOCIETY

Just as modern industrialism in the western world profoundly affected such distant places as China, India, and South Africa in the nineteenth century, so industrial leaders in the great cities of America affected life in every distant hamlet in the land. They controlled the railroads that brought the farmer's produce to market, the flour mills that ground his wheat, the slaughterhouses that purchased his pigs, the machine shops that supplied his tools, the shoe factories that made his shoes, the salt and sugar refineries that supplied his table with these necessities, and the oil refineries that gave him kerosene by which to read. There was in America no miner who did not depend upon machine-made tools, no lonely cultivator who did not strive in vain to keep his sons on the farm, his daughters from some wicked metropolis.

The growth of the railroads, the perfection of the telephone and Atlantic cable, the development of the telegraph, the improvement of postal and express services in the decades after the Civil War, all gave businessmen almost instantaneous communication with every department of their far-flung economic empires—with their lieutenants at the sources of raw materials, their managers at fabrication centers, their salesmen in the markets of the nation and the world. Often they had but to sit in their offices in great cities and press the proper buttons, call the proper clerks, dictate the pertinent letters, and their wishes would be transmitted to the proper subordinates and carried out a hundred, a thousand, three thousand miles away. No village was too distant to escape the influence of New York, Chicago, St. Louis, or San Francisco. No region was too secluded to escape the net cast by the imperialists of every great center to catch the labor, capital, and natural resources of the ever more accessible hinterlands.

While the new technology was annihilating distance, helping to speed and centralize the administration of proliferating business enterprises, businessmen were developing new techniques designed to accelerate these trends. They were coming more and more in their fiscal transactions to deal in stocks and bonds, in rights to property rather than in physical property itself. They were using checks canceled through central clearinghouses, rather than cumbersome commercial paper. Their commodity transactions were increasingly conducted through negotiable bills rather than in raw products themselves. In almost all our large cities in these decades commodity exchanges began bringing buyers and sellers into immediate contact, standardizing quality, codifying trade practices and developing systems of business ethics that speeded all transactions by making unnecessary the legal paraphernalia of competitive contract making—the jargon, the endless details, the interminable oaths and affidavits. There was little need, now, to go to the warehouses to test the quality of the wheat or to the docks to test the cotton. Varying qualities were classified by the exchanges and offered for what they were. As in stocks, frauds were perpetrated. Poor produce was passed off as the best, just as unauthorized stocks were sold as gilt-edged securities. But the markets responded each time with better regulations. Their very existence depended upon trust, upon the faith businessmen had in the reliability of their representations. It was axiomatic, therefore, that the exchanges must extend themselves to preserve this trust. They were generally successful in doing so, though raiders like Gould, who depended upon this general faith for the success of their own malpractices, frequently did their unwitting best to shatter business confidence.

While the centrifugal force of expanding industrialism was extending the power of American businessmen to the farthest reaches of the land, other industrial factors were drawing more and more people each year to the centers from which this force issued. Rural mills and forges closed down in the decades after the Civil War, and their owners went to work in Minneapolis or Pittsburgh; cobblers went to Lynn and Rochester; packers, to St. Louis and Chicago. Once thriving villages in every section of the land were left deserted while their residents thronged to the cities seeking the bright lights, the education, the glowing opportunities that were promised them. There they joined with aliens imported from every section of Europe to create an adequate labor supply for enterprising businessmen. At least as important in drawing business to the cities were the rate policies of the railroads. It was to the advantage of individual roads to keep business as decentralized as possible, so that they might charge monopoly rates from as many points as they could make dependent solely upon their lines. By overcharging businessmen at these points, however, the railroads forced them to move their plants to the larger cities, where alternative lines were available and competitive rates were in force. By becoming great distributing centers for the products of farms, mines and factories, metropolises also offered businessmen advantages in purchasing raw materials, fuel, and machinery. All these conditions brought businessmen swarming to the great cities of the East and Middle West, whose continual growth gave additional incentives by bringing always more and more buyers and sellers together, enhancing the value of urban real estate, combining the funds of tens of thousands into great capital available at reasonable rates for industrial and speculative enterprises.

While business expansion and business competition were drawing millions to the cities of America, technological inventions and improvements were encouraging city life. Refrigerator cars on the railroads after 1875 helped to feed large landless populations. Structural steel, introduced in the late seventies, helped to house them in their work. Urban rapid transit, beginning in 1869 with the Ninth Avenue Elevated in New York, helped them to move quickly and cheaply to and from their offices and factories.

It is impossible to exaggerate the role of business in developing great cities in America, and it is impossible to exaggerate the role of the cities in creating our business culture. The cities subjected hundreds of thousands of people to identical pressures, at the same time exporting to every rural river valley, plain, and plateau uniform factory products. Creating a national market for standardized goods, they also created a national model of the successful man: the thrifty, shrewd, and practical clerk or mechanic who rose from the ranks to leadership. "The millionaires who are in active control," wrote Carnegie, "started as poor boys and were trained in the sternest but most efficient of all schools—poverty." And he held up as examples, besides himself, McCormick, Pullman, Westinghouse, and Rockefeller in manufacturing; Stanford, Huntington, Gould, Sage, and Dillon, in finance; Wanamaker, Stewart, Claflin, Marshall Field, Phelps, and Dodge in merchandising.[35] Boys in the cities saw the stately mansions of these great men, saw their princely carriages, their gigantic offices and stores. Boys on the farms heard of them or studied their photographs in newspapers and magazines that were achieving national circulation. They read how these leaders of business society had acquired their rewards, and the ambitious set out to emulate them. Thus the ideals of our business leaders became the ideals of the great majority of the people, though only a few were themselves endowed with talent for leadership.

[35] Carnegie, *Empire of Business,* pp. 108–109.

VIII

THE BUSINESS OF POLITICS

WHILE industrial business was being consolidated into great units and winning for itself unassailable national supremacy, the business of politics, for a decade and a half after the Civil War, levied a heavy toll upon it. The general public, through federal, state, and local taxation, continued, of course, to contribute the largest amounts toward the support of professional politicians. But industrialists and railroad men especially were forced to pay extraordinary sums for political benefits, and frequently were blackmailed by threats of regulation or withdrawal of government aid. Faced with dissolution under the sectional and religious pressures of the fifties, the two-party system had now been firmly reestablished, with the new Republican party almost as strong in the federal government as the Democrats were later to become in the "Solid South." Victory in the war and paternalistic legislation during the conflict had won for the Republicans a stanch nucleus of party regulars, and expanding government functions had given Republican leaders much new patronage to barter for the support of opposition bosses as well as thousands of new officeholders to tax for lavish contributions to party chests. The politicians in power, therefore, could treat businessmen simply as customers, selling political support at the highest price the traffic would bear, depending mainly upon a nation's gratitude and party discipline for the perpetuation of their tenure.

As the relations between government and business became more and more complex, however, and agrarians and reformers organized protesting blocs within the major parties and radical "third" parties outside them, the older spoilsmen lost their grip. They alienated businessmen by the audacity of their pecuniary demands, the public by their unremitting high taxes, and all respectable elements in society by their unrelieved record of corruption. The depression following the panic of 1873 made political levies continuously more burdensome, so enlarging the ranks of the disaffected that by the 1880's the opponents of the spoilsmen were strong enough to take control into their hands. Symbolizing the change in American politics was civil service legislation in the states and Congress, beginning first on a very small scale to remove government jobs from party control. This relieved government employees from party taxation, forcing politicians thereafter to go to industrialists and railroad men for more and more of their campaign funds. It permitted directors of national corporations, therefore, to exercise more control over the personnel of party tickets, the policies of party platforms, the actions of victorious candidates. Just as they had begun to bring order out of business anarchy, so great industrialists and railroad men began to end political piracy, no longer having to go to the governmental market to bid against one another for favors.

There was no unanimity among industrial businessmen in the 1870's and 1880's in the things they sought from political bargainers or political henchmen. Some wanted cheap money, others dear; some high tariffs, others low; some railroad regulation, others none; some subsidies and lavish grants, others strict economy. But discussion of such problems was now reserved for party councils. Politicians continued to fight bitterly for the spoils of office, but only in terms of personalities, conflicts over real issues being settled before they appealed to the voters—and settled almost always in the same way by Republicans and Democrats. Both recognized that industrial businessmen had become the best source of party funds, and both were eager, therefore, to serve them, the Republicans as the "ins" to maintain control of patronage and graft, the Democrats as the "outs" to strengthen their challenge for the spoils.

While in national affairs both parties thus were yielding to businessmen, in the states, especially the commercial farming areas of the Northwest, dissent from the trend of national politics grew constantly more violent. By winning in the national judiciary power similar to that which they exerted in the leglislative and executive departments, however, railroad men and great industrialists were able ultimately to ward off agrarian uprisings.

"NOTHING COUNTS EXCEPT TO WIN"

The combination of a great war and a rapid expansion of business after 1861 greatly extended the activities of political government and multiplied political officeholders. New excises entailed a host of new tax collectors. High tariffs made the customhouses hum with unwonted activity. Army and navy contracts opened employment to purchasing agents, inspectors, bookkeepers, clerks. Government munition factories gave work to thousands; homesteads and railroad grants occupied surveyors, recorders, clerical assistants; new internal revenue taxes, the growing budget, the expanding population, the constantly increasing immigration once the war was over, created new jobs in the Treasury, the post office, and the ports. The phenomenal growth of American cities with their new requirements in police and fire protection, their construction of sewage and lighting systems and new public buildings, their paving of streets, their administration of myriad state laws and municipal ordinances added thousands more to public pay rolls. Some of these jobs ended with the war, but most of them continued after 1865; and all were filled on the recommendations of ward or district leaders, city or state bosses, Senators in Washington or the national chairmen of the parties. In the decades after the Civil War politics thus became one of the great businesses of the nation, steadily employing thousands of workers, seeking profits like any other enterprise in a competitive society.

It has become customary to call the Republican party after the Civil War the party of "Big Business," the Democratic the party of reform. At no time, however, did either party have a monopoly of bankers, industrialists, railroad men, or reformers; and until the 1880's both were managed by politicians mainly for the benefit of politicians. Nothing shows this more clearly than the way in which the latter rigged the collection of customs "to annoy, vex and deplete" importers.[1] The excise on whisky, the politicians used not to supply the government with revenue, thus reducing other taxes, but to support their state machines— notably in Illinois, Indiana, Wisconsin, and Missouri.[2] The Democratic Tweed Ring in New York, the Republican Gas Ring in Philadelphia, the bosses of Washington, San Francisco, Cincinnati, and St. Louis, all taxed businessmen severely only to line their own pockets and those of their political partners. Certainly the Reconstruction governments in the southern states functioned for no business but that of the carpetbaggers, making industrialists and railroad men wary about venturing into the region. "A party," said Secretary Seward, "is in one sense a joint stock company in which those who contribute the most, direct the action and management of the concern."[3] Until the early 1880's contributions to both parties came mainly from officeholders and from candidates who depended upon the parties for support. Until then, therefore, the parties were run for their benefit, as was the government, which could not operate without them. "What are we here for," exclaimed a delegate at the Republican National Convention in 1880, "except the offices?"[4] "The source of power and the cohesive force" in American political parties, said James Bryce, "is the desire for office and for office as a means of gain."[5]

In the age of Johnson and Grant politicians dealt in federal lands, mining and lumber resources, protective tariffs, mail contracts, subsidies, and pensions. They could regulate business, tax it, or protect it from regulation or taxation. Some critics of American politics in this period have complained that in distributing their favors the politicians acted for the benefit of Big Business. But we have seen what it cost Huntington, for instance, to get land grants for the Central and Southern Pacific,

---

[1] Under the revenue law in force until 1874 whole shipments could be condemned for fraud on the basis of discrepancies that the importer could not prevent. Half of the money received from such condemnation was to be divided between the informant and the customs officials. (Martyn, *Dodge*, p. 290; Josephson, *Politicos*, pp. 96, 153–154.)

[2] Nevins, *Fish*, pp. 762–763.

[3] Beard, *Rise of American Civilization*, vol. II, p. 7.

[4] Bryce, *American Commonwealth*, vol. II, p. 106.

[5] Bryce, *American Commonwealth*, vol. II, p. 102.

what it cost him to avoid paying his government loans. In November, 1877, Huntington wrote to his colleague, Colton: [6]

> You have no idea how I am annoyed by this Washington business, and I must and will give it up after this session. If we are not hurt this session it will be because we pay much money to prevent it, and you know how hard it is to get it to pay for such purposes; and I do not see my way clear to get through here and pay the January interest with other bills payable to January 1st, with less than $2,000,000 and probably not for that. . . . I think Congress will try very hard to pass some kind of a bill to make us commence paying on what we owe the government. I am striving very hard to get a bill in such shape that we can accept it, as this Washington business will kill me yet if I have to continue the fight from year to year, and then every year the fight grows more and more expensive; and rather than let it continue as it is from year to year, . . . I would rather they take the road and be done with it.

Jay Cooke of the Northern Pacific, Ames and Durant of the Union Pacific, Tom Scott of the Texas & Pacific, all had similar tribulations. The politicians were eager to do business with Big Business men only because the latter offered the largest fees; in an age of fearful competition, such businessmen vied with one another in bribing legislatures, administrators, judges to gain any advantage over their rivals. Stevenson of Ohio said in 1873: [7]

> The House of Representatives was like an auction room where more valuable considerations were disposed of under the speaker's hammer than in any other place on earth.

A party needed only votes to win seats in Congress and in state and local legislatures in order to carry on this business of politics. And as long as a party had its share of the spoils it could control sufficient votes. Not only was every officeholder forced to contribute money to the party chest, but he had constantly to work for the party ticket, to drum up votes at election time, to work for the district between elections. The twenty-five hundred customhouse employees in New York City were the backbone of the Conkling organization. The internal revenue collectors operating from St. Louis were the zealous agents of

---

[6] Daggett, *Southern Pacific*, pp. 211–212.
[7] Josephson, *Politicos*, p. 118.

Logan of Illinois and Morton of Indiana. Ben Butler in Massachusetts, Zach Chandler in Michigan, Simon Cameron in Pennsylvania, each had his army of postal clerks and federal marshals trumpeting for the Republican stalwarts in his state. Add to them city and county officials—each not only a voter but a procurer of voters whose job depended upon his proficiency in the ward —and it is not difficult to understand how party loyalty was achieved and party discipline maintained.

Party funds were used to rent offices and halls, to pay clerical help, to print posters and pamphlets, for traveling expenses. Where this combination did not guarantee the necessary votes, they were sought through bribery and fraud. "There are men in New York whom you can buy to make a false oath for a glass of beer," declared Henry Butts, who investigated naturalization frauds during Tweed's regime.[8] Such oaths were required in the manufacture of citizens out of aliens and were made by the thousands when the machine was in danger. Between October 8 and October 23, 1868, for instance, Judge Barnard of the New York State Supreme Court naturalized 10,093 men, said the *Tribune*, "with no more solemnity than, and quite as much celerity as, is displayed in converting swine into pork in a Cincinnati packing house."[9]

From time to time in the 1870's businessmen rebelled against the excesses of bossdom, organizing "liberal" movements in self-defense. In 1871 Democratic lawyers, bankers, and industrialists like Samuel Tilden, August Belmont, and W. F. Havemeyer formed the New York Citizens' Committee to oust Tweed. In the same year Republicans like A. T. Stewart, William E. Dodge, W. and J. Sloane, and Arnold Constable combined to protest against Conkling and his Republican henchmen in the New York Customhouse. As soon as they achieved their immediate objectives, however, such movements collapsed. Merchants, manufacturers, bankers, and lawyers had other businesses than politics to attend to. Besides, they themselves cut too many corners to tolerate absolutely honest administrators. What they wanted, as Horatio Seymour put it in a letter to Tilden in 1871,

---

[8] Werner, *Tammany Hall*, p. 135.
[9] Werner, *Tammany Hall*, p. 134.

was "men in office who will not steal but who will not interfere with those who do." [10] Such men, however, were hard to find, especially among professional politicians.

THE END OF THE SPOILSMEN

The Republican party emerged from the war period as the savior of the Union, the emancipator of the Negro, the grantor of homesteads, railroad lands, and high tariffs. It had, therefore, strong emotional and material claims upon the affections of the American people. On the other hand, the Democrats, as the older party, had on their side traditional allegiances, old members and machines. While the loss of the South during radical reconstruction decimated their resources, the Democrats maintained their ranks in the North and controlled many states and municipalities. Between them, therefore, the two parties monopolized political offices and traded them as members of business pools traded market rights and divided profits. In Philadelphia, for instance, in 1881, Republican reformers appealed to the Democrats to support their candidate for Receiver of Taxes against the regular Republican ticket put up by the Gas Ring. For a share in the booty of the Ring the Democratic bosses refused. They preferred allowing the Republican organization to win rather than to jeopardize the whole system of political business by supporting an independent reformer.[11]

By the 1880's, however, the conditions that had permitted Republican Stalwarts to entrench themselves in the federal and state governments had run their course. The war was long since over. Reconstruction was complete. Southern Democrats had retrieved their civil and political rights, and federal troops supporting the carpetbag governments had been removed. In addition, the old Stalwarts themselves were dying or retiring from politics. Oliver P. Morton died in 1877, Zach Chandler in 1879, Logan in 1886. Simon Cameron, boss of Pennsylvania, seventy-eight years old in 1877, abdicated in favor of his son. In 1881 Conkling, refused patronage by Garfield, resigned from the

---

[10] Alexander, *Political History of New York,* vol. III, p. 311.

[11] Bryce, *American Commonwealth,* vol. II, p. 374.

Senate. In 1883 Ben Butler bolted from the Republican party to become Democratic Governor of Massachusetts, the next year becoming Greenback candidate for the Presidency.

In national affairs the Democrats had had no opportunities to develop such corruptionists as dominated Republican ranks, but many Democratic state and local machines had been second only to the carpetbag governments in their quest for political booty. As early as 1874, however, in the key state of New York, the "liberal" elements in both parties rewarded Democrat Tilden with the governorship for his prosecution of the Tweed Ring. In 1876 Lucius Robinson, a director of the reformed Erie Railroad, was elected in Tilden's place despite Tammany's opposition, and in 1882 Grover Cleveland became chief executive of the state. By 1884 the nation had followed the example of New York, sending Cleveland to the White House, the first Democrat to reside there since Buchanan.

Each of these political changes was a measure of the control businessmen were gaining over the major parties. American industry in the late seventies and eighties was employing each year more and more capital and labor, strengthening its pressure groups, clarifying its interests. Spencerian philosophers were spreading broadcast the ideal of progress through business competition, and businessmen were making the claims of the philosophers seem but the clearest common sense. "Life [in America] in the last forty or fifty years," wrote Godkin of the New York Nation in 1882, "has grown easier, pleasanter, and more luxurious. Life in the United States to the average man is a sort of paradise." [12] President Harrison in his inaugural address in 1889 spoke of American progress and prosperity as [13]

so magnificent in extent, so pleasant to look upon, so full of generous suggestion to enterprise and labor. God has placed upon our head a diadem and has laid at our feet power and wealth beyond definition and calculation.

The younger political leaders like New York's Tom Platt and Maine's "Czar" Reed had been bred in this atmosphere of

---

[12] The Nation, vol. XXXV, pp. 348–349.
[13] Josephson, Politicos, p. 441.

expanding business enterprise, while "reconstructed" southerners like Joseph Brown and Henry Grady were spreading its gospel through the South. "A nervous energy permeates all classes of people and all departments of trade and the spirit of enterprise never sleeps," declared a southerner of Atlanta in 1881. "We have challenged your spinners in Massachusetts and your iron makers in Pennsylvania," boasted Grady. "We have sowed towns and cities in the place of theories, and put business in place of politics." Augusta boasted of being "the Lowell of the South"; Columbus, "the Pittsburgh of the South"; Atlanta, "the legitimate offspring of Chicago": " 'Yes sir-ree, it's a regular little old metropolis . . . 89,000 people in the last census—and *Progress?* Gen-tle-men, *Progress? I'll* say *Progress!*" [14]

Besides "reconstructed" southerners, northern businessmen like Stanford of the Central and Southern Pacific and Depew of the New York Central were themselves entering Congress in the 1880's. And after the passage of the Pendleton Civil Service Act in 1883 the new politicians came increasingly to depend upon such businessmen to finance machine work. At the same time old ward heelers were being supplemented at election time by ambitious clerks and salesmen. Garfield had complained in 1870 that businessmen "want a representative in Congress that they can own and carry around in their pantaloons pocket." By 1880, however, he was asking and receiving the "assistance in the canvass of Rockefeller's force of five hundred oil-selling agents located all about Indiana." [15] In 1884 the Democrats also enlisted business aid. " 'What about this man Cleveland?' wrote James J. Hill, the western railroad builder, to Tilden. 'He is all right,' replied the corporation lawyer. Hill thereupon sent Manning [Cleveland's manager] $10,000—and telegraphed his associates in the West 'to get busy' for Mr. Cleveland." [16]

The transition from political business to business politics was not an abrupt one. It became evident roughly about 1876 with the Tilden-Hayes campaign when the bosses of each party felt the need to conciliate the electorate with candidates who were

---

[14] Woodward, *Watson,* pp. 86, 115, 123.
[15] Josephson, *Politicos,* pp. 113, 291.
[16] Pyle, *Hill,* vol. I, p. 426.

unassailable as "good machine men." It was complete by 1888 when Harrison was teamed with the New York banker Levi Morton to run against the New York gold Democrat Cleveland. In February, 1877, just before Grant left office, the western capitalist John H. Van Alen wrote that [17]

> no permanent revival of business . . . can be hoped for until important reforms are effected and an administration shall be organized on principles widely different from those which have governed the present one.

By 1882 those "reforms" had been so thoroughly "effected" that Henry Demarest Lloyd, after observing that "the Standard [Oil Company] has done everything with the Pennsylvania legislature except to refine it," could complain: [18]

> Rings and bosses are rising to the top in the evolution of industry as in that of politics. . . . A few individuals are becoming rich enough to control almost all the great markets, including the legislatures.

And by 1889, according to William Allen White, [19]

> a United States senator . . . represented something more than a state, more even than a region. He represented principalities and powers in business. One senator, for instance, represented the Union Pacific Railway System, another the New York Central, still another the insurance interests of New York and New Jersey. . . . Coal and iron owned a coterie from the Middle and Eastern seaport states. Cotton had half a dozen senators. And so it went.

Harrison's cabinet was sometimes called the "Businessman's Cabinet" because it included the merchant John Wanamaker and the marble king of Vermont, Redfield Proctor. But it was in the Senate that the change in American politics could now be seen most clearly. Among the great businessmen there by 1889 were the lumbermen McMillan and Stockbridge of Michigan and Philetus Sawyer of Wisconsin. From Ohio had come Calvin Brice, director of banks and railroads, and H. B. Payne, father of the Standard Oil magnate; from Nevada, James Fair the "Bonanza king" and John P. Jones, owner of silver mines.

[17] Josephson, *Politicos*, p. 239.
[18] Josephson, *Politicos*, p. 344.
[19] White, *Masks in a Pageant*, p. 79.

California sent the gold miner and newspaper publisher George Hearst. Together with William B. Allison of Iowa, Donald Cameron of Pennsylvania and Nelson Aldrich of Rhode Island— each a representative of banks, railroads, and other utilities— these men constituted a ruling clique that through the committee system of legislation controlled every bill that tried to run the gantlet of the Senate. And presiding over their activities was Vice President Levi Morton, who ranked with Belmont and Morgan as one of the greatest bankers in the land.

This august body was labeled the "Millionaires' Club" by contemporaries. What its members thought of themselves and their colleagues was felicitously expressed some years later by Senator Hearst: [20]

> I do not know much about books; I have not read very much; but I have travelled a good deal and observed men and things and I have made up my mind after all my experiences that the members of the Senate are the survivors of the fittest.

ELECTIONS WITHOUT ISSUES

As certain powerful business interests thus were capturing control of the major parties, other groups in American society were getting less and less representation in American government. Most important among these groups were the commercial farmers of the South and West. Others included silver miners who were at odds with eastern bankers over monetary inflation; ocean shippers who contended unsuccessfully with protectionists over the tariff; small manufacturers who were discriminated against by the railroads and harassed by competition from larger companies; and industrial workers whose collective bargaining activities were obstructed by state and federal courts.

From time to time these groups made demands upon the ruling interests, threatening them with agrarian uprisings and national political revolts. In the seventies the "Anti-Monopoly" Granger groups challenged Republicans and Democrats for control of many western states. In the late seventies and early eighties the Greenbackers, and in the early nineties the Populists, ran presi-

---

[20] Josephson, *Politicos*, p. 445.

dential candidates as well as candidates for local offices. More frequently the dissenting groups agitated within the major parties, seeking to pledge their platforms and tickets to revenue duties, income taxes, conservation of natural resources, regulation of transportation rates and industrial "Trusts." Sometimes they even demanded social legislation enacting the eight-hour day, the prohibition of injunctions in labor disputes, workmen's compensation, old-age pensions, factory and housing inspection, the abolition of child labor, minimum wage laws.

The more boldly the minority groups fought for such measures, however, the more vigorous was the opposition they encountered. In party caucuses and conventions, in legislatures, executive departments, and the courts they met the disciplined representatives of the ruling cliques, who had sufficient resources to beat almost any candidate, platform plank, or bill they disliked. The improvised organizations of the protestants could not compete with the major parties, nor could minority spellbinders overcome the inertia of most of the members of those parties. Mute testimony to the failure of groups outside the ruling interests lies in the Democratic and Republican platforms; the record of Republican and Democratic administrations tells that failure aloud.

In the seventies and eighties personal abuse, picnics, and parades enlivened presidential campaigns, while violence was the the determining factor in many close frays at the polls. The candidates generally were Civil War heroes hiding their political impotence behind manly beards while ward heelers whipped party regulars into line and editors and stump speakers "waved the bloody shirt" and "agonized more and more on the tariff." Party platforms gave no clue to the problems of the time, no hint of dissatisfaction in America, indeed no excuse for *two* parties except the quadrennial squabble for office to determine which group would be the stewards of the ruling interests. On no controversial issue did either party ever take a definite stand, and whenever either made a statement mentioning Money or Monopoly it was carefully vague. In 1880 the Greenback-Labor party denounced every attempt of Republicans or Democrats "to stir up sectional strife as an effort to conceal monstrous crimes against the people." In 1884 George William Curtis declared that "the platforms of the two parties are practically the same." [21] And Henry Adams wrote in a letter to an English friend: [22]

Every one takes part [in the election]. We are all doing our best, and swearing at each other like demons. But the amusing thing is that no one talks about real interests. By common consent they agree to let these alone. We are afraid to discuss them.

In March, 1883, the New York *Nation* declared that "the tariff was seized on by the Republican party as a substitute when they could no longer subsist on Ku Klux outrages and Southern wickedness." Lest the Republicans dominate this "issue" just as they did that of the "bloody shirt," the Democrats also "seized on" it. By 1888 both parties had so belabored the subject to the exclusion of everything else that the agrarian radicals that year denounced Cleveland's espousal of reduction as part of the usual game "to drown the outcries of a plundered people with the uproar of a sham battle over the tariff." [23]

Thus, as Lord Bryce said in his analysis of the American commonwealth, "there was no politics in politics." Democrats split with Democrats on some issues and Republicans with Republicans on others, but in the end Democratic representives of the ruling interests usually joined with Republican representatives of the same interests to defeat any threats to the continuation of their policies. Of Democrat Bland's bill for the "free and unlimited coinage of silver," introduced in 1877, Democrat Belmont declared that it was to "the whole civilized world . . . an act of repudiation . . . and cast a stain on our national credit." [24] With Belmont's aid, Republicans Sherman and Allison amended the bill to limit silver coinage severely and pushed it through both houses with the support of both parties. Dramatizing this confusion most clearly was the Greenback party, born in 1876 of the depression demand for expanded circulation of currency. In

[21] Nevins, *Cleveland*, p. 159.
[22] Josephson, *Politicos*, pp. 316, 364.
[23] Tarbell, *Nationalizing of Business*, p. 145.
[24] Josephson, *Politicos*, p. 262.

that year it ran Democrat Peter Cooper for President. In 1880 and 1884 respectively, Republicans Weaver and Butler carried the Greenback banner.

On the question of the federal income tax there was similar confusion though it received much less publicity. Schuyler Colfax and Roscoe Conkling, both Republicans, had been in favor of the income tax in 1861, and John Sherman in 1870 had "pled for its continuance on the ground that it was the only tax which distinguished 'between John Jacob Astor and the humblest citizen in the community.' " [25] By 1872, however, Republican Anti-Income Tax associations had been formed in New York and Philadelphia to lobby against the tax, and one New Yorker pressed Hamilton Fish for its repeal in terms of party expediency. He wrote: [26]

> I wish the income tax could yet be repealed. Our Union League has denounced it unanimously. They contribute very largely at elections, and . . . it is unfortunate this income tax is now to be called for.

The Democrats were similarly at war with one another on this issue though they were not very articulate until after the short depression of 1890. In 1891, the Ohio State Democratic convention adopted a plank in favor of the tax which was denounced immediately by the Democratic New York *Sun* as "a final outrage in the way of class legislation." [27] In the debate over the Democratic Wilson-Gorman tariff bill in the Senate in 1893, Democrat Hill of New York expressed his contempt for the income-tax provision in these words: [28]

> European professors announce to American professors, who publish and believe it, the birth of a brand new political economy for universal application. From the midst of their armed camps between the Danube and the Rhine, the professors with their books, the socialists with their schemes, the anarchists with their bombs, are all instructing the people of the United States in the organization of society, the doctrines of democracy, and the principles of taxation. Little squads of anarchists, communists, and socialists cross the ocean and would have us learn from them.

---

[25] Ellis, in *Mississippi Valley Historical Review*, vol. XXVII, p. 229.
[26] Ellis, in *Mississippi Valley Historical Review*, vol. XXVII, p. 229.
[27] Ellis, in *Mississippi Valley Historical Review*, vol. XXVII, p. 236.
[28] Ellis, in *Mississippi Valley Historical Review*, vol. XXVII, p. 238.

The contradictions in the records of the major parties only intensified the frustration of minority groups already offended by the silence of Democrats and Republicans alike on many of the issues that concerned the nation as as whole. We shall see that these frustrated groups were not easily cowed; but while they persisted in their fight against the railroads and the "trusts," and in their fight for equitable taxation and easy currency, they did not really have a chance to win.

THE DEFENSE OF NATIONAL BUSINESS

The contradictions in party records might confuse the voting public, and the silence of party platforms on many basic issues might only add to the confusion, but periodically even the politicians of the ruling business interests had to go to the public for votes. Simply for the right to continue in office, therefore, they had from time to time to make concessions to this public, passing laws which did not directly favor the leading interests. Big Business men were willing to yield such laws to keep their own politicians in power and also to forestall more stringent legislation later. Against the strict enforcement of these laws, however, the leading interests had to protect themselves, and in almost every instance the machinery they created for this purpose proved successful—but not always before business was forced to resort to expensive corruption and to make expensive compromises. To remove the sting from the Granger legislation of the late sixties and early seventies, for instance, agents of the railroads had to bribe the commissioners and legislative committees selected to regulate rates, or railroad politicians had to arrange to get friendly legislators elected or friendly commissioners appointed. In the meantime, the companies were forced to wage costly court trials until ultimate victory was won. Similar expenses were incurred by great national corporations in their efforts to sidetrack or defeat state legislative attacks upon their charters, or state suits alleging that their charters had been circumvented or ignored.

That business politicians were ultimately successful in defeating these early popular attacks upon Big Business corporations was clearly shown by the repeal of the "Granger" laws in Minnesota, Iowa, and Wisconsin within two years after they had been passed. The growing demand throughout the nation for *federal* regulation of railroads and industrial "trusts" also showed the strength of Big Business resistance in the states, while the Supreme Court's decision in the Wabash case in 1886 gave final legal sanction to such resistance, declaring that the states could not regulate, even within their own borders, any traffic that involved interstate commerce. Since these defeats for the opponents of Big Business only aroused stronger and stronger demands for federal action, however, new concessions had to be made by business politicians. Between 1874 and 1885, more than thirty measures were introduced in the House of Representatives providing for the regulation of interstate railroads; and some of these measures actually were passed, only to die in the Senate. By 1885, however, as memorials and petitions from chambers of commerce and citizens in eastern states were added to the flood of anti-railroad arguments and literature that had been coming from the Middle West for more than a decade, even the Senate had to yield. Its initial response was the appointment of the Cullom Committee to conduct a thorough investigation into all phases of the problem of federal regulation of the railroads. In 1886 this committee made its report, concluding:

It is the deliberate judgment of the Committee that upon no public question are the people so nearly unanimous as upon the proposition that Congress should undertake in some way the regulation of interstate commerce.

This recommendation, combined with the Wabash decision forbidding the states to continue with their regulations, set the stage for the Interstate Commerce Act, signed by President Cleveland on February 4, 1887.

The Interstate Commerce Act was greeted with cheers throughout the farm regions of the West and by small businessmen everywhere. But the cheers were premature. The Act was to be administered by the Interstate Commerce Commission, simply a fact-finding commission with no coercive powers. The Commission could issue "cease and desist" orders to interstate railroads charged by shippers or state commissions with giving discriminatory rates, rebates, or drawbacks to favored corporations, or with levying monopoly rates for short hauls, or with pooling traffic with other companies to keep up rates in competitive territories. But the commission had to appeal to the federal courts to enforce its orders; it could not enforce them itself. Thus the machinery was established for the obstructionism which the railroads soon became adept in employing. The commission's orders would be received, the accused railroad would pretend to comply with them, in the meantime continuing its old practices. The commission would then appeal to the courts for an injunction against the offending railroad, and the railroad would appeal the injunction. The court would hear the appeal and render its decision. Then the loser—either railroad or commission—would appeal to a higher court and finally to the United States Supreme Court, where a final disposition of the case would be made, on the average about four years after the original complaint was instituted. During all that time, the railroads would continue with impunity their old rate schedules, their pools, their systems of rebates and drawbacks, sometimes, indeed, making them even more burdensome upon complaining shippers in retaliation for their accusations. And in the end, the complainants would get no redress whatsoever. Between 1887 and 1905 the Supreme Court heard sixteen cases brought before it under the Interstate Commerce Act. In fifteen it found for the railroads.[29]

The "trust" movement among manufacturing corporations, as we have seen, came later in America than the development of interstate railroad systems, and efforts to regulate the "trusts" were commensurately delayed. By 1887, however, Louisiana had instituted suit against the Cottonseed Oil Trust and Nebraska against the Whiskey Trust. In 1888 New York attacked the Sugar combine, and in 1890 Ohio sued the giant of them all, the Standard Oil Company. All these actions were "successful," the "trust" being ordered dissolved in each case. In the meantime, in 1888 the House Committee on Manufactures began an ex-

---

[29] Ripley, *Railroads,* vol. I, p. 463.

tended investigation into various "trusts," and under Populist auspices a great "anti-trust" drive had gotten under way in the West with Kansas in the lead. In 1889 that state passed the first state "anti-trust" act; by 1893 it had been followed by others in fifteen states and territories.

The House investigation succeeded only in postponing congressional action on the "trust problem" and arousing heated discussions of it in many of the new periodicals and journals of the time. It was a problem fraught with complications, most of which the legislators did not understand. It was clear, however, as in the case of the railroads, that the politicians had to take some action. Senator Sherman defined Congress's predicament when he declared in 1890: [30]

They had monopolies and mortmains of old, but never before such giants as in our day. You must heed their appeal [the American people's] or be ready for the socialist, the communist, the nihilist. Society is now disturbed by forces never felt before. Congress alone can deal with the trusts, and if we are unwilling or unable there will soon be a trust for every production and a master to fix the price for every necessity of life.

Congress showed how willing it was to deal with the problem, passing without a murmur of dissent in July, 1890, the Sherman "antitrust" act which declared illegal any combination in restraint of trade or any attempt at monopoly. Sherman had little to do with writing the act that bears his name. It was written mainly by Senators Edmunds and Hoar, the latter remarking of Sherman: "I do not think he ever understood it." [31] Sherman, however, introduced the bill into the Senate and was active in pushing its adoption.

The Interstate Commerce Act was a sop to the malcontents in American political society, the minimum concession by Big Business politicians to a balking electorate. The act was "a delusion and a sham," admitted Senator Aldrich himself, ". . . an empty menace to great interests, made to answer the clamor of the ignorant and the unreasoning." [32] The Sherman Act was a similar

---

30 Hacker and Kendrick, *United States*, p. 282.
31 Josephson, *Politicos*, p. 459.
32 Stephenson, *Aldrich*, p. 68.

device designed to meet a similar situation. Of its passage through the Senate, Republican Senator Orville Platt of Connecticut, declared: [33]

> The conduct of the Senate . . . has not been in the line of honest preparation of a bill to prohibit and punish trusts. It has been in the line of getting some bill with that title that we might go to the country with. The questions of whether the bill would be operative, of how it would operate, . . . have been whistled down the wind in this Senate as idle talk, and the whole effort has been to get some bill headed: 'A Bill to Punish Trusts' with which to go to the country.

If the Sherman Act "were strictly and literally enforced," said Senator Cullom, "the business of the country would come to a standstill." [34] And Mr. Dooley, commenting on the Act, said: "What looks like a stone-wall to a layman is a triumphal arch to a corporation lawyer."

While both acts were designed for circumvention, however, and national business interests in fact had no difficulty in getting around them, they proved to be expensive nuisances that Big Business would have much preferred to avoid. Moreover, they were constant reminders that the protective armor of *laissez faire* had been dented at last, no matter how slightly, by the importunities of a harassed public. It was not long, therefore, before a movement was under way for the repeal of both acts. The Sherman Act, however, soon became an effective instrument in fighting labor organizations, and repeal talk was quieted. And by 1892 the better part of political wisdom, as far as the Interstate Commerce Act was concerned, also seemed to be for business to *use* the new government agencies for their own purposes rather than to attempt to crush them. That at least was the opinion of Attorney General Olney, who was so close to railroad men that he had accepted the Attorney Generalship from Cleveland only after getting permission from President Perkins of the Chicago, Burlington & Quincy. In December, 1892, Olney wrote to Perkins: [35]

---

[33] Coolidge, *Platt*, p. 444. For a divergent explanation see Clark, *Federal Trust Policy*, pp. 29 ff.

[34] Cullom, *Fifty Years*, p. 254.

[35] Josephson, *Politicos*, pp. 525, 526. See also Sharfman, *Interstate Commerce Commission*, vol. I, p. 35.

My impression would be that looking at the matter from a railroad point of view exclusively it [repeal of the Interstate Commerce Act] would not be a wise thing to undertake. . . . The attempt would not be likely to succeed; if it did not succeed, and were made on the ground of the inefficiency and uselessness of the Commission, the result would very probably be giving it the power it now lacks. The Commission, as its functions have now been limited by the courts, is, or can be made, of great use to the railroads. It satisfies the popular clamor for government supervision of the railroads, at the same time that that supervision is almost entirely nominal. Further, the older such a commission gets to be, the more inclined it will be found to take the business and railroad view of things. It thus becomes a sort of barrier between the railroad corporations and the people and a sort of protection against hasty and crude legislation hostile to railroad interests. . . . The part of wisdom is not to destroy the Commission, but to utilize it.

While national business interests were fighting lesser competitors and their agrarian allies on the battlefield of regulation, the bankers were also forced to energetic defensive measures against legislative meddling with the currency, and the protected manufacturing interests had to fight constantly against downward revision of the tariff. Both of these groups, in the end, proved as successful as the railroads and the "trusts" in maintaining their strong positions in our political set-up. Against the bankers, the representatives of the commercial farmers and the silver miners of the West succeeded in passing various currency and coinage bills in the seventies and eighties. And in 1890, in return for their votes on the McKinley Tariff, the "free silverites" got the Sherman Silver Purchase Act, which greatly enlarged the coinage of silver and the circulation of "silver" legal tender certificates. By 1893, however, under pressure from President Cleveland, who blamed the Silver Purchase Act for the decline of government gold reserves, the Sherman Act was repealed and the country returned to a single gold standard. This was a signal victory for the bankers who had tried so hard to convince the American people that "dear" money was the only "sound" money, that legislative tinkering with exchange was "immoral," that gold alone was the only "true" standard of value. Coming just when the panic of 1893 burst upon the land, this repeal set the stage for the dramatic struggle of 1896, when the bankers and their industrial allies in the East and Middle West ably defended their

victory, sending down to a crushing defeat William Jennings
Bryan and his free silver, debtor agrarian followers.

In defense of the "gold standard" bankers had to fight only
silver miners and debtor farmers. In defense of high tariffs,
industrialists had to fight the farmers, practically all the ship-
owners in the country and their banker allies as well as some
manufacturers. The Standard Oil Company, for instance, being
a great user of tin cans for kerosene and other products, carried
on an unremitting warfare against the tin schedule. Despite the
strength of the opposition, however, the high-tariff principle
was maintained even more successfully than the "gold standard"
right up to 1913, though a few concessions were made to special
groups. Before 1890 the demand for a reduced tariff received
important Congressional recognition only in the act of 1882
creating a presidential Tariff Commission to investigate the needs
of American industry, in the innocuous act of 1883, and in the
Mills bill of 1888 which passed the House as a low-tariff measure. Of the Tariff Commission appointed by President Arthur,
Senator Aldrich explained that [36]

there was a representative of the wool growers on the commission; there
was a representative of the iron interest on the commission; there was a
representative of the sugar interest on the commission; and those interests
were very carefully looked out for.

If the Tariff Commission was packed from the start with men
picked by the protected interests themselves, the Mills bill was
made safe in a different way. Introduced into the House as
a Democratic measure in response to Cleveland's "tariff issue"
message of 1887, this bill was passed by the Democratic majority.
In the Senate, however, at the urgent behest of James M. Swank,
secretary and leading lobbyist of the Iron and Steel Association,
the bill was amended so drastically that nothing remained but
the enacting clause, to which the Senate added what was virtually
its own tariff measure. In April, 1888, Swank had written to
Senator Morrill: [37]

---

[36] Stephenson, *Aldrich,* p. 431, note.
[37] Josephson, *Politicos,* p. 404.

To amend the Mills Bill in the Senate (in any form) would be a victory for the Democrats, who would make the most of it in the Presidential campaign. No matter how nearly perfect the Senate might make the Mills Bill it would still be the Mills Bill.

So adamant was the Senate, therefore, in insisting upon its version, and so firm was the House in objecting to it that the two-headed bill was allowed to die in the conference of the two houses.

Having resisted the efforts of the Democrats to win popular favor by reducing the tariff, the Republicans in the next election went all out to elect their own President and Congress. Money was spent like water, and illicit voting was rife; and in the end the indefatigable Matt Quay was able to notify Harrison that he had won out. "Providence has given us the victory," exclaimed Harrison when he learned the news. "Think of the man," Quay later expostulated to A. K. McClure. "He ought to know that Providence hadn't a damn thing to do with it." And he added that he supposed Harrison "would never know how close a number of men were compelled to approach the gates of the penitentiary to make him President." [38]

When the Republicans returned to Washington victorious after this hectic campaign, they were faced not only with the tariff question once more but with the huge surplus of idle government funds in the Treasury, piled up during a decade of prosperity from internal revenue, large customs receipts, and the parsimony of the Cleveland regime. To meet both situations the McKinley Tariff was passed. Rather than reduce the tariff to an *average* rate sufficient to meet the financial needs of the government, at the instigation of Senator Randall, Democrat from Pennsylvania, Congress enacted the most prohibitory protective duties in our history on certain schedules, while reducing revenue duties and broadening the free list only for the importation of goods which could not possibly be produced in the United States and could not, therefore, compete with any American products. Western opposition to this measure was angry and

[38] Josephson, *Politicos*, p. 433.

articulate, but westerners were bought off with the Sherman Silver Purchase Act.

By 1894, however, depression once again had sapped the confidence of the nation. Agrarians had learned the futility of the Interstate Commerce Act and the Sherman Anti-trust Act, and the Silver Purchase Act had been repealed. Populists had won many seats in Congress, Cleveland was once more in the White House, and the westerners had found in William Jennings Bryan the greatest orator of his day to tell their story to the nation. In such an atmosphere the Wilson Tariff was introduced in the House, moderately reducing rates on most commodities and carrying the hated income-tax provision. After many amendments had been proposed and defeated, the bill came to a vote and was carried only after revealing deep fissures in the ranks of both parties. Then the interests in the Senate got to work on it. When it finally emerged from "the mysterious recesses of the Democratic steering committee," it had become the Wilson-Gorman Tariff, representing, as Senator Aldrich admitted, "a switch to Protection, incorporating increases from 10 to 300 percent in a long list of items." [39]

Thus the "Millionaires' Club" in the Senate emasculated the last opposition measure of the three decades after the Civil War. But it was left to the Supreme Court in 1895 to administer the *coup de grâce*. The income-tax provision of the Wilson-Gorman Tariff Act had somehow weathered the storm of the Senate's attack; but it was immediately challenged in a suit which promptly came to the Supreme Court. By a five-to-four decision it was declared unconstitutional. This verdict, said Justice Harlan in his dissenting opinion, "did monstrous, wicked injustice to the many for the benefit of the favored few in particular states." The St. Louis *Post-Dispatch* declared: [40]

Today's decision shows that the corporations and plutocrats are as securely intrenched in the Supreme Court as in the lower courts which they take such pains to control.

[39] Josephson, *Politicos*, p. 545.
[40] Ellis, in *Mississippi Valley Historical Review*, vol. XXVII, p. 240.

THE HIGH PRIESTS

The structure of nineteenth century American law was old, complex, and rigid. Its foundations reached down to the English Middle Ages. Its framework was the eighteenth century elaboration of the laws of property necessary to the new commercial and industrial class. And only its superficial trimmings were added in nineteenth century United States. The doctrine of *stare decisis* (decision by precedents) is the very essence of conservatism; the growth of a "common law" is a slow organic development permitting little change in any single generation. And American constitutional law itself was based essentially upon precedents and mainly upon precedents of *English* common law.

The men appointed to judgeships in the United States generally have been educated to think only in terms of the existing *legal* environment. They have represented most strongly what Veblen called "trained incapacity": the incapacity to evaluate events except in the restricted light of their own training. There have been, of course, lawyers and judges who could see the structure of the law objectively in its relation to the rest of society, but such men have never made up a majority of the United States Supreme Court or any other large bench.

The justices of the United States Supreme Court, in particular, have usually been men over fifty who had built up profitable legal practices, or who had had brilliant political careers. They generally have come from moderately distinguished middle-class families, and their views must always have been traditional enough to satisfy a majority of the Senate. As the most profitable type of legal practice by far, in the last seventy-five years, has been corporation law, a great majority of the members of our highest court during that period had previously served corporations well. Among those who ascended to the bench after political rather than legal careers there have also been many who knew the needs of business best. In the hands of such middle-class gentlemen, therefore—gentlemen learned in the legal traditions of the past and immersed in the conservative attitudes of their own times—has lain the power to determine beyond all appeal the proper social and economic interpretations of the studiedly vague statutes passed by Congress. And in the hands of the leaders among such men has lain almost equal power. For to the determination of the cases set before them the justices of the Supreme Court have brought not only their learning and experience but also their personalities, and the element of leadership has played an important part in the decisions of the court from the start. The history of the court under John Marshall showed this clearly. Since Marshall there have been other leaders, not all of them Chief Justices but all of them helping to shape the opinions of their colleagues. Upon each successive court such leaders have imposed a continuity of attitude and interpretation that otherwise might have been lacking, thus adding to the stability of the highest law of the land. On the other hand, this very continuity itself often has been a strong bulwark against change in accordance with constantly changing social conditions.

In 1865 the United States Supreme Court was composed of four Democrats and five Republicans. Three of the Justices had been born in the eighteenth century, two during Jefferson's first administration, all the rest before 1820, when industrialism first began to make itself felt as a major force in American life. Faced with the problems created by the national expansion of business and the new relations between business and the federal and state governments, these men were at a loss to deal with them. Fearful of extending the jurisdiction of the federal courts to cover a torrent of cases involving abridgment by the states of the civil rights of the Negroes as well as the privileges and immunities of all other citizens, they persisted in interpreting the Fourteenth Amendment in the narrowest sense, thus leaving businessmen and business corporations, as well as Negroes, without any protection from state regulation of elections, for instance, or state regulation of railroad or warehouse rates.

An attitude so out of tune with that of national business, Congress, the Chief Executive or the people, however, could not long endure, though even as late as 1879 the reluctant court was still handing down "narrow" interpretations favorable to the anachronistic theory of "states' rights" and against federal action.

Then the overdue change took place abruptly. Vacancies in the Supreme Court brought the appointment by Garfield and Arthur of three men more attuned to the pervasive spirit of the time. Furthermore, among the three was Horace Gray, former Chief Justice of the Supreme Judicial Court of highly industrialized Massachusetts. Like other leaders of his day, Gray was an ardent nationalist, a firm believer in the Spencerian doctrines of progress through free competition. And it was he who in 1884 read the famous decision in *Juilliard* v. *Greenman* which made explicit the change in interpretation which had been hinted at in several minor cases during the previous three years, a decision which well symbolizes the deep change in the court's attitude.

Juilliard v. *Greenman* tested the right of the government to issue paper money in time of peace and to give it legal-tender status: in other words it tested the constitutionality of the farmer's inflationary demands. In the spirit of John Marshall, Justice Gray made this problem, of vital importance in itself, the vehicle for radically broadening the interpretation of the Constitution. Before a packed gallery, which thought it likely that the eminently "sound-money" court would decide against inflation, Justice Gray read: [41]

Congress has the power to issue the obligations of the United States in such form . . . as accord[s] with the usage of *sovereign governments.* The power, as incident to the power of borrowing money or issuing notes of the government for money borrowed, of impressing upon those bills or notes the quality of being legal tender for the payment of private debts, was a power universally understood to belong to *sovereignty,* in Europe and America, at the time of the framing and adoption of the Constitution of the United States.

An immediate victory for the inflationists at a time when they seemed no longer a real menace, this decision pierced in one sharp thrust the whole "states' rights" constitutional theory. It demolished the idea of a federal government of *delegated* powers only, and took from the states their own cherished claims to sovereignty. What, indeed, could remain to the states if the federal government possessed all the authority of European

---

[41] Commager, *Documents,* vol. II, p. 115.

centralized governments in connection with every power "incident" to the clauses of the Constitution!

This was a revolutionary decision: one that had in essence been long awaited. If it shocked the country, almost as great a shock came with the simple announcement that "Mr. Justice Field will deliver a dissenting opinion." For this meant that Gray's decision had been carried in the court by a vote of eight to one! Only three new justices had come to the bench since the earlier series of states' rights decisions. Yet the states' rights majority had disappeared, at least partly because of the influence of Gray's masterful presence.

During the next fifty years the Supreme Court adhered firmly to the new doctrine of nationalism for the benefit of business in its contests with the states. In the Wabash decision of 1886, as we have seen, it forbade state regulation of interstate railroads. In the Milwaukee & St. Paul Railroad case of 1890 it adopted a substantive view of the meaning of "due process" in the Fourteenth Amendment, giving corporations recourse to the federal courts to test the confiscatory character of *intrastate* rate regulation. In *Smythe* v. *Ames* in 1897 the Court went on to indicate some general basis for determining a fair rate of return on property subject to *state* regulation. This was forthright nationalism, a new spirit in the law of the United States, and its application was not for long restricted to the field of regulation. In a series of decisions federal officers were broadly protected from action in the state courts, blanket federal injunctions were upheld in labor disputes, corporations were recognized as "persons" to be protected by the federal government under the Fourteenth Amendment, and the states were prevented from restricting hours of labor except in the direct interest of public health. Thus the court at last caught up with the spirit of the seventies and eighties as expressed in business enterprise and Congressional legislation. It had begun, on the one hand to advance the doctrines of nationalism to protect business from the states. And on the other hand it had begun to manifest its allegiance to the Spencerian doctrines of competitive individualism to protect business from interference by the federal government. Against these two bulwarks the doctrine of public interest made slow progress.

IX

THE RISE OF FINANCE CAPITALISM

BY 1893 American business leaders like Huntington, Rockefeller, Havemeyer, and Carnegie had far outstripped their respective rivals. They had created tremendous economic empires for themselves in older industries and had accelerated the decline of competition in every line in which they had become involved. Their political representatives had captured control of the major parties from the older spoilsmen and had successfully resisted the challenge of other groups seeking political leadership. In the meantime, in scientific laboratories throughout the world, new wonders were being prepared which were soon to revolutionize the physical aspects of American life and create new enterprises in American business. The gasoline motor was patented in the United States in 1878. Electric light and power appliances were improved enormously in the 1880's. After 1875 light, strong alloys of iron, chromium, nickel, aluminum, manganese, and copper had begun to be used in growing quantities in American industry.

In the two decades following the panic of 1893 these new developments absorbed increasing amounts of domestic and foreign capital, but compared to the older key industries like railroads and steel they made comparatively small demands upon the large savings of the nation. These savings grew tremendously in this period, encouraging the directors of banks, trust and insurance companies to seek new opportunities for investments. And as more and more railroads and industrial "trusts" began to seek the advantages of "bigness" through combinations requiring much new capital, such opportunities were not difficult to find. While new inventions, new industrial and chemical processes, therefore, were creating new outlets for investment capital, expansion and consolidation in older lines continued to give the major impetus to American economic development.

The more the industrial leaders in America became dependent upon investment bankers for funds, the shallower became their control over their own businesses; and by 1907 a few financial titans like Morgan, Rockefeller, Baker, Stillman, Schiff, Warburg, the Guggenheims, and Ryan had gained dominant positions in the directorates of most of the key enterprises in the land. Leading American industrialists had successfully checked the political efforts of the farmers and other groups to regulate American business, but by 1907 many of these industrialists had succumbed to the more stringent regulation of a few private bankers who had learned how to monopolize the most important avenues to capital.

If access to American savings gave the bankers control of many of our older key industries, it also gave them responsibility for developing new lines at home capable of using such savings in long-term expansion once the great consolidations were completed, or of finding opportunities outside the country to put those savings to profitable use. By 1907 the latter alternative had begun to seem the more attractive one; but investors were reluctant to discard their traditional isolation and their suspicion of foreign governments. By then, the United States had apparently reached the stage England had reached a quarter of a century before, the stage France and Germany had reached by the 1890's, the stage that had created among these older nations of Europe intense competition for control in "backward" areas of the temperate zone and ultimately in every section of the earth. Between 1907 and 1914 complaints of hard times had become constant in the United States. The continent had been filled in from coast to coast, and no new cities were clamoring for building materials and transportation facilities. The railroad system had practically been laid, the heavy industrial plant needed no immediate expansion, and attractive investment opportunities at home seemed to be declining in number. The bankers, however, persisted in their belief that the business uncertainty after 1907 was but a temporary dislocation like all previous business depressions. They were slow, therefore, in endorsing the imperial ventures of the State Department under Roosevelt and Taft, letting the government take the lead in trying to open foreign opportunities for expansion and following only reluctantly. The result was that after 1907 there was no vigorous business activity in the United States until the outbreak of the World War.

A TECHNOLOGICAL REVOLUTION

The western world in the last decades of the nineteenth century was a world of wood, iron, coal, and steam. Its industry was wasteful and inefficient, deafening and unwieldy. Already, however, American industrialists were beginning to yield to the possibilities of a new day. Well endowed technological colleges were applying chemistry and physics to the problems of manufacturing and communication. Highly trained scientists and engineers were discovering new wonders in nature, inventing new processes to make them available, new machines to make them profitable to business enterprise. Ideas for most new appliances and for improvements in old ones continued to come from mechanics actually employed in factories, but "theoretical" scientists were claiming more and more attention from alert businessmen. Great corporations were beginning either to set up laboratories of their own or to subsidize research in the nation's schools and colleges. In 1907 Theodore N. Vail, president of the American Telephone & Telegraph Company, described the original aims and pioneer work of his corporation in this field. He said:[1]

From the very commencement we had our experimental department . . . whose business it was to study patents, study the development and study these devices that either were originated by our own people or came to us from the outside. Then early in 1879 we started our patent department, whose business was entirely to study the question of patents and the patentability of these devices, to examine all patents that came out with a view to acquiring them, because, as I say, we recognized that if we did not control these devices, somebody else would, and we would be more or less hampered in the development of the business.

The example of the telephone company was followed by electrical corporations like Edison and Westinghouse, whose success also depended upon control of patents, and engineering firms like

---

[1] Danielian, *A. T. & T.*, p. 95.

the Baldwin Locomotive Company and steel companies like Carnegie's, which were eagerly seeking improvements in steam and electric engines and in the quality of steel. In each of these lines great advances had been made before the panic of 1893. Incandescent bulbs had been invented, making electric lighting available to homes as well as to great offices and city streets. Alternating current had been proved practical, making possible power transmission over long distances. Electric traction systems had won commercial success in half a dozen American cities. Steam engines had gained in efficiency and speed, steel alloys had gained in toughness and malleability, and patents had been taken out for the commercial production of aluminum, "the third most abundant element on the earth's crust." [2]

To these revolutionary changes in technology in the earlier period, Frederick W. Taylor was adding new ideas in industrial management. As foreman of the Midvale Steel Company in 1882 he had begun detailed analysis of each "job" in the factory. To each minute phase of the "job," he sought to apportion its precise decimal of total cost. He campaigned for constantly increasing mechanization, for atomic division of labor, for piecework wage systems. Taylor was highly successful in applying his program, but unlike the technological improvements of his times his ideas were slow in gaining currency among American industrialists, for the latter were making adequate profits without experimenting in plant management. By 1911, however, when Taylor first published his book on scientific management, profits had dwindled, the rate of industrial expansion had fallen, and industrialists had begun to look for opportunities to reduce costs. Then Taylor's ideas began to have as great a vogue in America as they had already had in Europe for a decade.

These late nineteenth century innovations, important as they were, soon proved to be but the first steps in the new progress of industrial technology. In the twentieth century the high-speed tool steel developed by Taylor and White in 1902 worked a quiet revolution in cutting machinery and hence in the productivity of mechanized industries. Open-hearth furnaces continued to replace

---

[2] Mumford, *Technics and Civilization,* p. 230.

the more cumbersome and expensive Bessemer converters at such a rapid rate that steel production increased 150 per cent in the first decade of the new century. The production of electric power and the number of its users grew at an equally rapid rate. Giant hydroelectric stations erected at Niagara Falls at the turn of the century were soon followed by others on the rivers of New England and the South, while additional steam generating plants swelled the total electrical horsepower used in industry to 13,-000,000 by 1912. By that year 40,000 miles of electric railway and trolley track, worth nearly $5,000,000,000, tied city and country ever more closely together. A new transportation industry seemed to be developing that promised to reenact the earlier role of the steam railroads as a consumer of private capital, but at this point a still newer form of transportation requiring far less initial capital, checked the progress of the trolley car. That was the automobile.

Nonexistent on a commercial basis before 1897, the automobile industry during the next twenty years was to employ on a grand scale many of the earlier technological advances and, as much as any of them, was to work enormous changes in American life. For glass, rubber, and the alloys out of which body and engine parts were made, automobile manufacturers depended upon new chemical and electrical knowledge and new electrochemical processes. Ultimately automobile manufacturers became the greatest users of each of the commodities that went into automobile production, and labor in automobile assembly plants became more highly routinized and mechanized than in any other type of factory.

American experience and American environment favored the automobile industry. From the nation's earliest days carriage companies had been training men in the manufacture of bodies, wheels, and springs. In the 1880's and 1890's tricycle and bicycle companies had developed pneumatic tires. Since the early nineteenth century manufacturing through the assembly of interchangeable parts had trained mechanics and factory managers in such work, and since the 1850's the production of farm and factory machinery and railroad locomotives had developed familiarity with engines. Perhaps even more important were the great distances in America, the demand for constantly increasing speed and the presence of a middle class sufficiently prosperous to purchase thousand-dollar articles. No comparable class brightened the prospects of the automobile industry in Europe, nor did English or French farmers, for instance, have to travel to cities a hundred or more miles away. European urban dwellers also rarely had to go such distances to visit relatives and friends.

Since the beginning of the industrial revolution in America, most enterprises in almost every *new* industry had started with shoestring financing. The automobile industry was no exception. So great were the initial profits, however, that by 1910 about sixty companies were producing cars. Most prominent among their products were the Olds, Ford, Maxwell, Reo, Buick, Cadillac, Studebaker, and Packard. Efforts to check cutthroat competition among these companies were already under way, and the first successful automobile mergers were completed by William C. Durant in 1908 and 1909. Durant combined Buick, Cadillac, and Oldsmobile with many smaller companies under the name of General Motors. In trying to add to his line the Maxwell and the Ford he sought the financial aid of J. P. Morgan & Company and was refused. Durant had boasted to the bankers that 500,000 automobiles would soon be sold annually. They thought he was mad. "If he [Durant] has any sense," said George W. Perkins, "he'll keep such notions to himself if he ever tries to borrow money." [3]

Durant was no technician and no administrator. He was a promoter. And the bankers who lacked confidence in the future of the new industry had even less confidence in him. Their suspicions were justified when Durant in 1910 invested $8,000,000 in General Motors' plant expansion and $30,000,000 in new supplies. To justify such expenditures General Motors would have had to increase its business 500 per cent in a single year. Not even General Motors could grow that fast, and the new corporation was on the edge of bankruptcy almost as soon as it had come into existence. Durant was thus hard pressed for funds once again, and once again he encountered the bankers' coldness.

---

[3] Corey, *Morgan,* p. 386 note.

After touring the money centers of the country without success, however, he finally got aid from Lee Higginson & Co. and J. & W. Seligman & Co. Their onerous terms reveal once more what the "money trust" thought of the new industry and its most energetic entrepreneur. For a five-year loan of $15,000,000 General Motors paid the bankers $2,500,000 in cash and the equivalent of $4,000,000 in securities. The bankers also retained a first mortgage on the company's assets to secure this loan. And, perhaps most important, they insisted that Durant surrender leadership of the company to the bankers' trustees, who were to control its business for the duration of the loan.

As early as 1908 Henry Ford was already one of the great automobile producers, and Durant's failure to include him and Briscoe (of the Maxwell Company) in his merger left General Motors vulnerable to stiff competition. In 1909 Ford started to produce his Model T, and this competition became very severe indeed. Mass production of a single model permitted Ford to cut his costs drastically, and depending for profits upon volume of sales he slashed his prices as quickly as he cut his costs. Fords sold for $950 in 1909. In 1913 they sold for as little as $550. In that period Ford sales jumped from 10,607 to 168,000, the latter figure representing more than one-third of the output of the automobile industry in 1913. In 1914 Ford's showing was still more remarkable. That year 248,000 Fords—45 per cent of the total automobile production—were sold at $490 and up. They returned a profit of $30,338,000—20 per cent above the banner year 1913.[4]

Such performances pushed the automobile industry past its pioneering stage. Shoestring successes became fewer after 1910. National sales campaigns were undertaken to correct the prejudice against the grotesque and greasy "horseless carriage," and the common man as well as his wealthy neighbor began to enjoy the new contraption and to use it in his work. Construction and maintenance of roads and highways by state and federal governments aided the new industry as much as earlier public assistance had helped the railroads. And it was not long before the rail-

---

[4] Kennedy, *Automobile Industry*, pp. 73–75.

roads themselves were threatened by this new means of transportation. How great a threat the automobile might become to
railroad passenger traffic was suggested by the figures for 1915.
That year the wholesale value of all automobiles produced was
$700,000,000—more than the gross passenger revenue of all
American railroads for the same twelve months.

THE CONSOLIDATION OF BUSINESS GOVERNMENT

Electric and gasoline motors and electric power were trans-
forming American life in the years between 1893 and 1913. The
industries that produced them, however, were still new, speculative, and apparently unstable. Capital, therefore, was not so
readily drawn to them and it remained for older lines—railroads
and steel especially, but also oil, farm machinery, sugar, meat,
and tobacco—to continue as most attractive to American investment capital. Such capital increased at an unprecedented rate in
this period, at the very time, however, when shrinking percentages
of new funds were required to finance plant expansion. This
left larger and larger amounts available for speculation and for
the financing of unproductive mergers and reorganizations.

In the 1870's and 1880's, as we have seen, mergers were made
in American industry mainly to check cutthroat competition. In
the half-decade after the panic of 1893, railroad combinations
were made for the same reason. After 1898, however, in railroads as well as many other lines, mergers began to be made
for more positive purposes. Prices in that year resumed their
upward trend all over the world, profits multiplied, and cutthroat
competition declined. Because of earlier mergers and the elimination of many firms through failures during the recent depression, competition in many industries was further curtailed. Despite the return of prosperity, however, the *rate* of growth in
American capital-goods industries had perceptibly begun to fall;
the demand for capital for *productive* purposes had at last begun
to slow down. Railroad building was extensive after 1898, but
most of it was for double tracking, new sidings and enlarged
terminal facilities—types of construction which were soon completed. In steel, much of the new capital went for modernization
of plants rather than for the construction of large *additional* pro-

ductive facilities. In mining, in the making of factory machinery, in the production of locomotives, and in other lines of heavy industry, the same tendency was apparent to a lesser extent, each line expanding at a rapid rate, but not quite in proportion to the *rate* of the late 1870's and the 1880's, not quite sufficiently to absorb the funds that were accumulating at ever greater speed in trust and insurance companies, commercial and savings banks. The new consumers' goods industries also failed to absorb these funds, and the government itself could find no use for them. They were left available, therefore, for speculative purposes. And since mergers proved the simplest way to create speculative opportunities, these funds began to find their way into the securities of new combinations instead of into their plants.

Capital is a commodity dealt in by bankers as mine owners deal in coal or copper, manufacturers in textiles or shoes. And it was the eagerness of bankers to find markets for the funds deposited with them or with financial institutions available to them, that gave great impetus to the consolidations that occurred in the United States between 1898 and 1903. As James J. Hill himself said in 1902:[5]

> The only serious objection to trusts has been the method of creating them—not for the purpose of manufacturing any particular commodity in the first place, but for the purpose of selling sheaves of printed securities which represent nothing more than good will and prospective profits to promoters.

This, however, was not the only factor encouraging centralization in American business, and leading among the others was the growing appeal to businessmen of sheer "bigness" itself. Through absolute control of an industry as in telephony and aluminum, or through partial control as in steel and other important lines, "bigness" promised proportionate control over supply and demand and hence over prices and profits. It seemed to promise, also, great savings in purchasing machinery, raw materials, transportation services, and commercial credit. In bargaining with labor, in organizing production, in marketing finished commodities and in smoothing out seasonal fluctuations, it

[5] Corey, *Morgan*, p. 285.

seemed to offer similar economies. The completion of American railroad and telegraph nets made "bigness" still more attractive, permitting from central offices remote control of factories scattered all over the country and making available to one great corporation all the advantages of proximity to power, raw materials, cheap labor, and markets.

The fear of corporations already endowed with these apparent advantages of "bigness" broke down the opposition of many independent industrialists to participating in giant mergers, and the failure of the federal government to enforce the antitrust acts seemed to give such mergers legislative and judicial sanction. Though many states also had antitrust acts and tried to enforce them more strictly than the federal government, their efforts were nullified by the existence of many other states with no such laws. In competing for corporate business, the lax states reduced restrictions in corporation charters to the disappearing point. They permitted interlocking directorates, encouraged the creation of giant holding companies and allowed such companies to do business anywhere. New Jersey was the leader in this movement, and so attractive were its corporation laws after 1889 that each of the seven "Greater Industrial Trusts" of 1904 (so classified by Moody to distinguish them from the lesser combinations), with a total capital of more than two and a half billion dollars and with control of approximately 1,528 plants in every section of the land, had a New Jersey charter.

Though the pools, trusts, and large corporations of the seventies and eighties created a profound fear of monopoly throughout the nation and brought about the passage if not the enforcement of antitrust acts, this early trend toward consolidation was but a feeble beginning compared to the activity of the half-dozen years after 1898. By 1893, twelve great companies with an aggregate capital of less than a billion dollars had emerged from all the activity of the previous two decades. By 1904, there were no fewer than 318 industrial combinations—one of them (Morgan's United States Steel Corporation) capitalized for more than $1,400,000,000. Of the rest, there were ten with capitalizations above $100,000,000 and thirty others capitalized for more than $30,000,000. All told, with an aggregate capital above seven and a quarter billion dollars, these 318 industrial companies controlled 5,288 separate plants. In addition, besides steam railroads, there were 111 public utility combinations by 1904, all but 14 of them organized after 1893. They controlled 1,336 plants with capital in excess of $3,700,000,000. Overshadowing both these groups were the steam railroads themselves, the largest single type of enterprise in America except farming. By 1904, 1,040 separate American railroad lines had been consolidated into six huge combinations, each of which, in turn, was allied either to Morgan or to Rockefeller interests, these giants between them controlling in railroads alone almost ten billion dollars of American capital.[6]

The usual procedure in organizing many firms into a merged giant corporation was for the directors of the new company to purchase with its new common stock the assets of the combining companies, to pay in common stock also the fees of the promoters who brought the combiners together and the fees of the bankers who worked out new financial structures. The bankers also received commissions in stock as well as cash for advancing whatever funds might be needed to consummate the transactions and for floating the bonds by which the new corporation continued to acquire working capital. In this way, between 1898 and 1904, for industrial consolidations alone, over four billion dollars in *new* securities were issued.[7] Since the new common stock was valueless and the new bonds were unnegotiable without markets, and since only the investment bankers had the facilities to create and organize such markets, the combiners even had they wished to do otherwise, had to come for aid to Morgan; or Kuhn, Loeb; or Speyer; Kidder, Peabody; Lee Higginson; Brown Brothers, or Belmont.[8] By purchasing strategic blocks of shares, such financiers had intrenched themselves in the directorates of life-insurance companies whose assets had grown from little more than a billion dollars in 1894 to almost five billion by 1913.[9] They also held controlling interests in other types of in-

---

[6] Moody, *Trusts,* pp. 453 f. These capital figures are rather meaningless but give a clue, at least, to relative size.

[7] Montague, *Trusts,* p. v.

[8] Myers, *Money Market,* p. 293.

[9] Brandeis, *Other People's Money,* pp. 9–12, 22.

surance companies with assets by 1913 totaling nearly eight hundred million dollars, and in trust companies which had grown in number from 228 in 1894 to 1,732 in 1913 and had resources on the eve of the World War totaling six billion dollars.[10] No national or state bank had anything like such resources at its command, none had the experience which private bankers had acquired over half a century in marketing government and railroad securities in the financial capitals of Europe and America. Besides, the national banks were forbidden to deal in common stocks and were too conservative until after 1908 to set up affiliates to market them.

Obviously, therefore, though not all of the consolidations in the years around the turn of the twentieth century were instigated by the investment bankers, almost all had to be underwritten by them. Part of the price they always demanded for such services, a price which could not be denied if the merger was to be successful, was that the banker or his representative must have a seat on the board of the new corporation. Thus a small clique acquired a voice in every one of the great "trusts" that came increasingly to dominate the everyday life of the nation. And since this voice was always that of the supplier of new funds, it soon came to be recognized as the dominating voice without the assent of which no important alterations of policy were ever undertaken.

THE "MONEY TRUST"

The private bankers first undertook corporate management simply to protect their railroad loans and investments from the havoc of competitive anarchy. Having reduced competition among the railroads by combining rival companies, however, they soon began, as we have seen, to pursue "bigness" in other lines as well, not only to create new investment opportunities but also to economize in production and marketing. Gradually, therefore, they came to make a veritable fetish of monopoly, sincerely believing in the end that it represented the only source of order in

---

[10] Perine, *Trust Companies*, pp. 269, 298.

mature capitalist society. These bankers did not care to meddle in the administrative details of the corporations they controlled, nor in the private lives of the citizens who were dependent upon such corporations for jobs or services. They sought, however, to maintain constant vigilance over the managers of their corporations and especially a rigid supervision of their financial policies.

The bankers did not hesitate (as in the case of the New York, New Haven & Hartford Railroad) to burden profitable companies with bankrupt properties when this seemed necessary to effect consolidations. They did not hesitate (as in the case of A. T. & T.) to purchase at any price, or to suppress or tangle in endless litigation, industrial patents that threatened to attract new firms to stabilized markets. By controlling the financial policies of giant industries and the financial resources of banks, trust and insurance companies, they were able to dominate simultaneously the users of capital and the collectors of capital. Thus they could regulate from the very heart of the economic system all its business activities. Incidentally, they made large personal fortunes through commissions by getting loans for their industrial corporations and by bringing borrowers to their financial corporations. More important, however, was the fact that they monopolized the major credit resources of the nation and therefore controlled the nation's growth. Woodrow Wilson was quick to see that the bankers thus had worked a virtual revolution in the United States, perfecting the techniques by which the system of free enterprise was being brought to a close, by which expansion was being controlled and enterprise circumscribed. "The great monopoly in this country," he said in 1913, "is the monopoly of big credits. So long as that exists, our old variety and freedom and individual energy of development are out of the question." [11] Earlier, in an address to the American Bar Association in 1910, Wilson said: [12]

Most men are individuals no longer as far as their business, its activities or its moralities, is concerned. They are not units but fractions; with their individuality and independence of choice in matters of business they have

---

[11] Edwards, *Finance Capital*, p. 193.
[12] Ripley, *Main Street and Wall Street*, p. 3.

lost their individual choice within the field of morals. They must do what they are told to do, or lose their connection with modern affairs. They are not at liberty to ask whether what they are told to do is right or wrong. They cannot get at the men who ordered it—have no access to them. They have no voice of counsel or protest. They are mere cogs in a machine which has men for its parts. And yet there are men with whom the whole choice lies. There are men who control the machine as a whole and the men who compose it. There are men who use it with an imperial freedom of design, whose power and whose individuality overtop whole communities. There is more individual power than ever, but those who exercise it are few and formidable, and the mass of men are mere pawns in the game.

The imperial leader of the new oligarchy was the House of Morgan. In its operations it was ably assisted by the First National Bank of New York (directed by George F. Baker) and the National City Bank of New York (presided over by James Stillman, agent of the Rockefeller interests). Among them, these three men and their financial associates occupied 341 directorships in 112 great corporations. The total resources of these corporations in 1912 was $22,245,000,000, more than the assessed value of all property in the twenty-two states and territories west of the Mississippi River, more than twice the assessed value of all property in the thirteen southern states.[13] Not always in sympathy with Morgan and his allies were Schiff and Warburg of Kuhn, Loeb & Co., and their client Harriman, who himself had accumulated sufficient capital to become an independent financial factor in the money markets of the country. Morgan had to tolerate the competition of Kuhn, Loeb because the latter company, like his own, had powerful foreign banking connections. He did not, however, have to yield anything to the Guggenheims, the Moores, Whitney, Ryan, Field, or Gates, all of whom in this period, backed mainly by their own personal fortunes, sought from time to time to battle Morgan for control of some key corporations. These lesser financiers fought roughly among themselves for dominance in industries left to them by the great "Money Trust," and as long as they were content to limit the range of their interests they were allowed to fight unmolested. Let them once impinge upon the empire of their superiors, how-

---

[13] *Money Trust Investigation*, 1913, vol. III, Report, p. 89.

ever, and they were punished. For such *lese majesty* Morgan in 1907 forced John W. Gates out of the Tennessee Coal & Iron Company the better to preserve "harmony" in steel. In 1908 he coerced Thomas Fortune Ryan into selling control of the Equitable Life Assurance Society lest its stock, as Morgan said, fall "into hands that might prove injurious." [14] It is possible that personal prejudices prompted Morgan's coldness toward the Guggenheims and Ryan; there can be little doubt that lack of social prestige hurt these less important financiers. For all their social, religious, and economic divergences, however, all investment bankers agreed with Morgan on the question of monopoly, and in times of panic they were willing, when permitted, to work with Morgan and his allies to preserve the integrity of the greater or smaller economic empires over which they ruled.

The very occurrence of financial panics in the United States after the emergence of the "Money Trust," however, seems to indicate that, for all their power and all their faith in the stabilizing influence of monopoly, the great bankers were neither infallible nor omnipotent. John Claflin said in 1901: [15]

With a man like Mr. Morgan at the head of a great industry, as against the old plan of many diverse interests in it, production would become more regular, labor would be more steadily employed at better wages, and panics caused by over-production would become a thing of the past.

As early as 1903, however, a 65 per cent decline from the "highs" of 1898 in industrial stock prices on the New York exchange had ended in a financial panic.[16] Within four years a panic even more severe again decimated values. And after 1907 there was no real business recovery until 1915. Panics destroyed the faith in securities that was so essential to the success of the operations of the "Money Trust," yet the members of that "Trust" not only could not avert panics; their very policies were calculated to bring them on. Only by maintaining constantly rising security markets could Morgan and his associates float the enormous

14 *Money Trust Investigation*, 1913, vol. II, pp. 1069–1070.
15 Edwards, *Finance Capital*, p. 189.
16 Montague, *Trusts*, p. v.

stock issues of their new combinations; yet the higher the markets would rise, the harder investors would strain to enlarge their holdings, the more sensitive they would thus become to any hint of contraction and the more likely they would be to sell out in a panic when actual contraction took place. By 1903 and again by 1907 the investors had thus overreached themselves. Tempted by the "Money Trust" with larger and larger issues until they were frightened by the size of their own holdings, investors were stampeded into selling in 1903 by revelations of fraud in the formation of Schwab's "Shipbuilding Trust" and the consequent failure of the market to absorb the stock of Morgan's International Mercantile Marine combine. In 1907 the success of a bear raid on United Copper created a similar selling stampede.

The inability of the leading bankers to achieve stability in the economy of the nation, their inability to take the steps obviously necessary to achieve such stability, was perhaps their greatest failure. It was not, however, their only one. Morgan, Baker, and Stillman disclaimed responsibility for panics and depressions on the ground that their power was less than absolute and hence their control less than perfect. Quite correctly, they explained their acquisition of leadership as a natural evolution from the necessities of the economic situation in America and the world. And since they had thus not seized power in response to any social crusade, they felt immune from responsibility for general social welfare. For the welfare of their own companies, however, they had publicly assumed obligation; on the credit of such obligation they had been able to gather up billions of dollars of the public's money, and for their failure to maintain the integrity of such investments they could not escape blame.

In reorganizing and combining railroads especially, three principles avowedly dominated Morgan's activity: First, to guarantee solvency for the future, fixed charges must be reduced to a figure that could be met under all conditions, with the payment of dividends on common stock relatively of minor importance. Second, a general "community of interest" must be established among major companies so that costly competition would be replaced by cooperation. Third, the House of Morgan must dominate the boards of directors of the reorganized companies. In the creation of the Southern Railway System, in the reorganization of the Erie, Baltimore & Ohio, Reading, and almost every other railroad in which Morgan was interested, the *last two* of these principles were religiously observed.

Morgan's usual procedure in dealing with fixed charges was to compensate bondholders for accepting reduced interest rates by giving them additional securities in common and preferred stock, both cheap to print and carrying no specific obligations. In this way, while funded debts were momentarily scaled down, capitalizations were increased to such an extent that the possibility of acquiring new working capital by selling stock (the safest method for soundly managed corporations) was obliterated. For new money the reorganized roads could only return once again to issuing bonds, to ballooning once more their funded debts. And that is exactly what they did. "In 1890 the funded debt of American railroads exceeded their stock capitalization by only $165,000,000. By 1918 this excess had grown to $2,929,-000,000, an increase of 1,675 per cent in the amount of difference." [17] Total capitalization, in the same period, had risen 137 per cent, capital stock only 108 per cent and funded debts 165 per cent. As William Z. Ripley testified before the United States Industrial Commission as early as 1899: [18]

> . . . the result was that through the reorganization you have got more stock and bonds than you had before you went into it; whereas the real cause of the receivership and of disaster was that they had too many stocks and bonds in the first place.

In applying these principles of financial reorganization, Morgan was not alone among the investment bankers; nor did any of them restrict such operations to railroads. The result of their procedures was brought home to the investing public as early as 1903 when thirty-seven new industrial "trusts," capitalized for more than $600,000,000, were already "disintegrated" or defunct, and thirteen others, capitalized for an additional half-billion dollars, were in financial difficulties. [19] The discontent cre-

---

[17] Campbell, *Railroad Reorganization*, p. 322.
[18] Campbell, *Railroad Reorganization*, p. 320.
[19] Moody, *Trusts*, p. 469.

ated by such conditions was aggravated by the failure of the United States Steel Corporation to pay common-stock dividends between March, 1904, and October, 1906, and by the failure of many other new industrial and railroad combinations to pay any dividends whatever. The outcome was that the marketing of new securities became increasingly difficult and the business of the bankers declined. They tried to save face in 1907 by blaming Theodore Roosevelt and his administration for their troubles. But Roosevelt replied: [20]

You say the fear of investors in railway securities must be dispelled; and you say that the people now have the impression that the greatest business interests (those of railroads) are imperiled. I am inclined to think that this is the case. If so, the responsibility lies primarily and overwhelmingly upon the railway and corporation people—that is, the manipulators of railroad and other corporation stock—who have been guilty of such scandalous irregularities during the last few years.

While reckless financing, the avowed bugbear of the "Money Trust," was chiefly to blame for the growing discontent with banker management in the years before the election of Wilson, it was not alone responsible. The bankers had disclaimed obligation for general social welfare, but they had frequently stated that many social benefits would result from their financial deals. And when these benefits, like corporation dividends, also failed to materialize, discontent increased rapidly. In many corporations controlled by the bankers, the anticipated economies of "bigness" had not been realized, while partial or complete monopoly also had failed to bring the savings expected. In addition, both "bigness" and monopoly had produced new difficulties of their own, all of which proved costly.

Perhaps the most important of the new problems was created by the passage of policy-making power from the leaders of separate productive units into the hands of men overloaded with directorships in a score or more of huge combinations. Men trained only in banking and finance now began to control manufacturing and transportation. Men to whom financial expediency was always the first consideration, now began to control the

---

[20] Edwards, *Finance Capital,* p. 192.

strategy of long-run planning in production and service. This change gradually dulled the initiative of erstwhile American entrepreneurs and straitened their inventive and organizing genius. It left them, when they remained as managers of plants that were once their own, simply bureaucrats in huge organizations, unable, without consulting their financial superiors, to adopt new methods or to discard costly old ones in plant operation or management. Since these superiors either were unavailable, or else were opposed to experimenting with new schemes, lest it disturb their financial arrangements, conservatism became as characteristic of many branches of American industry as recklessness had become characteristic of finance. "It is a well-known fact," said a Memorial to the Inventors' Guild in 1911, "that modern trade combinations tend strongly toward constancy of process and products." [21] About the same time, the *Engineering News* commented: [22]

We are today something like five years behind Germany in iron and steel metallurgy, and such innovations as are being introduced by our iron and steel manufacturers are most of them merely following the lead set by foreigners years ago. We do not believe this is because American engineers are any less ingenious or original than those of Europe, though they may indeed be deficient in training and scientific education compared with those of Germany. We believe the main cause is the wholesale consolidation which has taken place in American industry. A huge organization is too clumsy to take up the development of an original idea. With the market closely controlled and profits certain by following standard methods, those who control our trusts do not want the bother of developing anything new.

President Wilson had this to add:

I am not saying that all invention had been stopped by the growth of trusts, but I think it is perfectly clear that invention in many fields has been discouraged, that inventors have been prevented from reaping the full fruits of their ingenuity and industry, and that mankind has been deprived of many comforts and conveniences, as well as the opportunity of buying at lower prices.

Nothing, perhaps, shows the lack of enterprise of banker leadership as dramatically as the refusal of Morgan to finance

---

[21] Brandeis, *Other People's Money*, p. 102.
[22] Brandeis, *Other People's Money*, pp. 102, 103.

General Motors and the failure of General Motors, after Lee Higginson & Company had advanced funds, to keep pace with the Ford people in the production and marketing of automobiles. The initiative for drastic price cutting, for rapid expansion of markets, for the development of mass production and belt assembly lines, all came from manufacturers who knew automobiles and factories, not from bankers who knew only stocks and bonds. But at least as important as the failure of the bankers to stimulate the adoption of new inventions and the growth of new industries, were their agreements to limit speed on the railroads without reducing rates, and their failure to keep their lines, plants, rolling stock, and machinery in anything better than minimum repair. In addition, banker control led to frauds and defalcations that grew out of insufficient attention by responsible officers to the details of management. But most important of all was the bankers' failure even to try to check the loss of human life.

Especially weak in this respect was their administration of the railroads. The rate of fatalities per passenger carried on American lines even after bankers assumed control was exceeded only by the roads of Canada and Russia.[23] Adoption of adequate brakes, signals, and switching devices, and of steel passenger cars in place of wooden ones, usually waited upon severe accidents which called to the public's attention the condition of the monopolistic lines over which they rode. The same was true of mills, ships, and mines, where costly safety apparatus was rarely supplied until a series of injuries and deaths made their adoption imperative. Commenting on this condition, E. A. Ross declared in 1907 that the failure to observe fire regulations, to install safety devices in factories and in mines and on railroads, to inspect unseaworthy boats, might take a fearful toll in lives, but none of those involved in the process realized that they were guilty of manslaughter.[24] The reason was that while the corporation in the new organization of society had grown from a simple financial device to the only apparent doer of things, the law had not yet adjusted itself

[23] Campbell, *Railroad Reorganization,* p. 336.
[24] Morison and Commager, *Growth of the American Republic,* vol. II, pp. 358–359.

to the requirements of the new corporate society. You could not jail a *corporation* for crime, and you did not yet hold directors, themselves private persons, responsible for the acts of *other* "legal persons."

The same incompetence that shackled the law in dealing with corporate manslaughter shackled the stockholders of corporations in dealing with corporate management. And since corporate management was becoming actual national management, this meant not only that the bankers, through their financial operations, had worked an economic revolution in the United States, but that they were in the act of working also a drastic political revolution. The *Bankers' Magazine* itself admitted as much in 1901 when it said: [25]

As the business of the country has learned the secret of combination, it is gradually subverting the power of the politician and rendering him subservient to its purposes. . . . That [government is not] entirely controlled by these interests is due to the fact that business organization has not reached full perfection.

That business organization, by such a criterion, had not yet reached full perfection by 1906, 1910, or 1912, became increasingly clear to the businessmen themselves; but that it was gradually approaching such perfection was being made equally clear to the public, especially the investing public. Convinced by steady propaganda either that its common stock "had no value at all, actual or prospective, except through reorganization," or that the value of common stock would be enormously enhanced by some merger, investors were prevailed upon, in almost every consolidation, to exchange their stock for trustee certificates and thus to allow their votes to be cast by an exclusive voting trust composed of the interested bankers or their appointees. [26] Though such voting trusts were supposed in almost every case to terminate when the reorganization or consolidation was completed, they became instead permanent bodies directing the affairs of the new corporations. Morgan constantly avowed his intention of terminating such trusts when "a majority in amount of the stock re-

---

[25] *Bankers' Magazine*, vol. LXII, p. 498.
[26] Campbell, *Railroad Reorganization*, p. 152.

quested it." To organize such a majority, however, among stockholders scattered all over the world, was enormously difficult.
Henry P. Davison, a Morgan partner, admitted to the Pujo
Committee "that he could not name any case in which the stockholders in a great railway system had been able to oust the
incumbent management; individuals such as Harriman, Morgan
or Hill could buy control of railroads and oust the officials, but
for ordinary stockholders to band together for that purpose was
unheard of." [27]

If the "owners" of the corporations thus were stripped of
control, so, of course, was the public which the corporations were
presumed to serve. And since the financial empires represented by
such corporations were rapidly becoming the dominant force in
the nation, America's democracy was profoundly threatened.
This condition, combined with all other sources of discontent
with the administration of the "Money Trust," aroused widespread protest. Magazines like *McClure's* and the *Arena* were
flooded with literature hotly critical of the bankers. Such books
as Brandeis's *Other People's Money,* Lawson's *Frenzied Finance,*
and Richard T. Ely's *Monopolies and Trusts* also took the
bankers to task. The Houses's Pujo Investigation in 1912 supplied writers and speakers with an inexhaustible arsenal of information with which to attack the "Money Trust," but, as
we shall see, this flood of protest hardly obstructed the operations
of the bankers. It did, however, call to the attention of the
people the nature of the changed society in which they lived.

BEYOND CONTINENTAL FRONTIERS

By the last decade of the nineteenth century the United States
had constructed her essential factories and transportation systems,
had filled up and opened to cultivation most of her good arable
land, had charted practically all her high-grade mineral deposits. American industry had conquered the continental wilderness, had ceased to use up domestic as well as foreign capital,
had stopped returning the high profits of the old days of mighty

---

[27] Campbell, *Railroad Reorganization,* p. 160.

expansion. "The nation is made—its mode of action is determined," exclaimed Professor Woodrow Wilson in 1897. Then he went on to ask, "Where do we go from here?" [28]

> What we want to know [he said] is what is the nation going to do with its life, its material resources and its spiritual strength? How is it to gain and keep a common purpose in the midst of complex affairs . . . ? How is the nation to get definite leadership and form steady effective parties? . . . How shall we settle questions of economic policy? Who is to reconcile our interests?

As we have seen, the bankers and Big Business men gave one answer and promised to make it the only one. Another group in American society, however, was ready to turn to its own uses the bankers' consolidation of American business. The concentration of economic and financial control in a few strong hands, the completion of the transcontinental railroad, telegraph, and telephone systems, the development of national news services like the Associated Press, of national markets for magazines, books, and standard factory products, had diminished American sectionalism, had helped create a new spirit of nationalism in the country and with it a renewed sense of patriotism. To men who had scorned pecuniary ambitions or had been jostled uncomfortably in pursuit of them, here at last was a new avenue of approach to the American people, a new channel through which to satisfy personal longings for power. Here was a new national temper for early Progressives to exploit in their efforts to make the nation deeply ashamed of the "corruption" of its politics, of the "self-seeking" of its business leaders. Here was a new national temper for the Progressive firebrands—for Roosevelt, Hay, and Beveridge—to enlist against the "cowardice" of our foreign policies in the heyday of business politicians, to enlist in support of an embattled crusade for the right and the just, in support of a "splendid little war" with Spain, in support of shouldering at once the white man's bayonet and the white man's burden.

Throughout the eighties, as our trade expanded with Latin

---

[28] Josephson, *President Makers*, p. 25.

America, the Oriént, and the islands of the seven seas, American publicists, American philosophers and American ministers began to enlarge our ideas of "Manifest Destiny," began to popularize the dream of an American empire upon which the sun would never set. Navalist Mahan, Spencerian Fiske, Congregationalist Josiah Strong, each in his own terms, sought to fire the American people with zeal for ships, colonies, and power, with a firm belief in the inevitability of America's conquest of the world. The Anglo-Saxon was "divinely commissioned to be, in a peculiar sense, his brother's keeper," cried Strong in 1885.[29] In a paragraph he epitomized the budding feeling of his times:[30]

Then this race of unequaled energy, with all the majesty of numbers and the might of wealth behind it—the representative, let us hope, of the largest liberty, the purest Christianity, the highest civilization—having developed peculiarly aggressive traits calculated to impress its institutions upon mankind, will spread itself over the earth. If I read not amiss, this powerful race will move down upon Mexico, down upon Central and South America, out upon the islands of the sea, over upon Africa and beyond. And can any one doubt that the result of this competition of races will be the "survival of the fittest"?

Strong's book, *Our Country,* sold more than 170,000 copies in English and many more thousands in other languages.[31] Fiske reached the thousands of subscribers to *Harper's.* And Mahan had the ear of certain interests in the State Department. Such propaganda, however, bore little fruit in the 1880's. Conditions for overseas expansion were not yet mature. Smoldering sentiments of nationalism were not yet ready to burst into flame in a holy war. The hearts of the people were turned elsewhere, still too much devoted to domestic affairs to burn with imperialistic ambitions and jingoistic aims. But in another decade, in an atmosphere of diminishing economic opportunities at home, and of great concentrated business units equipped to finance and administer distant enterprises, America was ready to listen to the war cries of aristocrats starved for power and journalists hungry for circulation. In the midst of the bleak depression after 1893,

---

[29] Strong, *Our Country,* p. 210.
[30] Strong, *Our Country,* pp. 222–223.
[31] Pratt, *Expansionists of 1898,* p. 19.

for the first time in such circumstances, America had no new West to which to look for hope, no new prairies to gridiron with railroads, no new inland markets to develop for expanding factories. Accustomed in the prosperous days of the eighties to hear sung the songs of empire, America was now ready to heed the bloody thunder of Roosevelt, the righteous eloquence of Hay, Beveridge, and Lodge.

Though not all of them were well-born, each of these new leaders had pondered with Henry Adams over "democracy's neglect of the well-born and intelligent," and while Adams was content to note this neglect, the others yearned to rectify it. They abhorred the manners of market place and countinghouse and the self-made men who ruled there, and, ambitious beyond the power of yachting, polo, or the sport of kings to satisfy, they sought compensating prestige in other fields. None offered greater possibilities of power and glory than war and the diplomacy of conquest, and for none (except militaristically!) was America so well prepared. In the midst of panic and depression and what they thought was a looming revolution of farmers and workers, these Progressives took up the theme of Strong and Fiske and Mahan. With the aid of Pulitzer, Hearst, and the Cuban rebellion, in 1898 the war they sought was theirs.

Some time before 1898 Mrs. Roosevelt had asked Cecil Spring-Rice: "Do you remember how we used to call Theodore the Chilean Volunteer and tease him about his dream of leading a cavalry charge?"[32] Now the time for teasing was past. A few days after the battle of San Juan Hill, a friend wrote Mrs. Roosevelt from Cuba:[33]

No hunting trip so far has ever equalled it in Theodore's eyes. . . . When I caught up with him the day after the charge . . . he was revelling in victory and gore. . . . He had just "doubled up a Spanish officer like a jack-rabbit" just as he retired from a block house—and he encouraged us to "look at those damned Spanish dead."

Some years after the victory, "mourning the decadence of the British and American people," Roosevelt told Spring-Rice:[34]

[32] Pringle, *Roosevelt*, p. 167.
[33] Pringle, *Roosevelt*, p. 195.
[34] Pringle, *Roosevelt*, p. 176.

In the Spanish war . . . our generals . . . had to grapple with a public sentiment which screamed with anguish over the loss of a couple thousand men . . . a sentiment of preposterous and unreasoning mawkishness.

Roosevelt had declared as early as 1895 and almost incessantly thereafter that "this country needs a war." Beveridge had announced that "we must obey our blood and occupy new markets and . . . new lands." And Hay had gloried in the prospect of our "splendid little war." [35] These men, however, for all their adoration of the "military virtues" and their detestation of that "flabby, timid type of [commercial] character which eats away the great fighting qualities of our race," could not alone have plunged America into military conflict.[36] Nor would the assistance of Hearst and Pulitzer have been sufficient, with their blood-curdling competition in exaggerating the atrocities of "Butcher" Weyler, and in building into unescapable causes of war the De Lôme letter and the sinking of the *Maine*. For though Roosevelt and his fellow "ruffians" and "bullies," as President Eliot called them, hated the "green-grocer imagination" of many Americans, such Americans had yet to be reconciled to the great adventure.[37] And though he hated equally those who placed dollars and cents and American lives before intangible honor and national glory, these also had to be wooed at least from their opposition to conflict.

Roosevelt craved a war to give the nation "something to think about which isn't material gain." Yet to win consent to the war, he and Beveridge had to supplant their shrill jingoism with materialistic arguments. Such arguments failed completely to convince the great bankers who, thinking dispassionately in terms of taxes and trade, of the ratio between the costs and profits of war, held out for "peace at any price," just as they had held out for peace during the "Venezuela affair" three years before. Among middle-class businessmen, however, the jingoes' argument that American prosperity might depend upon colonial expansion began to have effect. And to win the allegiance of such

---

[35] Pringle, *Roosevelt*, p. 167; Bowers, *Beveridge*, p. 68; Josephson, *President Makers*, p. 83.

[36] Pringle, *Roosevelt*, p. 168; see also pp. 172–173.

[37] Pringle, *Roosevelt*, p. 168.

businessmen the final propaganda shots were fired. In what was virtually his war message on April 11, 1898, the equivocal Mc-Kinley thus rationalized his decision: [38]

The right to intervene in Cuba may be justified by the very serious injury to the commerce, trade and business of our people, and by the wanton destruction of property and devastation of the island.

And on April 27 Beveridge clinched the argument with this warning and this boast: [39]

American factories are making more than the American people can use; American soil is producing more than they can consume. Fate has written our policy for us; the trade of the world must and shall be ours.

Thus America was plunged into her first foreign war in more than half a century, her first war of any kind in more than thirty years. Mainly as a result of it, we acquired, by 1900, Porto Rico, the Philippines, Guam, Wake, and Hawaii. We secured definitive title to American Samoa and were in the act of establishing protectorates over Panama and Cuba. We had become a Caribbean power, a Pacific power, a Far Eastern power, ambitious to wield a "big stick" in the World's affairs, to mediate disputes between august emperors and to enter such disputes as an equal. The upstart republic, with a flourish worthy of Barnum himself, had declared itself ready at last to consort with the Hapsburgs, Hohenzollerns, Hanoverians, and Romanoffs of Europe.

"Expansion is a new idea with us. The defense of our rights is an old habit," declared the *New York Times* in July, 1898, in the very midst of a war in which we were hard pressed indeed to name what rights of ours we were defending.[40] And expansion certainly was no "new idea," as every one knew who had watched the extension of our borders three thousand miles from the Atlantic to the Pacific. What was new in 1898 was that American jingoes, with the blare of trumpets and the aid of a five-year depression, had at last brought the people to support their policy

---

[38] Commager, *Documents,* vol. II, p. 184.
[39] Bowers, *Beveridge,* p. 69.
[40] Bailey, *Diplomatic History,* p. 515.

of bellicose overseas imperialism. However, just as they had failed until the very last moment to win over to their war most American bankers and Big Business men, so these jingoes failed after the war to win the wholehearted backing of such bankers and businessmen.

Ever since the early 1890's, when Japan began seriously to enlarge her navy, American diplomats had been urging the need for a "two-ocean" fleet to defend our western as well as our eastern shores. Now that we had acquired territory in the Far East itself, the need for such a fleet became even more apparent. To facilitate the operation of such a fleet, communication lines much shorter than those around the whole of South America had to be found. For almost half a century proposals had been made for joining the Atlantic and the Pacific by a canal across either Panama or Nicaragua, and a private French corporation had actually begun construction work only to fail because of medical as well as engineering and financial difficulties. By 1900, however, a canal had become extremely important to American defense, and the United States government was prepared to overcome all obstacles to its completion. Not least among these obstacles were the political ones: the acquisition of land for the canal, and the acquisition of control over surrounding territory both on the mainland and on the islands of the neighboring seas to protect the canal from foreign threats. Thus, just as the State Department under Hay in 1898 had been most aggressive in taking colonies from defeated Spain and other powers, so the State Department after 1898 under Hay, Elihu Root, and Philander C. Knox was most aggressive in seeking American penetration into Panama, Cuba, Nicaragua, Haiti, and Santo Domingo.[41] By waving the "Big Stick" at European nations interested in western hemisphere events, by arranging timely Latin American revolutions, by interfering in foreign elections and appropriating foreign customs, the American government sought to make the Caribbean exclusively an American sea and the canal exclusively an American enterprise. And until 1913 we kept the sea of diplomacy in a rich and foamy lather with our vigorous

---

[41] Griswold, *Far Eastern Policy,* pp. 29, 133–135.

efforts to secure these ends. In order to protect what political gains it made the government sought to stimulate economic penetration; and in order to encourage and protect possible economic investments it sought additional political controls. Bankers and industrialists were urged by the State Department to promote national defense by engaging in enterprises in regions around the canal. And ambassadors, ministers, consuls, and ship captains were ordered to assist such enterprises with every means at their command.

Only after the American government had guaranteed adequate returns on investments and military and naval protection of property, however, did American businessmen venture much in the Caribbean area. Even then their investments were limited, except in Cuba and Mexico where they had already acquired extensive holdings and poured in millions of dollars. If American businessmen did not jump at opportunities in the western hemisphere, their reluctance to invest in the Far East, where the United States government could give no guarantees, was much more marked. Bankers who were too conservative to finance American automobiles naturally shied away from Philippine electrification projects or Chinese railroads. Manufacturers and shippers who had a flourishing trade with Canada or Europe naturally hesitated to extend large credits to Chinese importers. To be sure, during the depression after 1893 Americans had learned to look abroad for customers, and in 1897 the Annual Report of the State Department's Bureau of Foreign Commerce declared that we were beginning "what may be termed an American invasion of the markets of the world." To be sure, almost unknown to the general public, Americans had been reaching out gingerly for new economic worlds to conquer, for new areas and new enterprises to absorb their own surplus capital. But these shifts in our trade and our investments were only part of our normal economic evolution. The war and its hectic aftermath served only to interrupt this evolution. It did not accelerate it. And despite all the efforts of Hay and Lodge and the "dollar diplomacy" of Willard Straight, Knox, and Taft, American financiers remained cool toward most enterprises in many parts of Latin America and everywhere in the Orient.

Only after 1907—ten years after the war with Spain—did Morgan and Harriman yield grudgingly to the entreaties of our energetic diplomats. And then only because the panic of that year convinced them that the number of rich new opportunities at home had really begun to decline. Even so, compared to domestic demands, foreign markets for American capital remained infinitesimal until the First World War. The major success of all our fishing in diplomatic waters in the years before 1914 seems to have been the construction of the Panama Canal. But even in accomplishing this feat we succeeded also in creating a profound suspicion of American "justice" and American "righteousness" in the nations of the western hemisphere.

X

COMMERCIAL FARMERS IN AN INDUSTRIAL AGE

MEN are in business, according to Gras and Larson, when they "make a living *chiefly* out of providing goods and services for exchange with others." [1] On this basis early American farmers living on nearly self-sufficient farms, relying on local services for milling, smithing, tanning, and lumbering, were not businessmen. But even in the colonial period the great southern plantations were business ventures. In addition, many wheat, corn, and cattle farms in the valleys of the Chesapeake, Susquehanna, Delaware, and Hudson rivers and truck farms near big towns were business enterprises. The shift from local self-sufficiency to specialization and distant marketing, therefore, particularly in new western areas after 1850, was simply an extension of business agriculture in the United States. Sometimes, when a railroad or canal brought new transportation to the back country, specialization took place rapidly; more often it occurred gradually as industrialism built up surrounding cities, and lower shipping costs widened markets.

While specialization in cash crops meant higher living standards, it also meant increased dependence upon stable weather conditions and greater vulnerability to market fluctuations. Individual farmers, however, had little choice in determining whether or not to run these new risks. As expanding industries sent factory products into rural areas, local services upon which farmers depended were killed off. Local fulling, weaving, and flour mills closed down, local foundries and smithies that made farm and household implements were abandoned. Unless farmers could buy the new city goods in the market, therefore, their economic and social positions deteriorated, and for those who

---

[1] Gras and Larson, *Casebook*, p. 3.

would at least maintain their standard of living there was nothing to do but grow *cash* crops.

Many farmers to be sure, especially in some hilly areas of the South, East, and older Middle West, did not take this alternative; and in these regions, as the soil was exhausted and local enterprises shut down, the population and the standard of living declined. In 1920 about 25 per cent of American farms were in these retrogressive areas, and they maintained the original self-sufficient system with only slight changes.[2] The settlement of the prairie states and the Great Plains following the Civil War, however, opened up enormous new areas that were cultivated on a business basis practically from the start, and thus made the great majority of American farmers business farmers with many business problems in common. It is in the story of this majority, therefore, that we are chiefly interested. The cattlemen, who were the first producers to occupy the Plains, were usually large business enterprisers investing substantial amounts of capital, often foreign capital, in the conversion of the prairie grass into beef to feed the rapidly growing urban populations of Europe and the United States. But it was not long before large portions of the cattle ranges were enclosed and put under cultivation by farmers who were brought West by the railroads. These farmers bought farms on credit from land companies. They were in debt for mortgages to local lenders and banks. And they devoted their energies to raising wheat for world markets. Thus they were as completely subject to the agencies of industrial business as a Minneapolis merchant or manufacturer.

Though farming, especially in the West, became a great business, the commercial farmers themselves—their characteristic individualism heightened by their dispersion over the prairies and the Plains—almost always came off second best in their financial jousts with industrialists and financiers. Almost continuously after the Civil War, therefore, large numbers of discontented cultivators were seeking ways and means to check their growing indebtedness. Through political regulation of elevator and railroad rates, and through cooperation among

---

[2] Except where otherwise noted, the figures are from *Statistical Abstracts of the United States.*

themselves in marketing and banking, they sought to reduce their costs. Through diversification of crops they sought to increase their incomes. None of these stratagems, however, brought relief to the whole farm community or to those most in need of assistance. And even in the twentieth century, when new conditions made agrarian prosperity possible, the staple farmers failed to reduce their burdensome debt.

Up to 1933, at least, the farmer remained one of the few true competitors in a business society that steadily was becoming less and less competitive. Hence, he almost alone was subject to the classic laws of the *laissez faire* market to which those around him paid lip service only. If he could not solve the problems of production and distribution under rigorous competition, he was doomed as a property owner. He might then become a tenant or a wage laborer, or abandon farming altogether, and one of these courses was the fate of the majority of Americans born on the farm.

PLANNING AND PLANTING

The failure of the farmer after the Civil War permanently to improve his position was due mainly to the complexities of his business problems. From the very start he had to plan his crops carefully, in relation to soil, rainfall, and temperature. Corn, for example, needed at least eight inches of rain during the growing season, and a mean summer temperature of over 65 degrees. Even the hardiest varieties of wheat need a certain minimum depth of subsurface moisture at planting. Yet these conditions are not constant, and in dry areas like western Kansas or Oklahoma they were present in some years and absent in others, present in one township and lacking in the next. In well watered, fertile areas like Illinois and Iowa, on the other hand, the cultivator was faced with even greater problems in selecting the particular crops which would yield the maximum cash returns without impairing the fertility of the soil.

The mechanization of cereal production after 1850 introduced also the problem of buying new machinery if new crops were to be attempted, and hence the necessity for careful calculation of the initial cost of equipment, its probable earning power, and its length of life. Obviously it would not pay to purchase a reaper, twine binder, or complete harvester if only a few acres of wheat were to be planted; yet if they were not purchased reliable arrangements had to be made for renting such equipment when it was needed for the harvest. And in addition to the problems of new equipment, there were those of new skills and new information.

These difficulties led directly to a third general consideration: the proper apportionment of labor and machinery to acreage. What should be done by hand? When should horses be replaced by a tractor, a team and wagon by a motor truck? The heaviness of yield per acre, and the subsidiary activities that could be carried on in the time saved by machine cultivation had a direct bearing on the solution to these problems. So elusive were the answers, however, that, historically, probably more American farmers went bankrupt from overmechanization than from under-mechanization.

The value of the land was in some respects the key factor controlling adjustments in all the others, and, like rainfall, it was subject to continual change. The able farmer did not cultivate crops that failed to show a reasonable return on the money the farm would bring if offered for sale. If he wished to continue to grow his usual crop despite rising land values, therefore, he would sell out ond go to an area where land prices were lower. The inefficient farmer on the other hand, failing to recognize the cause of his difficulties, might compensate for unsuccessful seasons by increasing his mortgage. Ultimately, with the proceeds from his poorly planned crops, he would find himself unable to meet the high taxes and interest, and he also would be forced to migrate. It was indeed very difficult to be efficient in determining the best adjustment of crops to land values in fertile areas, so complicated were the factors involved. The problems of rotation, availability of certain types of markets, competition within the market area, availability of equipment and labor, all were variables that had to be considered each year. Wheat, for example, would not be a good major crop on most $200-an-acre land; yet, grown in limited quantities in rotation with corn, it had its place.

The problems of the commercial farmer were still far from solved even when he made a success of the year's *production* by harvesting excellent crops, for then he had to sell his produce in a market subject to wide fluctuations from year to year from forces over which he as an individual had no control. This was the final obstacle to his success.

MARKETING AND CREDIT

In the latter half of the nineteenth century, as the legend of America spread among the freed serfs and peasants of Europe and colonizing agents of railroad and land companies began to offer transportation and credit to farmers at home and abroad, an endless stream of Scandinavian, German, Hungarian, and Polish immigrants and easterners poured across the Mississippi, seeking their fortunes on the prairies and the plains. With horses, wagons, tools, and stock, they embarked on their interminable trek. Those who survived settled down at last on railroad or speculator land, only a few being lucky enough to find free homesteads near water, transportation, or towns.

Starting with mortgages on their quarter-sections, many of these settlers had to get additional credit for seed, machinery, and fencing. To raise funds for the first year's sustenance, for barns and houses to replace sod huts thrown up against the first year's weather, they had to pledge their chattels and initial crops. Only local moneylenders would accept such pledges, for the settlers had no direct access to eastern financial institutions and no standing in them. And the only cash crops which they could easily grow with the resulting funds, because of labor and marketing conditions, were wheat and corn in the more southerly regions and wheat alone to the north. Thus the average commercial farmer encountered his first dilemma in relation to the problem of credit. Without credits at high rates he could not grow wheat for the market. Burdened with such rates, he could not make wheat pay.

The farther west the wheat farmers went, the more acute became the problem presented by this dilemma, sheer distance from the Atlantic coast not only aggravating credit difficulties, but adding new obstacles as well. As the center of wheat production in America was pushed steadily toward the Rockies, wheat farmers were removed farther from the great cities of Europe, farther from the manufacturing centers of the East, farther from the capitals and booming mill towns of the Ohio and Mississippi valleys, where they were destined to find their ultimate markets. The farther they moved from such centers of population, the more dependent they became upon sources of information available only in their vicinity. As the price of grain fluctuated in Liverpool, New York, Chicago, or Minneapolis, the international broker knew about it immediately; the exporter, the jobber, the commission man, and the local merchant would soon learn of it; but the farmer in North Dakota or Montana, for instance, as late as 1890 had access to no such information, just as he had no access to news of his competitors' crops in every wheat-growing part of the world. The more he needed easy access to county seats and community churches where he might talk with his neighbors, the more distant were these centers of civilization. The more he needed newspapers, magazines, and regular mail routes through which he might learn of market conditions at home and abroad, the more inaccessible they were.

On the same fall day in 1874, there was a spread of twenty cents in the price of wheat between Minneapolis and Breckenridge, one hundred seventy-five miles to the northwest.[3] The conditions which permitted this spread were repeated in subsequent decades as new wheat lands were occupied. The remote farmer's ignorance of his market was responsible for part of this difference. Much of the rest could be charged to transportation costs. Just as distance from organized communities reduced the farmer's familiarity with his ultimate market, so it reduced also his means of access to that market, leaving him in the end in a sparsely settled region where a single line of river boats or a single railroad company had no competition for freight. The farmer himself rarely shipped his wheat on such lines, his transportation problem ending when he sold his wagonloads to the local merchant. The price he received, however, was profoundly influenced by the rates such merchants had to pay for monopolistic

---

[3] Larson, *Wheat Market*, p. 158.

short hauls to the nearest shipping terminals. As distance from these terminals increased, the price at the local merchant's fell proportionately, leaving many farmers, after their work was done, once again a little more deeply in the debt than they had been when the new season began.

Of course, not every wheat farmer in the American West was doomed to failure by this combination of high credit and transportation charges and ignorance of world markets. And even for the majority who could not make a net profit from crops alone, there seemed always a way out. As the younger sons in large farm families matured, the more ambitious among them joined with the majority of the 13,000,000 immigrants who arrived between 1865 and 1900 to seek western lands for themselves. Augmenting the ranks of these eager land seekers was a continuous stream of discontented eastern farmers and their own ambitious offspring. And all of them together created in the trans-Mississippi a persistent land boom which ebbed only in drought or depression years, and reached in 1886 the frantic proportions of the earlier days of western speculation. The result was that, while prices of all commodities were falling in the decades after the Civil War and prices for farm products were falling faster than the rest, the demand for farms steadily increased and the farmer's equity in his land increased proportionately. While they were forced periodically to the verge of bankruptcy by their dealings with the organized businessmen in the wheat and money markets, many farmers thus were able to save themselves by negotiating new mortgages or by selling their farms at good prices. In a typical Nebraska township, twenty years after its initial settlement, more than 50 per cent of the original cultivators had sold out; 77 per cent of the remaining *resident* owners owed mortgages.[4] By 1890, there were on the farms of Kansas, Nebraska, the Dakotas, and Minnesota as many mortgages as there were families in the five states.[5]

Faced with the necessity of paying cash for his family's food and clothing, for wagons, horses, and harness, for installments and interest on his machinery and other fixed charges on his land,

---

[4] Bentley, *History of a Nebraska Township,* p. 64.
[5] Hicks, *Populist Revolt,* p. 24.

the wheat farmer was fortunate in thus being able, in poor crop years, to raise money outside the wheat market. In the end, however, such good fortune only postponed the day of reckoning for many cultivators; and when that day came the costs of the postponement were onerous indeed. For eight years before 1886, the Great Plains had had such extraordinary rainfall that responsible geologists predicted a permanent moistening of the climate of the region. And so optimistic had farmers become that, encouraged by abundant eastern capital, they had steadily increased their mortgages in order to buy more land and machines. In the winter of 1886, however, the wet weather ended. Extreme cold and violent blizzards decimated the cattle on the overstocked ranges. And the following summer intense heat and parching drought killed the wheat and forage. To the hopeful farmers who had poured over the plains in the years of plenty and paid land speculators as much as $6,000 for quarter-sections, this was a fateful summer. To the railroads that had issued new bonds to finance extensions of their lines across the booming plains, it meant the beginning of retrenchment. To the banks and insurance companies that were charging high commissions and 8 to 10 per cent interest for land loans, it marked the end of a profitable branch of their business. And when this year 1886 was followed by a decade of intermittent drought and extreme changes of temperature, panic ran across the smitten area. The rush to the West soon was sharply reversed. Thousands who only a few years before had hopefully sought imagined wealth in central Kansas and similar areas, now retreated from the scorched or frozen earth. Equity in land disappeared. Farms mortgaged to the limit were foreclosed. Settlers who had tided themselves over lean years by expensive borrowing, lost their homesteads.[6] Literally the Middle Border had shriveled up, had withered and turned to dust.

To the ranks of those defeated by Nature soon were added those who were crushed by their ties with eastern business institutions and their dependence upon world business conditions. For in 1893 to drought and frost was added financial panic and, for

---

[6] Hicks, *Populist Revolt,* pp. 29–35.

the next five years, business depression. During these years wheat fell to its lowest price in our history, and homesteads fell with it. Truly the business of farming seemed too complicated, too dependent for success upon the caprices of man and Nature.

Paralleling the great dispersion of grain farmers over the prairies and the plains, was the enormous extension of cotton areas in the Gulf states and the Mississippi valley as far as the northern boundary of Arkansas. And paralleling the problems of the wheat farmer were those of the cotton cultivator. Aside from the complexities of farm management the troubles of both could be traced to large crops, rising fixed charges, especially for land, and falling prices, the nadir in wheat coming in 1894 when a bushel that yielded $1.05 in 1870 brought 49 cents, the bottom in cotton being reached in 1896 when a crop nearly six times that of 1866 brought $51,000,000 less. North and east of the cotton lands were tobacco planters, and south and east of wheat areas were corn and hog farmers. All of them had become businessmen devoting their energies to the cultivation of staples for sale at a profit. While corn farmers had not surrendered entirely the self-sufficiency that was once typical of American rural life, and tobacco planters were too few in number to be of special national interest, the new wheat and cotton farmers constituted large groups, unorganized, highly individualistic, inexperienced in business, ignorant of the vagaries of organized national and international markets and absolutely dependent upon them. Among no other groups was credit so necessary and so dear, among no others was distribution so complicated and so costly. By the middle nineties, the problems of these wheat and cotton farmers had come to be of national importance. Before that time, especially in the West, many local attempts to ameliorate their condition had been undertaken.

The earliest of these attempts revolved about the Granges, secret societies formed after 1867 to break down the farmer's insularity and to educate him in scientific farming. In some states, in order to alleviate capital and credit shortages, the Granges set up cooperative banks, life and fire insurance companies. To reduce the prices of tariff-protected commodities manufactured by "trusts," they set up cooperative stores and cooperative farm machine factories. To reduce middlemen's profits and the fees of monopolistic elevators, they organized cooperative marketing agencies, some of which shipped wheat directly to Chicago, New York, and Liverpool. But perhaps most important were the efforts of the Granges to reduce transportation and storage charges. Having mortgaged their farms to invest in railroad bonds and having paid taxes and assessments to help the states make similar investments, the wheat farmers especially felt they deserved cheap and efficient service. As early as 1869 these farmers won in Illinois the promise of such service through a maximum rate law and a railroad commission to administer it. Though originally without a political program, the Granges soon became engaged in seeking similar laws in other states and improvements in existing legislation. So efficient were they that, despite strong railroad opposition, they elected enough governors and legislators in Illinois, Wisconsin, Minnesota, Missouri, California, and Iowa to enact between 1871 and 1878 laws regulating railroad rates, nominally ending discrimination between long competitive hauls and short monopolistic ones, between great shippers and small.

In the chain of productive activities which create out of the raw materials of the soil the finished commodity for the ultimate consumer, that group which is least efficiently organized always gets the smallest share of the profit. That was true of the master craftsman in his relations with merchant capitalists; it was true of the small manufacturer in relation to the railroads; and it was preeminently true of the isolated cereal farmer in his relation to the town merchant, the jobber, the commission man, the railroad and elevator operator, the great broker in the primary market and the processor who turned his product into the world's food. The activities of the Grange constituted the grain farmer's first organized effort to remedy his unenviable position. And on the whole this effort proved futile. For want of sufficient working capital, most of the western cooperative stores and factories soon shut down. Through superior political experience, superior knowledge of the law, superior financial means, and adept bribery and corruption, the railroads were able to emasculate the laws seeking to end rate discrimination. And through the continuance of such discrimination, private elevator operators were able easily to defeat their cooperative marketing competitors. The history of the Granges is the history of the failure of makeshift organizations among independent agricultural enterprisers, in their fight against other business forces, richer, more closely integrated, more accustomed to cooperating until their objectives were attained.

In sympathy with a secular decline in prices in every part of the occidental world, American railroad rates in the late seventies had also begun to decline, and the construction in the eighties of competitive roads in most parts of the old wheat belt accelerated this reduction. Simultaneously, however, unfair grading systems, speculative trading in grain futures in the Chicago "Pit," and increasing monopoly among elevator operators combined to deprive the wheat farmer of as great a percentage of the consumer's price as before. While the average corn farmer received about 40 per cent of this price, the dairy farmer about 50 per cent, and the cattleman nearly as much, the wheat farmer, according to one estimate, received on the average no more than 17 per cent. The Granges had failed to increase this proportion by reducing railroad charges. In the eighties, new attempts at cooperative marketing also failed substantially to increase this percentage. In the meantime, the farmer's money income fell steadily as wheat prices sagged, and the price of improved farm land rose steadily as settlement thickened. The result was that problems of management became more complex, cheap land became more and more difficult to acquire, and tenancy increased.

Though the cotton South after the Civil War had always had a much larger percentage of tenants than the West, southern tenancy also increased steadily in the eighties because of falling crop prices and mounting credit charges. And for farmers in both areas, after the failure of political or cooperative devices, there seemed to be only one way to preserve their lands. That was to diversify their crops. Since wheat and cotton could no longer sustain the heavily mortgaged land upon which they grew, wheat and cotton farmers were urged to try other products which, through more intensive cultivation, would yield a greater return per acre. They were urged especially to try dairying and truck farming to supply near-by industrial towns. There was, however, one hitch; the shift to new products required new capital, and new skills. Since those who most needed diversification were those most heavily in debt and presumably least skillful, it offered no solution to them. Besides, there were other obstacles. Much wheat land in the West was unsuitable for other cash crops and was already too expensive for cattle and sheep raising. In the South, the average farmer owed a great deal to the merchant of the "country store." Since the merchant wanted real, hard cash above all, and since cotton at whatever price was the only sure bringer of cash, the planter was not permitted to speculate in the cultivation of the other products about which he presumably knew nothing.

Cooperative, political, and technical devices thus failed to ameliorate the condition of the debtor wheat and cotton farmers. But as they shifted to cheaper and cheaper land on the moving western frontier they left available for men with more money or credit great areas in the Mississippi valley. Here, north of Tennessee, especially in Wisconsin, Illinois, and Indiana, dairy farmers moved in. Equipped with adequate capital for intensive farming, they were also sufficiently few in number to cooperate successfully among themselves and sufficiently strong to resist the impositions of monopolistic railroads or monopolistic marketing agencies. Early they organized their own trade associations, the first being the Illinois & Wisconsin Dairymen's Association of 1867. They also organized cooperative cheese factories, creameries, and milk distributing companies, all of them successful in expanding local markets. In the meantime, for those who continued to specialize in grain, conditions got increasingly worse, rising fixed charges and falling prices reaching their widest spread between 1896 and 1897.

THE MISUSE OF PROSPERITY, 1897–1920

Impoverished by drought and depression and defeated in politics, the staple farmer, late in 1896, was confronted with a bleak and ominous prospect.[7] All his devices had failed to alleviate his increasingly difficult position, and now he was bankrupt not only of funds but of ideas. At the very nadir of his dejection, however, his position had begun to change. The seemingly interminable aridity on the western plains ended in 1897. At the same time, the world depression had run its course. In addition, American population was beginning to increase faster than improved farm acreage, and the producer of grain staples thus became less and less dependent upon foreign markets. Prices for produce and land began to rise, and the differential between income and fixed charges began to be more comfortable. For the first time in thirty years, by this sudden turn of events, staple farmers were enjoying the prospect of a prolonged period of prosperity.

During the first fifteen years of the new era these favorable trends continued. Even Nature smiled upon the cultivator as generally good rainfall helped raise the per-acre yield of wheat despite the movement to poorer land. In addition, the mature industrial economy offered the western farmer new luxuries and conveniences such as telephones, automobiles, phonographs, attractive magazines, and household appliances for which to spend his larger cash income. The spread of country trolley lines made the cities and their educational facilities, better markets, and exciting amusements available to many farmers for the first time. Had the cereal farmer diversified production to the greatest possible extent he might have enjoyed these favorable trends indefinitely and been able to break away from dependence on export altogether. Nor would this achievement have been bad for the economy as a whole. The United States no longer needed the foreign purchasing power that cereal and meat exports had provided in the nineteenth century. In addition, the decline of competition from our own agricultural products would have helped build up our *industrial* exports, which returned far greater profits to the nation.

But this wholesome diversification failed to take place prior to the First World War. As long as export markets existed for wheat, pork, cotton, and tobacco, farmers adhered to the tradi-

---

[7] See chap. VIII, pp. 16p ff.

tional routines rather than risk new crops with their greater rewards but more exacting demands upon thought, skill, and labor. The prevalence of farm tenancy was in no small degree responsible for this failure. For both economic and psychological reasons tenants are naturally loath to work hard to improve land they do not own, and as long as rents are paid under existing conditions, landlords are equally unwilling to have tenants experiment with crops that may be beyond their skill as cultivators. With 50 to 65 per cent of the farms in the cotton belt tilled by cash tenants or share-croppers in 1910 this inertia was particularly noticeable in the South. But even in Illinois and the northwest central states over 30 per cent of the farmers were tenants, and the effect there was more pronounced than the figures reveal. For it was in the rich fertile sections, where land values were high and the land best suited to varied cultivation, that tenancy was most frequent. This situation goes far to explain why, during the prewar years, the increase in the sale of eggs, milk, and vegetables fell 20 to 50 per cent behind population growth. It explains why a commentator surveying the scene in 1910 could write: "American agriculture must develop enormously along new lines if it is to save the nation from hunger." [8]

The failure of the new lines to develop rapidly was in part a result of the World War and its immediate aftermath. Even before the war, however, more liberal homestead laws, higher crop prices, heavier rainfall, and plentiful mortgage money had started hectic real estate booms that spread wheat production into the grass lands of western Kansas, Oklahoma, and northern Texas while prospective cotton planters moved as far west as the Rio Grande. Thus months before the shot at Serajevo a wheat crop had been planted that was to produce a harvest surpassing all previous records by a hundred million bushels. The war, of course, with its blockade of Russia, and devastation of farming areas in France, gave impetus to acreage extension, while high labor costs and soaring prices for wheat and corn removed the stimulus to diversification in the more fertile areas. The United States government also played an active part in the ex-

[8] Schmidt and Ross, *American Agriculture*, p. 363.

pansion. The Smith-Lever Act of 1914 brought county agents of the Department of Agriculture right to the farmer's door with scientific information on how to increase production, and the Farm Loan Act of 1916 brought government lending agents close on their heels. Unfortunately, the mortgages easily negotiated with these lending agents were based upon costs and prices that were not to be maintained in the following years of peace. In 1918 wheat farming returned, on the average, thirty-two dollars an acre. But the resumption of normal production in Europe and the limited buying power of the Continent in the twenties sharply curtailed the market for American wheat, and the western farmer soon found himself once again confronted with the problems of the nineties. The rudely awakened cultivator found his mortgage payments 200 per cent higher than before the war, his taxes about 140 per cent higher and his income only 75 per cent higher.[9]

THE END OF AN ERA

In 1920 slightly more than half of our western farms were unmortgaged, and life on such farms during the boom years of the twenties was more comfortable and interesting than ever before. Improved free education, radios, moving pictures, and automobiles ended the cultural isolation of remote farms. Electricity and gasoline motors supplied running water and lightened household tasks. The tractor made possible the cultivation of big acreages with less labor in field or barn. Farm bureaus, marketing cooperatives, and farm clubs not only gave cultivators a larger part of the food dollar but also a more interesting social life.

The brighter outlook of the more fortunate, however, could not compensate for the many dark aspects of the farm picture after 1921. Immigration restriction, the disappearing export market, and the decline in all commodity prices began to reduce land values in specialized wheat areas. Farm economists had for the first time fully to realize the extent to which the pros-

---

[9] Limber, *Crop Land Usage*, p. 105.

perity of American agriculture had been based upon profits from real estate rather than from crops. Agricultural enterprisers had for the first time to adjust their plans to constantly falling land values. The price of farm land in South Dakota fell 55 per cent in the twenties, and prices in surrounding states were hardly more stable. At the same time, mortgages and taxes continued to mount. Thus the mortgaged farmer, accustomed in earlier days to seeing his equity increase, now saw it rapidly decline. He no longer had the chance to sell out at a profit and to try again to make farming pay in some cheaper area farther west. The inevitable result was the conversion of owners into tenants at a more alarming rate than ever. In Louisiana, Arkansas, Oklahoma, and Texas, the most recent boom areas, by 1930 almost two-thirds of the cultivators were tenants, and many remaining "owners" continued in possession of their land only at the pleasure of local banks or lending agencies. In the Dakotas, a 50 per cent increase in tenancy occurred during these "good" years.

While rising fixed charges for land thus oppressed the small or marginal farmer, the widespread use of the gasoline tractor after the World War made his competitive position still more unfavorable. Either he had to compete without machinery, and thus with higher labor costs, against mechanized farms, or else he had to use his tractor on smaller plots of cheap land and thus still have higher costs per bushel.

The commercial farmer obviously was a businessman in a highly complicated line, and prior to 1933 he was in the most fiercely competitive of all major businesses. Whereas industrial prices after 1929 were to a considerable degree controlled by the mechanics of limited competition, the farmer's price structure disintegrated and the essentially unstable farm situation exploded. With farm prices in 1932 at half the already unsatisfactory levels of 1926, taxes and mortgage payments could no longer be met in large sections of the farm area. As early as 1929 the government had embarked upon a policy of supporting prices by temporarily removing cereal surpluses from the market; but the victory of the more advanced agrarian reformers in the elections of 1932 brought about much wider government activity. The Agricultural Adjustment Acts and crop loan legislation really ended the era of free and unrestrained competition among farm enterprisers, and introduced the kind of limitations on production and prices that trade associations had always aimed at in industry and Big Business had finally achieved.

XI

INDUSTRY AND LABOR

THE difficulties of commercial farmers after the Civil War centered chiefly around the problems of distribution—the problems of marketing and shipping crops. The difficulties of factory workers arose mainly from changes in the organization and techniques of production. Factory workers multiplied more than ten times in the second half of the nineteenth century—a rate far too rapid for social adjustment. Men like Andrew Carnegie or Jay Gould, brought up to be workers or farmers, found themselves the employers of thousands of men. Country towns whose citizens were educated to think in terms of rural values became great industrial centers. The new urban workers drawn from American farms or foreign countries needed education and guidance, but in keeping with *laissez faire* ideas neither government officials nor businessmen were willing to assume the necessary leadership. Into the resulting no man's land stepped the labor organizer, striving to protect labor through institutions of its own devising.

Expansion was the dominant motif of nineteenth century America. When the rate of physical expansion was high, "good times" and good jobs were available for all those able to do skilled work. When expansion lagged, good times turned to bad and many jobs disappeared. The great majority of workers in this period professed the same social objectives as their employers, especially when declining prices increased "real wages" and improved the general standard of living. It might have been possible, therefore, for labor and capital to work out satisfactory relationships had the basic economic situation continued unhanged, for both workers and employers in the nineties looked to trade agreements and state arbitration as possible remedies or industrial strife.

Unfortunately, however, the economic situation, as we have seen, was radically changed in the new century. Prices began to rise after 1897 and profits tended upward while real wages lagged. After the panic of 1907, the slowing down of the rate of economic expansion became very noticeable, and too little new investment in productive enterprises, coupled with steadily increasing plant efficiency, began to threaten employment. In this atmosphere new social theories arose. Consumers' goods industries, it was said, had to be stimulated to replace railroad construction or long-term mining developments, if employment was to continue to expand at least as fast as the population. But consumers' goods industries could succeed only if there was a wide distribution of purchasing power. Thus high wages had to be paid, spending had to take the place of saving, consumption had to be emphasized instead of production, and millions of dollars had to be diverted from investment in raw materials and machines to investment in advertising and sales organization. Everything that seemed a menace to the generation of employers brought up to think that efficiency meant minimum wages and maximum production, now began to appear socially desirable.

Neither labor nor capital, however, could be expected suddenly to execute such an intellectual somersault, and the result was confusion of doctrine and practice. On the one hand high wages, welfare expenditures, and social services began to receive a certain amount of attention from progressive employers, but only because they believed that such changes would pay higher dividends. On the other hand, efficiency engineering, the speed-up, and the stretch-out all tended to increase production faster than wages and faster, therefore, than consumption. Labor turnover was fought by employers as a major evil, yet they spent millions of dollars to finance associations designed to prevent unionism with its tendency toward job stability. Consequently "welfare capitalism" became suspect among the workers, and no satisfactory adjustment between them and the employers could be made. The failure of businessmen to solve this most crucial problem of industrialism during the age of free enterprise opened the door to state intervention in the days of the New Deal.

THE BROADENING GULF

In the middle of the nineteenth century, America was a nation of small and medium-sized businesses. An ironworks in New York that employed over a thousand workers was one of the biggest plants in the country.[1] The usual New England textile mill employed two or three hundred operatives. The McCormick factory in Chicago, the largest producer of agricultural machinery, had fewer than three hundred regular employees in the early 1850's and was managed by Leander McCormick and four foremen.[2] No shop or mill was so large that the manager could not know the older workers, and in most cases the manager was also the owner or an active partner. At this stage the "personal relation in industry" could be a reality. By 1914, however, this stage was passed. The Ford plant then employed over fifteen thousand men. Shops with six to eight thousand employees had become common in many lines of industry. Most of the big companies which accounted for three-quarters of the nation's industrial production had several plants, all of them divorced from the central business office. Thus the individual plant manager might not be a person of any great authority in the company, and the ultimate direction of wage and hour policies might rest with New York or Chicago bankers, as far removed from the workingmen as the President of the United States.

Nine million immigrants came to America between 1880 and 1900, and some twelve million more by 1914. From the nineties on, eastern and southern European types predominated, and the industrial centers were their destinations. By 1909, in twenty-one important branches of industry nearly two-thirds of all the workers were immigrants or Negroes.[3] Within the shop this meant that they did almost all unskilled and some semiskilled work, whereas the skilled jobs and minor administrative positions were reserved for native white Americans. "That job is not a hunky's job, and you can't have it," was the answer given to intelligent

---

[1] Albion, *New York Port*, pp. 150–151.
[2] Hutchinson, *McCormick*, vol. I, p. 308.
[3] *History of Labor*, vol. III, p. 41.

foreigners who aspired to rise above the ranks of common labor.[4] Thus a wedge of racial discrimination was driven into the labor force, leaving overbearing small bosses on the top and rebellious foreigners resenting their social inferiority at the bottom. Furthermore, new arrivals from Europe continually menaced the job security of those already employed. Even in good years the eastern factory towns had their starving fringes of immigrants who had not yet found work. The Holyoke, Massachusetts, *Transcript* observed in the summer of 1873:[5]

There is one pitiful and miserable sight which we have seen night after night in front of the fruit and vegetable stands. . . . It is a drove of poverty-stricken children, often girls, clad only in one or two ragged and dirty garments down on their hands and knees in the gutters, greedily picking out of the mud and dirt and eating the bits of spoiled and decaying fruit which have been thrown away as worthless. . . . Judging by the famished looks and actions of the children we are sure there must be poverty and misery and destitution in their wretched living places that only the sufferers know.

Jobs in big factories with increasingly high-speed machinery became ever more monotonous and dangerous. Repetitive motions dulled concentration while slight miscalculations often meant disaster. Perhaps the peak of severity in this warfare between men and machines was reached in the early years of the twentieth century. A reliable authority writes: "The accident rate was higher, in all probability, between 1903 and 1907 than at any other time or place."[6] The pressure of the Progressive reformers for employer liability laws helped to stimulate the introduction of some safety devices in the following years; but even in 1913 deaths from industrial accidents totaled 25,000, and injuries nearly 1,000,000. Without compensation insurance, possibly without relatives in this country, the families of dead or disabled immigrant workers were left to shift for themselves.

Another grave element of insecurity was the seasonal character of production. Few plants operated at an even rate all year round, and workers, both skilled and unskilled, were used to

---

[4] Interchurch World Movement, *Steel Strike*, p. 136.
[5] Green, *Holyoke*, pp. 125–126.
[6] *History of Labor*, vol. III, p. 366.

having more than two months off without pay. Most managers tried to keep at least a minimum force of skilled workers who were continuously rehired, but semiskilled and unskilled workers came and went as opportunity fluctuated. Professor Slichter found the turnover in 105 plants between 1912 and 1915 averaged nearly 100 per cent.[7] The fact that President Frank Disston of the Disston Saw Company felt that a 34 per cent annual turnover among 3,600 workers was a figure to be proud of in a company having model relationships, casts additional light on the usual situation.[8] Thus no one company was responsible for the old-age or sick periods of the ordinary worker, and any continuous insurance plan by a single company would break down through the annual or biennial severance of relations.

Most businessmen failed voluntarily to face the total situation brought about by loss of personal contact, immigrant labor, monotonous work, industrial accidents, insecurity of employment and old age. Most businessmen, therefore, failed to take adequate steps to alleviate these conditions. This led directly to the rise of militant unionism, political interference, and radical reform movements. To be sure, businessmen were caught in a dilemma. Safety devices, company medical staffs, health and accident insurance, and the maintenance of large working forces during slack periods all cost money. Shop committees, rest periods, and shorter hours were felt to menace the volume of production. No single entrepreneur or corporation could assume the burden of higher costs entailed by these changes without losing ground to his competitors, and no business leaders were able to persuade trade association members to take joint action. Only as some reform showed a profit would there be any wide adoption. Thus the way was left open for "outsiders," in the name of humanitarianism or the rights of the workers, to interest themselves in employer-employee relations, and labor was unavoidably challenged to better itself by its own efforts.

---

[7] *History of Labor*, vol. III, p. 331.
[8] *Handling Men*, p. 80.

LABOR'S WELFARE CAMPAIGNS

American labor worked under severe handicaps in its efforts at self-betterment. New processes and new machines continually displaced old skills and old jobs. The "march of the iron men" from the 1860's on was terrifyingly rapid to the eyes of skilled labor. Many of the crafts were in a continual stage of readjustment. They were always on the defensive, always striving to hold some advantage, some vested right that revolutionary changes in technology and business methods threatened to take away. Unionization could help in preserving status, in giving a greater measure of security. But while attempts to "freeze" the situation might work well in backward or hand-labor industries like building and construction, or tolerably well in slowly changing industries like railroading, they were inevitably doomed to defeat in progressive ones like chemistry, metallurgy, or electricity. Furthermore, industries like textiles, mining, or packing needed only a few skilled workers, the great majority being susceptible of easy replacement from the annual supply of new immigrants.

Under such conditions, accentuated by geographical dispersion of the working force, racial and linguistic antagonisms, and a relatively high level of job opportunity for displaced workers, it is not surprising that unionization or other collective efforts on the part of labor progressed but slowly.

Prior to 1898 unions presented no serious challenge to the exclusive control of labor policy by management. The older national craft unions, such as the printers, hatters, stonecutters, and railway engineers, went back to the 1850's; but they embraced only a few thousand skilled workers, men who had good bargaining power in any case. The Knights of Labor had appeared menacing to business control when its membership reached 700,000 in the recovery year 1886, but this one big union composed of Negroes and whites, skilled and unskilled, had melted away in the heat of its own internal controversies. The managers employing skilled workers next became alarmed over the rapid growth of the new American Federation of Labor, which doubled its small membership between 1886 and 1892, reaching some 250,000 by the latter year. But the ensuing depression arrested its progress, and defeats in strikes and legal battles made it seem less menacing. In 1898, the first full year of recovery from the depression of the nineties, the total union strength, including the railroad brotherhoods and other independents, was less than 500,000 among 17,000,000 non-agricultural workers.[9]

Then a great upswing in labor organization took place with a speed that seemed to portend the complete unionization of American industry. Nourished by the spread of German and British labor theories, business prosperity, and rising prices, encouraged by "progressive" politicians and social reformers, A.F. of L. unions scored a five-fold increase in membership between 1898 and 1904. Stiffening employer resistance and other factors checked the growth of the union movement at this point, but 8 to 11 per cent of the labor force remained organized until the time of the World War in comparison with the meager 2.5 per cent of 1898.

The organized efforts of two million unionized workers had surprisingly little effect on the movement of real wages. The drastic price decline from 1865 to 1897 that put pressure on businessmen and farmers greatly benefited labor, as wage rates showed remarkable rigidity. In some industries the pay for a day's unskilled labor remained fixed at the customary $1.25 or $1.50 quite regardless of price movements.[10] Meanwhile money wages for skilled work, responding to scarcities brought about through the rapid rate of industrial expansion, tended to advance slightly. By 1892 labor's living standard in terms of income and price levels was higher than it had ever been, or was to be prior to the end of the First World War. If business's hardship had been labor's boon in the late nineteenth century, the reverse was true after 1898. Rapidly rising prices as usual outstripped general wage advances even in some of the highly unionized industries, and by 1914 the average American worker had 5 or 6 per cent

9 *History of Labor,* vol. II, p. 522 note; vol. IV, p. 13.
10 *Industrial Commission,* 1901, vol. I, *passim.*

less purchasing power than in 1899 despite a gain of almost 20 per cent in the real per capita income of the country.[11]

Relative failure in the field of wage relations was not, however, a crucial blow to the idea of unionization. Collective action by labor had roots far more complex than simple questions of wages or hours. Men whose necessary feeling of self-importance, of belonging to some meaningful or responsive social structure, had been weakened by submergence in great impersonal factories and urban slums responded eagerly to opportunities for restoring themselves through group activity. Labor unions were but a part of the mass movement into clubs, lodges, and fraternal orders. Working for the union and empowering the delegates to do battle with the boss was a reassertion of the individual's power over his environment. The mutual benefit policies of the unions gave a feeling of security in the face of industrial accidents and seasonal unemployment, while union "socials," dances, picnics, and lectures offered stimulating leisure-time activity.

But even in the years of greatest union membership between the Civil War and the First World War these benefits were only for a few. From 89 to 99 per cent of non-agricultural labor was always outside the union ranks, shifting for itself, fighting its own battles on a single shop basis, depending upon employers, savings banks, private insurance companies, or fraternal orders for security. For this great majority rising real wages were at least partly offset during the latter nineteenth century by deteriorating living and working conditions. The bad sanitation and disagreeable working conditions of big mechanized plants were duplicated in the increasingly congested urban slums. Decent housing was simply not on the market for the unskilled workers of most cities. The free amusements of the small city—hunting, fishing, swimming, and picnicking—were either impossible in the industrial metropolis or else cost money for trolley fares and special tickets. The vaudeville, burlesque, or movie shows that the family was educated to crave, all cost money, as did store clothes with their frequent changes in style. The increasing emphasis on consumption goods in our economy after 1900 was a hard-

---

[11] *History of Labor*, vol. III, p. 83, and Douglas, *Real Wages*, p. 130, for wage estimates; National Industrial Conference Board, *Studies*, p. 83, for income.

ship to the average worker, who was unable to increase his purchases.

THE PROPHETS OF RADICAL CHANGE

The monopolistic trend of factory technology, so conveniently ignored by the dominant philosophers of Spencerian progress, was readily seized upon by certain intellectuals in America after 1865 as proof of the ultimate doom of competitive capitalism. Unwilling to stand for the control of economic life by government-regulated monopolies, the radical philosophers assumed that the ultimate solution must be a socialist democracy controlled by the white-collar and manual workers.

From the seventies on, socialist writers and speakers created an increasing stir of apprehension among conservative editors, professors, ministers, and business leaders. Distinguished novelists like Howells, Bellamy, Harris, Garland, and Norris either professed their belief in ultimate socialization or wrote popular stories that questioned the values of competitive capitalism. A number of Protestant ministers led by W. D. P. Bliss called themselves Christian Socialists, and helped, at least, to feed the growing strength of social criticism of business and its labor policies in the more liberal church organizations. Even academic economists like Richard Ely and John R. Commons, trained in the German concepts of state paternalism, seemed ready to advocate radical interference with existing business practices.

To a great many non-intellectual Americans this tendency seemed like one great concerted attack upon property and the American way of life. The hated word "socialism" covered everything from social democratic reforms through doctrinaire Marxism to anarcho-syndicalism. Yet in reality the radicals were too hopelessly weak and divided to warrant any grave concern by nineteenth century American property owners. No combination even of avowedly socialistic parties ever polled 100,000 votes or built a strong local machine prior to 1900. Neither the A.F. of L. nor the Knights of Labor ever officially embraced the doctrines of Marx, Lassalle, Bakunin, or Most. The anti-socialist influence of the Catholic Church was stronger among the leaders of both these union organizations than any counter force working toward socialism.

After 1900, however, the talk and writing of the previous twenty years seemed about to have practical results. The Industrial Workers of the World, standing for both the One Big Union idea and a vague kind of violent anarcho-syndicalism, showed considerable strength in the West during the depression of 1908 and 1909. Although its paid-up membership was insignificant, it gained prestige as an organizing agency for unskilled labor, and its principal leader "Big Bill" Haywood became a national figure in the years before the War. On a more impressive scale Eugene V. Debs, a native-born railroad labor leader, was building an American Socialist party upon a broad non-doctrinaire base. Supported by the western anarcho-syndicalists, many ex-Populists and groups of German and American workers in the industrial centers, Debs won almost 900,000 votes for President in 1912, and his showing seemed to presage a permanent American Labor party. Furthermore, the Socialists had built local machines of real strength in some cities. Victor Berger, a Socialist, representing the Milwaukee, Wisconsin, district in Congress, and Emil Seidel, Milwaukee's mayor, were only the most prominent of about a thousand Socialists occupying public offices.

But the Socialist party in the year of its greatest triumph was already foundering on the same rocks of sectional feeling and diversity of interest that had wrecked all other farmer-labor parties. The older eastern Socialists led by the wealthy Morris Hillquit of New York City were unwilling to continue cooperation with syndicalists like Haywood who condoned violence; yet in expelling the I.W.W. group these more conservative leaders lost much of the western strength of the party. The European war with its challenge to the doctrine of non-cooperation in "imperialist" struggles, and the split over the Russian Revolution, simply strengthened the disintegrating tendencies that had already started late in 1912.

THE EMPLOYERS' CAMPAIGN OF RESISTANCE

Unionization far more than radicalism was the continual worry of American employers. They all shared an almost psychopathic fear of having to meet the representatives of labor on a footing of equal authority, and a similar fear of labor gaining a position strong enough to influence management. "I do not believe," said President Meisel of the Kidder Press Company, "that a manufacturer can afford to be dictated to by his labor as to what he shall do, and I shall never give in. I would rather go out of business." [12] His was the old conception of the employer as the host inviting the worker to come and make use of his property, but only on the conditions that the owner of the property should dictate. In the manager-owned plants of a hundred or fewer employees, the backbone of nineteenth century business, this dictatorship furthered the aim of American society for progress, expansion, and elimination of the "unfit." Saving for future investment was the prime requisite for the achievement of this aim, and such saving was most easily arranged under a system of high profits and low wages.

The transition to twentieth century conditions of big organizations, minute labor specialization, greater mechanization, and unused savings broke down the old situation and the old rationale. The employing official in the big company was a career man trying to make a reputation for efficiency as measured by the balance sheet. With capital no longer "scarce," low wages advanced only the interests of this official, not those of society in general. New managerial devices and new slogans were needed if morale was to be maintained, but management refused to believe that recognition of the A.F. of L. was the proper solution.

Pro-union employers were largely confined to lines like building and public contracting, in which local unionization affected all companies equally and outside competition was nonexistent, or to industries like workmen's clothing and equipment, where the customers were union men. The great majority of employers,

---

[12] *Industrial Commission*, 1901, vol. VII, p. 352.

especially those selling in the national market, feared the effects of unequal application of union standards and felt that they must resist unionization in their plants until all their competitors had been forced to submit. The traveling delegate, the spearhead of the union drive, was naturally seen as a prime business menace. As President Fry of the National Glass Company saw it, the unions were managed by demagogues: "They are generally too lazy to work themselves and want what they call a snap or easy position." Such unions, he thought, robbed the workers of independence and character.[13] This fear of the national unions reached such heights among employers like the shoe manufacturers of Marlboro, Massachusetts, that they shut down their plants for almost two years and practically ruined themselves rather than accept unionization.

Really big business organizations like the "trusts," which in general used the most highly mechanized processes, had little trouble winning their own labor battles unassisted by any outside organizations. But among smaller industrialists national union drives could be countered effectively only by national employer associations. Such organizations, sometimes superseding older regional associations, began to appear in the middle eighties paralleling the growing influence of the Knights of Labor and the new A.F. of L. From then on the number and complexity of such bodies steadily increased. Employers, free from worries about dualism and additional dues, could well afford to belong to their own industrial association, the League for Industrial Rights and the National Association of Manufacturers. All could be counted on to cooperate in case of labor troubles.

The great upswing in A.F. of L. membership from 275,000 in 1898 to 1,675,000 in 1904 spread consternation among small employers, many of whom were already suffering from the pressure of semi-monopolistic competitors. Secret "Citizens Alliances" arose throughout the Middle West in 1902 and 1903 to prevent unionism from invading the smaller cities. David M. Parry, the president of the National Association of Manufacturers, coordinated these local bodies into the Citizens Industrial Associa-

---

[13] *Industrial Commission*, 1901, vol. VII, p. 101.

tion, with a special educational bureau, and carried on such a vigorous anti-union campaign that the A.F. of L. ceased to expand in the country as a whole and actually began to lose members in the small-city areas. Many forces aided the N.A.M. in these outlying centers. National unionism threatened local autonomy and custom; A.F. of L. locals, especially in the building trades, often fell under control of bosses allied with corrupt politics and racketeering; unskilled and Negro workers resented the exclusiveness of the Federation and made up an adequate non-union labor force.

The checking of union growth, and the consequent swing of the A.F. of L. toward political action made progressive legislative programs now appear as the chief danger to business. Accordingly the N.A.M. focused its attention more closely on state politics in particular, and scored notable successes in blocking legislation. President Kirby advised the members of the N.A.M. convention of 1909: [14]

If you have a batch of bad bills before your legislature and can arrange with your committee for a general hearing and will request Mr. Emery to come and appear before the committee he will be glad to do it, and I can assure you that no objectionable bill will pass through the hands of any committee after Mr. Emery has had a chance to tell them what it is. If he gets a chance at them I will promise you the bill is dead from that moment.

And a Mr. Hatch of Indiana testified that this was no exaggeration: [15]

In the recent legislative session in Indiana we had both houses in the hands of the opposing party, and I think the largest list of malicious class bills ever presented. The general subjects might be classed under employer's liability, master and servant, assumption of risks, fellow servants, our old friend anti-injunction, aesthetics and hygiene in factories, and everything of that kind, and we thought we were up against it; but through the insistent persistence of Mr. Emery we were able to prevent every one of those bills from going to the Governor.

This James A. Emery, a man little celebrated by historians, was unquestionably one of the great lobbyists of the twentieth

---

[14] Bonnett, *Employers' Associations*, p. 313.
[15] Bonnett, *Employers' Associations*, pp. 313–314.

century. Aided by Daniel Davenport, legislative counsel of the League for Industrial Rights, he did much to perfect pressure-group techniques. In the Republican Convention of 1908, for example, the Resolutions Committee adopted a plank pledging the party to legislation protecting labor from arbitrary injunctions and Sherman Anti-Trust Law prosecutions, but hastily rescinded its action when Emery engineered a flood of thirty or forty thousand telegrams of protest daily.[16] *American Industries,* the magazine of the N.A.M., boasted that these two men, Emery and Davenport, were able for the period 1902 to 1912 to secure the defeat of practically all bills urged for enactment by the officials of the A.F. of L.[17]

The N.A.M. was, of course, more than an anti-labor organization. It was interested in protecting its members from all menaces to orderly and traditional methods of profit making, and in securing all possible aid for small and medium-sized business. Hence the cutthroat employer who paid wages below those that would attract workers in most areas met the condemnation of the association. Voluntary adoption of safety devices, workmen's compensation, and other ameliorative devices were urged upon members in order to remove the necessity for state regulatory laws. In fact the association affirmed over and over again that it was not anti-labor or even anti-union, but merely opposed to the bad practices of American unions.

But neither the educational nor the lobbying efforts of the N.A.M. and other business groups were sufficient to prevent organized reformers from pushing labor legislation through the state legislatures. In spite of the opposition or apathy of the A.F. of L., which professed to fear state action, laws regulating hours of labor and workmen's compensation were passed in state after state after 1900. But at this juncture the courts came to the aid of business and imposed effective barriers to such regulation. Limitation of hours violated the constitutional guarantee of "freedom of contract," and the courts were loath to admit that public health was involved sufficiently to justify such extensions of state police power. Not until 1908 was a general state

---

[16] Bonnett, *Employers' Associations,* pp. 325, 326.
[17] Bonnett, *Employers' Associations,* p. 456.

ten-hour law for women upheld by the United States Supreme
Court, and then only after an exhaustive and masterly brief by
Louis D. Brandeis had persuaded a majority of the justices that
public health really was involved. Finally in 1917, in *Bunting* v.
Oregon, Mr. Justice Holmes spoke for a majority of the court
in sustaining a ten-hour law for men on the grounds of public
health and the general practice of civilized nations. But at the
end of the World War there were still five states without any
regulation of hours of labor.

A more serious judicial barrier was that imposed against
workmen's compensation laws. Mining, railroads, and high-speed
factories produced a bloody industrial warfare between workers
and machines. The boom from 1903 to 1907, and the employment of thousands of new immigrant workers, brought American
industrial accidents to an all-time high for any country, yet prior
to 1910 provisions for safety in the factory, other than fire protection, were negligible.[18] There was no practical way in which the
worker could safeguard himself or his family. Personal accident
insurance was too costly for the average worker, and the common-
law doctrines of "assumption of risk," "contributory negligence,"
and "fellow servant" responsibility kept him from collecting from
his employer even if he could meet the expense of legal action.
With Germany leading the way in 1884, the nations of Europe
had met this problem by compelling the employer to take out
insurance; but in America the state laws for that purpose, passed
from 1902 on, were held to involve deprivation of property
without due process of law and to violate "freedom of contract."
The adoption of a limited compensation law for federal employees in 1908 and the investigation of the subject by some
thirty state commissions between 1909 and 1913 finally aroused
business to the necessity of voluntary action if compulsory legislation was to be successfully resisted. United States Steel, for
example, which had paid nothing or only the equivalent of funeral
expenses in the case of most married workers' deaths, made it a
policy in 1910 to pay one and one half to three years' wages to the
dependents.[19] Thus, while the Supreme Court adhered to its

---

[18] *History of Labor,* vol. III, pp. 319, 366.
[19] Fitch, *Steel Workers,* pp. 196–197.

former attitude up to 1917, the passage of the state laws doubt-less stimulated the movement for safer factories and adequate compensation.

But the courts prior to 1936 never relaxed their rigorous *laissez faire* attitude sufficiently to allow such European antidotes to bad income distribution as old-age pensions, health and un-employment insurance, and maternity benefits. In defense of the tardiness of American humanitarianism it was urged that our higher standard of wages allowed workers to save money with which to regulate these matters for themselves. Confronted with the figures, most executives would have had to admit that the average worker did not receive enough to keep up with the "American standard of living" and still have any adequate sum left over for saving. Yet the outgrown morality of thrift and personal self-sufficiency so dominated these community leaders that they truly felt that the whole structure of society would be menaced by facing the facts—just as it was, in truth, menaced by not facing them.

WELFARE CAPITALISM

American entrepreneurs after 1865, absorbed in the problems of expanding markets, new construction, and falling prices, had always given too little attention to improving shop methods, handling materials, or increasing labor efficiency. And judged by continental European standards American plant management by the 1890's was backward. In the twentieth century, however, thoughtful American businessmen, assaulted by both labor and middle-class organizations, condemned by muckrakers, and badg-ered by comparisons with the more efficient managers of Europe, became increasingly aware of bad working conditions, low em-ployee morale, and haphazard shop methods.

That these problems now received new attention is shown by the publishing of two hundred and forty volumes on business management between 1900 and 1910 and the founding of the Harvard Graduate School of Business Administration in 1908.[20]

---

[20] *History of Labor,* vol. III, pp. 303, 308.

Best known among the students of efficiency was Frederick W. Taylor, originator of time and motion studies, functional foremanship, and "scientific" adjustment of employee relationships. Inspired by his general findings, up-to-date managers rationalized assembly lines, introduced piecework payment wherever possible, and offered special incentives for speed. The increase in production was often amazing. President Ommer of the Recording and Computing Machines Company wrote in 1917:[21]

> For some time the men on our turret lathes who were turning out standard pieces had been able to average only 190 pieces a day. By time studies we decided it was possible for them to do 375 pieces. We set this standard and the men were able to attain it. . . .
>
> Not long ago we had a style show. . . . The gowns were offered as prizes for excellent work. In this particular case, the effect was so direct and immediate that the output increased 100,000 pieces in two weeks. The girls showed themselves what they could do when they needed to, *and since that time the production has never fallen below these records.*

Similarly the United States Steel Company, in addition to paying by the amount produced, urged on its crews with contests among the various plants. Whether by such contests, rewarded only by prestige, or by the policy of gradual piecework wage cuts, the Steel Company raised production per worker greatly in the early twentieth century.[22]

While sound in theory, and useful in leading to more careful study of production problems, scientific management failed to produce labor harmony. For one thing, the full set-up of the Taylor system was so elaborate that the great majority of managers were never willing to install it completely. Nor was it possible to reduce explosive human relations to scientifically measurable quantities. There was no place *within* the Taylor system for unionism, and experience proved that without it there could be no "scientific," that is equal, contact between individual workers and the boss. To laborers scientific management signified the speed-up, pay reductions, and the breakdown of collective bargaining; and they set their faces against it.

---

[21] *Handling Men*, pp. 47, 52.
[22] Fitch, *Steel Workers*, pp. 185–190.

As early as the nineties a few employers were discovering that nine hours' work under good conditions might produce more than ten, that fatigue might be profitably lessened by rest periods, and that labor turnover might be cut by pleasanter working conditions. They discovered that even expensive welfare work, if intelligently carried on, might pay dividends. Good conditions, special facilities, and short hours not only increased production, but permitted wage cuts. Up to 1908 only some million and a half workers had been affected by new experiments along these lines, but the labor shortage during the World War gave enormous impetus to welfare activities, and the allied study of personnel management.

The first aim of personnel work was to hire the right man; the second, to keep him on the job. For the latter purpose it proved valuable to stimulate the old conditions of personal contact between the "Big Boss" and the worker. President Ommer reported of his 8,000-employee plant: [23]

Our factory workers are, if I may say it, like a happy family. All the girls know me and I know a great many of them by name. I want them to feel at home with me.

Hundreds of companies set up personnel departments during the war period, and applied aptitude tests to prospective employees. Labor turnover and its causes received scientific study, and in the five years after the war 2,750 volumes appeared on personnel administration.[24] While the depression of 1921 and 1922 and the reappearance of a labor surplus caused many managers to lose interest, the best features of both scientific shop procedure, and personnel selection had meanwhile been incorporated into American business policy.

Profit sharing and stock purchase at rates below the market were other devices used to speed work, indoctrinate employees, and reduce turnover. Many companies found these devices worked well with foremen or administrators, but failed when applied to labor as a whole. The usual worker reaction was that if the company could distribute profits it could afford to pay higher

---

[23] *Handling Men*, p. 51.
[24] *History of Labor*, vol. III, p. 330.

wages, and that the higher wages were preferable to an unpredictable annual bonus. Unfortunately many companies could not resist the temptation to cut basic wages if large profits were being distributed, to take back with one hand what they gave with the other. Stock purchase plans failed to benefit greatly the average worker, as he simply lacked the resources for investing any considerable amount. Furthermore, the various schemes usually diminished the worker's freedom by making it necessary for him to remain with the company if he were to profit from the special arrangements.

Welfare work, profit sharing, and stock distribution all impeded the spread of national trade unionism, but a still more positive check was unionization by order of the company itself. In 1904 the Nernst Lamp and American Rolling Mill companies led the way in setting up shop councils to represent their employees. As other companies adopted similar plans with added features, the form of the company union began to emerge. By 1912 an administrative "expert," John Leitch, had gone into the business of selling to executives with a taste for high-sounding names and elaborate ceremonies a ready-made union plan known as Industrial Democracy. The Rockefeller union, established at the Colorado Fuel and Iron Company after the bloody strike of 1914, and a careful study by the Rockefeller Foundation set a pattern for the modern company union. But it was the World War that gave the great impetus to shop representation plans. Since the government demanded that the war industries bargain collectively with their employees, it was a case of setting up a company union or else having the A.F. of L. establish itself in the plant. Led by General Electric some hundred and twenty-five large companies met the wartime situation by forming their own unions. At first Samuel Gompers felt that creation of such company organizations might be the first step toward trade unionism, but by 1919 the A.F. of L. realized its mistake.

Many business leaders never were convinced of the value of welfare expenditures. One prominent executive wrote in 1917:[25]

Profit sharing is probably impotent in its direct effects to stimulate output. While the workman may hope that everybody will work hard enough

---

[25] *Handling Men*, p. 154.

to increase his share of the profits, he hardly grasps the point of his working harder to increase everybody's share. It is beyond his field of vision.

The average manager, harassed by cost accounting and the demands of directors for maximum profits, feared to lay out money for welfare policies unless they would surely show some immediate return. Although many employers subscribed to the abstract theory that high wages were good for the economy as a whole, both traditional training and the demands of the market worked against the payment of wages higher than those necessary to secure the needed labor or to hold off union organizers.

Approached by management with larger production at less cost as the ruling consideration, welfare programs defeated themselves. The workers soon found that profit sharing and special rewards were accompanied by the speed-up and wage cuts, that better factories, houses, and sanitation were accompanied by surveillance and antiunion drives, that stock sales at special rates were accompanied by provisions binding the beneficiary to the company. Thus the workers became suspicious of all new techniques introduced by management. Workers soon learned that company unionism gave no true representation since the delegates who did the bargaining were paid by the employer rather than their own constituents. Nor would any employers, save a handful of "eccentrics" like Edward Filene, permit any labor participation in managerial decisions.

Here was the real crux of the failure of management and labor to reach a generally satisfactory relationship. The native American worker was educated in the schools and in his political and social life to think in terms of democracy. From this environment he brought to his job the idea that the majority should control, that each worker should be represented when decisions were made. Business on the other hand had been built around the tradition of leadership, the ideal of the vigorous, strong-willed, decisive entrepreneur. Strict obedience to authority from above and a free hand for the man at the helm was as much the rule of business as of the army or navy. Nor was it easy to see how industrial democracy would function even if it could be instituted. There was the essential conflict between wage costs and profits in meeting market prices. There was the conflict between expansion policies on the one hand, as against either pay increases or dividend payments on the other. Only an "impartial" judge could pretend to pass upon a "fair" adjustment of these factors, and where was such a judge to be found? The political state with its democratic control and need for conciliating mass constituents could hardly provide impartial tribunals from the standpoint of management. Labor trouble, therefore, represented merely one aspect of the broader conflict between social-democratic theory and the ideal of free business enterprise.

XII

INDUSTRY AND THE CITY

IN THE decades of prodigious expansion, when the United States teemed with economic opportunities and capital was almost always scarce, American businessmen had no use for humanitarian labor policies that seemed more costly than efficient. Likewise, they had no use for expensive urban improvements and city planning that seemed to offer gains only in aesthetics and health at the cost of higher taxes. The city is the home of modern industry in the United States as well as in Europe. And in so far as American culture has been a business culture it has found its most profound expression in our cities. American farmers have lived off city markets, American workers have lived off jobs in the cities, American factories have found their labor and their leaders here, and American artists of every kind, when they have found patronage, have found it in the cities. Cities have been the centers of wealth and fashion, poverty and disease from the times of Memphis, Athens, and Alexandria to the days of London, Paris, and New York. The intelligent and ambitious of every culture have come to seek their fortunes there. In industrial America they made the city the symbol of intense competition, of heightened individualism in business matters and uniform failure in most aspects of community life. One of Henry Blake Fuller's characters said of Chicago in 1895:[1]

This town of ours is the only great city in the world to which all its citizens have come for the common avowed object of making money. There you have its genesis, its growth, its end and object; and there are but few of us who are not attending to that object very strictly. In this Garden City of ours everyone cultivates his own little bed and his neighbor his; but who looks after the paths between? They have become a kind of No Man's Land and the weeds of rank iniquity are fast choking them up.

---

[1] Fuller, *With the Procession*, p. 248.

"The city is the nerve center of our civilization. It is also the storm center," wrote Josiah Strong, in 1885. And he continued: [2]

Dives and Lazarus are brought face to face; here, in sharp contrast, are the *ennui* of surfeit and the desperation of starvation. The rich are richer, and the poor are poorer, in the city than elsewhere; and, as a rule, the greater the city, the greater are the riches of the rich and the poverty of the poor.

In the cities, the problems of our culture have been intensified. If the United States grew rapidly in the industrial age, our cities grew many times as fast. If business conditions, from time to time, threw the nation into the depths of depression, in the cities social distress was most acute; and in times of prosperity extravagance and luxury were more prominent in the cities than anywhere else. Mines, forests, and fertile fields have paid fabulous tribute to absentee owners in the cities, but the increment in the value of city land has also yielded great returns, and city dwellers through rent, service charges, and the general cost of living have contributed a steadily greater portion to the income of urban business. The first great American fortune—that of the Astors—was accumulated mainly through rising land values in New York. Other great fortunes have also been made through this source, that of Marshall Field in Chicago being a notable example. Yet for every success in city real estate as well as in every other branch of city life, there have been scores of failures; and, even for those who managed to survive, hardships have been multiplied. Problems of growing traffic, congestion in living and working areas, problems of parks and housing, leisure and crime, poverty and disease—all these continued to be neglected by intensely individualistic urban communities in the age of industrial expansion. And city governments, through which amelioration of the worst conditions might have been sought, were always more corrupt and inefficient in this age than state or federal government in the United States and more corrupt than city governments anywhere else in the western world.

The concentration of wealth and power in a few metropolitan areas meant that economic life in many American cities was con-

---

[2] Strong, *Our Country,* pp. 179, 181–182.

trolled from afar by absentee directors who lived in security and comfort in one region while utterly neglecting civic responsibilities in places where their corporations owned factories, railroads, or power plants. This concentration of wealth and power also meant that painters, writers, journalists, and educators seeking the patronage of the rich and powerful were drawn in ever increasing numbers to the great cities, which thus exerted a powerful cultural influence upon the whole country. Just as our national business leaders directed our economy from places like New York or Chicago, so our nationally important newspapers, magazines, schoolbooks, and fiction originated almost exclusively in one metropolis or another. America, once a nation of farmers and small shopkeepers, agrarian in politics and provincial in spirit, had become by 1900 a land of big cities connected with one another by railroad, telegraph, and telephone and dominant in our national life.

THE FAÇADE OF BUSINESS CULTURE

Architecturally, the American city represented a national failure. In building a new urban world in the age of great industrial expansion, American businessmen created only a series of ugly barracks, containing indiscriminately factories, stores, workers, and employers. As Lord Bryce said, "American cities differ from one another only herein, that some are built more with brick than wood, and others more with wood than brick." [3] American architecture, to be sure, was no worse in the latter part of the nineteenth century than that of Europe. But being richer and comparatively unencumbered by the dead hand of the past both in existing buildings and in outworn traditions, Americans probably had the greater opportunity for successful innovation. That they failed to use it is apparent at every turn, but nowhere more apparent than in the widespread application of old styles of church architecture like Gothic and Romanesque to small houses and large business buildings. This produced a veritable parody on architecture that perhaps reached its climax in the three-story

---

[3] Bryce, *American Commonwealth*, vol. II, p. 686.

Victorian-Gothic railroad stations that dotted English and American landscapes alike.

Occasionally, in the hands of masters like Hunt, Richardson, and McKim, old styles were applied successfully in the construction of public buildings or large private mansions, where low cost was not the ultimate aim. But the ordinary architect-builder in the Gilded Age succeeded only in revealing his own lack of imagination and the philistinism of his client. On the whole, the buildings were worse in the small cities where less congestion made land cheaper and larger plots gave "architects" more scope. Here they could erect detached monstrosities characterized by Bill Nye as products of "mental hallucination and morbid delirium tremens," whereas the demands of solid block construction in metropolitan areas at least required plain uniformity and resulted mainly in drabness. One has only to compare the largely unembellished rows of brownstone or brick houses in New York, Philadelphia, or Baltimore with the detached dwellings of near-by Paterson, Trenton, or Norristown to judge the bankruptcy of average small-city architects who had money to spend and large open spaces to adorn.

The saving uniformity of style in large cities, however, mirrored another curse of construction undertaken simply with a view to market considerations. This was the standard-size lot. Usually twenty or twenty-five feet by a hundred, this lot dictated the proportions of almost every building. Even when the same owner erected a whole block of tenements or middle-class houses, he would erect them as a series of lot-size units so that they could be sold separately if desired, without violating any of the established real estate customs. Hence all the advantages of large-scale design for the apportionment of light and air or the achievement of larger architectural unity were thrown away, despite the complaints of some of the better architects and intelligent city planners.

In farming or factory production, maximum profit and maximum social efficiency may in the long run be closely allied. In city building and city planning, however, and in many other social activities, they are in conflict. A city planned and directed for social efficiency would have to be built directly contrary to the interests of real estate speculators, railroad companies, and certain retail interests. The most densely populated sections where land values would be highest, would at the same time require the broadest streets to accommodate heavy traffic, the largest parks and the greatest number of them, the most liberal provision for light and air. They would require the setting aside of valuable property for communal uses in non-profit developments, for recreation, for general health and protection from disease. In America, until well into the twentieth century, these considerations were ignored by businessmen who, in their quest for maximum returns from minimum costs, saw no need for long-range planning and built on every available foot of ground. When intelligent plans were early adopted, as in Chicago, Cincinnati, or St. Louis before the Civil War, land set aside for public use had been given up "to the realty gambler before half the 19th century was over." [4] And thereafter, in those places as in Manhattan, when there was any plan it was the gridiron plan, according to which, as Lewis Mumford says, "every street becomes a thoroughfare, and . . . every thoroughfare is potentially a commercial street." "The tendency towards movement in such a city," he continues, "vastly outweighs the tendency towards settlement. . . . The rectangular parcelling of ground promoted speculation in land-units and the ready interchange of real property: it had no relation whatever to the essential purposes for which a city exists." [5]

Urban congestion feeds upon itself. We have already seen what forces were at work constantly making big cities bigger.[6] Within each great metropolis similar forces were operative. As a section became thickly populated, greater and greater utility enterprises brought water, gas, and electricity; more and more transportation arteries were directed there; and increasing numbers of businesses flocked there to take advantage of constantly improved facilities. Eventually, neighboring residential regions were overrun, land values soared, and more and more intensive construction had to be undertaken in order to pay for higher

---

[4] Mumford in Stearns, *Civilization in the United States*, p. 8.
[5] Mumford in Stearns, *Civilization in the United States*, pp. 7–8.
[6] See Chap. VII, pp. 152 f.

taxes and service charges. Under such pressures, private dwellings that had accommodated single families were remodeled into tenements that housed eight or twelve, or else were destroyed to make room for warehouses, office buildings, and factories. Living conditions steadily deteriorated in such regions, and those who could afford to, moved away. Thus many industrial and white-collar workers were pushed steadily farther from their working places, often into cheaper and poorer regions, while richer employees or employers found their way into ramifying suburbia. The areas of our cities were constantly increased by this outward flow of population, until in the twentieth century many of our urban centers "melted" into one another, forming enormous metropolitan regions like those around New York, Philadelphia, Chicago, or Los Angeles. Workers' transportation costs multiplied, time spent in transit grew steadily, and the noise, dirt, and congestion of subways, "els" and streetcars took their toll of energy and health.

As great as was the movement of population to the peripheries of our cities, however, it was never greater than the influx into the cities from outside. Thus, while the nineteenth century "growth" had a decentralizing tendency, congestion continued to increase. The result was that land values grew higher all the time and utilization of land became always more intensive. So dense, in the end, was the network of electric, telegraph, and telephone wires, electric cables, elevated structures, and tracks in many cities, so thick was the pall of smoke and soot from factory chimneys and railroad locomotives that ran through many important streets that the sun shone but dimly in them and artificial light was required day and night. And under the streets was such a complex of water pipes, gas pipes, and sewers that here was a labyrinthine city in itself.

As congestion increased, however, it ultimately forced architects and city governments to adopt attractive and healthful innovations. Overcrowding and inflated land values in central metropolitan areas inevitably "squeezed up" the skyscraper, while the skyscraper itself forced city planners to adopt zoning and setback regulations lest city streets become deep caverns, as dark as mines and stifling for lack of air. The height of buildings in the United States had been slowly increasing since the early sixties, but in the eighties a rapid elevation took place. Ten- and twelve-story apartment and office buildings became common in New York and Chicago. Supported only by masonry walls, these early "paleotechnic" monsters reached as high as one hundred and fifty feet. As iron beams were introduced to give added support to the lower stories, however, still greater heights were achieved. This marked the beginning of the revolution in building techniques, and the revolution was completed with the construction of the Tacoma Building in Chicago in 1887. This building did not surpass some of the masonry structures in height, but it was the first building in the world with an all-steel framework, thus becoming the genuine prototype of the modern skyscraper.

For the first time since man had started to erect tall buildings he was freed from dependence upon stone support, and the vistas thus opened up must have staggered the imagination of thoughtful architects. For the fifteen years, however, until Louis Sullivan was commissioned to build the Schlesinger-Mayer structure in Chicago, no new departures in design followed the revolution in technology. And after that it was another twenty years before Sullivan's lead was widely followed. Until after the World War almost all buildings were constructed so as to *disguise* the fact that they depended upon steel framework. The trim steel shell was buried under layers of heavy surface stone that had nothing but an ornamental function, and enormous amounts of insipid carved detail obscured the bold simplicity of steel design.

Working in the exciting atmosphere of Chicago, which in 1890 was one of the most congested cities in the country and had just passed Philadelphia as runner-up to New York in size, young Louis Sullivan hoped to achieve a far more difficult goal than the erection simply of taller and taller buildings. He hoped to produce a native American school of ornamentation that might ultimately become the international style of modern industrialism. He sought the profound meaning of the American spirit and the techniques with which to express it in structural plans and ornamentation. Only a few original designs, however, have appeared in the course of ten thousand years of recorded history. Since the fall of the Roman Empire only the Gothic of the Middle Ages has been added. And in America of the late nineteenth century Sullivan was doomed to failure. Industrial America did not yet know its own spirit, and there was nothing for Sullivan to find. He has been called the "Whitman of architects" because of his lyrical faith in the future of the United States. But nowhere could he find in his time the substance of his American ideal, nowhere any real clue as to the form its crystallization in steel and stone should take. Yet Sullivan continued to experiment with designs of native American grains, plants, flowers, and the motif of the wheel, contributing ideas at least to other American architects if not finding the meaning of American life for himself. And in his one large creation in Chicago, the Schlesinger-Mayer building of 1901, Sullivan by his extensive use of glass, at last designed a building which any one could see was not supported by stone. His emphasis on horizontal layers has been followed in countless office buildings, schools, and warehouses to this day. He inspired Frank Lloyd Wright to experiment with the simple horizontal designs that won him international acclaim.

PROSPERITY OF THE "UPPER HALF"

One of the most striking results of industrial enterprise after the American Civil War was the great increase in the numbers and wealth of the middle and upper classes. Prosperous merchants and planters of an earlier day who, with incomes of ten or twenty thousand dollars a year, had set modest standards of elegance and public virtue, were overwhelmed by new industrial magnates and railroad barons with annual incomes of from fifty thousand to a million dollars. An entirely new upper class of "self-made" men was created within a generation, and so rapid was their ascent to power that few members of this class received any training in the social responsibilities of great wealth. The very qualities that brought them financial success were such as to make them least concerned with social welfare, and thus they never developed the imagination and breadth of view necessary to a benevolent ruling class. The result was that most of these businessmen shirked their social responsibilities or delegated them to underlings who dared not risk any innovations or unorthodoxies—a situation deadly to the patronage of living art as well as to education and politics.

Except for the construction of a few lavish country estates, the disposal of these great new fortunes was an urban phenomenon. Some millionaires like Rockefeller or Carnegie followed the paternalistic pattern of feudal lords by investing in libraries, universities, research foundations, and other enterprises where dividends took the form of public esteem. The great majority of the *nouveaux riches*, however, kept their investments on a business basis except for expenditures on "conspicuous living"— usually dictated by the social ambitions of wives and families. "Conspicuous living" reached absurd heights in the United States during the "gay nineties"—a decade marked on the other hand by five years of depression and widespread unemployment. Entertainments such as the notorious Bradley-Martin ball occurred in this period while upper Fifth Avenue in New York City was lined by grandiose palaces that rivaled those of titled families of Europe. High-priced architects like McKim, Meade, and White studiously reproduced ancient forms in limestone and marble, while some millionaires like Morgan and Frick decorated interiors with the most costly art treasures.

Rich Americans spent more money on art during the thirty years from 1880 to 1910 than had ever been spent by a similar group in the world's history. Painting, sculpture, and allied disciplines, however, languished in the United States from lack of appreciation and subsidy since most of this expenditure went to purchase the "gilt-edge securities" of foreign art. Works of technical brilliance alone, like those the Spaniard Fortuny, brought prices in the late 1890's up to forty-two thousand dollars, while among American painters only George Inness was sufficiently popular to receive ten thousand dollars for one picture. Most of his works sold for less than five thousand, and the works of few other Americans brought even that much.[7] One reason for this was that the millionaires did very little purchasing for

[7] *American Art Annual*, vols. I–III.

themselves. Collecting was entrusted to agents or dealers who, like the shrewd businessmen they were, sought maximum commissions by handling only the most reliable goods at the highest possible prices. Comparatively unknown American artists, therefore, had little chance to sell their works, for they had scant access to the market.

There was, to be sure, a small cultured group in the upper middle class made up of successful professional men, lesser executives, and their wives, that was interested in the American spirit and its representation in stone or oil, in sculpture or painting. But while this class grew steadily in size its *surplus* wealth was small, its outlook conservative, and its purchases, therefore, modest and mainly along traditional lines. In the end its influence was to straiten creative expression rather than to stimulate it, and artistic young men who refused to exercise their talents by building railroads, operating mines, or buying and selling securities, and who chose to pursue other than the literary muses, had a hard time in the United States. Even when they found a potential market, they could satisfy it only by compromising with their spirit and checking any experimentation in technique. No wonder most of them fled to Paris or turned, bitter and depressed, to other occupations.

In literature and in the theatrical arts, the conditions for success were somewhat better in the United States. Books or plays were much cheaper than painting or statuary, and as the leisured groups, especially among women, grew in size, they spent more and more time reading and attending the theater in large cities. Public taste was almost as restricted in these fields as in the fine arts, but the symbolism was simpler, actual social conflicts could be popularly dramatized, and a vicarious participation in exciting events could be had at little cost. And as experience with books increased, taste gradually improved and gifted novelists like Hamlin Garland, Frank Norris, Jack London, Stephen Crane, Edith Wharton, and Theodore Dreiser found adequate markets for their works. As the trend toward monopoly led to more and more frequent questioning of the value and validity of traditional American ideals, most of these writers helped maintain a continuous attack upon railroad corporations, investment bankers, great land companies, grain brokers, monopolists of public services. Novels, and to a lesser extent plays, gradually became vehicles of social protest, and as such they attracted many readers or spectators who had no genuine interest in art but were harassed every day by the problems with which literary artists dealt, and to which they seemed to offer solutions.

Industrial cities greatly increased the menaces to family life that had been alarming social critics as early as the 1830's. A large number of children was not an economic asset in the city, particularly among the upper classes where the wage labor of women and children was taboo. And as the family as a productive unit declined in importance, its social stability was also reduced. City hotels, restaurants, and boarding houses offered substitutes for family living, and as houses of prostitution flourished in almost all cities, patronized by many members of the "best families" as well as the lower classes, many women at least believed the incentive to establishing respectable homes was reduced and the creation of legitimate families was retarded. Though the middle-class home survived despite these conditions, its functions were profoundly altered as higher incomes and cheap immigrant servants gave the mother and daughters of the household a chance to spend more time in outside activities. Thus the whole organization of family life was changed, the home became less and less the center of social functions, and upper-class women began to take a much more active part in American life outside the home itself.

Similar developments took place in England, Germany, and other industrial nations, but a force peculiar to America made this change much more important here. This force was the frontier tradition in relation to the respect and privileges accorded to women. Women were scarce in the pioneer West and on the rugged frontier they alone were able to preserve some semblance of the amenities of life that busy empire builders completely neglected. Thus they were conceded a natural supremacy in all matters relating to taste, manners, and the arts. They were made themselves the symbols of conspicuous leisure by men too busy to indulge in it. Even in older centers that had long ceased to be affected by frontier conditions, these attitudes and habits persisted. The ordinary businessman, his mind full of plans for expansion and progress, made no pretense of leadership in the fine arts or the social and cultural life of his family and community. Such matters were for the entertainment of the ladies, and the ladies were left to set cultural standards. As upper middleclass families became smaller and the tasks of the home were relegated to servants, however, women refused any longer to confine their activities to the harmless cultivation of poetry or music; given money and leisure in the cities, they expanded their interests to the larger areas of politics and social reform. The American woman, whom Thomas Beer called the "Titaness" and whom cultured Europeans looked upon with amazement not unmixed with horror, thus began to assert her rights to an equal partnership with men in society.[8] Women's humanitarian, temperance, suffrage, and equal-rights movements, as we shall see, gained momentum, and the General Federation of Women's Clubs, formed in 1889, became a force to be reckoned with by politicians and business leaders.[9]

For the young men of the upper middle class, larger family incomes meant the possibility of prolonged education either at home or abroad. Many of them took advantage of the opportunity, and American cultural life was enriched by their experiences. German-trained scholars like Richard Ely, Simon Patten, Herbert B. Adams, and Edwin Seligman brought back new conceptions of "social science" and helped to "Germanize" American colleges, while graduates of the Ecole des Beaux Arts like Richardson and Hunt carried the higher learning into the arts. Johns Hopkins and Harvard universities pioneered in duplicating the European system of graduate education in the United States, and they were soon joined by a score of other universities. The general enthusiasm for organized learning manifested itself in such diverse forms as the great Chautauqua movement for adult education, and the formation of learned societies such as the American Historical Association in 1884 and the American Economics Association in 1885. The endowments of these gradu-

---

[8] Beer, *Mauve Decade*, pp. 17-65.
[9] See chap. XIII, pp. 277 ff.

ate schools, libraries, scientific publications, and the entire organization of higher learning were the products of expanding industrialism, the contributions of industrial business.

HOW THE OTHER HALF LIVED

There can be no question that during the fifty years from 1865 to 1915 the standard of living for *all* classes in the United States was apparently on the up-grade. Nor can there be any doubt that the upper third of American society was, from every material standpoint, enjoying a richer and more varied existence. But for the other two-thirds, including most of the farmers and manual workers, the real improvement, if any, is hard to estimate.

As prices declined from 1865 to 1898 real wages for unskilled labor rose, as we have seen, because of a remarkable rigidity in wage rates.[10] Meanwhile, because of such factors as scarcity and unionization, even money wages for skilled labor tended to advance. From 1898 to 1915, however, the trends were reversed. As prices rose, wages failed to keep pace and real earnings fell. Despite an increase in this period of 60 per cent in the per-capita wealth of the United States, therefore, the average worker was perhaps 5 per cent worse off in 1915 than in 1890 in terms of real purchasing power. On basis of these considerations, the year 1890 might be taken as the peak of prosperity before the World War.[11] Yet the census figures for that year present a very disquieting picture. C. B. Spahr estimated that of the 12,-500,000 families in the United States in 1890 11,000,000 received an average annual income of $380.[12] Because farming families had means of subsistence outside their money incomes, this figure is not as alarming as it appears; but it certainly shows a condition far removed from the comfortable assumption that everybody lived well during the period of great industrial expansion. Furthermore, many new anxieties harassed the industrial family. At least a quarter of the urban workers were unemployed for a

---

[10] See chap. XI, p. 234.
[11] Douglas, *Real Wages,* tables, pp. 120, 129, 130, 177 and 178.
[12] Spahr, *Distribution of Wealth,* pp. 127–128.

considerable part of each year. Sometimes the force in a plant might vary between 200 and 1,000 with the seasonal demand for its product. In bad years there was always the danger of no employment at all.

Steady income, however, is only one of many factors to be considered in estimating a standard of living. One has to take account, for example, not only of how much money a man makes in relation to prices, but also what satisfactions are available, even regardless of price. Decent housing simply was not on the market for unskilled workers in large cities. No worker could buy proper light, air, and sanitation if such things did not exist in the parts of the city available to him. Nor could he buy healthful or safe conditions of work where they did not exist. According to the Lynds,[13]

a superintendent in a leading plant employing 200 men in 1890, when asked if working conditions gave rise to a good many accidents, exclaimed:
"I should say they did! We kept a horse and buggy busy all the time taking men from the plant to the doctor."
"Not literally, of course?"
"No, not literally, but we used to have one most every day."

Yet conditions on the job where a man spent the majority of his waking hours were certainly a very important part of his standard of living even if his tendency to dramatize himself as really "living" only in his leisure time might obscure the fact.

City work deprived increasing millions of the free and simple amusements of the country where church picnics, spelling bees, harvest festivals, fishing, hunting, and swimming afforded excellent relaxation. The inadequate substitutes that the city could offer for such diversions all were less conducive to health and cost money for admission tickets, rentals, or trolley and subway fares. Thus the city took its toll in diseased and stunted children, lost physical vitality, and worn nerves. By 1870 the infant mortality rate in New York was 65 per cent higher than in 1810, and New York was better off in the matter of disease than southern cities like Memphis, Birmingham or New Orleans.[14]

---

[13] Lynd, *Middletown*, p. 69.
[14] Mumford, *Culture of Cities*, pp. 171–172; Nevins, *Modern America*, p. 323.

Apparently, comfortable or even barely healthful living conditions for the lower third of America's population in the nineteenth century were getting scarcer even as the nation became richer. Yet so strong was the doctrine of progress among the upper and educated classes that even some of the more thoughtful among them could not see what was really happening in America. Andrew Carnegie said in 1887: "I defy any man to show that there is pauperism in the United States." [15] Yet the federal census had such a classification, and even as he spoke destitute farmers in Kansas and Nebraska were actually starving to death. And William Graham Sumner, the great academic exponent of absolute *laissez faire*, could declaim: "It is constantly alleged in vague and declamatory terms that artisans and unskilled labor are in distress and misery or under oppression. No facts to bear out these assertions are offered." [16] One wonders if so erudite a sociologist had failed to read the various books and committee reports on the tenement problem in New York and other large cities. Robert Hunter, in his volume *Poverty*, declared in 1904, after a description of the low standard of living of respectable American city workers: [17]

I have not the slightest doubt that there are in the United States ten million persons in precisely these conditions of poverty, but I am largely guessing and there may be as many as fifteen or twenty million!

Yet his greatest complaint was our lack of knowledge. "But ought we not to know?" he cried. And he continued: [18]

If poverty were due to purely individual causes, it would perhaps be fair to deny the moral necessity of national inquiries at periodical intervals into the condition of all the people and especially of the poor. But no one knowing the many active social causes of individual poverty and misery could deny this necessity in a democracy of professedly Christian people. To neglect even to inquire into our national distress is to be guilty of the grossest moral insensitiveness.

Slum overcrowding was the most spectacular evil of the city in the age of free enterprise, and it is not surprising that our

---

[15] David, *Haymarket Square*, p. 10.
[16] David, *Haymarket Square*, p. 10.
[17] Hunter, *Poverty*, p. 11.
[18] Hunter, *Poverty*, pp. 11–12.

uncontrolled industrial development fostered the worst possible conditions. New York City's Sanitary District "A" in 1894 averaged 986.4 people to the acre for 32 acres; that is, about 30,000 people in a space of five or six city blocks. Bombay, India, possessing the next most crowded area on the surface of the earth could show only 759.7 people per acre and Prague, with the worst slum section in Europe, only 485.4.[19] In the United States, Chicago, Boston, Cincinnati, Cleveland, and many smaller cities had limited areas practically as congested as New York. In little Holyoke, Massachusetts, a town of 11,000 inhabitants in 1870, one block of High Street housed one hundred and five persons in seventeen upstairs rooms—ten people sometimes in one room —yet it was less than a mile to open woods and farm land.[20] Obviously, it was not lack of available space alone that produced slums, but also the natural effort of competing businessmen to collect the maximum rent from valuable land and buildings. The real cause both of slum conditions and of resistance by property owners to the enforcement of any legislation to improve urban housing was that old-style tenements in New York in the eighties, for example, paid their owners an annual profit of 40 per cent.[21]

Socially conscious reformers continuously attacked these conditions in the nineteenth century, but their exposés and agitations for improvement were met by politicians who allayed public discontent by passing laws that either were meaningless in their verbiage or remained unenforced. Such symbolic gestures were the creation of the Board of Health in New York City in 1866 and the enactment of the first of a series of tenement-house laws in 1867. These laws applied only to new buildings and thus made it more difficult for improved houses to compete with the old dilapidated rookeries. A scheme used for generations by organized tenement-house owners and their political representatives was to get reform groups interested in erecting new "model" tenements rather than in attacking existing buildings. When such projects were completed it was usually found that rents had to

<hr>

[19] Ford, *Slums and Housing*, vol. I, p. 187.
[20] Green, *Holyoke*, pp. 115–116.
[21] Ford, *Slums and Housing*, vol. I, p. 166.

be higher than in the old buildings, and hence new accommodations were beyond the reach of any but skilled workers and lower middle-class families. It was not until after 1908 that New York City had any effective tenement regulation. Most other cities were even more tardy in enacting effective measures.

While tenements supplied cheap apartments for the lower classes, for urban society as a whole teeming slums proved very costly. Disease was rife in them, undermining the labor supply and menacing the prosperous classes. Memphis lost almost 10 per cent of its population in 1873 in an epidemic that started in its slums, and the sewage that oozed from the unpaved streets of New Orleans spread typhoid among rich and poor alike.[22] Slums were breeding grounds for criminals of every caliber and thus greatly increased costs for urban police protection. The lack of sanitation facilities in refuse-littered wooden barracks and in the inaccessible alleys between them constituted dangerous fire hazards which raised the costs of insurance and fire control all over the city. In effect, by thus levying heavy charges upon the health and finances of our cities, tenement-house owners for their own benefit were exploiting the rest of the city's population. Yet so unorganized was the average city's populace, and so unaware of the ramifications of all aspects of city life, that it did little to improve conditions.

WHY THE CITIES WERE MISGOVERNED

The mechanics of national politics are usually so well concealed that the actors go through their parts with apparent spontaneity. On the smaller stage of municipal politics, however, the machinery becomes quite obvious, and Lord Bryce, Andrew D. White, Lincoln Steffens, and scores of other critics in the latter part of the nineteenth century raised a chorus of indignation over the shame of municipal government in the United States. Their attitude was clearly expressed by President White of Cornell who wrote in 1890:[23]

---

[22] Nevins, *Modern America*, p. 323.
[23] Schlesinger, *Rise of the City*, p. 392.

> With very few exceptions the city governments of the United States are the worst in Christendom—the most expensive, the most inefficient, and the most corrupt.

After the Civil War politics in the cities even more than in the nation was regarded in the United States merely as incidental to the pursuit of industrial wealth. Important executives of national and international corporations had no time to waste performing local functions which could easily be handled by men who, they thought, could not succeed in business but got along well with the lower classes. As the character of municipal leaders changed accordingly from the days of Edward Livingston and Philip Hone to those of Tweed and Croker, the ambition of respectable middle-class men of principle to mix in apparently sordid affairs became less and less. Occasionally, to be sure, there were exceptions, reformers who rose to temporary power through coalitions of middle-class taxpayers when conditions got intolerably bad. Such reformers were Carter Harrison of Chicago, Seth Low of New York, and Tom Johnson of Cleveland. Each of these men successfully "cleaned up" his city but never for long could he keep it "clean" against the pressure of the old corrupt party machine and its supporters among businessmen who had large amounts of money to spend for elections and special favors like contracts for public works or monopolistic franchises for public utilities. Lincoln Steffens had this finally impressed upon him in Boston, of which he wrote: [24]

> What Boston suggested to me was the idea that business and politics must be one; that it was natural, inevitable, and—possibly—right that business should—by bribery, corruption, or—somehow get and be the government.

While the decline in the character of municipal officers was partly responsible for the increasing corruption of municipal governments, more important was the application of traditional constitutional procedures to administrative functions. Checks and balances in government worked quite satisfactorily where large matters of policy had to be decided, but in municipal government division of powers led only to irresponsibility and buck

[24] Steffens, *Autobiography*, vol. II, p. 606.

passing. The division of authority over the city treasury and the administration of city police power among mayors, department heads, aldermen, councilors, and magistrates simply created situations like that pictured in the famous Nast cartoon showing Tweed and his fellow officeholders standing in a circle, each pointing to his neighbor in answer to the question, "Who stole the people's money?" Furthermore, the practice of *electing* almost all the important city officials often produced administrations that even well intentioned mayors were powerless to control.

But the difficulties in municipal government were more fundamental even than the apparent form of administration. The government of American cities was really conducted by the political machine controlled by a "boss" who held no office, but ran it through his lieutenants and his army of paid machine workers. Here was the core of municipal power. The "boss" was the businessman in politics, the man who set the prices for special favors, sold the franchises, and guaranteed a controlled electorate. He was the man who made it possible to conduct government in the interest of the upper middle class in spite of a great lower-class electorate. He was not unique in the United States. His work was less obvious in England because of his greater respectability and in Germany because of less local democracy. But in English and German cities as well as American, he helped to preserve the established structure of society. Unopposed by well managed machines and efficient party bosses, the eleven million American families with an average income of $380 a year might well have voted themselves all kinds of remedies, well or ill advised, for their relative poverty. They might also have elected such radicals as Henry George or Eugene Debs to municipal offices. Against the bosses, however, such radicals could get nowhere, and the bosses, for their success in reconciling equality at the polls with inequality in property, were allowed their price in graft. A reform movement might prove worth while every now and then to keep the boss in his place, but really to eliminate him was unthinkable.

From his own point of view, the boss's most important task was periodically to "sell" to the electorate his own candidates for municipal offices. This was the key to his success, and his work was made easier in typical American cities by our constantly shifting population and our large numbers of European immigrants. The young men who flocked to the city looking for jobs were neither acquainted with the local political situation nor interested in it. Often they intended to leave as soon as they had made some money, so that the future of the city was no concern of theirs. The immigrant workers drawn to centers like Pittsburgh, Chicago, New York and Philadelphia, lacking all knowledge of local politics or customs, were easily won to the support of the machine by minor favors. Nor was the rule of the boss an unmixed evil. *Sub rosa* he dispensed to the classes denied equal opportunities a justice that made life more tolerable. He became the guardian of the needy and the politically "regular" poor, while a large part of the bill was paid by the middle class.[25]

THE IMPERIALISM OF URBAN CULTURE

The economic triumphs of urban industrialism naturally were accompanied by the victory of city culture over the folkways of village, town, and farm. By 1890 erstwhile "lords of the soil" had become "hayseeds," "bumpkins," and "rubes." Crossroads merchants and yeoman farmers who, a few generations before, had run the United States, now had as little cultural influence as they had economic power. In control were manufacturers, bankers, railroad executives, and corporation lawyers, under whose influence the American people had developed urban modes of dressing, living, speaking, and thinking. General mail order catalogues after 1872 spread city customs while personal contact undoubtedly brought about much of the change. Traveling salesmen, national business executives, and workers visiting their families back home were missionaries of urban culture; and their influence was all the greater because the wealth of city businessmen and the bigness of city affairs gave prestige to all things pertaining to the metropolis. In addition to these subtle, untraceable influences, however, journalism and public education were continuously at work spreading the gospel of the city.

[25] Steffens, *Autobiography,* vol. II, pp. 617–620.

Under the influence of Joseph Pulitzer, E. W. Scripps, and William Randolph Hearst, the drab metropolitan paper of the 1860's and 1870's was transformed into the yellow journal of the nineties with its front-page pictures, color printing, magazine sections, comic strips, sports departments, and women's pages. These journals were read by millions of the lower classes who had never bothered with newspapers before. They helped standardize modes of speech and dress as well as political and social opinion. Under their influence, slang phrases could sweep the country overnight and patterns of thought could be as easily altered as cuts of clothing. These metropolitan newspapers did not circulate widely outside urban areas. By the 1880's, however, S. S. McClure and a number of other farsighted journalists had started syndicates that could supply small-town and country papers everywhere with the same features, telegraph and cable news that appeared in the metropolitan press, and with the same urban bias. Besides, all small-town editors read some of the metropolitan papers and passed their ideas along to the millions of readers outside the big cities.

Another important vehicle for urban culture was the national slick-paper magazine. The original among these was the *Ladies' Home Journal,* edited by Edward Bok after 1889. Bok was the first to show that a ten-cent or fifteen-cent illustrated monthly or weekly, with lively stories, many pictures and clever special features could gain a nation-wide circulation. So successful was he that the venerable *Saturday Evening Post* as well as *McClure's* and *Munsey's* all soon applied the same techniques to magazines of even wider scope. Not only did the poetry and fiction carried by these magazines have to follow a rigid moral code and glorify traditional American ideals, but their advertisements helped standardize the national taste while their editorials contained no opinions that might offend purchasers of expensive space.

The trend from individual to collective enterprise that marked American business after the Civil War was as apparent in journalism as in oil, steel, or railroads though it occurred at a slower rate. By the 1890's city papers came to be published by large corporations for the financial benefit of stockholders and directors. They became primarily profit-making enterprises rather than vehicles of private opinion. And their advertising revenue by 1890 was their most important source of income. Thus journalism took its place in the ranks of Big Business. Soon it was marked by trade associations, combinations, and overcapitalized mergers, and just as control of capital and credit came to be concentrated in the hands of a few city bankers, so influence over opinion came to be concentrated in the hands of a few city journalists.

As early as 1887, the American Newspaper Publishers Association was formed. By 1910 it had become one of the most powerful pressure groups in the country. Not only did it wield direct influence, but it also sponsored organizations like the International Circulation Managers Association in order to achieve better integration in the industry. Newspaper combinations were of two sorts. One type was made up of separately owned papers receiving identical services from organizations like the Inland Press Association. Perhaps more important were the large corporations dominated by men like Scripps, Hearst, or Munsey and owning outright large numbers of papers. E. W. Scripps, the founder of large-scale chain journalism, controlled nine papers in 1900 and twenty-two by 1910. Unlike Hearst, Scripps gave wide discretionary powers to local editors and argued that membership in the chain strengthened rather than weakened their independence. It was true, however, that editors in Scripps's chain as well as Hearst's and smaller chains had ceased to be individual critics and had become, however subtly, the mouthpieces of big corporations directed in most cases from New York or Chicago.

Formal school education, like journalism, has always been a useful device for strengthening the grip of any culture and it was not neglected by urban leaders in the great age of industrial expansion. The use of American schools as bulwarks for the existing order of society is as old as America itself. In the early nineteenth century, as we have seen, New Englanders sought almost from the start of American industrialism to impose the ideals of eastern cities upon the merchants and farmers of the West. After the Civil War similar intentions dominated urban educators in relation not only to farmers but also to city workers. Standard textbooks, written to a large extent by people associated with city schools and distributed by publishing houses in New York, Boston, and Philadelphia were bound to convey urban mores and business ideas, and it early became a matter of policy for educational agencies to see that contrary ideas were shut out. As John Eaton, national Commissioner of Education, pointed out after the railroad strikes of 1877, "the school could train the child to resist the evils of strikes and violence and . . . capital should 'weigh the cost of the mob and the tramp against the expense of universal and sufficient education.' " [26] In 1888 the Reverend A. D. Mayo in a circular of the Bureau of Education urged the organization of southern schools and curricula along such lines that northern capital could be attracted by the dependably educated working classes.[27]

Business led the drive in the late nineteenth century for the training of skilled artisans and mechanics in the public schools and at the public expense. The objective was education for industrial efficiency. As J. B. Taylor wrote in 1900 in the *Educational Review,* "The whole drift of present educational thinking is to produce the efficient man, the man related by forceful needs to the world without." [28] And William H. Maxwell, superintendent of schools in New York City, in 1905 expressed his optimistic approval of such educational objectives. "In a community," he wrote, "in which every man had been trained to his highest efficiency the evils of monopoly and poverty would be alike impossible." [29]

Despite the interest of businessmen and official educators in directing education along carefully chosen lines, outside the South between 1870 and 1910 there were only moderate gains in school attendance. In education as in all other aspects of industrial society, there was great reluctance to plan ahead, to develop institutions or programs the benefits of which were not obvious and immediate. Many businessmen questioned whether any education beyond the three "R's" was a good thing for

---

[26] Curti, *American Educators,* p. 219.
[27] Curti, *American Educators,* pp. 210–211.
[28] Curti, *American Educators,* p. 231.
[29] Curti, *American Educators,* p. 231.

potential industrial workers, whether it would not in the end make them discontented with doing only the menial tasks of industrial society. Many other businessmen balked at the diversion of capital from industry to education, at the taxes necessary to build extensive school systems and to run them efficiently. They were eager to influence the personnel and curricula of existing schools, but in the end their thoughts were mainly on business rather than education, more on the use of urban institutions for immediate economic ends than for future social welfare.

By drawing so many millions into our cities, by forcing reluctant private enterprisers to engage in such communal activities as organizing municipal police, fire and sanitation departments, and schools, the growth of industrialism in the United States helped to weaken American individualism. But it had failed as yet to correct the faults of individualism with better adjusted social ideals. For the economy of the farm, industry had substituted the economy of the factory; for provincialism it had substituted nationalism. For selfish individualism, however, it had as yet failed to find a substitute. As Lincoln Steffens said: [30]

Instead of leading a city or a nation to a career, leaders who won the faith and the votes of the mob used them to make careers for themselves. All leaders do it: captains of industry, doctors and attorneys, editors, priests —all the natural leaders of society are making successes of themselves and so—a failure of democracy. This isn't right. Our ideal is individual, not social, success, and that's what has to be changed, this ideal. We have got to get the leaders to have a more social ideal, and I have come to Boston to develop one in all your leaders here.

[30] Steffens, *Autobiography,* vol. II, p. 616.

XIII

PRESSURE POLITICS IN AN
AGE OF REFORM

BETWEEN 1890 and 1910 the investment bankers controlled more and more of the key industries of the nation, and the ruling oligarchy, as we have seen, became a smaller and more exclusive group. Topped by Morgan and Rockefeller, it included in the end hardly any one but their associates and allies. Almost Jovian in their economic power, these leaders successfully invaded politics and high society. Already a few of them had been admitted to the awesome Knickerbocker Club, while many others had joined the magnificent Metropolitan or the lesser Union League. Mainly vigorous, self-made men still adding to their imperial domains, they were as yet unhampered by incompetent relatives who later were to be installed in important places simply because of family connections. By marrying their daughters to the impoverished nobility of Europe, however, they were giving a monarchic gloss to their democratic fortunes, and by intermarriage among themselves they were retaining the power of those fortunes within the family ranks. In 1910 there were still seats at the top in American business, politics, and society for enterprising and ambitious young men of lower-class origin. There had never been a time in American industrial society, however, when those seats seemed so few and the holders' heritage so important.

As control of the American economy and American politics thus fell into fewer and fewer hands, the number of industrial workers subject to this control became steadily larger. Combination led inexorably to the increasing "bigness" of monopolistic corporations; and "bigness" in capital, plants, and programs meant also "bigness" in labor force. While monopoly, therefore, was to create in a short time grave problems of leadership at the top, it created, almost immediately, equally grave problems of superintendence at the bottom. The labyrinthine financial entanglements of corporations capitalized for hundreds of millions of dollars, and producing innumerable commodities in plants all over the world, required the most complicated systems of cost accounting. In these systems, devoted almost exclusively to considerations of profit and loss, the workingmen had no more claim to special attention than raw materials or machines. In Colorado mines or Alabama factories directed from New York, for instance, workers had no more opportunity to protest to their employers than if they had been made indeed of mute and insensitive copper, iron, cotton, or wood. In smaller industries the situation was not much different, the workers, immigrant and native alike, being set off in clearly marked slums, each year more overcrowded, more vulnerable to disease, more likely to encourage crime or vice among young boys and girls striving to get to the other side of the tracks.

While the growing masses of industrial labor thus were coming to realize the comparative permanence of their status and the leaders of finance were becoming intensely conscious of their own social estate, the fringes of the urban middle class were also becoming clearer, and the composition of the groups within this class was becoming more clearly defined. Made up of smaller industrialists and merchants and their white-collar workers, of men who lived on modest inherited incomes and professional men—ministers, teachers, scholars, lawyers, doctors, writers, and artists, the educated and well born and their leisured wives— this class had no unity, but its members suffered in common the fear of having their independence abridged by monopolizing Titans from above or else engulfed by a surge of socialism from the ranks of labor below. Truly conservative, they opposed equally the collectivism of great trusts and the collectivism of trade unions; and they shared a profound belief in free capitalism, equal economic opportunity, fair trade practices and the protection of property. Inheritors of the victory of the English Parliament over the Stuart kings, they insisted also upon the supremacy of laws over men or institutions, and they had a naïve belief in the efficacy of legislation to achieve their ends.

In a society as complex as that in America in the decades around the turn of the century, however, it was one thing to have a set of fixed beliefs and quite another to vote them into effect. And while the Progressive movement was essentially the effort of this urban middle class together with the yeoman farmers of the West to escape subservience on the one hand to great capitalists and on the other to the great mass of workers, the attempt to do so through legislation had some unexpected results. The attacks upon the railroads, the industrial trusts, the monopolists of currency and credit, and the despoilers of the public domain won vigorous support from the middle class. The attempt to end the threat of revolution from below, however, by ameliorating the conditions under which labor worked and lived, sundered this class. Child labor was the source of profits in many industries, large and small. So were long hours and cheap female labor. The installation of protective devices in factories was costly, as were contributions to pension funds for aging or injured employees. Many factories had poor lighting, ventilation, and sanitation, and many more were firetraps. But to improve them was expensive, just as it was expensive to remodel old tenements and to limit the number of families that were to occupy them. Not only were slum conditions sources of high profits to tenement owners, but such conditions had been allowed to fester through the systematic cooperation of municipal and state governments. The attack upon the slums, therefore, aroused not only middle-class businessmen but also their political allies. Businessmen and politicians had a horror of socialism. Their devotion to immediate gains, however, was stronger and they determined to protect those gains, whatever the social consequences.

While maturing industrialism was responsible for the growth of many social evils, it was also responsible for producing wealth and leisure for groups that could attack such evils. Ministers, teachers, writers, artists, and thousands of prosperous women had no large financial stake in child and female labor, long hours, sweatshops, saloons, tenements, and slums. Long before 1900, in

England, Germany, Australia, New Zealand, Switzerland, and Holland, such members of the middle class had encountered and had begun to correct similar evils. In America at last they now were prepared to face them. The federal government in the United States attracts the most colorful leaders and handles the most spectacular issues. By the Constitution, however, the federal government was forbidden to deal with most of the problems that directly concern a majority of the people. These problems were left to the states and cities, and it was there that the Progressive movement accomplished its most important results. We have heard much of Roosevelt, Beveridge, and Wilson. Our historians would have been more equitable had they recorded instead the deeds of Jane Addams, Lillian Wald, Sarah Decker, Felix Adler, Robert De Forest, Florence Kelley, the Reverend E. G. Murphy, Robert Hunter, Katherine Edson, Josephine Goldmark, Ben Lindsey, Alice Woodbridge, and Mrs. Charles Russell Lowell. These were the men and women who fought and in many cases defeated the organized business opposition to reform in the states and cities of the nation. Under their leadership the Progressive movement soon took the form of a humanitarian crusade, and they, not the "trust-busters," were our great Progressives.

THE PROGRESSIVES ORGANIZE

Though they were battling for the social, economic, and political rights of man, for the preservation of individual freedom and private initiative, the Progressives were forced to concede to the enemy that only in union was there strength. To conquer the interests arrayed against them they had, like those interests, to organize and combine. Individuals in business could no longer compete with corporations, and individuals in reform could no longer compete with groups of corporations. The strength of Progressivism, therefore, was in its associations, and between 1897 and 1914, Progressive societies multiplied rapidly in number and membership. Child Labor committees, Consumers' leagues, Charities Aid societies, church organizations and women's clubs appeared in all our industrial cities and states and formed national associations with branches everywhere. They employed professional social workers, secretaries, treasurers and sent trained lobbies to state capitals and to Washington. They sent practiced lecturers to address groups all over the country, published their own periodicals, and competed successfully for space in popular journals. Some of these groups started merely as community philanthropic organizations. All of them ended in the van of social movements. Typical, of course, were the women's clubs. At her inaugural as president of the General Federation of Women's Clubs, suffragette Sarah P. Decker said in 1904:[1]

Ladies, you have chosen me your leader. Well, I have an important piece of news for you. Dante is dead. He has been dead for several centuries, and I think it is time that we dropped the study of his inferno and turned attention to our own.

A committee appointed in Illinois by the State Federation of Women's Clubs, aided by the Cook County Child Saving League, had already led the successful fight in that state for the Child Labor Law of 1903. Other branches were soon to fight for similar legislation in New York, California, Colorado, and the South while the Federation itself groomed for specialized activities many members of more parochial associations.

Men suffered most from the harsh conditions of modern industrialism; but the plight of women and children in the factories and on the streets engaged the sympathy of humanitarians to a greater degree, and they became the chief beneficiaries of the Progressive movement. Child labor legislation antedated the twentieth century. As early as 1813 Connecticut had a vague law relating to the education of working children, and by 1899 twenty-eight states (none of them in the South) had some statutory provisions affecting their employment. None of these laws, however, provided adequately for enforcement, and none touched the employment of children outside factories. Most of these laws failed to distinguish between hazardous and safe occupations and accepted the affidavit of a parent as proof that a child had reached the legal minimum age. The hour and educational provi-

---

[1] Filler, *Crusaders for American Liberalism*, p. 261.

sions invited evasion and the exemption of many industries from the operation of the laws nullified even their nuisance value.[2]

In the next decade, however, great progress was made. The "first child labor committee in the United States" was organized in 1901 by the Reverend Edgar G. Murphy, a Protestant Episcopal minister of Montgomery, Alabama. In 1902 the New Jersey Consumers' League and the State Charities Aid Association began a vigorous campaign to close the gaps in existing laws and to tighten up the state inspection. In New York the Child Labor Committee, with Robert Hunter of the University Settlement as chairman, started a similar campaign. In 1904 the National Child Labor Committee was formed with Felix Adler as president and Samuel McCune Lindsay as secretary, and this group made the fight a national one. By 1910, it had working with it twenty-five state and local committees in twenty-two states in addition to the National Consumers' League, the General Federation of Women's Clubs, and the American Federation of Labor. The result was the enactment in forty-three states, between 1902 and 1909, of new child labor laws or far-reaching amendments to old ones. These laws and amendments made for compulsory education, the eight-hour day for children above the minimum age, the abolition of night work.

In its 1901 investigation, the New York Child Labor Committee found that of the state's 1,500,000 children between the ages of five and eighteen 450,000 were not in school. Of these, only one-tenth worked in factories. Of the remainder who were employed, newsboys, bootblacks, peddlers, delivery and messenger boys were protected by no laws whatsoever. The New York Child Labor Act of 1903, therefore, was designed to cover them as well as factory workers. It protected all children employed in a "mercantile establishment, business office or telegraph office, restaurant, hotel, apartment house, or in the distribution or transmission of merchandise or messages." The man who introduced this bill in the Legislature wrote to Robert Hunter that its passage

---

[2] *History of Labor,* vol. III, chap. II.

was due solely to the magnificent campaign waged by you. So thoroughly was the work done that all opposition was silenced through fear of opposing the intelligent public opinion that had been aroused.[3]

Pennsylvania and Delaware soon followed New York with more general laws, Delaware in 1909 being the first to declare directly that "no child under the age of fourteen years shall be employed or suffered to work in any gainful occupation."

Similar progress was made in the regulation of women's working conditions. Such regulations were gradually extended to cover stores and restaurants as well as factories, and under them the working day was reduced from ten to eight hours and the working week from sixty to forty-eight hours. Lobbying vigorously for such legislation and threatening boycotts of recalcitrant companies were the consumers' leagues. In Illinois, however, Florence Kelley and her Hull-House following were the most effective campaigners, while in California, fired by the slogan "Let us be our sisters' keepers," Katherine Edson and her State Federation of Women's Clubs led the fight.[4]

Unlike the child labor laws, the acts regulating hours for women encountered the hostility of the courts. The protection of children was early interpreted as a proper function of the state's police power; the protection of women was deemed interference with the freedom of contract. The decision of the United States Supreme Court in *Muller* v. *Oregon* (1908), however, finally gave judicial sanction to laws affecting women's working conditions, and after 1909 most of the legislative progress in this field was made. In 1908 only thirteen states had laws regulating women's hours; by 1917 all but eight states had such laws.

Progressives everywhere, however, learned early that the enactment of laws was only the first step in eradicating evils. By 1910 detailed statutes had been placed upon the books in many states covering not only child and female labor but also public health, workmen's compensation, minimum wages, and factory and tenement construction, but none of these laws appreciably

---

[3] *History of Labor,* vol. III, p. 407.
[4] *History of Labor,* vol. III, p. 515.

improved the working or living conditions of those who now came under the state's care.

It has been estimated that, around 1900, twenty per cent of the people of New York and Boston had each year to apply to public agencies for some sort of relief.[5] In 1893 more than half the residents of New York were "tenement dwellers," many of them living in houses that paid their owners 25 to 40 per cent profit. In 1903, 14 per cent of the families of Manhattan were evicted from their homes.[6] Each year around the turn of the century, one in every ten persons who died in New York was buried in Potter's Field.[7] New York was typical of all other industrial cities, and neither in New York nor elsewhere were conditions much improved in the next decade.

For some of this distress business could be held responsible. Low wages, irregular employment, unprotected machinery, unsanitary factories, and crowded sweatshops steadily undermined the living conditions of industrial workers. As long as immigrants continued to pour in by the million each year, however, supplying the factories with cheap and docile labor and the slums with uncomplaining tenants, businessmen ignored their responsibilities. Not only did most of them leave the care of their sick and poverty-stricken to philanthropists, but they placed every obstacle in the way of ameliorative activities. To placate aroused and enlightened voters, legislators had to enact laws that were anathema to themselves and their business supporters. They did not, however, have to enforce such laws. And though the Progressive statutes passed in the first decade of the twentieth century steadily improved in quality and scope, appropriations for their enforcement remained as inadequate as ever, inspectors as venal as before, the courts as unsympathetic as old men could be who had been nurtured on the harsh and inadequate doctrines of Spencerian *laissez faire*.

---

[5] Hunter, *Poverty*, pp. 23–24.
[6] Ford, *Slums and Housing*, vol. I, pp. 187–190.
[7] Hunter, *Poverty*, p. 25.

MEETING BUSINESS RESISTANCE IN THE STATES

To combat the activities of the Progressives, middle-class businessmen after 1900 began themselves to organize. Between 1901 and 1905 old associations like the National Metal Trades, the National Founders, the United Typothetae, the National Erectors, and the National Association of Manufacturers became "belligerent" for the first time in their attacks upon social legislation. In 1902 and 1903, to supplement the activities of such groups and the activities of chambers of commerce throughout the country, businessmen also formed the Citizens Industrial Association of America, the Citizens Alliances and the Anti-Boycott Association (later the League for Industrial Rights).[8] When the Progressives sent lobbyists to state capitals, these business organizations fought them with veterans schooled in the art of influencing legislation. If the humanitarians wrote magazine articles and published books, business organizations threatened to have their members remove their advertisements from the magazines, and subsidized books giving their own point of view. Not only did business organizations combat proposed Progressive legislation but they developed positive plans of their own. Men like Daniel Davenport of the Anti-Boycotters and James A. Emery of the N.A.M. became well known in Washington for their zeal in pushing laws for the incorporation of trade unions and for their liability under the Sherman Act.[9] Even when Progressive laws finally were passed by reluctant legislatures, these business associations attacked them, working actively for the repeal of wage and hour laws that had not yet been thrown out by the courts.

The strength of business associations, the enormous wealth they had to call upon, and their growing sophistication in the employment of propaganda and pressure politics, all contributed to the decline of the Progressive movement in the states. Accelerating this decline was the abandonment of Progressivism

---

[8] Bonnett, *Employers' Associations*, p. 24.
[9] Bonnett, *Employers' Associations*, p. 456.

by leaders like Steffens and Upton Sinclair, both of whom became Socialists in the belief that some form of collectivism was unavoidable.[10] Others like Ray Stannard Baker and Ida Tarbell also learned that to reclaim the old age of free competition was impossible, and they abandoned reform for the collectivism of the right, hating socialism with middle-class intensity, preferring the rule of regulated trusts.[11] The depression of 1913–1915 robbed the Progressive movement of the source of most of its funds, and the European war took away the glamour it had had for many once enthusiastic supporters.

Before it surrendered to waning enthusiasm, to the pressure of organized business, and to swelling patriotism, however, the Progressive movement won victories in the years after 1910 that made its earlier gains look small. In 1911 and 1913 many new laws were passed strengthening the education requirements for working children, lowering women's hours still further, and abolishing night work for minors and females. In the same years, the National Consumers' League and its local subsidiaries started the successful drive for minimum wages for women, nine states adopting such laws for the first time. By 1913 also, the Charity Aid societies in twenty-one states had forced the passage of workmen's compensation laws so designed as to close the gaps in previous legislation and to serve as patterns for subsequent acts. But most important of all was the creation in Wisconsin in 1911, and in seven other states by 1915, of special boards to administer the hundreds of laws already on the statute books.

Just as the social problems of mature industrialism were making *laissez faire* untenable, so the enforcement of social legislation was making rigid separation of government powers impossible. To carry on their new work the states had to have new agencies, and with the creation of industrial commissions after 1911 state legislatures began to give administrative bodies in the executive department legislative as well as judicial powers. After creating these commissions the legislatures quit trying to control the details of factory labor administration by passing more and more

---

[10] Steffens, *Autobiography,* vol. II, pp. 631, 634.
[11] Chamberlain, *Farewell to Reform,* pp. 140–141.

specific laws; they quit trying to enforce such laws through inquisitorial inspectors and the courts. Instead, they set up general standards and gave the new commissions broad powers for the maintenance of those standards. Inspectors, instead of acting as policemen, became expert advisers to individual firms.[12] They enforced the detailed specifications made by professional commissions, at the same time developing for the commissions much clearer conceptions than politicians ever could acquire of the needs of both labor and capital. Dealing at first only with problems of safety and health, these commissions gradually came to administer the whole range of factory regulations, including hour and wage laws. By 1931, twenty states had adopted this system, not all of them with equal success. But even in the weaker states, according to Dr. John B. Andrews of the American Association for Labor Legislation, they represented improvements. After investigating the activities of such commissions in 1930 Andrews concluded: [13]

It seems clear that the delegation of administrative code power [to industrial commissions] does not in itself guarantee definiteness and completeness in the resulting protective standards. But it is equally true that even the most elementary codes sometimes represent a step in advance of existing conditions and of any protective legislation which could be hoped for in the same states.

The countless battles waged by the Progressives to get from the supposed "representatives of the people" social legislation for "the people's" good led not only to a great expansion of the activities of the government but also to changes in its character and personnel. The creation of expert administrative commissions is one example of this, but there were others of a different nature. To make democratic reforms successful, the reformers had constantly to fight for more and more democracy, occupying themselves with campaigns for the direct primary, the initiative, referendum, and recall, the short and secret ballot, the direct election of Senators, and corrupt practices acts.[14] This aspect of

---

[12] *History of Labor*, vol. III, p. 644.
[13] *History of Labor*, vol. III, p. 654.
[14] La Follette, *Autobiography*, p. 204.

the Progressive movement in the states is sometimes featured as most important. But it was only a means to the ends we have discussed. In many cities and states all of these reforms were won, introducing into politics not only new methods but new men. Just as businessmen gradually adapted themselves to the new social legislation, however, and perfected the means to circumvent or soften it wherever possible, so the political bosses in most cases were able to get around the intent of much of the new political legislation. This legislation served in the end to complicate the bosses' problems, not to eradicate them, served to bother the bosses, not to exterminate them. Like other Progressive laws these measures were pushed by middle-class pressure groups, prominent among them being the Good Government leagues and the American Woman's Suffrage Association. Without their contributions it is possible that some Progressive social legislation could not have been enacted. Rarely, however, did such groups succeed in preserving the force of social legislation when it was attacked.

THE NATIONAL THEATER

When asked in 1915 if corporation directors and stockholders were responsible for labor conditions, J. P. Morgan replied that they were not.[15] And while mystery still enshrouds the political activities of the great financiers, there is little evidence that they interfered in state contests between middle-class reformers and middle-class businessmen over Progressive social legislation. Morgan, Rockefeller, Harriman, and Baker had passed the stage when their fortunes depended upon sweated labor, when their international empires could be much harmed by local laws. Roosevelt always feared that "the big financiers . . . outside their own narrowly limited profession, are as foolish as they are selfish." But their "foolishness" apparently fell short of heightening the antagonism of humanitarians by deliberate opposition to their program.

If the ruling oligarchy was content to let little business suffer

---

[15] Corey, *Morgan*, p. 420.

the brunt of the Progressive attack on social problems, however, it was prepared itself to resist little business when small manufacturers, shippers, and western commercial farmers joined muckrakers and reformers in assaulting the trusts, the railroads, and the banks. As early as 1899 Roosevelt had written of the possibility of "heading some great outburst of the emotional classes which should at least temporarily crush the Economic Man." [16] And in the first decade of the new century he succeeded in organizing such classes and exalting their struggle for economic survival into a crusade for the right and the just. As the Progressives on the national scene became more and more militant, however, the bankers and great industrialists developed an *esprit de corps* of their own; and, continuing to defend as sacrosanct their exclusive control of hundred-million-dollar corporations, they came also to regard such corporations as sacred symbols of their power. To tamper with these institutions and with the tariff was to upset security prices, but more than that it was to assert the supremacy of political government over Big Business. That constituted the greater danger, and to avert it the bankers and great industrialists mobilized their forces. No one understood their spirit better than Frederick Townsend Martin, who wrote in 1911 in his *The Passing of the Idle Rich:* [17]

The class I represent care nothing for politics. . . . [But] touch the question of the tariff, touch the issue of the income tax, touch the problem of railroad regulation, or touch the most vital of all business matters, the question of general federal regulation of industrial corporations and the people amongst whom I live my life become immediately rabid partisans. . . . It matters not one iota what political party is in power or what President holds the reins of office. We are not politicians or public thinkers; we are the rich; we own America; we got it, God knows how, but we intend to keep it if we can by throwing all the tremendous weight of our support, our influence, our money, our political connection, our purchased senators, our hungry congressmen, our public-speaking demagogues, into the scale against any legislature, any political platform, any Presidential campaign that threatens the integrity of our estate.

Ably led in the Senate by Nelson Aldrich and in the House by Speaker "Uncle Joe" Cannon, the legislative forces of Big

[16] Josephson, *President Makers*, p. 98.
[17] Martin, *The Passing of the Idle Rich*, p. 148–9.

Business obstructed effective railroad legislation until 1910, tariff reductions until 1913, antitrust legislation until 1914. After the investment bankers had consolidated most of the nation's railroads into a few great systems and no longer needed to curry patronage by special favors, the House and Senate passed the Elkins Act of 1903, making shippers as well as carriers subject to prosecution for rebating. In 1908 they passed the Aldrich-Vreeland Act permitting banks to issue currency on corporate as well as government bonds and postponing radical banking legislation until a monetary commission under Aldrich himself could investigate world conditions and foreign practices. After touring Europe in the company of Henry Davison of Morgan & Company and George Reynolds of the First National Bank of Chicago, Aldrich and his commission submitted a report in forty volumes to which the writers of the Federal Reserve Act made constant reference.

While the national administration thus was impeding the Progressive program and enacting conservative legislation, the federal courts were making the enforcement of existing regulatory laws very difficult. Throughout the reign of Roosevelt no railroad was forced to alter its rates except after a tedious and expensive suit by a complainant; no industrial combination was so effectively broken that with different legal arrangements it could not function much as it would have, had the courts not acted. Even when the Supreme Court did force the Standard Oil Company in 1911 to split into twenty-nine parts, they continued to function with such synchronization that they might almost have remained one company. By introducing the "rule of reason" into this decision, the Court seemed to imply that hereafter it would be even less severe than it had been. And in the United States Steel Corporation case, started in 1912 and decided in 1920, the Court showed this implication to be true. It ruled that, while the great company controlled about 40 per cent of the steel industry, it was not acting in "unreasonable" restraint of trade.

While Big Business was thus being protected against Progressivism in Congress and the courts, Roosevelt was doing little besides making bold speeches, bandying vague threats and irresponsible charges, waving the Big Stick at domestic "malefactors of great wealth" and foreign imperial adventurers. Under pressure from him Congress in 1903 created the Department of Commerce and Labor with a subsidiary Bureau of Corporations. In 1906 it passed the Hepburn Act enlarging the jurisdiction of the Interstate Commerce Commission but giving it little new enforcement power.[18] In 1906 Congress also adopted its first Pure Food and Drug Act. This act only postponed effective legislation and was a defeat for those truly interested in the purity of American meats and the integrity of American advertising. In 1902, with the aid of Mark Hanna, Roosevelt settled the coal strike; and at his behest Congress that year enacted the eight-hour day for federal employees. Except for his notable achievements in conservation, that is the paltry record of Roosevelt's two "Progressive" administrations.

Big Business had learned early that, as Elihu Root reputedly said of him, Roosevelt's "bark is worse than his bite." [19] Roosevelt had started his political career at the suggestion of Cabot Lodge, had worked as Governor of New York in cooperation with "Boss" Platt and as Vice President and President under the direction of Hay, Cannon, and Quay in addition to his earlier mentors. Roosevelt worried Big Business men by his erratic personality, by his seeming independence of party machinery if not party principles. Throughout his career he was verbally chastising "Big Financiers" or sneering at their "glorified pawnbrokers' souls." While he constantly affronted their dignity, however, he rarely obstructed their plans. Roosevelt's great contribution to Progressivism was educational. By his platform espousal of the Progressive program he made it as popular as he was himself. But, as far as Big Business was concerned, that popularity was comparatively harmless as long as Roosevelt was its keeper. In Wisconsin, La Follette had forced railroad representatives to retire from politics, had routed the regular Republican machine, had made the "Octopus" bear its share of taxation and submit to rigid regulation of rates and service. But Roosevelt was no La Follette, and Big Business men knew it.

While Roosevelt frequently compromised with party bosses,

[18] Jones, *Trust Problem*, p. 327.
[19] Josephson, *President Makers*, p. 158.

it was part of their strategy in handling him to make him think that he always maintained his independence. But there was no compromise in his selection of Taft as his successor, for so great was Roosevelt's personal popularity that the party dared name no candidate other than the man Roosevelt would heartily endorse. It was Taft's misfortune, however, to inherit along with the Presidency the business uncertainty after 1907 and the Democratic-Progressive Congress after the election of 1910. Taft was at least as conservative as Roosevelt, and much less adept at seeming liberal, but his single administration was marked by more Progressive legislation than both of Roosevelt's. He ended, however, profoundly out of sympathy with the reformers and feared for his political ineptitude by their opponents.

During Taft's regime the Progressives provided the country with parcel post and with postal savings banks despite the cry of "socialism" raised throughout the land by the express companies and local bankers. During his regime Congress supplemented Roosevelt's eight-hour day for federal employees with additional social legislation: it created the Bureau of Mines to supervise working conditions and force the adoption of safety devices; it enacted rules for the adoption of safety appliances on interstate railroads; it created the federal Children's Bureau under the direction of Julia Lathrop of Hull-House; it raised the Labor division of the Commerce Department into a separate department with a secretary of its own. In promoting the Progressive campaign for more democracy Congress enacted a law making compulsory the publication of party campaign contributions; it submitted to the people what was to become the Seventeenth Amendment to the Constitution making for the direct election of Senators; and in the House, Democrats and Insurgent Republicans reformed the Speakership, relieving the holder of that office of the power to name the Rules Committee and thus to determine the order of House business and the fate of all legislation. But perhaps the most important Progressive measures of Taft's administration were the Income Tax Amendment, submitted to the voters in 1909 and the Mann Elkins Act passed by Congress in 1910. The latter at last gave the Interstate Commerce Commission the right to suspend changes in railroad rates without waiting for shippers' complaints and without having first to go to court. The income tax, opening the way for taxation according to ability to pay, had long been the *bête noire* of the rich, and they had long been protected against it by the Supreme Court. In 1909, however, the Progressives prepared to get around the court's objections by submitting an Amendment to the people. By 1913 a sufficient number of states had approved the Amendment. In the light of subsequent events one can hardly overestimate its effects on federal fiscal policies.

This great burst of Progressive legislation was equaled by judicial activity in the same period. Taft's Attorney General, Wickersham, brought ninety antitrust suits in four years, as compared to forty-four in Roosevelt's seven years. During the administration of neither President were criminal proceedings successful against officers of any corporation for Sherman Act violations.[20] But Taft's men went after bigger game than Roosevelt's and collected bigger fines.

Though much of the Progressive legislation of his regime had Taft's blessing, none of it had the benefit of Presidential leadership. By his failure to oppose the Aldrich amendments to the Payne low-tariff bill of 1909 Taft early in his administration aroused the suspicions of the reformers, and when he then toured the West boasting that the Payne-Aldrich Act was the best tariff ever enacted in America their distrust flared into open hostility. The western Republican Progressives were still more deeply offended when Taft sought a reciprocity tariff with Canada which would allow Canadian agricultural staples to enter the United States at favorable rates, here to compete with the produce of American farms. Republican schism was completed when Taft sustained Ballinger of the Interior Department against the accusations of Gifford Pinchot in 1911. Pinchot's accusations arose out of his suspicion and the suspicion of his fellow Progressives that Ballinger and Taft were trying to undo Roosevelt's great conservation measures.

Under the Forest Reserve Act of 1891 authorizing the President to set aside timberland reserves, Harrison, Cleveland, and

---

[20] Jones, *Trust Problem,* p. 444.

McKinley withdrew from sale or settlement about 45,000,000 acres. Roosevelt in one swoop reserved 150,000,000 acres outright and 85,000,000 additional acres in Alaska as well as in the United States pending a geological survey of their resources. In addition, under the Reclamation Act of 1902 Roosevelt had set up by 1906 twenty-six irrigation projects; he had tightened the administration of the land laws, created the United States Forest Service in the Department of Agriculture with Pinchot as its chief, charged rents for grazing privileges on the public domain, created the Inland Waterways Commission of 1907 to investigate the whole problem of flood control, irrigation, reforestation, and power development. In 1908 he had called the first conference of state governors and national conservation societies to synchronize all conservation activities.

When Taft came into office as Roosevelt's successor it was expected that he would at least protect the gains made. Ballinger, however, as Taft's Secretary of the Interior, decided that Roosevelt had withdrawn some land without sufficient justification, and he immediately aroused the antagonism of the Progressives by reopening such land, including coal sites in Alaska in which Morgan and Guggenheim were interested. Ballinger had a record as a lawyer for parties dealing in public lands, and the muckrakers now jumped on him and Taft for catering to special interests. *Collier's* for instance carried the headline: "Are the Guggenheims in Charge of the Department of the Interior?" [21] The case soon became a *cause célèbre* throughout the nation, tainting the Republican party once again with scandal. Pinchot added fuel to the muckrakers' fire by making speeches everywhere. And Taft, in supporting Ballinger against Pinchot, did his Secretary's cause no good and brought abuse upon himself. In the end Ballinger was "vindicated" by a congressional investigation in 1911, but by then Taft's meager popularity had almost disappeared, and with it went the chances of his party in the next election.

---

[21] Josephson, *President Makers*, p. 314.

THE "NEW FREEDOM"

Through control of party patronage alone the President of the United States, if he chooses, can be one of the most powerful rulers in the world. And if, besides being a shrewd politician he has an attractive personality, he can exercise his power without too much restraint by his party colleagues or the interests they represent. For he is in a position from which he can always appeal to the voters directly if he breaks with his party machine. It was partly because of such considerations that La Follette was never allowed to become President, and it was partly because of such considerations that the real meaning of the election of 1912 lies in his defeat even before he could become a candidate.

As early as 1910 many leading Progressives were working to win for La Follette the regular Republican presidential nomination, and in January, 1911, they formed the National Progressive Republican League, ostensibly to promote his chances.[22] In October of that year they held a "convention" in Chicago to name La Follette as the "logical candidate" and to indicate to the bosses of the regular machine that they would accept no conservative in his place. As the La Follette drive gained momentum, however, the conservative "standpatters" of the party began to prepare Taft delegates for the regular Republican convention. In the meantime another group claiming to be awed by the growing Socialist vote and frightened by the Russian revolution of 1905 began to meddle in politics, seeking at once to undermine the dangerously conservative Taft and the dangerously radical La Follette. Leading this group were the former Morgan partner George Perkins and the newspaper publisher who had made a fortune in the "Steel Trust," Frank Munsey. Aiding them were the wealthy Amos and Gifford Pinchot, the "Carpet King" Alexander Smith Cochrane, T. Coleman du Pont of the "Powder Trust," Medill McCormick of the *Chicago Tribune* and H. H. Wilkinson, president of Crucible Steel. The aim of this group, as Brand Whitlock noted in December, 1911,

---

[22] Pringle, *Roosevelt*, p. 548.

was "to bring [Roosevelt] out as candidate in order to head off
La Follette." Their strategy was to stampede the regular Convention into nominating the Rough Rider or, failing that, "to
smash the convention" and nominate Roosevelt in a rump convention of their own. They were forced to take the second
alternative and, lest Roosevelt hesitate to bolt, Munsey assured
him immediately that "my fortune, my magazine and my newspapers are with you." Urged by Borah not to take the step,
Roosevelt replied, "If they [the Progressives]don't nominate
me they will nominate La Follette." But La Follette had no intention of bolting the party, preferring to persist in his efforts to
capture the organization rather than leave it in the hands of Big
Business. Roosevelt, however, had found his excuse, and the Bull
Moose had its candidate.[23]

While this coup was being worked among the Republicans,
assuring Big Business a conservative candidate in either section
of the party, men like George Harvey, editor of *Harper's
Weekly* after Morgan's reorganization of the publishing house
in 1906, and Cleveland Dodge, a director of the National City
Bank, were working hard for "Doctor Wilson" among the
Democrats. What La Follette was to the Republicans, Bryan
was to their opponents while Wilson, as Governor of New Jersey,
seemed to have the same profound conservatism as Roosevelt.
Wilson seemed to know how to satisfy popular radicalism with
just enough concessions, without crusading against "soulless corporations" and arousing the zealots' fire.

In the Democratic convention it proved to be almost as hard
to nominate Wilson as it had been to nominate Roosevelt among
the "Standpat" Republicans. In the end, however, Bryan added
his strength to that of the New Jersey reformer, preferring him
to the conservative Champ Clark, and Wilson finally was named
to carry the Democratic standard against the split Republican
machine. It was the best Democratic opportunity since the
Civil War, and though Wilson polled fewer votes than Bryan
had polled even while losing in 1896, 1900, and 1908, he became,
for only the second time since 1860, a Democratic President rul-

---

[23] Josephson, *President Makers,* pp. 397–440 *passim.*

ing with Democratic majorities in both the House and the Senate.

Nothing illustrates better than the election of 1912 the subtle power Big Business could exert upon national politics, and yet nothing shows more clearly the concessions it had had to make in the previous decade. The era of the Arthurs, Garfields, and McKinleys had plainly passed, just as had the era of Grantism before it. The middle class had become organized and articulate with a program of its own and, in the Progressives of both major parties, had found leaders who were free of commitments to great political and financial friends. The middle class had found leaders who could capture the imagination of the voters without pledging concessions the "interests" would be reluctant to grant, and the middle class succeeded also in placing those leaders in office.

Wilson looked upon Cleveland as a "conservative Republican" and in 1913 claimed his own administration to be the first Democratic one since the Civil War. He was prepared, therefore, to carry out the policies that the southern and western wings of his party had favored for more than a generation. The power of Wall Street was to be curbed slightly in favor of Main Street, and the tariff was to be readjusted in favor of the consumer. There was nothing in this program to which the Democratic rank and file since Jefferson's time would not have agreed. The one new element was the respectable and vigorous leadership of Dr. Wilson.

No western radical but the ex-president of a conservative eastern university, Wilson was able to hold his party together as Theodore Roosevelt had done and at the same time to assume the role of prime minister in pushing an important reform program. Part of his extraordinary political power may have come from the fact that he did not try to interfere with the "bread and butter" side of organization work. House, Burleson, and Tumulty were allowed to distribute the spoils of victory on a realistic basis, and in return the Democratic caucus steam-rollered the President's "New Freedom" program through House and Senate.[24]

---

[24] Josephson, *President Makers*, pp. 471–473.

The "New Freedom" meant freedom to engage in equal competition, freedom for the small businessman against the "trust,"
the country banker against Wall Street, the importer against the
protected home producer, the worker in his contests with his
employer, and the farm cooperative in its contests with industrial
and commercial business. During the first two years of the new
administration, all these problems were dealt with by acts of
Congress.

The Underwood Tariff of 1913 established "competitive"
rates. It cut the duties on finished products, placed more raw
materials, including wool and sugar, on the free list, and substituted simple *ad valorem* schedules for the intricate specific duties
that had flourished since the Civil War. Perhaps its most remarkable feature was the fact that the Democrats jammed it through
the Senate with only two dissenting votes in their own party and
no important amendments.

The report of the Pujo Committee's investigation of the
"Money Trust," emphasizing the need for a new federal banking
law, was submitted to the Senate in February, 1913. For five
years there had been active discussion in and out of Congress
between Republicans and Democrats regarding the form of such
a law, and the Owen-Glass Act of 1913, enacted after consideration of the points brought out by the Pujo Committee, represented a final compromise. According to the terms of this act the
Federal Reserve System was created. The ownership of the
American banking system was to remain private, as Aldrich had
advocated for the Republicans. But there was to be no central
bank, and the topmost board of control was to be appointed by
the President, concessions to Bryan's point of view. The central
function of the system was to create an elastic currency based
upon business and agricultural assets rather than upon government bonds. All national banks were required to join, and other
banks were invited on certain conditions. A few of the large state
banks promptly accepted the invitation, but the great majority of
small local banks elected to stay outside rather than meet the
requirements for membership. In 1915, 30 per cent of all banks
in the United States with about 50 per cent of all banking assets
were within the system. By 1929, 65 per cent of the banks were

still outside, but they possessed only 20 per cent of the assets. Thus the law brought the bulk of American banking credit under the control and protection of the Federal Reserve System, but still left some sixteen thousand little banks beyond its jurisdiction. A few hundred of these failed almost every year.

Having dealt with the tariff and the banks, the Democratic Congress next turned its attention to the "trusts," and in 1914 passed the Clayton amendment to the Sherman Antitrust Act. The Clayton Act was a statute so framed that its meaning would depend altogether on its administration and interpretation by the courts. On the one hand it aimed to restore and preserve competition, not by breaking up all big businesses but by forbidding the practices by which large companies had stifled competitors. Price discriminations, tying agreements, and acquisitions of the stock of one company by another with the aim of curtailing competition were all forbidden. Interlocking directorates among banks with over $1,000,000 capital also were banned. On the other hand, the Clayton Act explicitly exempted labor unions and farm cooperatives from the operation of the Sherman Act, and forbade the use of injunctions in labor disputes except where necessary to prevent irreparable injury to property. To administer the new act a Federal Trade Commission was established with power to investigate questionable business practices and to issue cease and desist orders when necessary. The Commission could initiate investigations without waiting for complaints, but its orders could be enforced only through the United States Circuit courts. Thus the initial application of the law came to depend on the courts and, as we shall see, the courts in the twenties interpreted the function of the Commission so that the intention of its creators was reversed.

FAREWELL TO REFORM

Congress and the state legislatures, between 1910 and 1914, had enacted a large part of the Progressive program, and the approval of the Sixteenth and Seventeenth Amendments by the people had added their direct sanction of Progressive aims. It seemed then that there was not much further to go along the

Progressive road before reaching socialism—one of the things the Progressive movement, from the very start, had been undertaken to avoid. If the national leaders of the movement were thus in the same dilemma by 1914 that the state leaders had faced a short time before, the war helped to relieve them of their anxiety, substituting a new purpose for the one they had pursued with such apparent success. Theodore Roosevelt promptly became, as he had been twenty years earlier, an ardent advocate of war and a willing convert to fusion once more with the Republican Old Guard. With the defection of their only possible victor in a presidential campaign, the Progressive party slumped woefully in the elections of 1914, and the professional politicians in the party knew it was time to follow Roosevelt back to the Republican bandwagon. In effect this meant that Roosevelt and Perkins, having disciplined Taft and prevented a radical third party, abandoned the Bull Moose as an animal that had outlived its usefulness. And the only ones hurt by the abandonment were a few men like Beveridge who had taken reform too seriously.

All this does not mean that liberal legislation was no longer passed after 1914, or that all Progressives disappeared from state governments and the halls of Congress. But after 1914 Federal Progressive legislation was special in character, and was almost invariably connected in some way with Allied victory or national preparedness. Examples of this type of legislation were: the La Follette Act governing conditions of maritime employment; the Adamson Act creating an eight-hour day for railroad employees and opening the way for possible federal administration of the whole network; the Farm Loan Banking Act; and the Federal Aid to Highways Act. The last measure marked the beginning of what was to become an enormous federal subsidy to state internal improvements, passed by an old-fashioned southern Democratic administration.

The election of 1916 kept Wilson in office; but there was little of the old Progressive spirit in the campaign, and the reunited Republicans won a plurality in the House of Representatives. The politicians who had led the old movement were either dead or devoting themselves to the problems of war in state capitals or in Washington. The attitude of the administration had veered from trying to restore competition to trying to speed production of war materials, and the Attorney General was not inclined to interfere with essential industries. As in 1898 a foreign war was to prove the surest answer to domestic discontent.

XIV

THE CLIMAX OF FINANCE
CAPITALISM

FOR a hundred years before the World War, Americans had poured billions of dollars into transportation and manufacturing plants, into the exploitation of unparalleled natural resources from which no immediate returns could be expected. To keep up the supply of funds for such enterprises, Americans had been lectured constantly on the virtue of frugality and thrift. By 1913, however, savings were mounting faster than new investments in productive enterprises. Population continued to multiply, but employment and wages had ceased to expand. Recapitalizations at higher levels had taken the place of actual railroad building, and general construction was in the doldrums. The United States, after 1900, like England, Germany, and France, needed new openings for investment in long-term economic developments; up to 1913 she had failed to find a sufficient number.

For a few years the Great War relieved the pressure on the economic systems of the combatants, affording private enterprise ample opportunity to employ its total savings in the production of goods. The war, however, proved to be only a temporary expedient. In England and the United States, and to a greater degree in other countries, governments in the "prosperous" twenties had to supplement private industry with public works to keep many of their people employed, and with public doles to keep them fed. In the United States, government construction of streets, highways, and public buildings in the decade after the war used more capital and employed more men than any single line of private enterprise.

Some of the most important changes wrought by the war were in industrial technology and business organization, and in the twenties these were developed to a very high degree of efficiency.

Their net result, however, was to increase the productive capacity of American industry tremendously, without at the same time increasing the capacity of many Americans to buy. Like the staple farmers, many American industrial laborers became relatively poorer in the twenties. The number of new workers constantly outran the number of new jobs. Unprecedented savings in the costs of production pushed profits, executive salaries, and bonuses to new heights, but industrial wages after 1922 remained practically stationary. As more and more goods poured off the modern speeded-up assembly lines, therefore, the number of new purchasers failed to expand. Those people who *could* buy were already well stocked, while those who most needed goods failed to share in the general prosperity.

There were two ways in which great American corporations and upper middle-class dividend collectors could put their growing incomes to productive use. One was to expand the "home market" for American commodities to such an extent that great domestic plant expansion would be required and our economic system would be revitalized. The other was to expand the foreign market by finding new long-term investment opportunities abroad. By frenetic advertising and high-pressure salesmanship they sought the first objective. By some energetic measures in the western and eastern hemispheres beyond our own continental boundaries, they sought to accomplish the second. In neither, however, were they successful. Rich Americans could not shed their traditional habits in a year or two, and while they purchased many more commodities than they needed they also poured billions into insurance premiums and accounts in commercial and savings banks and trust companies. At the same time, those without money (and their number was considerable) could not buy, however attractive the commodities offered or the advertising that whetted their desires. And just as Americans were traditional savers so were they traditional isolationists. While they accumulated savings in financial institutions and accumulated profits in the treasuries of giant corporations, therefore, they also invested abroad too little to cause much expansion in our industrial plant.

Failing to find productive uses for all their savings either at home or abroad, Americans turned more and more to speculation. The war and the previous depression had caused widespread neglect of private construction, and once hostilities ceased the optimism in this field became so great that a building boom soon was under way. Speculation in land and mortgages became rife, and prices skyrocketed as idle savings were poured into fabulous real estate projects. In the meantime, rising prices in the stock and bond market attracted increasing amounts of capital, and soon a boom was in progress here too. Holding companies and industrial trusts fed the new plungers with more and more securities, but still prices soared. The upswing was so regular, and so confident was every one in its continuance that many industries flourished merely because of extensive commodity purchases based upon paper profits in the stock market. Thus our whole economy soon became geared to the rise and fall of security prices. And when these prices soared so far beyond any reasonable valuation of corporation assets that the slightest wisp of uncertainty would send the market tumbling, our whole business structure was in danger of collapse.

In 1929 this collapse occurred, and the results were even worse than any one had anticipated. The depression that followed was perhaps the most severe in our history, and recovery was impeded not only by the depth of the fall and the growing fear of political interference but by the rigidity introduced into business mechanisms, prices and wages during the previous decade.

THE FIRST WORLD WAR

"Freedom of the seas" was one of the major planks in the democratic credo of the United States, and when Germany by unrestricted submarine warfare sought to close the ship lanes of the Atlantic to Anglo-American wartime trade we joined the armed conflict against the central powers. Before that we had already become the "arsenal of the Democracies," supplying the Allied combatants with an ever lengthening list of war materials. To pay for these, Britain, France, and Russia had sent us all the gold they could spare. Their bankers had ransacked every portfolio for American securities to exchange for American goods. Their speculators had raided every European exchange for American dollars, which had soared with each shipment of wheat, cotton, oil, ordnance, and ammunition. America, which had always been Europe's debtor, was thus becoming the greatest creditor nation in the world. And our industry and agriculture, which had always strained to service our foreign debts with larger and larger exports, were on the way to finding those debts dissolved and that incentive to enterprise gone.

This was one of the major changes wrought by the war in American business and American life, and its effects were augmented once we entered into hostilities ourselves and enlarged our assistance to the western powers. Redressing the balance, however, were other wartime changes that stimulated American enterprise in various ways. The cessation of German exports of coal-tar products—dyes, medicines, and industrial solvents—led to their production in the United States, revolutionizing our coke-making industry. In many other lines by-products took on new importance when imports were cut off. Our entrance into armed conflict led to the confiscation of German patents previously honored here, which gave an extra impetus to our chemical industry. By destroying industrial plants and private homes in Europe, and by preventing normal peacetime construction and repair in Europe and America, the war created new opportunities for private capital once hostilities ceased. Aside from such indirect costs, it has been estimated that actual expenditures during the war amounted to eighty billion dollars in gold. In so far as men were employed to produce that much in war goods and to use those goods in combat, the war stimulated private enterprise everywhere. The United States bore about one-quarter of this cost and reaped proportionate benefits. This gave a needed fillip to our steel, shipbuilding, shipping, and munitions industries and most of all to our staple farming. It helped put idle capital and idle men to work and thus stimulated other lines as well.

To eliminate waste in many industries, the War Industries Board, set up in 1917 to direct America's war economy, insisted upon standardization in peacetime manufactures. This limited style competition in many lines. To simplify the enforcement of its rules in thousands of factories throughout the country, the board also found it convenient to deal with businessmen through their trade associations. This narrowed price competition as well. In addition, all antitrust suits were halted during the war, and semi-monopolistic corporations frequently received extra consideration in war contracts because of their ability to make large and rapid deliveries. Besides encouraging new industries, therefore, and creating new opportunities for private capital in older ones, the war led to a sharp reversal in the attitude of the government toward free competition and business enterprise.

For war purposes the federal government took over the railroads, telegraph and telephones. It regulated prices and labor, passed strict espionage and sedition acts, and set each citizen to spy upon his neighbors. The schools, the press, and the movies were harnessed to the war propaganda machine. Nearly five million men were taken from other employment to serve in the Army and Navy while thousands of others were caught in enemy territory and interned "for the duration." The hardships imposed or the improvements created by these conditions ended in most cases with the armistice and the dismantling of the war machine. Not so, however, the effects of the war upon American corporation finance.

Many peacetime industries shut down during the war. Many others reduced operations. But manufacturers, shippers, brokers, agents, and commission men who could get war orders got rich; corporation profits in war lines multiplied, creating surpluses in spite of taxation. This meant that many companies which once had to go to investment bankers for funds could now finance out of their own resources all their future needs. It meant that, while members of the "Money Trust" might continue to sit on boards of directors, their power at meetings would be much reduced. The war created many new fortunes and thus greatly enlarged the investing public. By selling this public billions in Liberty bonds, the government during the war trained it to deal in securities. Had corporation profits declined and the quest for investments slowed down, this training might have become useless. Since profits continued to mount, however, and new outlets for long-term expansion failed to appear, the stock market itself tended to become the major recipient of savings. The great boom in holding company and other corporate securities followed directly from this.

A REVOLUTION IN BUSINESS TECHNIQUES

The chemical industry was the most important young industry to be stimulated by the war, and after 1918 it grew rapidly. In 1920 the Chemical Foundation was formed to lobby for high tariffs, and in 1922, under the Fordney-McCumber Act, prohibitive rates were won for most of the products of the new line. By 1929 Du Pont, Allied Chemical, Union Carbide, and smaller companies were producing acids, plastics, metallic alloys and "allied products" valued at $3,750,000,000.[1]

Besides opening new opportunities for industrial activity during and after the war, chemistry joined with electricity to revolutionize other industries. In extracting and refining copper and iron ores new chemical methods and new electrical machines provided tremendous savings. The same was true in drilling oil wells and cracking petroleum. New electrochemical operations propelled the automobile, motion picture, radio, and telephone industries to gigantic heights and greatly increased the importance in our economy of refrigerators, washing machines, and other household appliances. Improvements in parts and processes, made possible only through the application of chemistry and electricity, steadily increased the efficiency of gasoline motors, while new economies were found each year in the production of electricity itself. Between 1920 and 1929 the amount of fuel used to generate electric power rose about 25 per cent. The production of kilowatt hours increased more than 100 per cent.

While electricity thus helped to revolutionize industrial *technology* in the twenties, it also worked radical changes in the *organization* of factory production. In 1914 "perhaps 30 per cent of factory machine equipment was electrified; in 1929 the total was approximately 70 per cent."[2] By allowing even distribution

---

[1] Shannon, *Economic History*, p. 742.
[2] Kirkland, *Economic Life*, p. 645.

of power throughout enormous plants, electricity decentralized production within the factory, and by permitting the transmission of power over tremendous distances it freed the factory from the river valley and the coal field. Electricity made much more efficient the "straight-line" system of production, the conveyer belt and the assembly line. It opened the way to economies in the manufacture of interchangeable parts never dreamed of by Eli Whitney. It put a premium upon scientific management and the standardization of jobs and commodities. Factories could now be set up very near raw materials. New workers could be recruited easily to handle simplified routine tasks. High wages could be paid because electric machinery between 1919 and 1929 doubled the work that could be done by a single pair of hands. For the same reasons technological unemployment increased.

Since markets for goods failed to expand in the twenties at the same rate as technological improvements and productive capacity, and since competition thus threatened to become ruinous, many new trade associations were formed, each with its own code of "fair practices" and the machinery for enforcing it. We have seen how trade associations were started before the war to engage in lobbying activities and to make agreements limiting competition. We have seen how these associations and many new ones acquired respectability during the war. In the twenties, innumerable industries that previously had been freely competitive became partly monopolistic for the first time, and the government, which had heretofore frowned upon all organized efforts to "restrain trade," blessed the new order. The "Rugged Individualist" Herbert Hoover was the leading sponsor of these cooperative activities in the twenties. In its decision in the Maple Flooring Manufacturers case in 1925 the Supreme Court joined him. The court said:[3]

We decide only that trade associations or combinations of persons or corporations which openly and fairly garner and disseminate information as to the cost of their products, the volume of production, the actual price which the product had brought in past transactions, stocks of merchandise on hand, approximate cost of transportation from the principal points of shipment to the points of consumption, *without however reaching or at-*

---

[3] Maple Flooring Manufacturers Association et al. *v.* U. S., 268 U. S. 563.

tempting to reach any agreement or any concert of action with respect to prices or production or restraining competition, do not thereby engage in unlawful restraint of commerce.

This dictum declared in so many words that trade associations might limit competition however they pleased, provided only that they did not admit that that was their intention. It gave *carte blanche* to as great a revolution in business techniques as anything connected with the laboratory or the factory.

Trade associations tried to regulate competition in industries which had a multiplicity of small firms. In other lines where a few companies led the field regulation required no such elaborate machinery; and in lines dominated by one or two great corporations it required no machinery at all. There were in the late twenties, for instance, only half a dozen cigarette companies, led by R. J. Reynolds and American Tobacco. Price wars among these companies might demolish one or two, but the government, under the Clayton Act, was likely to restrain the victor from absorbing defeated rivals. Better, therefore, for all to adhere to a price that would allow a fair profit for each and to limit competitive activities to such fields as advertising and packaging. This was easy to arrange when only a few companies were involved. In the steel industry, where one great company was dominant, it would have been foolhardy for any little corporation to embark on price competition with the "leader." Thus, without any collusion whatever, United States Steel Corporation prices became the prices throughout the industry.

These innovations in factory techniques and business organization brought large profits to many corporations already burdened with undivided surpluses, and the measures taken by them to use up these profits brought further changes in business practices and business management.

"Why won't it be in the future as in the past, all the money you make and more, put back into the business?" asked Frederick H. Prince, the Boston railroad executive, of Charles Schwab, chairman of the board of Bethlehem Steel in 1923. Schwab replied: "In the old days we were building and building; in the future we shall not require so much building." [4] To employ the

---

[4] Barron, *More They Told Barron*, p. 298.

profits that once went into expansion, many companies in the twenties began for the first time to erect plant hospitals, to improve sanitary conditions in their factories, to construct dwellings, clubhouses, theaters, athletic fields, and playgrounds for employees.[5] More important, many corporations enlarged their expenditures for scientific research, and many others spent millions on it for the first time. New laboratories were set up, and old ones were extended. Large contributions were made to technical colleges and technical divisions of great universities. Fellowships and endowed chairs in physics, chemistry, and engineering were multiplied, and courses in industrial management, public relations, and marketing became common in the curricula of schools of higher education. "We have no experimental shop comparable with the motor companies," said President Vauclain of the Baldwin Locomotive in 1927, "but we are experimenting all the time in every way."[6] In 1925 the United States Chamber of Commerce reported 527 separate research projects being carried on by sixty-eight different trade associations.[7] By 1928, 600 firms in forty different lines of manufacture were spending $12,000,000 a year on scientific investigations.[8] In 1930 Bell Telephone Laboratories had nearly 5,900 technical and other workers and a budget of $23,547,000.[9] Eastman Kodak, Du Pont, and General Electric were not far behind.

The quest for economies and greater power had led, before the war, to the worship of "Bigness" in American industry and to the development of immense corporations. Many of the new scientific investigations after the war discovered uses for industrial refuse, and expansion through the manufacture of by-products added new giants to the list. Still more were added when many corporations began to use undivided profits in vertical integration. Kroger Grocery, for instance, purchased bakeshops, canneries, packing houses, sausage factories, and coffee roasting plants. Such integrated corporations were better equipped than

---

[5] For additional reasons for these activities, see chap. XI, pp. 244–247.
[6] Barron, *More They Told Barron*, p. 316.
[7] *Recent Economic Changes*, vol. II, p. 499 note.
[8] *Recent Economic Changes*, vol. I, pp. 108–109.
[9] Danielian, *A. T. & T.*, pp. 92, 205.

smaller rivals to take advantage of new production methods and to develop them to their limits. In the twenties big corporations grew, on the average, three times as fast as smaller ones. The faster they grew, however, the greater became their problems of management, and here too new techniques were evolved —techniques which, like those in production and distribution, had their origins before the war but became highly sophisticated after the war was over.

As early as 1911 Frederick Taylor had written in his volume on scientific management: [10]

> No great man can (with the old system of personal management) hope to compete with a number of ordinary men who have been properly organized so as efficiently to cooperate.

In the twenties this became a maxim with corporation leaders. As plants were scattered all over the world, and as the number of commodities produced by single corporations steadily increased, highly specialized vice presidents appeared by the dozens in each large company. Some directed the manufacture of one group of commodities, some the manufacture of other groups; some managed sales, others research; some purchasing, and still others plant maintenance and construction. The old separation of ownership from management continued to grow wider in the twenties, but the new separation of powers within management grew faster still. Only Henry Ford held out against the change. In the places once occupied by the Vanderbilts, McCormicks, Rockefellers, and Carnegies were bankers and bankers' sons, financial managers, and a multiplicity of less powerful men—each of whom knew little of the business outside his own department.

The chief recommendation of Taylor's plan was that it so routinized business procedures that a number of commonplace men together could handle situations that had grown too complex for any one to handle alone. But this also had its drawbacks, which became increasingly clear as the twenties unfolded. The separation of corporation financiers from those in charge of industrial operations permitted a company to be pulled two ways

---

[10] Taylor, *Scientific Management*, pp. 6–7.

at once until it was sometimes impossible to tell whether its primary function was industrial production or security manipulation. Besides, if every officer was a specialist, who could understand the business as a whole? And if work was perfectly systematized, so that it required little ingenuity, where was the incentive to enterprise? On this point, J. B. Sheridan, a public relations man for important utility companies, wrote in 1927: [11]

> We are raising a lot of thoroughly drilled "yes ma'ms" in the big corporations who have no minds of their own; no opinions. As soon as the old individualists die, and there are not so many of them left, I think the corporations will have a lot of trouble in getting good executives. After a man has served twenty to thirty years in one of these monstrous corporations he is not liable to have a mind of his own.

To coordinate the activities of such proliferating corporations, "industrial engineers" were employed in greater and greater numbers. Personnel directors took on new duties and responsibilities. A great internal literature of business appeared, to bolster the morale of men in high and low places who could not discern out of the welter of corporate practices any clear-cut corporate objectives for which to strive. As early as 1910 Woodrow Wilson had said that a "modern corporation is an economic society, a little economic state—and not always little, even as compared with states." [12] By the twenties the truth of this observation was clear to every one. The great corporations had their own politics, their own internal diplomacy, their own bureaucracies and hierarchies of power. They had their own court conflicts and court scandals, their own hereditary offices and strategic marriages, their own ministerial cabinets composed of men brought up occasionally from the ranks and their own pensioners who played polo or sailed yachts, held balls and horse shows while great corporate machines ground out profits or consumed capital.

In 1927 a director of General Motors said that "bankers regard research as most dangerous and a thing that makes banking hazardous, due to the rapid changes it brings about in industry." [13] Bankers have always been the most conservative

---

[11] Thompson, *Power Trust,* p. 14.
[12] Ripley, *Main Street and Wall Street,* p. 6.
[13] Kirkland, *Economic Life,* p. 647.

men in our society. They frowned on foreign investments when the nation was looking for opportunities to put capital to work. They shied away from new industries like oil or automobiles until more adventurous promoters proved them to be "good things." They allowed the state and federal governments to take over highway construction because they could not adjust themselves to a rate of return on money lower than the long established one. Ever since Morgan began his consolidations of the railroads their quest had been for stability in business, and though they never achieved it their domination over American industry until the war broke out put a damper on costly innovations. In the twenties, however, banker control of productive activity declined. New research went forward in all fields, and rapid changes were made. New technological devices increased profits, new restrictions on competition protected them, and new techniques in management channelized them into the hands of those who already had a great deal of money to spend.

THE SEARCH FOR NEW OPPORTUNITIES

For every hundred people in American cities in 1920 there were only thirteen bathtubs and six telephones.[14] One American family in every three had an automobile but not one in ten thousand had a radio.[15] Almost no farmhouses and but one in every ten city homes were wired for electricity; only in such homes, therefore, were there potential customers for washing machines, vacuum cleaners, refrigerators, floor lamps, incandescent bulbs, fans, and flatirons. If American manufacturers could expand the markets for all these commodities, there was a chance that they could not only run their factories almost at full capacity but use their profits in steady plant expansion. If manufacturers could reach more and more Americans each year with new comforts and luxuries, if they could make these into such necessities of daily life or standards of social position that few could do without them, there was a chance that they could employ the tens of thousands of new workers seeking jobs each year, that they could

---

[14] *Recent Economic Changes,* vol. I, p. 67.
[15] Kennedy, *Automobile Industry,* p. 113.

also employ the billions of dollars in savings that were piling up in their treasuries and those of banks and insurance companies.

It was this chance that was behind the tremendous advertising campaigns of the twenties, behind the quest for good-will and the emphasis on "service," behind the growth in installment selling and personal credit plans. In 1897, when the House Ways and Means Committee was busy drawing up schedules for the Dingley Tariff Act, Louis D. Brandeis tried to get the committee to give some consideration to the "consumer." He was "greeted with jeering laughter." [16] By 1920, however, the consumer had become the likely savior of private enterprise in America. And so much was done to encourage him in his new role that the "public relations counsel" became the key man in many companies.

Through newspapers, magazines, billboards, radios, and motion pictures this new "expert" fashioned new wants, stimulated social competition, created discontents, and offered tempting amulets and charms to spirit them away. Each year a new gadget in an automobile, a new speaker in a radio set, a new noise muffler in a vacuum cleaner, or electric fan was designed to make last year's model obsolete, a stigma of social inferiority, a public confession of inability to "keep up with the Joneses." Premiums, prizes, and gifts were offered for continued patronage, "down payments" were steadily reduced, "trade-in" allowances increased, credit terms extended over longer and longer periods. "There is no detail too trivial to influence the public in a favorable or unfavorable sense," [17] said Edward Bernays, perhaps the ablest public relations man. Factories must be kept immaculate and open to inspection by the consumers of their goods. Corporation labor policies and "financial dealings" must receive favorable publicity. [18] Even

the personality of the president may be a matter of importance, for he perhaps dramatizes the whole concern to the public mind. It may be very important to what charities he contributes, in what civic societies he holds office. If he is a leader in his industry, the public may demand that he be a leader in his community.

---

[16] Josephson, *President Makers*, p. 10.
[17] Bernays, *Propaganda*, p. 71.
[18] Bernays, *Propaganda*, p. 71.

In 1882 William Vanderbilt in a moment of pique could say, "The public be damned," and get away with it. In the 1920's such a remark might have wrecked an economic empire. Samuel Insull knew this when he said:[19]

It matters not how much capital you may have, how fair the rates may be, how favorable the conditions of service, if you haven't behind you a sympathetic public opinion, you are bound to fail.

Like many other things in the twenties this interest in the consumer was not entirely new. As early as 1899 the National Biscuit Company was placarding the nation's magazines and newspapers with Uneeda Biscuit. In 1903 Cadillac was advertising everywhere its "smartest of runabouts," "speed range four to thirty miles an hour." "Camel cigarettes are here," boomed R. J. Reynolds Company in 1914. "Atlantic Gasoline puts pep in your motor," said the Atlantic Refining Company in 1918.[20] In the twenties, however, advertising found new outlets, developed new techniques and new experts. It became a great business itself, paying on the average higher salaries than the industries whose products it tried to sell. By its patronage it could make or break newspapers, magazines, and radio chains, thus wielding a potent club over the country's communication facilities. Even Calvin Coolidge was impressed with its strength, carried away as he was by the seemingly flush times over which he ruled, from his traditional New England moorings, from the thrifty and frugal habits of his forebears. In an address in 1926 Coolidge commended advertising:[21]

It makes new thoughts, new desires and new actions. . . . It is the most potent influence in adopting and changing the habits and modes of life, affecting what we eat, what we wear, and the work and play of the whole nation.

Whatever else advertising could do, however, it could not itself create buying power. It could regiment the nation's taste and marshal the nation's purse behind selected products, but it

---

[19] Bernays, *Propaganda*, pp. 74–75.
[20] Hower, *Advertising Agency*, pp. 313, 314, 321, 323.
[21] Hower, *Advertising Agency*, p. 155.

could not more evenly distribute the national income by increasing the proportion going to the poor. All kinds of attractive commodities might roll off assembly lines at ever accelerating rates, and all kinds of attractive advertising might whet the appetite of every one for those commodities. Only those could buy, however, who had the cash or credit, and in the twenties this group failed to increase sufficiently. Installment payments might allow thousands to buy who could not pay at once the whole cost of expensive objects. But as such purchases increased, more and more of the national income went for interest payments instead of additional goods from retailers' shelves and showrooms. The same was true of purchases made with money borrowed from the "personal finance companies" that flourished in the twenties. Many corporations introduced systems of employee stock ownership and employee participation in dividends. But the number of securities distributed to workers always remained small, and the dividends the workers received added little to their purchasing power. Many bills were introduced into Congress to raise the price of farm products and thus to raise farmers' income. But these failed of adoption, and the farmers remained a poor market throughout the decade.

While advertising thus was failing necessarily to enlarge for any long period of time the "home market" for American goods, and while it was failing also, therefore, to enlarge the home market for investment capital, a few Americans were beginning to look abroad for opportunities to sell the products of our tremendous industrial plant and to invest the profits that that plant was returning. Here too, however, the ultimate result was to be failure.

Until 1898 American "imperialist" investments had been limited mainly to the development of the American West. We had little capital to invest in foreign securities or in American enterprises in foreign lands. At the outbreak of the war with Spain there were but fifteen American factories in all of Europe, and in 1900, though Americans owned abroad property worth $455,000,000, all but $15,000,000 of this was in the western hemisphere.[22] During the next twelve years our direct foreign

[22] Beard, *National Interest,* pp. 207, 209.

investments more than tripled in value, but even that total hardly surpassed the capitalization of the United States Steel Corporation alone. American businessmen still were satisfied with the "home market" for capital and goods, still were eager to protect that market behind high tariffs, still were suspicious of foreign governments whose politics they did not understand. As long as Americans continued to patronize American railroads, to buy American manufactured goods and to supply American factories with cheap labor, American industrialists had remained content to sell in the United States, to keep their money here, to attract as much foreign capital as they could, but to use it only in their own bailiwicks not in the realm of some foreign prince.

When the World War was over, however, and the farmer's purchasing power had collapsed, the time had come when it seemed that free enterprise in the United States could be saved only by the vigorous pursuit of new outlets for commodities and idle funds. Americans, eager to preserve their traditional system, were faced with the necessity of discarding their traditional isolationism. Just as they were being badgered on every side to spend and spend when they had always been taught to save, so they were being urged to invest and invest abroad when they had always shied away from foreign entanglements. The campaign to change American thrift into prodigality, as we have seen, met very limited success, and the campaign for vigorous imperialist enterprise was hardly more fruitful. To be sure, the British, the French, and the Dutch had long before 1914 beaten us to the most attractive areas for long-term developments. In the race for what was left, however, we also lagged behind, preferring the insecure paper profits of speculation in real estate and securities. Human habits and attitudes cherished for generations tend to persist long after the conditions that created them. In America our habitual dependence upon the "home market," even after it ceased to grow rapidly enough, and our traditional isolationist attitude operated as perhaps the greatest brakes on imperialist activity.

This is not to say that American bankers, industrialists, promoters, and prospectors withdrew in the twenties from economic enterprise outside the United States. It is only to explain why our expansion was so limited. Our long-term direct investments in foreign countries jumped sharply from $1,740,000,000 in 1912 to $7,477,735,000 in 1929; but the latter figure was equalled by the *net profits* of our corporate system for the *single year* 1928 and surpassed by the net corporate profits of 1929. In 1929 Americans owned abroad [23]

cattle ranches, fruit and rubber plantations, tobacco farms and sugar centrals, pulp and paper mills, fishing fleets and packing centers, mines and smelters, oil wells and refineries, almost every conceivable public utility . . . automobile plants, chemical works and electrical enterprises, a wide variety of food, leather and lumber processors, plants for the construction and assembly of all sorts of machinery, enterprises fabricating metal, rubber and textile products, stone, clay and glass works.

Yet this seemingly gigantic property, built and developed over many decades, could have been purchased with the amount of capital used to buy new securities of American corporations in the single year 1926.

By that year South America had absorbed 20 per cent of our foreign investments. There the Big Four in American packing were involved in the Argentine meat trade. Ford dominated the small Brazilian rubber production, and the United States Steel controlled Brazilian manganese ore. Bethlehem Steel owned extensive iron mines in Chile, where the Guggenheims and du Ponts controlled copper and nitrate deposits. The Guggenheims and the National Lead Company invested heavily in Bolivian tin; and 97 per cent of American holdings in Peru, Colombia, and Venezuela were in the oil deposits of those countries. [24] Yet in 1929 the assets of A. T. & T. alone were worth very nearly *three times* as much as the whole of America's direct investments in South America, and there were five other non-financial American corporations the assets of *each* of which surpassed those investments in value. [25] In 1930 Alfred P. Sloan, Jr., boasted that General Motors had invested altogether "something like $50,000,000 in overseas operations." [26] This sum was equal only

---

[23] Beard, *National Interest,* p. 208.
[24] Kirkland, *Economic Life,* p. 617.
[25] Berle and Means, *The Modern Corporation,* pp. 20–23.
[26] Laidler, *American Industry,* pp. 178–179.

to about one-fifth of that corporation's *net* income for 1929 alone.[27]

Long-term industrial developments in backward areas require steel, heavy machinery, tools, and other equipment. They stimulate the heavy industries that produce such commodities, thus toning up the whole of a nation's economy. They are much more effective, therefore, than loans to mature countries in maintaining high rates of productive activity at home. America's long-term developments in the twenties, however, were too small to act as a tonic to our tremendous industrial plant. And since our loans to other governments and some private corporations abroad after 1921 were not even as great as our direct investments in backward areas, their effect upon our economy was even less significant.

THE FABULOUS BOOM OF THE TWENTIES

The failure of American industry to utilize its usual proportion of American savings and the failure of foreign opportunities to take up the slack in our long-term investments left America in the twenties with increasing amounts of unused capital available for speculation. Experience with Liberty bonds had made holders of such capital willing to experiment in corporate securities, and the steady rise in stock and bond prices had crowned their experiments with success. By the late twenties the demand for new speculative opportunities had become so great that holding companies and investment trusts were able to sell more than a billion dollars' worth a year in stocks and bonds that had little but other common stock behind them. Even then the supply of securities remained insufficient, and prices soared almost out of sight as intense buying continued.

"Pyramided" holding companies would have delighted the great promoters of earlier days. Their appearance was delayed until the twenties because their formation required a great congregation of security speculators. Once this condition was met, there appeared Giannini's Bancitaly Corporation, the Van Swer-

---

[27] Kennedy, *Automobile Industry*, p. 221.

ingens' railroad system, Sidney Z. Mitchell's Electric Bond and Share Company, and the famed Insull Empire of electric utilities. These were four of the largest, but only a few among hundreds. The structure of each was so complicated that even Owen D. Young, expert corporation lawyer and experienced board chairman of General Electric, despaired of understanding them. Of the Insull agglomeration he said: [28]

> It is impossible for any man to grasp the situation of that vast structure . . . it was so set up that you could not possibly get an accounting system which would not mislead even the officers themselves.

One of the companies at the bottom of the Insull Empire was the Georgia Power Company. This was an operating company that produced electric power and light, sold it to factories and homes, employed industrial labor and paid industrial wages. Its assets consisted of land, buildings, equipment and good-will. To control *all* these assets, another corporation had only to control, at most, *half* of the voting stock of the Georgia Power Company. This the Seaboard Public Service Corporation did. And this was all it did.

The entire "plant" of the Seaboard consisted of an office from which its directors bought and sold securities. And just as the Seaboard could control *all* the assets of the Georgia Power Company by controlling *half* of its stock, so the National Public Service Corporation could control all the holdings of the Seaboard by controlling only *half* of the latter's own *voting* stock. In turn the National Public Service Corporation, itself only an "office" company, was controlled by the National Electric Power Company. The latter, therefore, controlled the Georgia Power Company as well, with an infinitesimal investment sufficient only to purchase enough voting stock in the next lower holding company.

Still higher in the Insull hierarchy was the Middle West Utilities Company—another nonentity in terms of its own "plant," a giant corporation in terms of the assets it controlled. The Middle West Utilities Company was a great holding company which "held" stock in many other holding and operating com-

---

[28] Allen, *Lords of Creation*, p. 280.

panies, one of which was the National Electric Power Company. Thus it also controlled the Georgia Power Company.

Still the end of the maze is not in sight. Higher yet was Insull Utility Investments, Inc., which was formed in 1928 to control not only the Middle West Utilities Company but three other giants: the Public Service Company of Northern Illinois, the Commonwealth Edison Company, and the Peoples Gas, Light & Coke Company. And beyond even this company, the network of whose holdings was so intricate as to defy intelligent unraveling, was the Corporation Securities Company of Chicago, a "super-super-super holding company" called "Corps" for short.

This "Corps" controlled Insull Utility Investments, Inc., by owning almost 30 per cent of its stock. Yet Insull Utility also held 12.5 per cent of "Corps" stock, a controlling interest. Another 1.2 per cent of "Corps" stock was held by the Middle West Utilities Company. Commenting on the Insull structure, Frederick Lewis Allen exclaimed: [29]

A pyramid, was it? But what sort of a pyramid has a lower step partly resting upon the step above it? A family tree, was it? (Financiers often refer to parent companies.) But in what sort of a family is the child a part-parent of the father?

The value of the "pyramided" holding company device to the promoter becomes clear when we realize that a single dollar invested by Insull in the voting stock of the Insull Utility Investments, Inc., controlled $1,750 in assets of the Georgia Power Company. And this was only one such company among scores in the whole set-up. The outline we have drawn, for all its apparent complexities, is a very much simplified representation of the corporate morass that was the Insull Empire, a simplified representation of companies within companies, each owning other companies, which in turn controlled their "owners." And Insull's was only one such Empire among scores, none quite so involved, but few so plain as to be comprehended in all their ramifications by one mind.

The possibility of lucrative security manipulation was the only incentive behind many of the holding company pyramids of the

---

[29] Allen, *Lords of Creation*, p. 280.

twenties. Men like Insull and Sidney Mitchell, however, actually expected great operating economies to accrue from centralized management of huge properties. They also expected great expansion in the electricity business to justify not only new stock issues but also holding company bonds whose fixed charges would have to be met out of the revenue of the bottom operating companies. In the end, neither the economies nor the expected rate of expansion materialized, and Insull's whole structure and many others erected on the same principles were in trouble.

The net effect of this multiplication of holding companies was to introduce into the seething security market enormous amounts of new paper and enormous sums of idle money to speculate in this new paper. Encouraging such speculation was the very liberal credit allowed by reputable banks to margin purchasers of questionable securities or of reliable securities at questionable prices. Encouraging speculation still further was the money poured into the "call market" by giant corporations which had no other current use for the large profits they were making. Standard Oil of New Jersey, Electric Bond and Share, and Cities Service Corporation, all advanced hundreds of millions of dollars to be used for brokers' loans. Still another incentive to heedless gambling were the "investment trusts," created to accommodate little plungers who could not afford to deal in large blocks of stock.[30] But perhaps the greatest impulse of all, aside from the actual accumulated capital seeking new opportunities, came from the security sales organizations set up by many notable banks with branches everywhere. As Bruce Barton said of Charles Edwin Mitchell, president of the National City Bank of New York: "Instead of waiting for investors to come, he took young men and women, gave them a course of training in the sale of securities, and sent them to *find* the investors." [31] By 1929 Mitchell was employing three hundred and fifty stock and bond salesmen, operating from offices in fifty-eight different cities "connected with New York headquarters by means of eleven thousand miles of private wire." His methods

---

[30] An investment trust sells its own stock to the public and with the proceeds buys stock in other companies. Thus the holder of a single share in the trust has the advantage of diversified security holding.

[31] Allen, *Lords of Creation*, pp. 312–313.

were contagious, and his organization was aped by many other groups, even older conservative houses like Kuhn, Loeb & Co. and Hallgarten & Company seeking customers all over the country.

The more widely stock is scattered among little investors, the smaller is the percentage of that stock required to control a company. It was partly because of this principle that Insull always sought the little speculator as the purchaser of his new issues. The same was true of A. T. & T., Pennsylvania Railroad, and other large companies. In addition, the more numerous the stockholders in a giant corporation, the more numerous its potential customers, its defenders against political regulation, its supporters against community pressures of various kinds, in schools, colleges, churches, and women's clubs. While new holding companies were luring many gullible neophytes into the security market, therefore, other corporations were also issuing new common stocks and "splitting up" older issues that had reached such prohibitive heights as to discourage new purchasers. As the number of speculators grew steadily, the prices of these new issues continued to spurt to astronomical figures at a rate all out of proportion even to the rate of profit in very profitable companies. At last an outlet had been found where new funds could be poured without limit, or so it seemed, and the security boom was on in earnest, prices soaring heedlessly in 1928, reaching their climax in September, 1929, collapsing finally in October of that year.

Accompanying the security boom in the twenties and in many ways intensifying it, was the real estate boom. Great speculation in land always marked periods of prosperity in America. Until the war, farm land had received most attention. In the twenties, the major boom was in urban property. Prices for farm land had reached their peak in 1920, and the market for farm mortgages had become saturated as early as 1922. In the cities, however, where the prewar business doldrums had slowed down new construction and where wartime prohibitions and high prices had prevented additional construction and repair for three years, opportunities were tremendous. New areas were awaiting development in regions where the automobile made it possible for city workers to live. New private homes and new apartment houses had to be built, new factories and new office buildings had to be erected, all to accommodate the increasing population of the nation as a whole, the increasing industrial population of urban manufacturing centers, the new industries themselves, and their promoters, publicity men, salesmen, and other white-collar workers.

So extensive were our initial needs in new construction at this time that a great field for long-term economic activity seemed to beckon to American enterprise. Huge undertakings were eagerly planned, large amounts of property were purchased for improvement, mortgages were sought to supply the necessary cash for material and still more land. A great wave of optimism surged through the building community, and the race was on to capture the biggest prizes. The banks, through their credit policies, did nothing to stop this growing speculation, and they themselves undertook some of the greatest ventures. Irving Trust, Bankers Trust, Farmers Trust, Central Hanover, and others sold large amounts of stock to pay for magnificent marble temples and huge office buildings. These they fondly hoped to fill with their new customers, tenants who were engaged in stock speculations of their own and in creating all sorts of private companies in real estate as well as in utilities, in domestic as well as foreign business. Matching the bankers in New York were the Rockefellers with their ambitious Radio City, Chrysler with his modern Gothic skyscraper, and Raskob and his colleagues with the Empire State Building, the biggest white elephant as well as the tallest structure in the world. Much smaller were thousands of other ventures, all of which together attracted greater amounts of cash and credit than these monster undertakings.

As this real estate activity became increasingly intense and prices for land and buildings soared, many real estate operators hypothecated their paper profits to acquire funds for stock speculation. Thus the two booms were joined. Furthermore, as stock prices continued to rise and paper profits increased, more and more installment purchases of consumers' goods were made on the basis of such profits. So extensive were these purchases among the middle class in the late twenties that the vitality of our entire economy came gradually to depend upon the steady ascent of security prices. When these finally collapsed the whole structure came tumbling down.

THE END OF PROSPERITY

When the economy of the United States was rapidly expanding, our depressions were almost always foreshadowed in the production-goods industries by contraction resulting from strained credit, high prices, and rising interest rates, all of which checked further construction. In our more mature economy of the twenties, however, most of these old-time danger signals were absent. There was uncertainty in some lines of business in 1927 and 1928 but this seems to have been dissipated when purchase of consumers' goods broke all records in 1929. Not since the war had there been such a good year in imports and exports. Interest rates were going up, to be sure, but that was partly due to the deliberate policy of the Federal Reserve Board. On the other hand, wholesale prices were showing a salutary downward tendency. When the situation in the stock market in 1929, therefore, precipitated almost of itself the amazingly rapid liquidation that occurred, the business community was astounded.

Following the stock market collapse in October came the second longest recession in our history, one surpassed only by the sixty-five-month depression of the 1870's. In different businesses the bottom was hit between August, 1932, and March, 1933, and the severity of the decline was closely connected with the new business developments of the preceding decade.[32] Stock prices fell more precipitously than ever before because greater savings had driven them higher than in any previous boom. Production-goods industries contracted more violently because avenues for further expansion were less obvious than in earlier years. And perhaps worst of all, the control over prices and production that had been established in so many industries to limit competition in the twenties, permitted a policy of price mantenance and drastic limitations in production. This removed one of the elements counted

---

[32] Mitchell and Burns, *National Bureau of Economic Research, Bulletin 69*, pp. 6–7.

on by classic theorists to restore prosperity: bargain prices that would encourage new expansion.

By the beginning of 1933 the outlook was worse probably than it had ever been before in America. The policy of drastic restriction of production in the semi-monopolistic industries accompanied with the "speed-up" and "stretch-out" to get more work out of those fortunate enough to have jobs, resulted in a staggering burden of unemployed, variously estimated at ten to twenty millions, but not counted for fear of the discouraging effect the true figure might have on both business and politics. The old elasticity seemed to have gone out of the system. Despite the fact that things could scarcely sink lower without complete paralysis of all economic functions, capital goods producers showed no inclination to justify classic theory by taking advantage of the situation and resuming expansion. As the rest of the world was in much the same condition, there were no promising outlets for activity abroad.

XV

THE LEADERSHIP OF BUSINESS

JUST as the steady accumulation of personal savings in the United States after the World War revolutionized American business techniques, so it worked profound changes in other parts of American life. Old habits were transformed by the new emphasis on spending. Old habitats were abandoned as consumers' goods industries sprang up in various sections of the country. The new technology created many leisure hours for industrial workers. It also increased the hardships and insecurity of those unable to keep pace with speeded-up factory processes. As cheap land became scarcer and agricultural depression persisted, more and more farm children sought jobs in the regions of the new enterprises. Urban and suburban population grew rapidly, and municipal problems multiplied. Old institutions took on new functions in the changed American environment, and new associations performed old functions on a revolutionary scale. The needs of modern towns and factories became sharply defined, and the objectives of schools, churches, and philanthropic foundations became clarified. Labor unions and employer associations adjusted their activities to the demands of the new era while men's and women's clubs and business associations found common purposes for which to strive.

Americans in the twenties, profoundly disillusioned by their venture into world affairs, were eager for a reaffirmation of traditional American ideals. But while they spoke bravely of "rugged individualism" and "private initiative" more and more of their activities became cooperative or communal. Their abandonment of traditional isolation to engage in the European conflict had resulted, once that conflict was over, in a resurgence of American nationalism. And as American borders were shut tighter and tighter against the influx of alien people and alien "ideologies," within those borders they strove to weld a "100 per cent American" culture of their own.

Since America's economy had become dependent to a large extent upon new consumers' goods industries and the success of these industries depended upon good public relations, it is not surprising that businessmen sought increasing social control. And since their "prosperity" won for them the confidence of a large part of the population, they became more than ever before the fountainheads of American ideas and the arbiters of American morality. Under pressure to put the Nation's savings to work in productive enterprises, American businessmen vigorously pushed their sales of automobiles, radios, and moving pictures. And as rapid urbanization and agricultural discontent weakened traditional agrarian individualism, the perfection of these new devices of communication together with the older newspapers and national magazines broke down local insularity. Metropolis and village, city and country, factory town and suburban park came increasingly under identical business influences. Provincial habits and customs crumbled. Radios, moving pictures and automobiles opened new interests to Americans everywhere but brought them also into a tighter network of ideas, habits, tastes. Just as local industries had succumbed in competition with national corporations and local stores had succumbed in competition with national chains, so local manners, eccentricities, self-dependence, and self-determination yielded in the twenties to pressures imposed by those seeking national markets for consumers' goods, national consent for business policies, national approbation for business politics. "The business of the United States is business," said Calvin Coolidge, the official oracle of the new era, and most Americans, impressed with the performance of the new business enterprises and indoctrinated with the belief in a magnificent future of ease and plenty, rallied to his slogan.

"Advertising, to be highly successful, must be continuous," wrote Bruce Barton, and American industrialists in the twenties spent fortunes continuously to strengthen the public's belief in the righteousness of business, its altruism and efficiency in handling public problems and giving public service. As business dominance became more and more stringent, however, it gradually became one of the main elements of business weakness, for it set up *spiritual* alienations in a people nurtured on a strong tradition of individualism, and it set up also *material* alienations among the large groups of workers and farmers who failed to share in business prosperity. On the surface the 1920's seemed much more an "era of good feeling" than the age of Monroe a century before, but on cotton and wheat farms, in industrial cities and old mining towns, the insecurity of the many walked hand in hand with the prosperity of the few. To improve their condition or to register their protests, industrial workers turned increasingly to violence. Deprived of their traditional beer by fanatical reformers and industrialists seeking greater productive efficiency, these workers were joined by many other groups in "antisocial" demonstrations against Prohibition. Youngsters shut out from the "normal" opportunities of an expanding economy found employment and self-respect in the new "rackets." Intellectuals were deeply offended by the Babbittry of Rotarians and Lions, and idealists in religion were shocked by their businessmen colleagues of the cloth. In an age dominated by a few giant corporations, nepotism and bureaucracy choked the individual initiative of the ambitious or lowly, and the old American myth of "office boy to president" came to have a hollow sound. Boasts of unlimited opportunities, "upward and onward forever" and "two cars in every garage" had no more substance behind them than holding company stocks. Stocks and slogans flourished in the twenties, but many who could not afford to purchase the stocks learned also to distrust the slogans.

When the stock market crashed in 1929, business leaders tried immediately to restore confidence with new optimistic pronouncements. After a year or two of abysmal depression, however, American manufacturers, merchants, bankers, and brokers could no longer deny that there were great discrepancies between their philosophy and their actions. Faced with obvious misery throughout the nation, they had to admit their inability to keep up American pay rolls, American purchasing power, American standards of living, and American morale. Most businessmen continued to fight the N.I.R.A., the S.E.C., the N.L.R.B., T.V.A.

and federal home and work relief. But some businessmen and most politicians, at least in 1933, were for the first time profoundly worried lest the age of individual enterprise, its fables, folklore and mythology, was finished. Actually it had ended long before when American business, under the leadership of international corporations, interstate trade associations, national chambers of commerce, and "booster" business organizations, had already become much more cooperative than competitive, much more social than individualistic.

THE DECLINE OF INDIVIDUALISM

For more than a century, American workers had been losing command of their workshops, their tools, their hours and conditions of labor. American farmers had been losing sovereignty over their land, their homesteads, and their children who ran off to the city. For fifty years small American businessmen had been surrendering control of local factories and forges while shopkeepers, at a much slower rate, had been yielding control over their stores and local markets. Factories and financial institutions had grown steadily in size and power, wealth had become more concentrated, insecurity more pervasive. In the twenties all these trends were rapidly accelerated, leaving more and more Americans dependent upon some agency other than themselves for the fulfillment of their elementary as well as their more cultivated needs, leaving them also subject to more and more storms and crises not of their own creation nor amenable to their own palliatives.

As American industry was consolidated into larger and larger establishments, scientific management became more widely adopted in American factories. Assembly line tasks became simpler, industrial jobs more monotonous, and youth, energy, and speed emerged as the strongest recommendations for industrial employment. Plant superintendents became increasingly responsive to delicate fluctuations in the productive capacity of individual operatives, and advancing age, illness, or outside worries became constantly more dangerous to industrial workers. Experience, skill, and training declined steadily in value, and larger and larger numbers of Americans thus became oppressed by the insecurity of their jobs and homes, by the uncertainty of their incomes, their supply of food and clothing, the futures of their children, their husbands and their wives.

Aggravating this condition were new refinements in cost accounting and the constantly growing sensitivity of corporate managers to the slightest changes in the business outlook. Pay rolls could now be reduced more promptly when the omens for continued expansion and continued profits looked bad, and employment, even for the most efficient workers, thus became more capricious. Local retailers and service men like barbers and tailors, already troubled by new chain-store competition, now were made still more insecure by the plight of the factory families to whom they looked for patronage. More and more Americans in the twenties thus became aware for the first time of their complete dependence upon national and even international conditions far beyond their control. They became aware of their dependence upon decisions made without any consultation of their needs by absentee managers meeting in places far distant from those where such decisions would have effect.

To the uncertainties of factory work were added those of urban and suburban living. In the twenties more Americans than ever before in our history moved from the country to the city. The proportion of home owners declined; tenancy increased in urban and rural areas alike; and urban mortgages skyrocketed leaving many with nominal title to their property but, considering the flimsiness of their equities and the urgency of interest and amortization charges, even less secure in their tenure than many renters. Overcrowding and undernourishment, crime and disease flourished side by side while taxes mounted to pay for new schools, new parks, new equipment for expanding police and fire personnel, new street pavements and new public buildings. The cost of urban living rose steadily as public services increased and functions once performed on the farm or in the cities by independent individuals came more than ever before to be carried on by new municipal bureaus or new public utilities.

Forced by the pressure of great savings to expand in every possible way the market for consumers' goods, American manufacturers after the World War learned to appeal to the unconscious desires of their potential customers. Prompted by advertising men who had studied Freud, they began to make profoundly uneasy those Americans who could not keep up with the Joneses, who could not purchase all the new symbols of respectable social position as determined by the social leaders of the new communities. To the uncertainties caused by fitful employment and urban dependence, therefore, were added in the twenties the burdens of constantly expanding debts incurred for the purchase of new automobiles, house furnishings, porcelain and chromium plumbing, radios, washing machines and refrigerators. "Human desires are the steam which makes the social machine work," wrote Edward Bernays, himself a nephew of Freud.[1] And as Bernays and other advertising men aroused desires for more and more of the luxuries of the day, these luxuries gradually became the signs of a "decent" home. Despite the strain placed upon most American family budgets, therefore, as many new devices as possible had to be purchased, lest one's daughter or one's wife fear to bring into her home her richer neighbors. The new fads and fashions, the new labor-saving devices and attractive house furnishings were not bad in themselves. The difficulty in the twenties was that while every one's appetite was stimulated, only a few could afford to buy. Among the great majority, some were discontented because they could not even appear to keep pace with their neighbors, others because they could only keep pace with great difficulty and nerve-racking worry about how to make ends meet and yet "maintain appearances."

While the growing consolidation of American industry and the increasing urbanization of American population aggravated the feeling of insecurity that pervaded American life in the twenties, this insecurity itself led to further inroads upon traditional American individualism and the practice of "self-help." Rotary, Kiwanis, Lions, and Elks all had great membership booms as small business competitors felt the need to boost one another's morale, with slogans like[2]

---

[1] Bernays, *Propaganda,* p. 52.
[2] Lynd, *Middletown,* p. 487.

United we stick, divided we're stuck.
United we boost, divided we bust.

At the same time, with football rallies, basketball games, and "community sings," many towns themselves were displacing the family and the home as the real focus of American activity. In the twenties "an outstanding Middletown clubwoman" exhorted a group of "Middletown" children: [3]

You must have community spirit. You must think that there is no finer town in the whole United States than this. There is no finer school than yours, no finer parents than yours, no finer opportunities anywhere than you have right here. People talk of California where there is sunshine all the year round, but I've lived in California, and give me Middle Western rains! I tell you there's no lovelier place on God's footstool than this old state of yours.

Membership in women's clubs in the twenties gave leisured females throughout the country charitable, educational, and business affairs with which to occupy themselves, and by 1926 three million women had grasped these opportunities. Church membership also increased steadily in all denominations as the older gospel of social reform gave way to the new gospel of business. Y.M. and Y.W.C.A.'s flourished as homeless young men and women from farms and villages came to seek work and respectable amusement in the great cities. As population became more centralized, religious, educational, and medical institutions began to pool their assets, consolidating like giant business corporations into larger units the better to serve increasing group needs. Not only private and public hospitals but even private medical practitioners, especially in the Middle West, combined in the twenties in "group clinics." By 1930 there were about one hundred and fifty such clinics with a personnel of two thousand physicians.[4]

Perhaps most important among all of these communal activities was the "community chest." The first of these was established in Cleveland in 1914 with $22,500 in funds. By 1919 there were twelve community chests in the United States. By 1930 there were 363, and they raised that year $75,108,792 to aid the grow-

3 Lynd, *Middletown,* p. 487.
4 Shryock, *Medicine,* pp. 397–398.

ing numbers of citizens of American cities and towns who, in whatever ways, could no longer help themselves.[5]

While many Americans and many American institutions thus were developing the social machinery to assist their countrymen in an age of declining self-dependence, other men and other institutions less benevolent in purpose began to look beyond the new unity of our local communities. Shrewdly capitalizing the spirit of nationalism, strong in America after the war, they tried desperately to forge a homogeneous *nation* of "white" skin, "Nordic" blood, Protestant religion and small-town prejudices. Dominant among these groups was the revived Ku Klux Klan.

Directing its attack upon different minorities in different parts of the country, the Klan was at once anti-Negro, anti-Semitic, anti-Catholic and anti-Wall Street. Its campaigns were aided greatly by its insistence, in an atmosphere of high tension during the radical revolutions in Europe after the World War, that "every method known to man has been used and is being used by alien-minded and foreign influence to halt our growth." [6] The mysterious sheet and grandiose ritual of the Klan fed the craving for romance and high adventure starved in the drab surroundings of American Middletowns and Zeniths. Klan parades, lynchings, beatings, and violent raids gave emotional outlets for the frustrations encountered daily by lower-class Americans, while Klannish myths about international Jewry, international bankers, the vaulting ambition and profound cruelty of the Pope and his hirelings, satisfied the ignorant in American small towns who were eager to find scapegoats for their own insecurity and discontent. The Klan claimed a membership of 4,000,000 at its peak in 1924. In that year its strength was demonstrated when a resolution denouncing its activities was defeated in the Democratic National Convention. When that convention sought to nominate Alfred E. Smith for the Presidency, the Klan lobbied vigorously and successfully to defeat him, Smith being a representative of everything the Klan hated: alien parentage, Catholic religion, New York upbringing. The bombast of Klannish pronouncements and one of

---

[5] *Recent Social Trends,* p. 1205.
[6] Lynd, *Middletown,* pp. 483–484.

the major objectives of Klannish activity are clearly shown in the following extract from a Klan address:[7]

This great country of ours—bounded on the north by the aurora borealis, on the south by the equator, on the east by the rising sun, and on the west by the hereafter—is American, thank God! We make our boys and girls live here twenty-one years before we allow them to vote, and we ought to do the same with all foreigners.

DIRECTING CORPORATE SOCIETY

Many Americans thus were finding, in associations of all sorts, outlets for the expression of those aspects of their individuality that were circumscribed by the monotony or insecurity of their jobs. Many other Americans, however, remained dissatisfied throughout the twenties, with their economic as well as their social situations, and it was against the attitudes and activities of these groups that businessmen felt most keenly that they must defend themselves. While a good deal of business propaganda and a good many of the activities of strictly business associations, therefore, had the objective, to be sure, of enlarging the markets for goods, services, and securities, businessmen also were seeking in every possible way to direct American thinking in lines more favorable to general business purposes in a consumers' goods economy. And on the whole, of course, they succeeded.

Unhampered by an entrenched military caste or landed aristocracy, businessmen encountered the opposition of no ancient vested interests. The booming prosperity of the twenties gave a magnificent gloss to the quality of their leadership, and their control of important avenues of communication permitted no strong heretical gospel to gain a foothold in the United States. "In making up its mind," said Edward Bernays, a group's "first impulse is usually to follow the example of a trusted leader." [8] And as business conditions improved steadily in the twenties and business propaganda had its cumulative effect, this "trusted leader" came to be the national Chamber of Commerce, the National Association of Manufacturers, the Edison Electric In-

[7] Lynd, *Middletown*, p. 483.
[8] Bernays, *Propaganda*, p. 50.

stitute, the American Bankers or the American Bar Association. The utility that gave a town its power and light, the corporation that gave it its jobs, the banker who gave it its credit, and the lawyer who negotiated its mortgages, all came to wield a steadily greater influence. And since each was in fact a representative of some national corporation or national association, the latter could influence with all the latest instruments of propaganda every county, city, town, and hamlet in the land. "As civilization has become more complex," wrote Bernays in 1928, "the technical means have been invented and developed by which opinion may be regimented." [9] And as America became more and more a nation of billion-dollar corporations seeking to sell consumers' goods, stocks, and bonds, her citizens felt increasingly the impact of those new "technical means" and regimentation went on apace.

The first object of business leaders in America in the twenties, just as it was the first object of *leaders* of all earlier societies, was to eliminate every shade of "radicalism." The threat of world revolution contained in Bolshevik propaganda, made American businessmen extremely sensitive to attacks upon the "American way of life." Supported by a growing middle class of white-collar workers and professional men and women, therefore, they helped to make the words "Socialism" and "Communism" taboo among all classes of society. Any discussion of postwar Russia was frowned upon in many schools and colleges; and any *favorable* discussion in classroom or factory, newspaper or magazine was likely if publicized to lead to a teacher's or worker's dismissal, to the withdrawal of business advertisements and the denial of commercial credits. The more the monopolistic corporations and national trade associations threatened free competition in America in the twenties, the more zealously were the competitive virtues reemphasized. As protective tariffs were restored to private industries and natural resources were reopened to private exploitation, the virtues of "rugged individualism" were more and more vigorously reaffirmed. Businessmen were not alone in the country-wide attack upon "un-American" ideas and

---

[9] Bernays, *Propaganda*, p. 12.

"subversive" organizations and activities. The *majority* of the people seemed to hug their old ways and old slogans more closely. Businessmen, however, paid the piper most of the time, and most often they called the tune.

While businessmen in the early twenties really feared the activities of "red" revolutionaries, it was part of the strategy of their propaganda to make the hatred of radicalism so profound in America that anything simply labeled "un-American" would encounter immediate public hostility. The most important victims of this strategy were the labor unions. Labor and capital in 1917 had made a truce for the duration of the war, and President Wilson, through the Industrial Conference of 1919, tried to make this truce permanent. When the Conference foundered, however, on the employers' insistence upon their right to hire and fire as they pleased without consulting union leaders, strikes, lockouts, shootings, and bombings once again began to mark industrial warfare in the United States, especially in the steel regions of Pennsylvania and the coal regions of West Virginia and Kentucky. Here then was business's opportunity. "The war taught us the power of propaganda," said Roger Babson, business's great forecaster, in 1921. "Now when we have anything to sell to the American people, we know how to sell it. We have the school, the pulpit, and the press." [10] In an atmosphere teeming with drawn-out strikes, industrial violence, and reports of lurid radical projects, business had first of all to sell the "American Plan." And none of Babson's propaganda media or methods were neglected in the campaign.

The "American Plan" was not a program for peaceful industrial relations. It was a set of attitudes, the most important of which was that the closed shop and collective bargaining were "un-American"—the first because it interfered with the owner's free use of his private property, the second because it limited the ancient right of the worker to contract individually for the sale of his labor. To indoctrinate the nation with these attitudes, American Plan associations were organized in every state and nearly every city in the country. Local chambers of commerce

---

[10] Beale, *Are American Teachers Free?* p. 546.

were enlisted in the work while such diverse groups as the American Constitutional Association in West Virginia, the employers' associations in Pittsburgh and Dayton, the Board of Trade in Scranton, and the Merchants' and Manufacturers' Association in Toledo were all very active. As early as 1920 there were forty-six open-shop associations in Illinois, twenty-one of them in Chicago alone. Michigan had twenty-five, Ohio seventeen. Other middle western states followed closely while the rest of the forty-eight soon joined the procession. In Louisville, Kentucky, two hundred firms subscribed $20,000 to educate its people in the justice of the open shop. In Tulsa, Oklahoma, the Open Shop Association, by September, 1921, had three thousand five hundred members. The great state of California was covered with propaganda emanating from Los Angeles while in Utah, Montana, Washington, and similar mountain and western regions where industrial concentration was limited, the Associated Industries carried the employers' banner.[11]

From the start thousands of farmers fell in with the "American Plan" campaign, expressing through the National Grange as early as 1920, their belief in the right of each individual "to work where his industry is needed at any time and at any wage which is satisfactory to him." [12] In 1921 the American Bankers Association added its weight and prestige by announcing in *Industry*, an employer periodical, that it favored allowing "every man . . . to work out his salvation and not to be bound by the shackles of organization to his own detriment." [13] And the National Association of Manufacturers also lent its aid to further this new "100 per cent American" cause, supplying funds and shrewd generalship. Within its ranks were trained lobbyists, good public speakers, able propagandists and representatives of every manufacturing line in the country. On its mailing lists were ministers, teachers, lecturers, editors, school superintendents, radio broadcasting companies, judges, legislators, governors, and mayors. It supported the use of injunctions in checking strikes and peaceful picketing, and spent hundreds of thousands of dollars annually in

[11] *History of Labor,* vol. IV, pp. 492–494.
[12] *History of Labor,* vol. IV, p. 491.
[13] *History of Labor,* vol. IV, p. 491.

fighting legislation designed to prohibit such injunctions as well as for other political and propagandist purposes.[14] In 1925 its president, John E. Edgerton, eloquently denounced labor leaders and labor unions in the following terms: [15]

The palatial temples of labor whose golden domes rise in exultant splendor throughout the nation, the millions of dollars extracted annually by the jewelled hand of greed from the pockets of wage-earners and paid out in lucrative salaries to a ravenous band of pretenders, tell the pitiful story of a slavery such as this country never knew before.

And he went on to admonish the members of his organization:

It is your duty to break the shackles that have been forged upon the wrists of those who labor with you by showing them in your daily contact and attitude that you are their best friends and that it is not necessary to them to follow the false leadership of designing pirates who parade in the guise of the workingman's friends.

So successful were the N.A.M. and its member associations in selling the "American Plan" that the United States Senate Committee on Education and Labor could report that by 1926, "having achieved the retardation of labor organizations, . . . the hectic effort to allay what had seemed to them impending radical revolution became unnecessary, and the association settled back to the quiet enjoyment of the fruits of their efforts during the years of prosperity." [16]

While American businessmen and American business organizations were preventing organized labor from winning the sympathy of the American people in the fight for the closed shop, businessmen were also engaged in the opposite direction, working vigorously to strengthen their own position in the country. To check the growth of American radicalism was only a negative achievement, simply a starting point for an animated pro-business drive. Negative too, was the successful effort to dispel the bad taste left in the public's mouth before the war by the muckrakers' revelations. Business needed positive good will, not simply dis-

---

14 Committee on Education and Labor, *Report*, pp. 42–43.
15 Committee on Education and Labor, *Report*, p. 31.
16 Committee on Education and Labor, *Report*, p. 43.

interest or tolerance. Businessmen had more and more consumers' goods to sell, more and more stocks and bonds to issue. They were open to attack by new political boards and commissions and, in some lines, by government competition. They needed the public positively on their side, and they spared no expenditure and overlooked few opportunities to drive home business's message.

Just as businessmen started to work first upon their operatives in the drive against radicalism, so too they started to work on their labor forces in the drive for respect and support for business policies and business practices. The extensive welfare activities of great corporations were designed in part to convince labor of the benevolence of its employers. Employee stock ownership was designed to divide among the workers a share of business profits and hence to inculcate among them a feeling of responsibility for the welfare of the company and the preservation of its good name. Employee participation in management through shop committees and company unions was planned once more to drive home the idea, as expressed by one industrialist, that employers and employees were really but "one great happy family." We have seen how President Edgerton of the N.A.M. admonished the members of his organization to prove in daily contacts their genuine friendship for their employees. Other leading industrialists urged the same practices upon their colleagues while hundreds of companies started "employee magazines" to develop an *esprit de corps* not generally found in large factories.

"An employee magazine serves the same purpose within a plant that advertising and salesmanship serve in getting the product sold," said one large firm. By 1925 nearly 500 companies, more than half of them engaged in manufacturing, were publishing employee magazines. The "good will" they won among the workers, their friends, and the public generally was enormous. "The employee magazine is the best means of correcting the 'soulless corporation' idea," said the management of a big textile company.[17] The editor of another of these journals said:[18]

---

[17] National Industrial Conference Board, *Employee Magazines*, p. 45.
[18] National Industrial Conference Board, *Employee Magazines*, p. 43.

A big organization in the minds of its employees is either a soulless, efficient, impersonal machine or human, sincere and vital. The distribution of the right sort of employees' magazine will do more to give employees the proper slant on their company and on their particular job than anything else I know of.

The "primary purpose" of employee magazines and the rest of the program of which they were a part was, as one firm succinctly expressed it: "Increased production of a better quality at a lower cost through the *stimulation of the human element in industry.*" [19] And so successful were the devices used to achieve this purpose that even as late as 1930 the A.F. of L. declared in its official periodical the *American Federationist:* [20]

Trade unions must cooperate actively with management to promote high productivity, elimination of waste, and lower cost of production in organized establishments. Only under these conditions can payment of the highest wages become possible.

But the conversion of labor to the business point of view was insignificant compared to the winning of the public, and indeed the campaign for good labor relations was often only one aspect of the larger pattern. As Bernays said in 1928, "the general public, apart from its function as potential customer, is influenced in its attitude toward the concern by what it knows of that concern's financial dealings, its labor policy, even by the livableness of the houses in which its employees dwell." [21] And so convincing was business's appeal to the general public in the twenties that Frederick Lewis Allen, a perspicacious editor of *Harper's,* could write that "the overwhelming majority of the American people believed with increasing certainty that business men knew better than anybody else what was good for the country." [22]

It was rarely necessary for business corporations or business associations to threaten withdrawal of advertisements from newspapers or magazines because of anti-business publicity. Editors

[19] National Industrial Conference Board, *Employee Magazines,* p. 21.
[20] Chapman, *Business and Banking Thought,* p. 122.
[21] Bernays, *Propaganda,* p. 71.
[22] Allen, *Lords of Creation,* p. 222.

and publishers, as we have seen, had themselves become Big
Business men, keenly aware of how to deal with their customers.[23]
They knew what stories to run and which to kill. They knew
which was the pro-business angle and which was not. They knew
the value of success stories and the costliness of unpleasant
truths. No word of theirs, except inadvertently, would shake
confidence in Florida real estate or some great stock flotation.
They would give no hint to the realty groups which were behind
"news" stories praising resort areas, or the food companies
which inspired daily articles on dietetics and public health. Railroads and other utilities purchased space in newspapers and
magazines not only to advertise their products but also to maintain their influence upon these tremendous vehicles of propaganda. And newspapers and magazines in turn responded to this
pressure, seeking to retain the good will of their customers just
as those customers sought the good will of the public.

Newspaper chains were a long time developing in the United
States. Syndicated articles and "canned" editorials emanating for
national consumption out of the offices of business propaganda
associations were a comparatively new aspect of American
journalism in the twentieth century. Only late in its history, therefore, had the newspaper business become Big Business. Such,
however, was not the case in radio. The first daily broadcast in
the United States started with the election returns transmitted
over station KDKA, Pittsburgh, on November 2, 1920. To attract audiences, sets were given away free to those who would
promise to stay at home and listen. By 1927, there were 732
broadcasting stations in the country and probably ten million
radio sets in American homes. Virtually all the long-wave air
lanes had been distributed, and network broadcasting was practically monopolized by two major companies, the National Broadcasting Company and the Columbia Broadcasting System. Almost
from the very start, therefore, radio was Big Business and had
begun to compete with newspapers and magazines not only in the
contest for business advertising but also in the effort to sell
business itself to the public. The National Broadcasting Company

---

[23] See chap. XII, pp. 269–270.

after its creation in 1926 was controlled by the Radio Corporation of America, and R.C.A. in turn was controlled by the General Electric Company. Incidentally the first president of N.B.C. was M. H. Aylesworth, earlier managing director of the National Electric Light Association, a utilities public relations agency. Almost from the beginning, therefore, network broadcasting was virtually closed to anything but messages acceptable to business. Permits for new stations became more difficult to obtain while rates for time on national hook-ups soared to such heights that only large companies could afford to use this newest instrument of special pleading. Their success with it was acknowledged by the head of the Public Relations Bureau of the Edison Electric Company of Boston, who said in 1930 that his company's "broadcasting station was the greatest builder of good will which the company ever had developed." [24]

The "news" content of newspapers and popular magazines were often puerile, while intellectuals scorned radio programs as fodder for "twelve-year-old minds." Both published and broadcast propaganda, however, was designed to influence American adults. To get at the youngsters other techniques were used. Community pressure and direct intimidation were often employed to make recalcitrant teachers toe the conventional mark. But more important, textbooks were written in accordance with business ideas, or corrected to get those ideas across.[25] Whole courses, especially in government and civics, were introduced to preach the business gospel, while business publications themselves were used in many schools. "We wish to reach the mind of the child while it is still plastic," stated the American Bar Association in 1924.[26] The utilities, said the Illinois Public Utility Information Committee, aim "to fix the truth about the utilities in the young person's mind before incorrect notions become fixed there." [27] This Illinois committee and its work "have been established as so entirely legitimate," testified Bernard J. Mullaney (Mr. Insull's "right-hand man in public relations matters") in 1928,

[24] Thompson, *Power Trust,* p. 411.
[25] Thompson, *Power Trust,* pp. 383–385.
[26] Beale, *Are American Teachers Free?* p. 533.
[27] T.N.E.C. *Monograph, no. 26,* p. 154.

"that its literature is used in the public schools without question."
"When the committee celebrated its second anniversary," he
continued, "it had passed the five million mark in pieces of literature distributed." [28]

"From birth to death," said *America's New Frontier,* a
pamphlet issued in 1929 by Insull's Middle West Utilities Company, "the modern man is served every waking hour by corporations of one kind or another." And it would take a book as long
again as this one to run the gamut of all the propaganda methods
used by these corporations to capture the good will of "modern
man" and to retain it. A. T. & T. and its twenty-one associated
telephone companies in 1926, for instance, had deposits in 4,549
banks scattered in almost as many communities throughout the
country. This organization, declared a representative of its treasury department, "regards the bankers as a class, as influential
citizens in their particular communities, whose friendship and
good will should be considered from a public relations standpoint." [29] Between 1925 and 1934, Bell Telephone companies
and the Western Electric Company paid dues totaling nearly
$5,000,000 for about eight thousand memberships in five thou-
sand different noncommercial organizations. The purpose of such
expenditures was explained as early as 1921 by H. B. Thayer,
then president of A. T. & T., of which Bell and Western Electric
were parts: [30]

Membership in such organizations as the United States Chamber of
Commerce, National Labor Organizations, and National Farmers Organizations, etc., local Chambers of Commerce, Rotary Clubs, etc., and
civic organizations of every description, improvement societies, neighbor-
hood groups, church clubs, consumers' leagues, etc., *afford unusual opportunities for establishing contacts with the leaders in general public activities and those who are molding public sentiment.*

Representatives of many lines of business, but especially the
utilities, were on university faculties, on Chautauqua and other
lecture courses, and on church councils. They endowed special

---

28 Thompson, *Power Trust,* pp. 272–274.
29 Danielian, *A. T. & T.,* p. 287.
30 Danielian, *A. T. & T.,* pp. 285–286.

chairs in universities and gave funds for special courses, underwrote football expenses and supplied star players to fill magnificent stadia. They financed learned foundations publishing authoritative reports by experts with a business turn of mind. They financed other foundations doing educational and welfare work in order to capture public sympathy. They sold stocks to an ever growing investing public and thus created a large group of protectors, and they showed free movies to any organization that would have them in order to strengthen still more the message of business to the business-minded American public. Judge Healy for the Federal Trade Commission in 1928 asked Mr. Oxley, Director of the Information Department of the National Electric Light Association: [31]

Do you know any means of publicity that has been neglected by your organization?
Answer: Only one, and that is sky writing. I don't believe that we have tried that with airplanes.

"I cannot understand," said a traveling companion to William Wrigley, Jr., "why you spend such huge sums in advertising Spearmint. Every one knows your gum now." Mr. Wrigley replied: [32]

The train we are on is probably running sixty miles an hour. What would happen if we should uncouple the locomotive? I'll tell you. We'd run a few hundred yards along the track and stop. The advertising I am doing is as necessary to remind people of Spearmint as the locomotive is necessary to the uninterrupted progress of this train.

This was the philosophy of business propaganda as well as direct commodity advertising. And business propaganda obviously had done its job well. True, there were heretical organizations like the National Child Labor Committee and the National Consumers' League, combating with business's own methods objectionable industrial practices. There was also a noisy farm minority pressing throughout the decade for aid to agriculture. But these only justified the continuance of business propaganda;

[31] Thompson, *Power Trust*, p. 270.
[32] Lichtenberg, *Advertising Campaigns*, p. 17.

they did not threaten the result. Public relations men had proved themselves to be the high priests of the new order, and even Jesus himself was enrolled in it. Among the chapter titles of Bruce Barton's *The Man Nobody Knows: A Discovery of the Real Jesus*, a "best-seller" in 1924 and for two years thereafter, were "The Executive," "The Outdoor Man," "The Sociable Man," "His Advertisements," "The Founder of Modern Business." Truly business propaganda had conquered heaven and earth in the fabulous twenties.

POLITICS DURING THE BOOM

Business associations in the twenties undertook many of their activities simply to broaden the markets for goods and new securities. Much business propaganda had the same objectives. But business's energetic quest for good will as we have seen, had other purposes besides encouraging great spending and invest-ment. And of leading importance among these other purposes was the acquiescence of the public in business politics. Business-men and business organizations had fought with the rest of the nation against socialism and communism right after the war, and they continued their political offensive against organized labor throughout the twenties. More specifically, however, business groups were interested in organizing public opinion behind their drives for high tariffs and other aids to business enterprises, behind their views on war debts and reparations. What we want in America, said Harding in 1920, "is less government in business and more business in government." [33] And business leaders sought above all to have the public agree to this reversal of Progressive tendencies. They wanted to merge and combine without hindrance by the Attorney General or the courts. They wanted as little regulation as possible of rates for electric power and light, illum-inating gas and water, railroad transportation, telephone and telegraph service. They wanted no municipal, state, or federal ownership of business properties which would compete with

[33] Kirkland, *Economic Life*, p. 682.

private enterprise or set up "yardsticks" by which private enterprise would be judged. "Canned" editorials and inspired "news" were among the most popular means employed by business organizations to impress their desires upon the public. The largest disseminator of such propaganda was E. Hofer & Sons of Salem, Oregon. This company serviced 14,000 daily and weekly newspapers "absolutely free of charge," underwritten as it was, according to Mr. Insull, by a number of large manufacturers and holding companies. Mr. Hofer himself told succinctly the purpose of his service: [34]

First, to reduce the volume of legislation that interferes with business and industry; second, to minimize and counteract political regulation of business that is hurtful; third, to discourage radicalism by labor organizations and all sorts of agitators; fourth, a constant fight for reasonable taxation by state, city and county government; fifth, a scientific educational campaign against all socialistic and radical propaganda of whatever nature.

Compared to business enterprise in an age of great corporations, politics is a volatile thing. Executive, administrative, and legislative departments frequently change their personnel while all political office holders are subject to meteoric shifts in the attitudes and opinions of the voters. Of all the cabinet members of 1921 only Andrew Mellon was in the same position in 1929. Three Presidents had been in office in that period, four Congresses had been elected, four Secretaries of State appointed, four Attorneys General, four Secretaries of the Interior, and so on down the list. Yet so profoundly pro-business was the national temper and so successful were business efforts in keeping the favor of the public, that other groups might combine, publish, speak, and vote, and still industrial business could assert itself above all competitors for public favor. Industrial pressure groups were not the only ones in the country. It is probable, indeed, that democracy cannot function without pressure groups. Prohibitionists, farmers, workers, teachers, consumers, all had their lobbies, their journals, their paid secretaries and expert propagandists. But business associations and business leaders were so powerful in the twenties that none of these groups could with-

[34] Thompson, *Power Trust*, pp. 323, 327.

stand them. Business had, as Babson said, "the press, the pulpit and the schools." It had, besides, the movies and the radio. Even more important, business leadership seemed "to deliver the goods"; as Frederick Lewis Allen said, the system "worked." The twenties were vexatious for large portions of our population. But nowhere, at any time in the world's history, had there been so much wealth so widely distributed. No wonder, then, that business pressures were most successful. No wonder that, while many groups in America won some laws in the twenties, very little legislation was passed that business opposed and very little legislation failed that business wanted.

Businessmen and their associations thus overshadowed all other groups in our society; and since business was having its best years in the twenties national politics was not very exciting, and most of the important federal problems were inherited from the war. Under the leadership of Andrew Mellon the wartime excess profits tax was repealed in 1921. After the mild recession of 1924, estate and gift taxes were repealed and publicity for income-tax returns was abolished. In the meantime the Treasury was finding loopholes in the income-tax laws which had been overlooked by businessmen, and tax refunds poured out of Washington. Many business interests thus succeeded in reducing their own tax burdens.

While they were settling their tax problems, businessmen were also winning their points in relation to the railroads and the merchant marine. Soon after we entered the war the government had taken over almost all the railroads in the country. Under the Esch-Cummins Act of 1920, after bills to continue federal operation were defeated, these roads were returned to their former owners. A "recapture" clause in the Esch-Cummins Act stated that 5.5 per cent was a fair rate of profit for railroads and one-half of all profits above 6 per cent was to be returned to the Treasury of the United States. Since neither Congress nor the courts could decide upon what basis this 6 per cent was to be computed, however, the railroads were free to make as much profit as they could while they entangled in litigation all efforts to put the "recapture" clause to work.

Just as the government had engaged in the railroad business

during the war, so it had engaged in ocean shipping, creating a huge merchant fleet to carry troops, munitions, and supplies to Europe and to maintain facilities for essential peacetime trade. When the war was over businessmen sought to get hold of this fleet. They undertook to convince the nation that the government should get out of business, that it should sell its merchant ships at great discounts to private corporations, that it should subsidize these corporations with generous mail contracts to enable them to compete with European shippers paying low wages, and that it should in addition lend these corporations extra sums to construct still more ships in order to make American commerce independent of foreign vessels. All this was done.

The Fordney-McCumber Tariff Act of 1922 was not passed to solve any vestigial war problems, nor were the still higher Smoot-Hawley rates of 1930 adopted for that purpose. These acts were more in keeping with the attempted "return to normalcy," which meant in G.O.P. terms the return to prohibitive protection for new and old industries alike. Incidentally, however, by closing our ports to foreign goods, these acts made the war debts practically uncollectable, and that pleased American manufacturers as well as the banking interests which had no desire to see European credit strained to service these old public debts, lest Europeans find it impossible as well to service new private loans.

By "normalcy," Harding probably meant also the rapid development of natural resources by private enterprise, though it was necessary to go all the way back to Grant's administrations to find precedents for the fraud and corruption that marked the leasing of oil properties in the early twenties. This distribution was not the only corrupt act of Harding's henchmen, but it certainly was the most scandalous illustration of government aid to business in a period when business leaders were making brave attempts to revive theoretical *laissez faire*. Besides tariffs and outright grants of natural resources, business interests in the twenties also won the cooperation of the "rugged individualist" Herbert Hoover in the establishment of a great clearing house for business information in the Department of Commerce. And while they were making that department virtually the greatest trade association in the world they were also turning the Federal Trade Commission, after 1925, into a research organization to discover ways in which business managers could cooperate more successfully.[35] The Federal Trade Commission had originally been formed to check violations of the Clayton Antitrust Act. Under business pressures it became an instrument for rationalizing such violations.[36]

While American business as a whole and particular Americans business groups maintained good relations with federal politics in the twenties, their most notable defeat came in the attempt to force the government to sell to private corporations the wartime power development at Muscle Shoals, Alabama. Senator Norris of Nebraska fought such proposals with a countermeasure of his own, seeking to get the government to complete the power plants already under construction and then to sell power to neighboring rural communities. Norris got his bill through both houses of Congress in 1928 only to have it pocket-vetoed by Coolidge, and again in 1931 to have Hoover not only veto it but protest to Congress that such legislation was "not liberalism" but "degeneration." [37] While Norris failed in his endeavors, businessmen failed in theirs, the Muscle Shoals works remaining idle throughout the twenties in the hands of the government.

It might be said also that "prohibition" was a defeat for business interests in so far as the distillers and brewers, a powerful industrial group, were of course dead set against it. Led by Henry Ford, however, quite a few industrialists supported the W.C.T.U. and its "dry" campaign, seeking to reduce drinking by their employees and thus increase productive efficiency and industrial output.

Similarly there were two sides to the immigration question. Businessmen had profited greatly from the constant stream of immigrants that had been pouring into the United States for more than a century right up to the World War. Steamship companies had built up a thriving trade carrying Europeans to America. The western railroads, as we have seen, had settled

[35] Burns, *Decline of Competition*, p. 579.
[36] Ripley, *Main Street and Wall Street*, p. 115.
[37] Parkes, *Recent America*, pp. 437–438.

their extensive lands with immigrants. For decades, immigration societies, financed by industrialists in eastern as well as western states, had found cheap foreign labor for American factories. Incidentally, the steamship companies determined to a large degree the type of immigrant that came at different periods by offering cheap transportation rates at European ports where steamship competition was intense. The railroads and heavy industries, on the other hand, helped determine the location of immigrants once they arrived in the United States. The railroads sought mainly farmers and sent them west. Steel mills sought mixed language groups in order to impede the exchange of ideas among their workers, thus to forestall unionization. Other industries sought the particular types of foreign workers that had already proved adaptable to their needs, while still others tried to select immigrants with special skills and training. With the outbreak of the World War, however, business lost this source of settlers and cheap labor, and the new quota and exclusion acts of 1921, 1924 and 1929 made the pre-war volume of immigration impossible to attain. Not all businessmen opposed these acts, though most business groups had fought all previous restrictive measures. Many industrialists in the twenties no longer needed additional foreign workers, while many other businessmen, like others in American society, had begun to fear the "foreign ideologies" which some of the new immigrants were bringing with them. The acts of 1921 and 1924, however, were triumphs for labor not business, victories for the unions which feared competition for jobs from men and women fleeing impoverished Europe after the war.

American businessmen also fought strongly against the payment of the veterans' bonus, fearing increased taxes to meet the demands of the erstwhile A.E.F. Yet here too was no clear-cut victory since bonus payments would certainly have increased the purchasing power of many families and hence broadened the market for factory commodities. Similarly the persistent defeat, either by presidential veto or by congressional rejection, of bills to increase farm prices certainly kept down the cost of living in industrial communities and thus was an excuse to keep down wages. On the other hand, such defeats probably hurt businessmen almost as much as they hurt the farmers, curtailing as they did the latter's ability to purchase new tools and machinery, to buy new household labor-saving devices, to keep up with the changes in fads and fashions in all lines of consumers' goods.

By emphasizing the "rule of reason" in the United States Steel Corporation case in 1920 the Supreme Court made it much more difficult for the government to prosecute combinations "in restraint of trade." By introducing a similar rule in rate cases involving railroads as well as other utilities, the court weakened greatly the power of the Interstate Commerce Commission and the large number of new public utility commissions in the states. By deciding that holding companies were not utilities even though they "held" control of tremendous operating companies, the court removed many great corporations from almost any surveillance by the law. While the Department of Commerce and the Federal Trade Commission were furthering business combination, therefore, the courts were also contributing their share, and the failure of the Department of Justice under Harding, Coolidge, or Hoover to prosecute violations of the Sherman and Clayton acts helped accelerate this tendency still more. The governmental agencies responsible for checking the growth of monopoly thus were used instead to encourage it. And the American public acquiesced in this retreat from Progressivism.

THE PROMISE OF THE ARTS

As long as capital for the production of goods and the payment of wages was scarce in the United States, money-making was a momentous social function. In the twenties, however, capital went begging for productive opportunities; yet never was the spirit of business more pervasive in our society. Never were more Americans seeking to "get rich quick," to make a lucky speculation, to pull off a successful promotion in one bold financial stroke. And with good reason—for never were there such great savings lying idle for the taking in some imaginative enterprise, and never were there such comforts, such marks of social distinction to be won if an enterprise were successful.

Industrial business in America and elsewhere had never won

the sympathy of literary artists. And in the twenties, the more dominant the spirit of business became, the less justification could American writers find for the current way of life. Dreiser wrote now with consummate pity of the defeated in the struggle for existence, while Sherwood Anderson, William Faulkner, Ellen Glasgow, and John Dos Passos—among those who remained to deal with the America they knew—were grim in their assays of business culture. On the other hand some of our greatest stylists and more original creators fled with Cabell to phantasy kingdoms like Storisende, or with Eliot, Fitzgerald, Hemingway, and Stein to Europe. Even Sinclair Lewis and H. L. Mencken, the arch-intellectuals of democratic America, while enjoying their feeling of superiority to the life about them, could do little but complain.

Many critics explain the disillusionment and despair that marked American literature in the twenties as a result of the World War and its grievous aftermath. But much of the spirit of our literature after the war was already apparent in the earlier decade when Edgar Lee Masters wrote his bitter *Spoon River Anthology* and Dreiser wrote many of his important works. The war left its mark upon the most sensitive minds in America and the world, but our writers' discontent was rooted in American life itself and not in our unsuccessful adventure in international affairs.

America in the twenties had ceased to build with the rapidity of past decades. Our economy had ceased to function with the vitality of a half-century before. Once our writers had looked forward to the time when we should be through building with all our might, when we should have reasonably satisfied our material needs, when we should begin to seek also the fulfillment of the spiritual promise of American life. In the twenties, however, our writers found little to justify hope. American industry had accomplished miracles of production, the "economy of abundance" had become a genuine possibility. But after centuries of scarcity it was impossible for businessmen in a single generation to shed their old acquisitive habits, to change overnight to a consumers' goods economy in which funds for investment were plentiful and the general welfare of society depended more on the even distribution of purchasing power than on the rapid accumulation of capital. It was this rather than the war alone that darkened the spirit of our writers. As Max Lerner wrote: [38]

> In so far as hopelessness characterized the post-war literary generation it was not just the hopelessness that came from glimpses into death and violence, but that which came from the gap between the promise of American life and the realities of American life in the nineteen-twenties when the economic structure was already rickety but still too tough to be subjected to real control.

Serious novel writing is an individualistic art whose greatest creations are individual characters. No wonder then that American novelists were pessimistic in the age of great combinations and the concentration of social and economic power. Unlike painters or sculptors, novelists need look to no rich patrons to engage their services or buy their works. Unlike musicians, they need no millionaires to underwrite expensive symphony orchestras or endow opera houses and concert halls. Painters, sculptors, and musicians flourished in America in the twenties when their talents at last found bountiful patronage and their works won greater attention than ever before. The serious novelists, however, got little encouragement from the new leisure class that until 1929 remained quite uncritical of the new trends in American democracy.

While painting, sculpture, and music benefited from new patronage in the twenties, they were overshadowed by the spectacular achievements in architecture, moving pictures, and industrial design. Educated Americans might take pride in the canvases of men like John Sloan, Eugene Speicher, or Alexander Brook, and feel that George Gershwin was making lasting contributions to the world's music, but the average citizen appreciated far more the collaborative and usually anonymous art which gave him his skyscrapers, his Hollywood features, his handsome automobiles, refrigerators, clocks, stoves, or radios.

The achievements of American architecture in the twenties were directly connected with the large volume of American savings and the great advances in American technology. We have

---

[38] Clarkson and Cochran, *War,* p. 186.

seen how corporations invested undistributed profits in new office buildings, factories, and laboratories while their officers built
suburban homes and contributed generously to the erection of
schools, colleges, hospitals, and museums. All this gave greater
opportunities to architects than ever before in history. Equipped
with reenforced concrete, glass, and steel, inspired by the models
of Sullivan and Wright in America and Saarinen, Le Corbusier,
and others in Europe, architects brought about the revolution in
building that had been impending since the development of the
steel skyscraper in Chicago in the 1880's. While the names of
certain leaders like Raymond Hood, Arthur L. Harmon, Frank
Lloyd Wright, and William Van Alen may stand out, this new
building was done primarily by companies for corporations.
Scores of architects worked out designs for large buildings in
the offices of leading architectural and engineering firms, and the
resulting structures were as much group creations as the Disney
films.

The motion picture, the greatest new art form of the twentieth
century, was dominated by American developments from the beginning, chiefly because we had the capital to invest in costly
technical experiments, and urban audiences large and prosperous enough to make high production costs return great profits.
Although the necessity to cater to mass markets may have interfered in some ways with artistic progress, big motion picture
production budgets led to rapid technical improvements which
in the early period were probably more important. Chemists,
electricians, fashion and stage designers, writers, directors, and
actors all contributed to the production of the new art while
tremendous advances in the mechanisms and techniques of photography enhanced its emotional and aesthetic appeal. In no
other field were the scientific, artistic, and financial resources of
our mature industrial culture combined to produce such popular
artistic results.

While business leaders were slow to adapt their wage and
profit policies to the new consumers' goods economy of the
twenties, they were quick to see that the aesthetic appeal of their
mass production commodities would help to keep markets active.
It was not until 1927, however, when Norman Bel Geddes

opened the first "industrial-design studio" in the country, that American art and industry combined forces. Before that time the sheer perfection of functional design had often led to the unconscious creation of beauty in industrial products. As early as 1864, James Jackson Jarves commented on this aspect of industrial culture in the United States. He wrote: [39]

The American while adhering closely to his utilitarian and economical principles, has unwittingly, in some objects to which his heart equally with his hand has been devoted, developed a degree of beauty in them that no other nation equals. His clipper-ships, fire-engines, locomotives, and some of his machinery and tools combine that equilibrium of lines, proportions, and masses, which is among the fundamental causes of abstract beauty. Their success in producing broad general effects out of a few simple elements, and of admirable adaptations of means to ends, as nature evolves beauty out of the common and practical, covers these things with a certain atmosphere of poetry, and is an indication of what may happen to the rest of his work when he puts into it an equal amount of heart and knowledge.

Broadening the path opened up by Norman Bel Geddes in the twenties, were Walter Dorwin Teague, George Sakier, Henry Dreyfuss, Raymond Loewy, Otto Kuhler, and a score of others, each designing or redesigning the everyday things used by Americans in their homes and offices, in transportation and communication. Cheap glass and tableware, unit stoves, refrigerators, and modern furniture all were reduced to their simplest industrial and artistic terms by these men. From their desks came also the most economical designs for typewriters, adding machines, electric fans, locomotives, Pullman cars, coaches, telephones, and, somewhat later, standard Western Union offices. For many years Frank Lloyd Wright had been urging architects to use the new technology in their designs, to use the machine, not attack it, to use its products boldly, not hide them under meaningless cornices and obsolete stone. Similarly Bel Geddes and others urged artists to cease *decorating* machines and machine products, to form machines themselves and the products of machines into new designs of abstract beauty. In almost everything around us these ideas have been applied, in ash trays, fountain

---

[39] Cheney, *Art and the Machine,* quoted in front.

pens, lamps, and toys, notably in the new abstract forms in painting and sculpture themselves where leaders like Picasso and Archipenko had already shown the possibilities of machine motifs.

Thus once again in the 1920's, after a lapse of centuries, form and function had been conjoined to give a new stimulus to art and a new appeal to industry and its products. The very industrial technology that was by its sheer cost alone helping to bring to an end the age of individual business enterprise was beginning to open up a new era of individual expression in corporate and collaborative arts. Nowhere was this more apparent than in the development of "streamlining," worked out by engineers alone in the quest for maximum speed in airplanes. The "ovoid gliding form" and "the smooth, continuous surface," which are the characteristics of a streamlined body,[40] might well be judged by future generations to be a creation in artistic design equivalent to the gothic worked out by earlier "engineers" in response to the need for light in large stone buildings. The industrial and artistic exhibitions at the Chicago Exposition of 1933 and the New York World's Fair of 1939 supported this view.

---

[40] Cheney, *Art and the Machine*, p. 100.

XVI

EPILOGUE

THE Age of Enterprise, as it developed in industrial America in the nineteenth century, had the advantage of revolutionary improvements in technology, a free labor supply, and free access to the markets and raw materials of the world. This age had begun in Europe when medieval restrictions on exchange and feudal restrictions on movement were swept away, when villeins and serfs in increasing numbers left the manors to seek industrial employment. It flourished when the web of mercantile restrictions was broken and commercial monopolists like the British and Dutch East India companies relaxed their grip on avenues of trade. The Age of Enterprise, theoretically, was a period of free competition in the pursuit of profits, free investment of those profits in productive industry. It was a period when constant technological advances opened apparently inexhaustible industrial opportunities and "the greatest good of the greatest number" seemed most likely to be served by men exploiting those opportunities to their limits.

Industrial enterprise was most successful in creating a free society in America because America with its tremendous material heritage had the greatest capacity for growth. America had incomparable resources to develop, seemingly limitless space to accommodate large numbers of workers and consumers. Expansion was the keystone of business freedom, and America had the greatest opportunities to expand. Even in America, however, by the middle of the nineteenth century there was no longer room in certain lines of enterprise for all who would enter those lines. And, as the century grew older, production in more and more industries periodically glutted markets, prices fell, and profits temporarily disappeared. Restrictions thus were placed upon free competition. Industrialists of their own accord entered into trade agreements, pools, and trusts. Voluntarily they surrendered the right to manufacture as much as they pleased, to sell where they pleased, to charge what the traffic would bear. They agreed to partition markets, curtail production, maintain prices, withhold investment in costly technological improvements. So numerous were these limitations upon economic freedom by the twentieth century, so powerful had the agencies that imposed these limitations become, that the age of free industrial enterprise seemed to be waning. By 1914 most of the traditional areas for profitable enterprise were closed to all but those who had access to large amounts of investment capital, and the control of such capital had itself become concentrated in very few hands.

The First World War, by stimulating expansion in old lines of heavy industry, postponed for a time the demise of the old system. And the "fabulous boom" of the twenties, through the development of new lines of consumers' goods, seemed to give free enterprise new life. We have seen, however, how the war strengthened the agencies curtailing economic freedom, how the conventions of thrift and frugality impeded the growth of consumers' goods industries. What America needed most in the twenties was wider distribution of purchasing power. What we had was rapid concentration of savings. We needed new, rapidly expanding productive opportunities, new ventures to employ our growing population; with few exceptions we had only new opportunities for speculation in land and securities, and the number of unemployed grew steadily. By 1928 only the purchasing power created by the paper profits of the great bull market kept business prosperous. When those profits suddenly disappeared after October, 1929, American business collapsed. And this time it was ten years before a new war gave fresh incentive to expansion; it was ten years before jobs once again became plentiful.

In these ten years profound social changes occurred. Under the New Deal the federal government became a great employer of men, the greatest user of the nation's savings, the greatest underwriter of debt. The government assumed much of the risk-taking activity of private enterprise. It assumed leadership in finance and construction. All in all, it took a solid stance beside private business in the planning of the nation's economic life.

We have described the century-long surrender in America of personal to institutional enterprise. We have seen how independent master workers, their journeymen and apprentices were absorbed into factories and harnessed to machine production; how individual entrepreneurs became bureaucrats in large corporations; how those corporations themselves were merged into vast financial empires through which small numbers of men controlled important sectors of the nation's economy. As the freedom of individual businessmen, if not of business itself, thus became curtailed in the United States, vigorous public efforts were made to check the concentration of wealth and power. Theodore Roosevelt confronted the private economic overlords with the power of the federal government; under Wilson, Congress, by one statute after another, tried to turn the nation back to the traditions of individual initiative and small private business. In spite of these policies, limitations upon individual economic opportunity grew in severity and the concentration of private economic power grew apace. The language of free competition persisted, but free competition itself had been sorely circumscribed. Orthodox economics continued to speak of *laissez faire*, but big business had restricted the mechanisms through which the traditional principles of *laissez faire* could operate.

This dichotomy between theory and practice could exist in the United States during the First World War and the twenties because prosperity created few pressing problems which government or business had to solve or which economics had to explain. Once depression struck in the early thirties, however, it was apparent that the old theories would no longer serve. By the end of 1932 American business had failed to respond to the low costs and low interest rates of the previous three years. The mechanisms of the free market had failed to operate effectively in situations of limited competition and rigid price control. Thus the depression lingered. The number of unemployed grew rapidly, industry languished, the burden of private debt became unbearable, and the banking structure trembled. Even when business spurted during one of the longest upswings in American history between 1934 and 1937, the unemployed by the latter year still numbered between seven and eight million. Apparently private enterprise was no longer able by itself to supply enough new jobs for the growing American population, no longer able to distribute the national income so that all Americans could have at least food, clothing, and shelter. Apparently even in a new "prosperity" work relief, home relief, and other forms of government aid had still to be supplied to indigent though able-bodied and ambitious Americans.

Unlike the Square Deal or the New Freedom, therefore, the government under the New Deal undertook in some areas to supplement private enterprise. It engaged in banking to supply business credit where private institutions refused. It engaged in low-cost housing projects where private builders held back. By arbitrarily removing large areas from cultivation the government raised the prices of farm staples where the traditional mechanisms of the free market failed to do so. By tampering with the currency the government also tried to raise prices for other commodities. The New Deal, to be sure, had its reform aspects, its National Labor Relations Board, and its Securities and Exchange Commission. The New Deal also tried to preserve many features of the system of private enterprise. But probably more important in the long run was the entrance of government itself into the businesses of banking, housing, and public utilities. More important than any reform measures was the assumption by the New Deal government of many functions heretofore performed almost exclusively by private enterprise.

That this new trend in American social relations cannot easily be reversed, seems clear. As Professor Larson of the Harvard Graduate School of Business Administration declared in 1941:[1]

Of one thing we may be certain. The old days of *laissez faire* are gone. A new age or system is in the making, which Professor Gras calls national capitalism, in which control and planning are largely in the hands of gov-

---

[1] *Bulletin Business Historical Society*, Vol. XVI, pp. 41–42.

ernment and only routine management to any great extent remains to private business. This growing union of business and government is probably no temporary development—the changes represent not only current difficulties but a new situation. The *trend* is obvious; we do not know how *far* it will go.

In a broad sense the Age of Enterprise in America may still be young. The "union of business and government" of which Professor Larson speaks may yet result in even greater opportunities, greater freedom, greater wealth for the multitude than did the hustling, optimistic economy based exclusively upon private initiative. Certainly the materials for a satisfactory economy are abundant in the United States.

BOOKS FOR READING
AND REFERENCE

With certain exceptions the "Bibliography" in the original edition of THE AGE OF ENTERPRISE contained only the titles of books and articles cited in the footnotes. In no sense was it a comprehensive list of the sources used by the authors in writing the volume. Since our first edition, the literature on the social history of industrial America has been greatly enriched, and in the following revised and expanded list of books and occasional articles we have cited many important new works as well as virtually all of those we first named. Some of the works in our earlier list have since been issued in later editions; but, since our footnote references were to the editions available when we first wrote, we have retained the original citations of publisher and date. It has, of course, been impossible in this new edition as it was impossible in the original edition to include every relevant work of merit. But we do feel that every work we have included does itself merit the serious reader's attention.

T.C. and W.M.

BIBLIOGRAPHY

Adamic, Louis, *Dynamite*. Viking, 1934.

Adams, Henry, *The Education of Henry Adams*. Houghton Mifflin, 1930.

Adams, James Truslow, *The Epic of America*. Little, Brown, 1931.

Albion, Robert G., *The Rise of New York Port, 1815–1860*. Scribner's, 1939.

—, *Square Riggers on Schedule*. Princeton, 1938.

Alexander, De Alva S., *Political History of the State of New York*. 3 vols., Holt, 1906.

Allen, Frederick L., *The Great Pierpont Morgan*. Harper, 1949.

—, *The Lords of Creation*. Harper, 1935.

—, *Only Yesterday*. Harper, 1931.

—, *Since Yesterday*. Harper, 1940.

Allen, James S., *Reconstruction*. International, 1937.

Ambler, Charles H., ed., "Correspondence of Robert M. T. Hunter, 1826–1876," *Annual Report, American Historical Assn.*, 1916, vol. II, Washington, 1918.

American Art Annual, New York, 1897–

American Iron and Steel Association, *Bulletin*, vols., I–XLVI, Philadelphia, 1867–1912.

Andrews, Wayne, *Architecture, Ambition and Americans*. Harper, 1955.

—, *The Vanderbilt Legend*. Harcourt, Brace, 1940.

Arnold, Thurman W., *The Folklore of Capitalism*. Yale, 1937.

—, *The Symbols of Government*. Yale, 1935.

Atherton, Lewis E., *Main Street on the Middle Border*. Indiana University, 1954.

—, *The Pioneer Merchant in Mid-America*. University of Missouri, 1939.

—, *The Southern Country Store, 1800–1860*. Louisiana State University, 1949.

Bailey, Thomas A., *A Diplomatic History of the American People*. Appleton, 1955.

Barger, Harold, *Distribution's Place in the American Economy Since 1869*. Princeton, 1955.

—, *Transportation Industries, 1889–1946*. National Bureau of Economic Research, 1951.

—, and Landsberg, H. H., *American Agriculture, 1899–1939*. National Bureau of Economic Research, 1942.

—, and Schurr, S. H., *Mining Industries, 1899–1939*. National Bureau of Economic Research, 1943.

Barnard, Chester I., *The Functions of the Executive*. Harvard, 1931.

Barron, Clarence W., *More They Told Barron*. Harper, 1931.

—, *They Told Barron*, Harper, 1930.

Beale, Howard K., *Are American Teachers Free?* Scribner's, 1936.

—, *The Critical Year*. Harcourt, Brace, 1930.

Beale, Truxton, ed., *Man v. the State*. Kennerley, 1916.

Beard, Charles A., *The Idea of National Interest*. Macmillan, 1934.

—, and Mary R., *America in Midpassage*. Macmillan, 1939.

—, *The Rise of American Civilization*. 2 vols., Macmillan, 1928.

Beard, Charles A., and Smith, George H. E., *The Old Deal and the New*. Macmillan, 1940.

Beard, Miriam, *A History of the Business Man*. Macmillan, 1938.

Beer, Thomas, *Hanna*. Knopf, 1929.

—, *Mauve Decade*. Knopf, 1926.

Benedict, Murray R., *Farm Policies of the United States, 1790–1950*. Twentieth Century Fund, 1953.

Benson, Lee, *Merchants, Farmers and Railroads*. Harvard, 1955.

Bentley, Arthur F., *The Condition of the Western Farmer as Illustrated by the Economic History of a Nebraska Township*. Johns Hopkins, 1893.

Berle, Adolph A., Jr., and Means, Gardiner C., *The Modern Corporation and Private Property*. Macmillan, 1933.

Bernays, Edward L., *Propaganda*. Liveright, 1928.

Berthoff, Rowland T., *British Immigrants in Industrial America, 1790–1950*. Harvard, 1953.

Billington, Ray A., *Far Western Frontier, 1830–1860*. Harper, 1956.

—, *The Protestant Crusade*. Macmillan, 1939.

—, *Westward Expansion*. Macmillan, 1949.

Bishop, James L., *A History of American Manufacturing from 1608 to 1860*. 3 vols. E. Young, 1868.

Bogart, Ernest L., *Economic History of the United States*. Longmans, Green, 1914.

Bonnett, Clarence E., *Employers' Associations in the United States*. Macmillan, 1922.

Bowers, Claude G., *Beveridge and the Progressive Era.*, Houghton Mifflin, 1932.

Brandeis, Louis D., *Other People's Money*. Stokes, 1914.

Bremner, Robert H., *From the Depths, the Discovery of Poverty in the United States*. New York University, 1956.

Bright, Arthur A., Jr., *The Electric-Lamp Industry*. Macmillan, 1949.

Bryce, James, *The American Commonwealth*. 2 vols., Macmillan, 1888.

Bulletin of the Business Historical Society, Boston, 1926–

Burke, Kenneth, *Attitudes Toward History*. 2 vols., New Republic, 1937.

—, *Permanence and Change*. New Republic, 1935.

Burlingame, Roger, *Backgrounds of Power*. Scribner's, 1949.

—, *Engines of Democracy*. Scribner's, 1940.

—, *March of the Iron Men*, Scribner's, 1938.

Burns, Arthur R., *The Decline of Competition*. McGraw-Hill, 1936.

Butler, Nicholas M., "Herbert Spencer's 'The Great Political Superstition,'" *Forum*, vol. LV, pp. 81–108.

Cadman, John W., Jr., *The Corporation in New Jersey*. Harvard, 1949.

Callender, Guy S., "Early Transportation and Banking Enterprises of the States in Relation to the Growth of Corporations," *Quarterly Journal of Economics*, vol. XVII, pp. 111–162.

—, ed., *Selections from the Economic History of the United States, 1765–1860*. Ginn, 1909.

Campbell, E. G., *Railroad Reorganization*. Columbia University, 1938.

Carman, Harry J., *Social and Economic History of the United States*, 2 vols., Heath, 1930, 1934.

Carnegie, Andrew, *Autobiography of Andrew Carnegie*. Houghton Mifflin, 1920.

—, *The Empire of Business*. Doubleday, Page, 1912.

Carpenter, Jesse T., *The South as a Conscious Minority*. New York University, 1930.

Carver, Thomas N., ed., *Selected Readings in Rural Economics*. Ginn, 1916.

Chamberlain, John, *Farewell to Reform*. Liveright, 1932.

Channing, William E., *Works*. American Unitarian Association, 1875.

Chapman, Charles C., *The Development of American Business and Banking Thought, 1913–1936*. Longmans, Green, 1936.

Charvat, William, "American Romanticism and the Depression of 1937," *Science and Society*, vol. II, pp. 63–82.

Cheney, Sheldon and Martha C., *Art and the Machine*. Whittlesey, 1936.

Childs, Marquis, and Cater, Douglass, *Ethics in a Business Society*. Harper, 1954.

Clark, Colin, *The Conditions of Economic Progress*. Macmillan, 1940.

Clark, John D., *The Federal Trust Policy*. Johns Hopkins, 1931.

Clark, Victor S., *History of Manufactures in the United States*. 3 vols., McGraw-Hill, 1929.

Clarkson, Jessie D., and Cochran, Thomas C., eds., *War as a Social Institution*. Columbia University, 1941.

Cleveland, Frederick A., and Powell, Fred W., *Railroad Finance*. Appleton, 1912.

—, *Railroad Promotion and Capitalization in the United States*. Longmans, Green, 1909.

Clews, Henry, *Twenty-eight Years in Wall Street*. Irving, 1888.

—, *The Wall Street Point of View*. Silver, Burdett, 1900.

Cochran, Thomas C., *The American Business System*. Harvard, 1957.

—, *Basic History of American Business*. Anvil, 1959.

—, "The Faith of Our Fathers," *Frontiers of Democracy*, Vol. VI, pp. 17–19.

—, *The Pabst Brewing Company*. New York University, 1948.

—, *Railroad Leaders, 1845–1890*. Harvard, 1953.

—, "The Social History of the Corporation in the United States," in *The Cultural Approach to History*, ed. Caroline F. Ware, Columbia University, 1940.

Cole, Arthur C., *The Irrepressible Conflict, 1850–1865*. Macmillan, 1934.

Cole, Arthur H., *The American Wool Manufacture*. 2 vols., Harvard, 1926.

—, *Business in Its Social Setting*. Harvard, 1959.

—, and Williamson, Harold F., *The American Carpet Manufacture*. Harvard, 1941.

Commager, Henry S., *The American Mind*. Yale, 1950.

—, *Theodore Parker*. Little, Brown, 1936.

—, ed., *Documents of American History*. Crofts, 1934.

Committee on Education and Labor, 76th Congress, 1st Session, Report No. 6, Pt. 6, Labor Policies of Employers' Associations—Pt. III, The National Association of Manufacturers. Washington, 1939.

Commons, John R., and others, eds., *A Documentary History of American Industrial Society*. 2 vols., A. H. Clark, 1910–1911.

—, and Associates, *History of Labour in the United States*, 4 vols., Macmillan, 1918–1935.

Coolidge, Louis A., *An Old Fashioned Senator: Orville H. Platt*. Putnam's, 1910.
Corey, Lewis, *The House of Morgan*. G. H. Watt, 1930.
Coulter, E. M., "Effects of Secession on the Commerce of the Mississippi Valley," *Mississippi Valley Historical Review*, vol. III, pp. 275–300.
Craven, Avery, *The Coming of the Civil War*. 2nd ed., University of Chicago, 1957.
—, "The Coming of War Between the States," *Journal of Southern History*, vol. II, no. 3, pp. 303–322.
—, *The Repressible Conflict, 1830–1861*. Louisiana State University, 1939.
Cullom, Shelby, *Fifty Years of Public Service*. A. C. McClurg, 1911.
Curti, Merle, *The Social Ideas of American Educators*. Scribner's, 1935.
—, *The Making of an American Community*. Stanford University, 1959.

Daggett, Stuart, *Chapters on the History of the Southern Pacific*. Ronald, 1922.
—, *Railroad Reorganization*. Houghton Mifflin, 1908.
Danielian, N. R., *A. T. & T.* Vanguard, 1939.
David, Henry, *History of the Haymarket Affair*. 2nd ed., Russell, 1958.
Davis, John P., *Corporations: A Study of the Origin and Development of Great Business Combinations and of Their Relation to the Authority of the State*. 2 vols., Putnam, 1905.
Davis, Joseph S., *Essays in the Earlier History of American Corporations*, 2 vols., Harvard, 1917.
Dewing, Arthur S., *Corporate Promotions and Reorganizations*. Harvard, 1920.
Dorfman, Joseph, *The Economic Mind in American Civilization*. 5 vols., Viking, 1946–1959.
—, *Thorstein Veblen and His America*. Viking, 1934.
Doster, James F., *Railroads in Alabama Politics, 1875–1914*. University of Alabama, 1957.
Douglas, Paul H., *Real Wages in the United States, 1890–1926*. Houghton Mifflin, 1930.
Dunbar, Seymour, *A History of Travel in America*. 1 vol. ed., Tudor, 1937.

Eddy, Arthur J., *The New Competition*. Appleton, 1912.
Edwards, George W., *The Evolution of Finance Capitalism*. Longmans, Green, 1938.
Eliot, Charles, "Spencer's Specialized Administration," *Forum*, vol. LV, pp. 709–743.
Ellis, Elmer, "Public Opinion and the Income Tax," *Mississippi Valley Historical Review*, vol. XXVII, pp. 225–242.
Emerson, Ralph W., *English Traits, Representative Men and Other Essays*. Dutton (Everyman's Library), 1908.
Emmet, Boris, and Jeuck, John E., *Catalogues and Counters: A History of Sears, Roebuck and Company*. University of Chicago, 1950.
Erickson, Charlotte, *American Industry and the European Immigrant, 1860–1885*. Harvard, 1957.

Facts and Factors in Economic History (articles by former students of Edwin F. Gay). Harvard, 1932.
Fahrney, Ralph R., *Horace Greeley and the Tribune in the Civil War*. Torch, 1936.
Faulkner, Harold U., *American Economic History*. Harper, 1924.
—, *The Decline of Laissez Faire, 1897–1917*. Rinehart, 1951.
—, *The Quest for Social Justice, 1898–1914*. Macmillan, 1931.
Fels, Rendigs, *American Business Cycles, 1865–1917*. University of North Carolina, 1959.
Filler, Louis, *Crusaders for American Liberalism*. Harcourt, Brace, 1939.
Fine, Sidney, *Laissez Faire and the General Welfare State, 1865–1901*. University of Michigan, 1956.

Fitch, James M., *American Building.* Houghton Mifflin, 1948.

Fitch, John A., *The Steel Workers.* Russell Sage Foundation, The Pittsburgh Survey, Charities Publication Committee, 1911.

Fite, E. D., *Social and Industrial Conditions in the North During the Civil War,* Macmillan, 1910.

Flynn, John T., *God's Gold.* Harcourt, Brace, 1932.

Foner, Philip S., *Business and Slavery.* University of North Carolina, 1941.

Ford, James, *Slums and Housing.* 2 vols., Harvard, 1936.

Foulke, Roy A., *The Sinews of American Commerce.* Dun & Bradstreet, 1941.

Freidel, Frank, *Franklin D. Rooosevelt.* 3 vols., Little, Brown, 1952–1956.

Fuller, Henry B., *With the Procession.* Harper, 1895.

Gabriel, Ralph H., *The Course of American Democratic Thought.* Ronald, 1940.

Galbraith, John K., *The Great Crash, 1929.* Houghton Mifflin, 1955.

Garrison, Wendell P. and F. J., *William Lloyd Garrison, 1805–1879.* 4 vols. Houghton Mifflin, 1894.

Gates, Paul W., "The Homestead Law in an Incongruous Land System," *American Historical Review,* vol. XLI, pp. 652–681.

—, *Fifty Million Acres.* Cornell, 1954.

—, *The Illinois Central Railroad and Its Colonization Work.* Harvard, 1934.

Gibb, George S., and Knowlton, Evelyn H., *The Resurgent Years: A History of Standard Oil Company (New Jersey), 1911–1927.* Harper, 1956.

Giedion, Sigfried, *Space, Time and Architecture.* Harvard, 1942.

—, *Mechanization Takes Command.* Oxford, 1948.

Goldman, Eric, *Rendezvous with Destiny.* Knopf, 1952.

Gompers, Samuel, *Seventy Years of Life and Labor.* 2 vols., Dutton, 1925.

Goodrich, Carter, *Government Promotion of American Canals and Railroads, 1800–1890.* Columbia University, 1960.

Graebner, Norman A., *Empire on the Pacific.* Ronald, 1955.

Gras, N. S. B., *Business and Capitalism.* Crofts, 1939.

—, and Larson, Henrietta M., *Casebook in American Business History.* Crofts, 1939.

Green, Constance M., *Holyoke, Massachusetts.* Yale, 1939.

Griswold, A. Whitney, *The Far Eastern Policy of the United States.* Harcourt, Brace, 1938.

Grodinsky, Julius, *Jay Gould.* University of Pennsylvania, 1957.

Hacker, Louis M., *The Triumph of American Capitalism.* Simon & Schuster, 1940.

—, and Kendrick, Benjamin B., *The United States Since 1865.* Crofts, 1939.

Hammond, Bray, *Banks and Politics in America from the Revolution to the Civil War.* Princeton, 1957.

Handlin, Oscar, and Flug, Mary, *Commonwealth: Massachusetts, 1774–1861.* New York University, 1947.

Handling Men, compiled and published by A. W. Shaw Co., Chicago, 1917.

Haney, Lewis H., *A Congressional History of Railroads in the United States,* 2 vols., Democrat Printing Co., Madison, Wis., 1910.

Hansen, Marcus L., *The Immigrant in American History.* Harvard, 1940.

—, *The Atlantic Migration, 1607–1860.* Harvard, 1951.

Harper's Encyclopedia of United States History. New York Tribune Edition, 10 vols., Harper, 1905.

Hays, Samuel P., *The Response to Industrialism, 1885–1914.* University of Chicago, 1957.

Hazard, Blanche E., *The Organization of the Boot and Shoe Industry in Massachusetts Before 1875.* Harvard, 1921.

Heath, Milton S., *Constructive Liberalism: the Role of the State in Economic Development in Georgia to 1860.* Harvard, 1954.

Hendrick, Burton J., *The Life of Andrew Carnegie.* 2 vols., Doubleday, Doran, 1932.

Hibbard, Benjamin H., *A History of the Public Land Policies.* Macmillan, 1924.

Hibben, Paxton. *Henry Ward Beecher.* Doran, 1927.

Hicks, Frederick C., ed., *High Finance in the Sixties.* Yale, 1929.

Hicks, John D., *The American Nation.* 2 vols., Houghton Mifflin, 1941.

—, *The Populist Revolt.* University of Minnesota, 1931.

Hidy, Ralph W., *The House of Baring in American Trade and Finance, 1763–1861.* Harvard, 1949.

—, "Anglo-American Merchant Bankers, 1815–1860," in *The Tasks of Economic History,* supp. issue of *Journal of Economic History,* Vol. I, pp. 53–66.

—, and Muriel E., *Pioneering in Big Business: History of Standard Oil Company (New Jersey), 1882–1911.* Harper, 1955.

Higham, John, *Strangers in the Land: Patterns of American Nativism, 1860–1925.* Rutgers, 1955.

Hill, Forest G., *Roads, Rails & Waterways: The Army Engineers and Early Transportation.* University of Oklahoma, 1957.

Historical Statistics of the United States, 1789–1945. United States Department of Commerce, 1949.

History of Labor. See entry under Commons, John R.

Hofstader, Richard, *The Age of Reform.* Knopf, 1955.

—, *The American Political Tradition.* Knopf, 1948.

—, *Social Darwinism in American Thought.* Rev. Ed., Beacon, 1955.

—, "The Tariff Issue in the Civil War," *American Historical Review,* vol. XLIV, pp. 50–55.

—, Miller, William, and Aaron, Daniel, *The American Republic.* 2 vols., Prentice-Hall, 1959.

Holt, Henry, *Garrulities of an Octogenarian Editor.* Houghton Mifflin, 1923.

—, "Herbert Spencer," *Unpopular Review,* vol. VIII, pp. 343–364.

Hoover, Herbert, *Memoirs: The Cabinet and the Presidency, 1920–1933; Memoirs: The Great Depression, 1929–1941.* 2 vols., Macmillan, 1952.

Hower, Ralph M., *The History of an Advertising Agency.* Harvard, 1939.

—, *History of Macy's of New York, 1858–1919.* Harvard, 1943.

Hubbard, Henry C., *The Older Middle West, 1840–1880.* Appleton-Century, 1936.

Hunt's Merchants Magazine and Commercial Review, vol. XXIX, New York, 1853.

Hunter, Louis C., *Studies in the Economic History of the Ohio Valley,* (Smith College Studies in History, vol. XIX, nos. 1–2). Smith College, 1934.

—, *Steamboats on the Western Rivers.* Harvard, 1949.

Hunter, Robert, *Poverty,* Macmillan, 1909.

Hutchinson, William T., *Cyrus Hall McCormick.* 2 vols., Century, 1935.

—, ed., *The Marcus W. Jernegan Essays in American Historiography.* University of Chicago, 1937.

Industrial Commission on the Relations and Conditions of Capital and Labor Employed in Manufactures and General Business, *Report.* 19 vols., Washington, 1901.

Interchurch World Movement, Commission of Inquiry, *Report on the Steel Strike of 1919.* Harcourt, Brace, 1920.

Jacobs, Lewis, *The Rise of the American Film.* Harcourt, Brace, 1939.

Jefferson, Thomas, *Writings,* ed., Paul L. Ford. 10 vols., Putnam, 1892–1899.

Jenks, Leland H., *The Migration of British Capital, to 1875.* Knopf, 1927.

Johnson, Arthur M., *The Development of American Petroleum Pipelines*. Cornell, 1956.

Jones, Eliot, *The Trust Problem in the United States*. Macmillan, 1927.

Jones, Fred M., *Middlemen in the Domestic Trade of the United States, 1806–1860*. University of Illinois, 1937.

Josephson, Hannah, *Golden Threads: New England's Mill Girls and Magnates*. Duell, Sloan and Pearce, 1949.

Josephson, Matthew, *Edison*. McGraw-Hill, 1959.

—, *The Politicos, 1865–1896*. Harcourt, Brace, 1938.

—, *The President Makers, 1896–1919*. Harcourt, Brace, 1940.

—, *The Robber Barons*. Harcourt, Brace, 1934.

Kennan, George, *E. H. Harriman*. 2 vols., Houghton Mifflin, 1922.

Kennedy, E. D., *The Automobile Industry*. Reynal & Hitchcock, 1941.

Keynes, John M., *The General Theory of Employment, Interest and Money*. Harcourt, Brace, 1936.

Kirkland, Edward C., *Dream and Thought in the Business Community*. Cornell, 1956.

—, *A History of American Economic Life*. Crofts, 1940.

—, *Men, Cities and Transportation: A Study in New England History*. 2 vols., Harvard, 1948.

Kistler, Thelma M., *The Rise of Railroads in the Connecticut River Valley*, (Smith College Studies in History, Vol. XXIII, Nos. 1–4.) Smith College, 1938.

Kouwenhoven, John A., *Made in America*. Doubleday, 1948.

Kuznets, Simon, *National Income and Its Composition, 1919–1938*. National Bureau of Economic Research, 1941.

—, *National Income: A Summary of Findings*. National Bureau of Economic Research, 1946.

La Follette, Robert M., *La Follette's Autobiography*. Robert L. La Follette Co., Madison, Wis., 1913.

Laidler, Harry W., *Concentration in American Industry*. Crowell, 1931.

Lambie, Joseph T., and Clemence, Richard V., eds., *Economic Change in America: Readings in the Economic History of the United States*. Stackpole, 1954.

Lane, Wheaton J., *Commodore Vanderbilt*. Knopf, 1942.

—, *From Indian Trail to Iron Horse*. Princeton, 1939.

Larson, Henrietta M., *Jay Cooke*. Harvard, 1936.

—, *The Wheat Market and the Farmer in Minnesota, 1858–1900*. Columbia University, 1926.

—, and Porter, Kenneth, *History of Humble Oil and Refining Company*. Harper, 1959.

Leuchtenburg, William E., *The Perils of Prosperity, 1914–1932*. University of Chicago, 1958.

Lewis, Cleona, *America's Stake in International Investments*. Brookings Institution, 1938.

Lichtenberg, Bernard, *Advertising Campaigns* (Modern Business Tracts, vol. XIII). Alexander Hamilton Inst., 1926.

Limber, Ralph C., *Economic and Technological Change in American Agriculture in Relation to Crop Land Requirements* (Ph.D. thesis, MS.). New York University, 1942.

Link, Arthur S., *Woodrow Wilson and the Progressive Era, 1910–1917*. Harper, 1954.

Lloyd, Henry D., *Wealth Against Commonwealth*. Harper, 1894.

Lynd, Robert S. and Helen M., *Middletown*. Harcourt, Brace, 1929.

—, *Middletown in Transition*. Harcourt, Brace, 1937.

McGrane, Reginald C., *Foreign Bondholders and American State Debts*. Macmillan, 1935.

—, *The Panic of 1837*. University of Chicago, 1924.

Macpherson, Hector, *Spencer and Spencerianism*. Doubleday, Page, 1900.

Martyn, Carlos, *William E. Dodge*. Funk & Wagnalls, 1890.

May, Henry F., *Protestant Churches and Industrial America*. Harper, 1949.

McMaster, John Bach, *The History of the People of the United States*. 8 vols., Appleton, 1883–1913.

The Master Workers' Book. Doubleday, Page, 1916.

Medbery, James K., *Men and Mysteries of Wall Street*. Fields, Osgood, 1870.

Meyer, Balthasar H., MacGill, C. E. and others, *History of Transportation in the United States before 1860*. Carnegie Institution, 1917.

Miller, H. E., *Banking Theories in the United States before 1860*. Harvard, 1928.

Miller, Sidney L., *Inland Transportation*. McGraw-Hill, 1933.

Miller, William, "A Note in the History of Business Corporations in Pennsylvania, 1800–1860," *Quarterly Journal of Economics*, Vol. LV, pp. 150–160.

—, "American Historians and the Business Elite," *Journal of Economic History*, Vol. IX, pp. 184–208.

—, *A New History of the United States*. Braziller, 1958.

—, ed., *Men in Business: Essays in the History of Entrepreneurship*. Harvard, 1952.

Milton, George F., *The Eve of Conflict*. Houghton Mifflin, 1934.

Mitchell, Broadus, *Depression Decade, 1929–1947*. Rinehart, 1947.

—, *William Gregg*. University of North Carolina, 1928.

Mitchell, Wesley C., and Burns, Arthur F., "Statistical Indicators of Cyclical Revivals," *National Bureau of Economic Research Bulletin 69*, May, 1938.

Money Trust Investigation, 3 vols., U.S. Congress House Committee on Banking and Currency, Washington, 1913.

Montague, G. H., *Standard Oil*. Harper, 1903.

—, *Trusts of Today*. McClure, Phillips, 1904.

Moody, John, *The Truth About the Trusts*. Moody Publishing Co., 1904.

Morison, Samuel E., and Commager, Henry S., *Growth of the American Republic*. 2 vols., Oxford, 1937.

Mott, E. H., *Between the Ocean and the Lakes: The Story of Erie*. Collins, 1899.

Mott, Frank L., *American Journalism*. Macmillan, 1941.

Moulton, Harold G., *Formation of Capital*. Brookings Institution, 1935.

Mowry, George E., *The Era of Theodore Roosevelt, 1900–1912*. Harper, 1958.

Mumford, Lewis, *The Culture of Cities*. Harcourt, Brace, 1938.

—, *The Golden Day*. Boni & Liveright, 1926.

—, *Technics and Civilization*. Harcourt, Brace, 1934.

Myers, Margaret, *The New York Money Market*, vol. I. Columbia University, 1931.

Nadworny, Milton J., *Scientific Management and the Unions, 1900–1932*. Harvard, 1955.

National Industrial Conference Board, *Employee Magazines in the United States*. New York, 1925.

—, *The International Financial Position of the United States*. New York, 1929.

—, *Studies in Enterprise and Social Progress*. New York, 1939.

Nevins, Allan, *The Emergence of Modern America, 1865–1877*. Macmillan, 1927.

—, *Ford*. 2 vols., Scribner's, 1954, 1956.

—, *Grover Cleveland*. Dodd, Mead, 1932.

—, *Hamilton Fish*. Dodd, Mead, 1936.

—, *Abram S. Hewitt*. Harper, 1935.

—, *John D. Rockefeller*. 2 vols., Scribner's, 1940.

—, ed., *Selected Writings of Abram S. Hewitt*. Columbia University, 1937.

Oberholtzer, Ellis P., *A History of the United States Since the Civil War.* 5 vols., Macmillan, 1917–1936.

Overton, Richard C., *Burlington West.* Harvard, 1941.

—, *Gulf to Rockies.* University of Texas, 1953.

Parkes, Henry B., *Recent America.* Crowell, 1940.

Parrington, Vernon L., *Main Currents in American Thought.* 3 vols., Harcourt, Brace, 1927–1930.

Passer, Harold C., *The Electrical Manufacturers, 1875–1900.* Harvard, 1953.

Paul, Randolph, *Taxation in the United States.* Little, Brown, 1954.

Paullin, Charles O., *Atlas of the Historical Geography of the United States.* Carnegie Institution of Washington and American Geographical Society of New York, 1932.

Pecora, Ferdinand, *Wall Street Under Oath.* Simon & Schuster, 1939.

Peffer, E. Louise, *The Closing of the Public Domain, 1900–50.* Stanford University, 1951.

Perine, Edward, *The Story of the Trust Companies.* Putnam's, 1916.

Phillips, U. B., *A History of Transportation in the Eastern Cotton Belt.* Columbia University, 1908.

—, "A Central Theme in Southern History," *American Historical Review,* vol. XXXIV, pp. 30–43.

Porter, Kenneth W., *John Jacob Astor.* 2 vols., Harvard, 1931.

Pratt, Julius W., *Expansionists of 1898.* Johns Hopkins, 1936.

Presbry, Frank, *The History and Development of Advertising.* Doubleday, 1929.

Primm, James N., *Economic Policy in the Development of a Western State: Missouri, 1820–1860.* Harvard, 1954.

Pringle, Henry F., *The Life and Times of William Howard Taft.* 2 vols., Farrar & Rinehart, 1939.

—, *Theodore Roosevelt.* Harcourt, Brace, 1931.

Pyle, Joseph G., *Life of James J. Hill.* 2 vols., Doubleday, Page, 1917.

Randall, James G., *The Civil War and Reconstruction.* Heath, 1937.

Raney, William F., *Wisconsin.* Prentice-Hall, 1940.

Ratner, Sidney, *American Taxation: Its History as a Social Force in Democracy.* Norton, 1942.

Recent Economic Changes in the United States (Report of the Committee on Recent Economic Changes, of the President's Conference on Unemployment, Herbert Hoover, chairman). 2 vols., McGraw-Hill, 1929.

Recent Social Trends in the United States (Report of the President's Research Committee on Social Trends). McGraw-Hill, 1934.

Redlich, Fritz, *History of American Business Leaders.* Edwards Bros., 1940.

—, *The Molding of American Banking, 1781–1910.* 2 vols., Hafner, 1947, 1951.

Rezneck, Samuel, "The Rise and Early Development of Industrial Consciousness in the United States, 1760–1830," *Journal of Economic and Business History,* vol. IV, pp. 784–811.

Riegel, Robert F., *The Story of the Western Railroads.* Macmillan, 1926.

Ripley, William Z., *Main Street and Wall Street.* Little, Brown, 1927.

—, *Railroads: Rates and Regulation* (vol. I); *Finance and Organization* (vol. II). Longmans, Green, 1912, 1915.

—, ed., *Railway Problems.* Ginn, 1907.

—, ed., *Trusts, Pools, and Corporations.* Ginn, 1905.

Robbins, Roy M., *Our Landed Heritage.* Princeton, 1942.

Rogin, Leo M., *The Introduction of Farm Machinery in Its Relation to the Productivity of Labor in the Agriculture of the United States During the 19th Century.* University of California, 1931.

Roosevelt, Theodore, *An Autobiography.* Scribner's, 1913.

Ross, Edward A., *Sin and Society.* Houghton Mifflin, 1907.

Russell, Robert R., *The Economic Aspects of Southern Sectionalism, 1840–1861.* University of Illinois, 1924.

Sakolski, Aaron M., *The Great American Land Bubble.* Harper, 1932.

Sandburg, Carl, *Abraham Lincoln: The Prairie Years.* 2 vols., Harcourt, Brace, 1926.

—, *Abraham Lincoln: The War Years.* 4 vols., Harcourt, Brace, 1939.

Schlesinger, Arthur M., *The Rise of the City, 1878–1898.* Macmillan, 1933.

Schlesinger, Arthur M., Jr., *The Coming of the New Deal.* Houghton Mifflin, 1959.

—, *The Crisis of the Old Order.* Houghton Mifflin, 1957.

Schluter, Herman, *Lincoln and Labor and Slavery.* Socialist Party, 1913.

Schmidt, Louis B., and Ross, Earle D., eds., *Readings in the Economic History of American Agriculture.* Macmillan, 1925.

Schumpeter, Joseph A., *Capitalism, Socialism and Democracy.* 2nd ed., Harper, 1947.

Seager, Henry R., and Gulick, Charles A., Jr., *Trust and Corporation Problems.* Harper, 1929.

Shannon, Fred A., *Economic History of the People of the United States.* Macmillan, 1934.

—, *The Farmer's Last Frontier.* Rinehart, 1945.

Sharfman, I. L., *The Interstate Commerce Commission.* 5 vols., Commonwealth Fund, 1931–1937.

Shlakman, Vera, *Economic History of a Factory Town* (Smith College Studies in History, vol. XX, nos. 1–4). Smith College, 1935.

Shryock, Richard H., *The Development of Modern Medicine.* University of Pennsylvania, 1936.

Slosson, Preston W., *The Great Crusade and After, 1914–1928.* Macmillan, 1930.

Smith, Walter B., *Economic Aspects of the Second Bank of the United States.* Harvard, 1953.

—, and Cole, Arthur H., *Fluctuations in American Business, 1790–1860.* Harvard, 1935.

Solomon, Barbara M., *Ancestors and Immigrants: A Changing New England Tradition.* Harvard, 1956.

Soule, George, *Prosperity Decade, 1917–1929.* Rinehart, 1947.

Spahr, Charles B., *An Essay on the Present Distribution of Wealth in the United States.* Crowell, 1896.

Spencer, Herbert, *The Principles of Biology.* 2 vols., Appleton, 1914.

"Herbert Spencer," *Outlook Magazine,* vol. LXXV, pp. 931–934.

Stalson, J. Owen, *Marketing Life Insurance.* Harvard, 1942.

Stearns, Harold E., ed., *Civilization in the United States.* Harcourt, Brace, 1922.

—, ed., *America Now.* Scribner's, 1938.

Steffens, Lincoln, *The Autobiography of Lincoln Steffens.* 2 vols., Harcourt, Brace, 1931.

Stephenson, George M., *A History of American Immigration, 1820–1924.* Ginn, 1926.

—, *The Political History of the Public Lands from 1840 to 1862.* R. G. Badger, 1917.

Stephenson, Nathaniel W., *Nelson W. Aldrich.* Scribner's, 1930.

Stevens, Frank W., *The Beginnings of the New York Central Railroad.* New York Central Railroad, 1926.

Storey, Moorfield, *Charles Sumner.* Houghton Mifflin, 1900.

Stover, John F., *The Railroads of the South, 1865–1900.* University of North Carolina, 1955.

Strassmann, W. Paul, *Risk and Technological Innovation: American Manufacturing Methods During the Nineteenth Century*. Cornell, 1959.

Strong, Josiah, *Our Country*. American Home Mission Society, 1885.

Summers, Festus P., *The Baltimore and Ohio in the Civil War*. Putnam's, 1939.

Sutton, F. X., Harris, S. E., Kaysen, Carl, and Tobin, James, *The American Business Creed*. Harvard, 1956.

Tarbell, Ida M., *The Nationalizing of Business, 1878–1898*. Macmillan, 1936.

—, *The History of the Standard Oil Company*. 1 vol. ed., Peter Smith, 1950.

—, *The Tariff in Our Times*. Macmillan, 1912.

Taussig, F. W., *The Tariff History of the United States*. Putnam's 1903.

—, *Some Aspects of the Tariff Question*. Harvard, 1934.

Taylor, Frederick W., *Principles of Scientific Management*. Harper, 1911.

Taylor, George R., *The Transportation Revolution, 1815–1860*. Rinehart, 1951.

Temporary National Economic Committee, *Final Report of the Executive Secretary*. Washington, 1941.

—, *Monographs*, nos. 1–43. Washington, 1941.

Terpenning, Walter A., *Village and Open-Country Neighborhoods*. Century, 1931.

Thompson, Carl D., *Confessions of the Power Trust*. Dutton, 1932.

Thompson, Robert L., *Wiring a Continent: The History of the Telegraph Industry in the United States, 1832–1866*. Princeton, 1947.

Thorelli, Hans B., *The Federal Antitrust Policy*. Johns Hopkins, 1955.

Tunnard, Christopher and Reed, Henry H., *American Skyline*. Houghton Mifflin, 1955.

Turner, Frederick J., *The Rise of the New West*. Harper, 1906.

—, *The United States, 1830–1850*. Holt, 1935.

U.S. Department of Agriculture, *The Farmers in a Changing World: 1940 Yearbook of Agriculture*. Washington, 1941.

Van Deusen, Glyndon G., *The Life of Henry Clay*. Little, Brown, 1937.

Van Vleck, George W., *The Panic of 1857*. Columbia University, 1943.

Veblen, Thorstein, *Absentee Ownership*. Huebsch, 1923.

—, *The Theory of Business Enterprise*. Scribner's, 1904.

—, *The Theory of the Leisure Class*. Macmillan, 1899.

Ware, Caroline F., *The Early New England Cotton Manufacture*. Houghton Mifflin, 1931.

—, ed., *The Cultural Approach to History*. Columbia University, 1940.

Wecter, Dixon, *The Saga of American Society*. Scribner's, 1937.

Weinberg, Albert K., *Manifest Destiny*, Johns Hopkins, 1935.

Wells, David A., *Recent Economic Changes in the United States*. D. Appleton, 1891.

Werner, M. R., *Tammany Hall*. Doubleday, Doran, 1928.

White, Bouck, *The Book of Daniel Drew*. Doubleday, Page, 1910.

White, William Allen, *Masks in a Pageant*. Macmillan, 1928.

Williamson, Harold F., and Daum, Arnold R., *The American Petroleum Industry, 1859–1899*. Northwestern University, 1959.

Woodward, C. Vann, *Origins of the New South, 1877–1913*. Louisiana State University, 1951.

—, *Tom Watson, Agrarian Rebel*. Macmillan, 1938.

Wyllie, Irvin G., *The Self-Made Man in America*. Rutgers, 1954.

Youmans, E. L., ed., *The Correlation and Conservation of Forces*. Appleton, 1874.

INDEX

A

Abolition, 89, 93–97, 103; and labor, 23, 36

Absentee owners, of early mill towns, 18, 63 f.; and the corporation, 70 ff.; and cities, 250 ff.; and insecurity, 327. *See also* Corporations

Adams, Henry, quoted, 124, 166, 205

Adams, Herbert B., 260

Adamson Act, 296

Addams, Jane, 276

Adler, Felix, 276, 278

Advertising, 1; and western lands, 108–110; and consumers' goods, 229, 299, 310 ff.; and public opinion, 269 f., 311, 324 f., 332 f., 341 f.; institutional, 324 f., 338; and insecurity, 328. *See also* Newspapers

Agrarians, fear manufacturing, 10; and politics, 29, 49 ff., 111, 118, 121, 164, 173 ff., 219 ff., 226 f.; individualism curtailed, 87. *See also* Agriculture

Agriculture, immigration and, 4, 215, 217, 225; and capital, 10, 55, 213 ff.; as best possible occupation, 10; expansion of, 13, 30 f., 52, 55, 138, 212, 217; and railroads, 40, 56 f., 77 f., 131, 215 ff.; western production, 56, Ch. X; and markets, 56 f., 215 ff.; mechanization, 56 ff., 111, 113, 213 f., 225 f.; specialization, 57, 211, 215 f.; and foreign debt, 138, 301; standard of living in, 211 f., 225 f., 325; credit, 212 f., 214, 215 ff., 222 f.; cooperatives, 212 f., 220 ff., 225; diversification, 213, 221 f., 223; in twentieth century, 213, 222 ff., 301, 325, 347 f.; planning and planting, 213–215; labor in, 214; middlemen in, 216, 220; prices, 216, 219, 222, 225, 347 f.; and land speculation, 217, 226; boom in, 217 f., 224 f.; mortgages, 217 f., 224 f., 226, 319; moisture and drought, 218; Granger movement, 219 ff.; income, 221, 223, 225, 325, 347 f.; tenancy, 221 f., 224, 226, 327;

dairy, 222; trade associations, 222; Smith-Lever Act, 225; Dept. of, 225; Farm Loan Act, 225, 296; Agricultural Adjustment Acts, 226 f. *See also* Agrarians

Airplanes, 353

Alabama, 48, 80, 96, 278

Albany, 6, 7, 114

Albion, Robert G., 73

Aldrich, Nelson P., 285, 286; on I. C. C., 171; on tariff, 174, 176, 289

Aldrich-Vreeland Act, 286

Allen, Fred L., quoted, 317, 337, 344

Allied Chemical Corp., 303

Allison, Wm. B., 164, 166

Aluminum, 184

America, Latin, 203 ff., 208 ff. *See also* So. America

American Assoc. for Labor Legislation, 283

American Bankers Assoc., 332; and "American Plan," 334

American Bar Assoc., 193, 332, 339

American Brass Assoc., 61

American Constitutional Assoc., 334

American Economics Assoc., 260

American Emigrant Co., 107

American Federation of Labor, 233 ff., 236 f., 238, 239, 246, 278, 337

American Federationist, quoted, 337

American Historical Assoc., 260

American Industries, 241

American Iron Assoc., 61

American Iron & Steel Assoc., 114, 174; *Bulletin,* 138, 139

American Newspaper Publishers Assoc., 270

"American Plan," 333 ff.

American Socialist Party, 237. *See also* Socialism

American Telegraph Co., 115

American Telephone & Telegraph Co., and science, 183 f., 306; and monopoly, 183 f., 193; assets, 314; stock holding in, 319; and public opinion, 340

American Tobacco Co., 305

371

American Woman's Suffrage Assoc., 284
American Workingmen's Party, 25 f.
America's New Frontier, 340
Ames, Oakes, 158
Amusements, business influence on, 1, 324; in cities, 235, 262
Anderson, Sherwood, 349
Andrews, John B., quoted, 283
Anti-Boycott Assoc., 281
Anti-Income Tax Assoc., 167
Antietam, 112
Appleton family, 21, 71
Archipenko, 353
Architecture, 251 ff., 257, 320, 350 f.
Arena, 202
Argentina, 314
Arkansas, 42, 96
Armour, Phillip D., 137, 146
Army, lack of, in North and South, 104; and labor, 106, 117; in Civil War, 112; transportation consolidation, 114–116; in World War, 302
Art, business influence on, 1, 72, 251, 256 ff., 348–353; in the West, 55; cities and, 251, 256 ff.; Big Business and, 257 ff., 351 ff.; middle class and, 258; women and, 258 ff., in 1920's, 348–353; and technology, 350 ff.; and industrial design, 351 ff.; "streamlining," 353. *See also* Architecture, Moving pictures, Music, Patronage
Art of Conversation, 37
Arthur, Chester A., 174, 179, 293
Aspinwall, W. H., 98
Assembly lines, 185, 299, 301
Associated Industries, 334
Associated Press, 203
Associations, to promote manufacturing, 10; for tariff, 16, 17; cooperative, 27; of white collar workers, 28; utopian, 89; anti-income tax, 167; social, 235, 328 ff., 331 ff.; women's, 260, 329; learned, 260 f.; newspaper, 270; Progressive, 276 ff.; "booster," 328 f.; Klan, 330 f.; Utility, 331 f., 339 ff.; "American Plan," 333 ff. *See also* Employer associations, Trade associations, Trade unions, Individual associations by name
Astor, John Jacob, 13, 68, 167
Astor, William B., 68, 94, 98
Astor, Mrs. William, 147
Astor family, 250
Atlanta, 162
Atlantic Monthly, 127
Atlantic Refining Co., 311
Auctions, mercantile, 8; land, 38
Augusta, Ga., 162
Automobiles, 185–188, 200, 225, 303, 324; and state aid, 187 f., 296; in 1920, 309

Avery, I. W., quoted, 162
Aylesworth, M. H., 339

B

Babson, Roger, quoted, 333, 344
Baker, George F., 182, 194, 196, 284
Baker, Ray Stannard, 282
Bakunin, Michael, 236
Baldwin Locomotive Co., 184, 306
Ballinger, Richard, 289 f.
Baltimore, 33; land values, 43; railroad terminal, 55; distribution center, 63; and the B. & O., 70; railroad debt, 80; bank failures, 86; architecture in, 252
Baltimore & Ohio R. R., 67; opened, 7 f.; to West, 55; cost, 68; and government ownership, 70; reorganization of, 197
Bancitaly Corp., 315
Bank of Belgium, 46
Bank of England, 45
Bank of the State of Indiana, 86
Bank of the U. S. (second), 40, 43, 77; removal of deposits, 43; stockholders in South, 49; and recharter, 50
Bankers, ignore manufacturing, 10; and southern trade, 35; local, 50; and silver, 173 ff.; and automobiles, 186 f.; and control of business, 188 ff., 197 ff. *See also* American Bankers' Assoc.; Banking; Banking, Investment; Panics
Bankers' Magazine, 76; quoted, 201
Bankers Trust Co., 320
Banking, in South, 33; early New York, 34, 85 f.; early western, 40, 85 f.; national, 40, 43, 49, 50, 77, 112, 294 f.; and panic of 1837, 41–49; early state, 42, 85 f.; statistics, 43, 192; loans, 43, 82; circulation, 43; failures, 45 ff., 86, 295; and cities, 63; and "Boston Associates," 71; savings, 76, 189; privileges to railroads, 77, 80; and panic of 1857, 81–86; deposit, 82; and Civil War, 91, 96, 112; new devices, 151; cooperative, 220; Aldrich-Vreeland Act, 286; Federal Reserve System, 294 f.; and real estate boom, 320; and public opinion, 332, 334, 340; and world war debts, 345; in 1930's, 357. *See also* Bankers; Banking, Investment; Panics; Trust companies
Banking, Investment, and panic of 1837, 41–49; early growth of, 52 f.; "Boston Associates" and, 70 ff.; after 1837, 76; after Civil War, 130; holding companies, 150, 300, 315, 316 ff.; leadership, 150, 182, 192 ff., 201, 273; reorganizations, 150, 187, 201 f.; com-

binations, 191; and social welfare, 196, 198 ff., 256 f., 308 f.; and voting trusts, 201 f.; and Spanish War, 206 f.; and foreign investments, 208 ff., 312 ff.; and World War, 302; and enterprise, 308 f. *See also* Bankers, Banking, Panics, Trust companies

Banks, *see* Banking

Baring Brothers, 76

Barker, Jacob, 74

Barnard, Judge, 159

Barton, Bruce, quoted, 318, 324, 342

Bashford, Coles, 81

Beaver Falls Mills, 146

Beecher, Henry Ward, 94, 100

Beer, Thomas, 260

Bel Geddes, Norman, 351 f.

Bell, Alexander Graham, 137

Bell Telephone Laboratories, 306

Bellamy, Edward, 236

Belmont, August, 76, 86, 94, 98, 159, 164, 166, 191

Bennett, James Gordon, 28, 103; quoted, 93 f.

Benton, Thomas H., quoted 40, 47; and railroads, 78

Berger, Victor, 237

Bernays, Edward, quoted, 310, 328, 331, 337

Bessemer process, 138

Bethlehem Steel Corp., 305; in So. America, 314

Beveridge, Albert, 203, 205, 276, 296; quoted, 206, 207

Biddeford, Me., 72

Biddle, Nicholas, 46, 48

Big Business, and Roosevelt, 126, 287 f.; and Wilson, 126, 193 f., 199, 292 ff., 308; and parties, 156 ff., 162 f., 168 ff.; and savings, 181 f.; and science, 181, 183 f., 306; growth of, 189 ff., 306 f.; bureaucracy in, 198 f., 230, 273 f., 307 f.; 325, 356; and imperialism, 203 ff., 313 f.; and arts, 257 ff., 351 ff.; newspapers in, 269 f., 337 f.; and Progressivism, 284 f., 292 ff.; World War and, 302. *See also* Banking, Investment; "bigness"; "trusts"

"bigness," economies of, 189 f., 198, 306 f., 317 f.; managerial problems of, 198 f., 230, 273 ff., 307 f., 325, 336 f.; and holding companies, 315 ff.

Biology, 121 ff.

Birmingham, Ala., 262

Birney, James G., quoted, 94

Black Ball Line, 33 f.

Blacksmiths, village, 3

Blair, John J., 109

Bland, Richard P., 166

Blatchford, R. M., 98

Bliss, W. D. P., 236

Bok, Edward, 269

Bolivia, 314

Bombay, India, 263

Bonds, *see* Securities

Bonus, veterans, 347

Booms, and labor organization, 26, 234; in 1830's, 41 ff.; railroad, 82–84, 131; Civil War, 91, 112–114; after 1898, 188 ff.; in agriculture, 218, 224 f.; in 1920's, 300, 315–321, 355; in 1930's, 357. *See also* Business Cycles, Depressions, Panics

Boone, Daniel, 38

Boot and Shoe industry, 9, 26 f., 59, 98, 113, 152

Borah, Wm. E., 292

Bosses, 154, 266 ff., 284

Boston, 7, 26, 33, 114, 115, 271; failure of 10 hour movement, 26; new business interests, 29; railroad terminal, 55; distribution center, 63; western investments, 72; and stock exchanges, 74; private bankers in, 76; clothing industry in, 113; and telephone, 137; slums, 264, 280

"Boston Associates," 20, 99, 109; invest in textiles, 13; and Puritan tradition, 21; dominate Massachusetts, 70 ff.

Boston Manufacturing Co., 71

Boston & Worcester R. R., 114

Bradley-Martin ball, 257

Brandeis, Louis, 202, 242, 310

Brazil, 314

Brice, Calvin, 163

Brickmakers, village, 3

British Iron Trade Commission, quoted, 146

Brokers, 8, 56, 216, 220, 318 f.

Brook, Alexander, 350

Brooks, Preston S., 97

Brougham, Henry, quoted, 11

Brown, Governor, quoted, 97

Brown, John, 97

Brown, John Carter, 109

Brown, Joseph, 162

Brown Brothers, 76, 191

Brown v. Maryland, 15

Brownson, Orestes, quoted, 23

Bryan, Wm. Jennings, 173, 176, 292 ff.

Bryant, William Cullen, 79, 89

Bryant & Sturgis, 13

Bryce, James, 265; quoted, 157, 166, 251

Buchanan, James, 78, 94, 102, 107

Buckminster, William, quoted, 57

Buffalo, 6, 8, 93, 114, 115; Erie Canal terminal, 7; distribution center, 63; telegraph in, 115

Bull Moose Party, 292, 296

Bunting v. Oregon, 242

Bureau of Corporations, 287

Bureau of Mines, 288

Bureaucracy, in politics, 157 ff., 282 f., 357; in corporations, 198 f., 230, 273 f., 307 f., 325, 356
Burleson, Albert S., 293
Business, influence on art and ideas, 1, 71 f., 89, 119–128, 247 f., 256 ff., 260 f., 332 ff., 339 f., 348–353; government aid to, 5, 11, 15 f., 42, 77 ff., 107 ff., 132, 301 f., 342 ff.; and political corruption, 16, 39, 67 ff., 78 ff., 110 f., 132 ff., 148, 154 ff., 158; and radicalism, 25 f., 88 f., 236 ff., 267, 332 ff.; organization and techniques, 28, 52 f., 57 ff., 67 ff., 140 ff., 184, 188, 198 ff., 243 ff., 298 f., 307 ff., 336 ff.; spirit, 29, 52, 74 ff., 161, 184, 198 ff., 243 ff., 307 ff.; and West, 30 f., 37, 39 ff., 49, 55 f., 108–110, Ch. X; and South, 32, 34, 49, 90–97; and science, 58, 183 ff., 306; combination, 61 ff., 130, 140 ff., 188 ff., 299; little, 62, 152, 164, 281 ff., 284 f.; and stock exchanges, 73 ff., 146 ff., 315 ff.; and secession, 91, 92 ff.; and Civil War, 91, 98 f., 100–117; and Republican Party, 105, 107 ff.; contract labor law, 106 f.; political leadership of, 111, 118, 129, 154 ff., 201, 324, 342–348; philosophy, 119–128, 161, 196 f., 247 f.; and social leadership, 119–128, 129 ff., 136, 142 f., 150 ff.; Ch. XII, 273, 324 ff., 331–342; and reconstruction, 157; men in Congress, 162–164; and I. C. C., 169 ff.; and anti-trust laws, 171 ff., 286, 289, 295, 305, 346, 348; bureaucracy in, 198 f., 230, 273 f., 307 f., 325, 356; and Progressivism, 203, Ch. XIII; and imperialism, 202–210, 312 ff.; and Spanish War, 206 f.; and welfare capitalism, 229, 232, 242 ff., 306, 336 ff.; and city planning, 252 ff.; and city politics, 156 ff., 266 ff.; public relations of, 310 f., 324 ff., 336 ff.; alienated groups, 325, 342; "booster clubs," 328 f.; and "American Plan," 333 ff.; and employee magazines, 336 f. See also Absentee owners, Combination, Corporations, Employers associations, Enterprise, Industry, Labor, Securities, Standardization, Tariffs, Trade associations, and individual industries by name
Business cycles, and labor, 24 ff., 228, 234 f.; ignorance of, 43, 136 f.; theory of, 44; and expansion, 44 f., 82 ff., 139, 182, 228, 321; after Civil War, 136 f.; in 1920's, 321 f. See also Booms, Depressions, Panics
"Businessman's Cabinet," 163
Butler, Gen. Ben, 118, 159, 161, 167
Butler, Nicholas Murray, 126, 128; quoted, 126

Butts, Henry, quoted, 159
By-products, and combinations, 143, 306 f.

C

Cabell, James B., 349
Cable, Atlantic, 151
Cabot family, 21, 71
Calhoun, John C., 16, 95, 121
California, 131, 164; nativism in, 65; gold, 82 f., 86; land grant, 132; Grange in, 220; Progressivism in, 277, 279; "American Plan" in, 334
California Wine Growers' Assoc., 114
Camden & Amboy R. R., 79–80
Cameron, Donald, 160, 164
Cameron, Simon, 159; abdicates, 160
Canada, 200, 289
Canals, in 1800, 3; early boom in, 7; government aid, 42; and panic of 1837, 46 f.
Cannon, "Uncle Joe," 285, 287
Cap and Hat Manufacturers Assoc. of New York, 114
Capital, competition for, 10, 133; new sources of manufacturing, 13; in South, 32 f.; eastern in West, 39 ff., 53 ff., 72, 93, 108 ff., 131; foreign, 41, 45 ff., 137, 181, 301; accumulation, 14, 49, 55, 76, 153, 188, 298 ff.; new outlets for, 53, 68, 181, 202–210, 309 f., 312 ff.; concentration of, 67–76, 113–116, 150, 190–202, 299, 305, 314 f.; in railroads, 68, 80, 83, 131, 133 ff., 137, 181; in securities, 73 ff., 133 ff., 189 ff., 315 ff.; and new industries, 181, 188, 298; in consumers' goods, 186 ff., 229, 309 f.; and speculation, 188 ff., 315 ff.; in government enterprise, 298 f. See also Banking, Investment; Corporations; Railroads; Securities; Speculation
Capital goods, see Production goods
Capital Land Agency of Topeka, 110
Capitalists, and early manufacturing, 4 f., 12 f.; in relation to South, 36, 90; English and panic of 1837, 41 ff.; eastern and panic of 1837, 41 ff.; and speculation, 52 f.; and panic of 1857, 81–86; and western lands, 107–111. See also Banking, Investment; capital
Carey, Matthew, 4, 10, 15, 17 f.
Caribbean policy, 207 f.
Carnegie, Andrew, 137, 181, 228, 307; on Spencer, 124; on railroads, 136; and depressions, 137, 145; and Bessemer process, 138; and competition, 145–146; on poverty, 153, 263; and philanthropy, 257
Carnegie Steel Co., 146; and science, 184
Cary sisters, 55

Cass, Lewis, 78
Catholics, 52, 65, 236; Klan and, 330
Cattle Raising, 212
Central Hanover Bank & Trust Co., 320
Central Pacific R. R., 55, 162; land
  grant, 108, 157, 158; corruption, 132;
  loans, 133
Chain Stores, see Merchandising
Chambers of Commerce, 306, 331; and
  "American Plan," 333 f.
Chandler, "Zach," 159, 160
Channing, William Ellery, quoted, 68
Charity Aid Societies, 276, 278, 282
Charleston, S. C., 32 ff., 101
Charleston & Hamburg R. R., 7 f.
Chase, Salmon P., 94
Chattanooga, 112
Chautauqua, 260, 340
Chemical Foundation, 303
Chemical industry, 301, 303 f.
Cherokee Indians, 109
Chesapeake & Ohio R. R., 135
Chesapeake Valley, 211
Chevalier, Michel, quoted, 20
Chicago, 93, 114, 151, 230, 254, 268,
  270; growth, 42 f.; and speculation,
  42 f., 250; and canals, 43; as rail-
  road terminal, 55; distribution center,
  63, 152, 216, 220; immigrants, 65;
  private bankers in, 76; telegraph in,
  115; "Pit," 221; city planning in, 253;
  skyscrapers, 255; slums, 264; reform
  in, 266; "American Plan" in, 334;
  Centennial, 353
Chicago, Burlington & Quincy R. R.,
  172
Chicago Daily Journal, quoted, 93
Chicago Exposition, 1933, 353
Chicago, Milwaukee & St. Paul Rail-
  way Co. v. Minnesota, 180
Chicago & North Western R. R., 115
Chicago, Rock Island & Pacific Rway.,
  83
Chicago Tribune, 291
Chicopee, Mass., 18, 63, 71
Child Labor, see Labor
Child Labor Committees, 276 ff.
Children's Bureau, federal, 288
Chile, 314
China, see Commerce, foreign; Far East
Chrysler, Walter P., 320
Chubb & Schenck, 76
Churches, lack of, 18; and imperialism,
  204; and Progressivism, 275 ff.; in
  1920's, 329
Cigarettes, see Tobacco
Cincinnati, 6, 7, 93, 117, 157; distribu-
  tion center, 63; clothing industry in,
  113; city planning, 253; slums, 264
Cincinnati Gazette, quoted, 62
Circulation Managers Assoc., 270

Cities, invest in factories, 11; housing
  in, 18, 28, 63 f., 235, 253 ff., 262 ff.,
  319 f., 327; lower class in, 20, 27,
  63 ff., 261 ff.; new problems of, 27 f.,
  53, 63 ff., 250, 323, 327; and individualism, 28, 249 f., 271 f., 326 f.;
  middle class in, 28, 56, 258 ff.; source
  of culture, 31, 87 ff., 150 ff., 249, 251 ff.,
  256 ff., 268 ff., 323; growth of western,
  42 f., 152 f.; land values in, 43, 250,
  253 f., 319 f.; agriculture and, 57 f.,
  212; disease in, 63 ff., 262, 265, 327;
  and distribution, 63, 151 ff.; and immigration, 63 ff., 159, 169, 268, 280;
  and mechanization, 63, 153, 184; poverty in, 63 ff., 231, 263; and railroads,
  80, 129, 132 f., 152, 251; upper class in,
  153, 256 ff.; government of, 156 ff.,
  250, 265 ff., 275 ff., 280, 284; electricity
  and, 184; amusements in, 235, 262;
  planning of, 249, 252 ff., 254, 264 f.,
  279 f.; education in, 251, 270 ff.;
  architecture in, 251 ff., 257; and family, 259; crime in, 265, 326, 327. See
  also Absentee owners, Housing, Labor,
  Poverty, Slums
Cities Service Corp., 318
"Citizens Alliances," 239, 281
Citizens Industrial Assoc., 239 f., 281
Civil Liberties, in Civil War, 118; in
  World War, 302
Civil Service Reform, 155, 162
Civil War, 54, 57, 58, 61, Ch. V; northern business and, 91, 98 f., 107-117,
  133; and West, 92 f., 100; abolition
  and, 93-97; precipitated, 104; and
  tariff, 105 f.; and government finance,
  105 f., 112; and labor, 106 f., 117 f.;
  and industrial combinations, 114 ff.;
  civil liberties in, 148; parties after,
  154, 156 ff.
Claflin, H. B., 153
Claflin, John, quoted, 195
Clark, Champ, 292
Clark, E. W. & Co., 76
Classes, new relations, 5, 27 ff., 53,
  273 f.; city lower, 20, 27, 63 ff., 261 ff.;
  appearance in labor movement, 22 f.;
  middle, 25 f., 28, 30 f., 118, 258 f.,
  274 ff.; war millionaires, 113, 114;
  city upper, 153, 256 ff.; fluidity of, 153
Clay, Henry, 4, 15, 16 f., 50; quoted, 12
Clayton Act, 295, 305, 346, 348
Cleveland, 6, 7, 8, 42, 93, 329; telegraph
  in, 115; oil refining, 143 f.; slums,
  264; reform in, 266
Cleveland, Grover, 161, 162, 163, 166,
  169, 172, 174, 175, 176, 289, 293
Cleveland Plain Dealer, quoted, 93
Climate, and water transportation, 6 f.;
  and agriculture, 211, 213 f., 218 f.

Cobblers, village, 3
Cochrane, Alexander S., 291
Colfax, Schuyler, 167
Collier's, quoted, 290
Colombia, S. A., 314
Colorado, 131, 246, 277
Colorado Fuel & Iron Co., 146, 246
Colt, Peter, 17
Colton, David B., 158
Columbia Broadcasting System, 338
Columbia University, 126, 128
Columbus, O., 54
Columbus, S. C., 162
Combination, and courts, 24, 141, 170, 286, 289, 304, 348; and overhead costs, 61 ff., 149 f., 189 f., 196 f.; in railroads, 61 f., 114, 115, 193; industrial, 61 f., 130, 138–146, 181 f., 188–192, 315 ff.; telegraph, 115 f.; and investment banking, 130, 181 f., 188–192; overcapitalization of, 139 f., 149 f., 197 f., 315 ff.; procedure in, 142 ff., 191, 316 ff.; vertical integration, 143, 306 f.; in automobiles, 186; and security speculation, 188 ff., 195 ff.; in journalism, 269 f.; in medicine, 329; in religion and education, 329. *See also* Banking, Investment; Big Business; "bigness"; Corporations; Reorganization; "trusts"
Commerce, Foreign, profits from in 1790's, 4; user of capital, 10, 209; declining value, 13; China trade, 13, 54; Supreme Court on, 15; Congress and, 15; New York City and, 33–35; packets, 33–34; World War and, 300 f. *See also* Imports, Exports, Tariff
Commerce, Interstate, Supreme Court on, 15, 169, 180; and Civil War, 98. *See also* Railroads, Shipping, Trade, Transportation
Commercial & Financial Chronicle, 138; quoted, 116
Commodity Exchanges, 151 f., 221
Common Law, 177; labor conspiracies, 24; and pools, 141; and factory accidents, 242 f.
Commons, John R., 236
Commonwealth v. Hunt, 24
Commonwealth Edison Co., 317
Communication, in 1800, 3; and labor organization, 26, 66; and business turnover, 28, 151; telephone and telegraph, 56 f., 59, 66, 115 f., 136 f., 151, 302 f., 309; uniform postage rates, 59; consolidation, 114 ff.; and centralization of business, 151; and nationalism, 203 f., 251, 324, 331 f.; and agriculture, 216; radio, 225, 303, 309, 324, 310, 311, 338 f.; and city culture, 251, 338 f.; advertising and, 310 ff. *See also*

Postal Service, Railroads, Transportation, Travel
Communism, 27, 89, 236, 332
Community chests, 329 f.
"Community of Interest," 196
Company towns, 18 f., 20, 63, 71 ff.
Company unions, 246
Competition, in 1800, 4; early industrial, 8 ff.; western influence on, 41; limitations on, 59 ff., 120 f., 130, 138, 140–146, 188 ff., 226 f., 304 f., 321 f., 354 f.; and overhead costs, 59 f., 63, 149 f., 189 f., 196 f.; railroads and, 114, 132, 133, 135 f., 143 f., 152, 158, 164, 169 ff., 196; and business philosophy, 119–128, 139 f.; and waste, 138 ff.; trade associations on, 139 f.; and courts, 141, 170, 180, 286, 289, 304, 348; and cities, 152 f., 249; in politics, 155, 157 f., 164; regulation of, 170 f., 286, 289, 295, 348; in automobiles, 186; and "money trust," 192 ff.; and welfare capitalism, 232; World War and, 302; and price leadership, 305, 321 f.; and oligopoly, 305, 321 f.
Comstock Lode, 137
Confederate States, 98, 101
Conkling, Roscoe, 158, 159, 160 f., 167
Connecticut, 16 f., 65, 277
Connecticut River, 6, 71
Conservation, 165, 289 f.
Conshohocken, Pa., 63
Consolidation, *see* Combination
Constable, Arnold, 159
Construction, and Civil War, 111 f., declining rate of, 182, 298; and labor, 233, 238, 240; regulation of, 254, 264 f., 279 f.; in 1920's, 319 f.
Construction companies, in railroads, 110 f., 131, 134 f.
Consumer Goods, importance of, 189, 229, 299, 309 ff.; and distribution, 229, 299, 324; expansion of, 299, 309 ff., 355; credit selling, 310; and fashion, 310; and culture, 324, 331 ff.; and farm prices, 347 f.
Consumers' League (N. J.), 278
Contract Labor Law, 106 f.
Cook County Child Saving League, 277
Cooke, Jay, 131; and Civil War finance, 112; and railroad politics, 158
Coolidge, Calvin, 348; quoted, 311, 324
Cooper, James Fenimore, 38
Cooper, Peter, 73, 167
Cooper, Thomas, 10, 121; quoted, 17
Coopers, village, 3
Cooperatives, communal, 27; agricultural, 212 f., 220, 222, 225; in medicine, 329

Cordage Trust (National Cordage Company), 142
Cornell, Ezra, 109
Corning, Erastus, 73
Corporation Securities Co. of Chicago, 317
Corporations, and Dartmouth College Case, 15, 15 n.; enter iron industry, 19; fractional interest in, 29, 71 ff.; separation of ownership and management, 29, 52, 67 ff., 146 ff., 189 ff., 201 f., 307, 319; growth of, 53, 70; in 1850's, 67–77; and property relations, 67–76, 129, 142, 146 ff., 188 ff., 315 ff.; "modern," 68 ff., 146 ff., 230, 315 ff.; general acts for, 70; Federal R. R. charters, 110; and investment banking, 130, 140, 150, 188 ff., 299 ff., 302 f.; individualism and, 143 f.; and by-products, 143, 306 f.; reorganizations, 147 ff., 188 ff.; and Fourteenth Amendment, 178; and science, 183 ff., 306; lax charters, 190; and bureaucracy, 198 f., 230, 273 f., 307 f., 325 f., 356; and criminal law, 200 f.; newspaper, 269 f.; public relations of, 310 f., 324 ff., 331 ff.; profits, 314; and call money, 318; and art, 351 ff. See also Big Business, "bigness," Combination, Holding Companies, Railroads, Securities, "trusts" and Individual Corporations
Corruption, and tariff, 16, 79, 156 f., 174 f.; and land sales, 39; and railroads, 67 ff., 78 ff., 110, 111, 132 ff., 148, 158; and securities, 74 f., 152; in Civil War, 118; after Civil War, 154 ff.; in cities, 158 ff., 265 ff.; and bureaucracy, 200; and Progressivism, 202, 280; Harding and, 345
Cost Accounting, 247, 327. See also Scientific management
Costs, decrease in manufacturing, 14, 59, 184 f., 187, 299, 304; southern marketing, 34 f.; overhead, 59–63, 149 f., 189 f., 196 f., 213 f., 219, 226; railroad, 68, 83, 131–135; and depressions, 137; and welfare capitalism, 232, 243–248. See also Business cycles, Scientific management
Cotton, 3, 219; spindles, 14, 61, 71; prices, 16, 35, 219; demand for, 32; acceptances, 45; and Civil War, 98; expansion of, 219; problems of, 219 ff.
Cottonseed Oil Trust (American Cotton Oil Trust, also The American Cotton Oil Co.), 142, 170
Coxe, Tench, 4, 10
Crane, Edward, 67, 75
Crane, Stephen, 258
Credit, early manufacturing, 8, 13 f.;

terms, 28, 37 f., 82; early facilities, 34 f., 56; and investment banking, 76, 192 ff.; deposit, 82; call money, 84 f., 318; and Civil War, 112; and government securities, 112; monopoly of, 191 ff.; agricultural, 212 f.. 216 f., 222; installment, 310, 328. See also Banking, Capital, Securities
Crédit Mobilier, 110 f., 131
Crimean War, 83, 84
Crises, financial, see Panics
Corn, 3, 213, 219
"Crittenden Compromise," 101
Croker, Richard, 266; quoted, 2
Cuba, 205 f., 207, 208 ff.
Cullom, Shelby, on Sherman Act, 172
Cullom Committee (U. S. Senate), quoted, 136, 169
Currency, circulation, 43, 86; in politics, 43, 164 ff., 173 f., 176; greenbacks, 105, 112, 164 ff.; Aldrich-Vreeland Act, 286; Federal Reserve Act, 286, 294 f.
Curtis, George Wm., quoted, 166
Cushing, Caleb, quoted, 94
Cushing, John P., 13

D

Dairy farming, see Agriculture
Dartmouth College v. Woodward, 15, 15 n.
Darwin, Charles, 121 ff.
Davenport, Daniel, 241, 281
Davison, Henry P., 286; quoted, 202
Dayton, O., 334
De Bow, J. D. B., quoted, 56 f.
Debs, Eugene V., 237, 267
Debts, southern, 32, 35, 91, 100, 112; foreign, 41, 45–49, 137, 181, 301; states default on, 48; municipal railroad, 80; Morgan and railroad, 197; and insecurity, 328; World War, 345; private, 1930's, 357. See also Capital
Decker, Sarah, 276; quoted, 277
De Forest, Robert, 276
Delaware, child labor law, 279
Delaware & Hudson R. R., 67
Delaware river, 6, 211
De Lôme letter, 206
Democratic Party, and Andrew Jackson, 50 ff.; and West, 93; and Civil War, 102, 160; and solid south, 154; and issues, 155, 165 ff., 173 ff.; Tweed Ring, 157, 159; and local government, 161; and Big Business, 162, 292; and Grange, 164; and Supreme Court, 178; and Woodrow Wilson, 292 ff.; Klan and, 330; and New Deal, 355 ff.
Depressions, 1817–1822, 11 f., 49; and labor, 25; 1828–1829, 25, 49; 1837–1843, 44–49, 54; and immigration, 66;

and secession, 91; and Civil War, 136 f.; 1893–1896, 150, 219; and parties, 155; 1907–1909, 182, 195; 1929–1933, 355 ff. *See also* Booms, Business Cycles, Panics.
de Tocqueville, A., 58
Denver Pacific R. R., 149
Depew, Chauncey, 162
Devyr, Thomas A., quoted, 14 f.
Dew, Professor, 95
Dillon, Sidney, 145, **153**
Disney, Walt, 351
Disston, Frank, 232
Disston Law Co., 232
Distribution, 27; and village merchants, 3, 55; by auctions, 8; of foreign goods, 8, 13, 32 ff.; by centralized markets, 63, 151 ff.; agricultural, 215 ff.; of consumer goods, 229, 299, 309 ff., 324; mail order, 268. *See also* Markets, Merchandising
Dodge, Cleveland, 292
Dodge, William E., 109, 153, 159
Dos Passos, John, 349
Dover, N. H., 18, 72
Douglas, Stephen A., 78; quoted, 102
Dred Scott Case (*Scott v. Sanford*), 96
Dreiser, Theodore, 258, 349
Drew, Daniel, 67, 69, 133 f., 148
Drexel & Co., 76
Dreyfuss, Henry, 352
Dunkirk, 55, 115
Du Pont, E. I., 17
Du Pont, E. I., de Nemours, Powder Co., 303, 306, 314
Du Pont, T. Coleman, 291
Duquesne Steel Works, 146
Durable goods, *see* Production goods
Durant, Thomas C., 158
Durant, Wm. C., 186 f.
Dutch East India Co., 354
Dwight family, 21, 71
Dyers, village, 3

E

East India Co., 354
Eastman Kodak Corp., 306
Eaton, John, quoted, 271
Ecole des Beaux Arts, 260
Economic theory, 119–128; and business cycle, 43 f.; and costs, 59 ff.; and consumers' goods, 229; and depression of 1930's, 321 f., 356 f.
Edgerton, John E., 336; quoted, 335
Edinburgh Review, quoted, 48
Edgar Thomson Steel Works, 146
Edison Companies, 183
Edison Electric Illuminating Co. of Boston, 339
Edison Electric Institute, 331 f.

Edmunds, George F., 171
Edson, Kathrine, 276, 279
Education, business influence on, 1, 37, 53, 260 f., 270 ff., 306, 332 f., 339 f.; workers', 19, 25, 247 f.; southern, 36, 271; and western lands, 108 ff.; college, 108 ff., 260 f., 306; Spencerianism and, 127 f.; in cities, 152, 251, 259 f.; rural, 219, 225; Germany and, 236, 260; secondary, 270 ff.; in World War, 302; and science, 306; and radicalism, 332; utilities and, 339 f.
Educational Review, 271
Electric Bond & Share Co., 316, 318
Electricity, 136, 181, 183 ff.; after World War, 303 f.; appliances, 303, 309
Eliot family, 71
Eliot, Charles W., quoted, 126, 128, 206
Eliot, T. S., 349
Elkins Act, 286
Elks, 328
Ely, Richard T., 202, 236, 260
Embargo, of 1807, 5
Emerson, Ralph W., 53; quoted, 54, 68, 70, 87, 88
Emery, James A., 240 f., 281
Emigrant Aid Co., 109
Employee magazines, 336 f.
Employers Associations, and labor, 66, 229, 239 ff.; and Progressivism, 281 ff.; in 1920's, 331 ff.; and "American Plan," 334 f.
Employers' Liability, 231, 279
Engineering News, quoted, 199
Engineers, 184 ff.; and financiers, 67, 199 f.; industrial, 308
England, *see* Great Britain
Enterprise, in 1800, 4, 354; industrial, 12 f., 71 ff., 136 ff.; New York shippers and, 33 ff.; and foreign capital, 41 ff., 137 f.; and West, 53 ff., 130 ff.; railroad, 53 ff., 130 ff.; "Boston Associates" and, 71 ff.; corporations and, 73; in South, 162; and Supreme Court, 15, 180; and new technology, 181, 183 ff.; bankers and, 186 f., 193 ff., 198 ff., 308 f.; agricultural, 212 ff.; government, 298 f., 301 f., 355 ff.; World War and, 301 f.; and expansion, 354 f.
Entrepreneur, *see* Enterprise
Erie Canal, effects of on American economy, 7; and New York City, 33; and West, 33, 36; and panic of 1837, 41 f.
Erie R. R., 8, 83, 133–134; to the West, 55; cost, 68; election fraud, 69, 70; fails, 85; combines, 115; Rockefeller and, 144; Gould and, 148; reorganization of, 197
Esch-Cummins Act, 344

Etiquette, 28, 37
Evangelists, 89
Everett, Edward, quoted, 37
Evolution, 121-128
Exchanges, *see* Commodity exchanges, Stock exchanges
Expositions, industrial, 58, 138
Expansion, opportunities for in 1800, 1, 354; and West, 38 ff., 53 ff., 130 ff., 215 ff.; and foreign loans, 41 ff., 137 f.; and business cycle, 45, 82 ff., 139; to Pacific, 52; and corporation, 67 ff.; after Civil War, 129 ff.; world, 130, 298; and depressions, 136 f., 139; and stock exchanges, 147; "Progress" and, 161, 162, 354 ff.; and Supreme Court, 178; and new technology, 181, 183; foreign, 182, 202-210, 312 ff.; slows down, 182, 188 f., 202 f., 229, 298 ff., 305 f., 354 f.; bankers and, 200; Wilson on, 203; agricultural, 215 ff.; Schwab on, 305; and consumer goods, 309 ff.; and freedom, 354 ff. *See also,* Capital, Industry, Railroads
Exports, importance of cotton, 34; and foreign loans, 137-138; agricultural, 223 ff.; and World War, 300 f.; in 1929, 321. *See also* Commerce, Foreign
Express business, 56, 59, 151

F

Factories, early difficulties, 8-12; woolen, 11; cotton, 11; iron forges, 11; sources of early labor, 13; prosper from tariffs, 18; and local industry, 27; western, 40; improved machinery, 57-59, 112 f., 183 ff., 303 f.; number of, 61; cooperative, 220; regulation, 200, 241, 275; electrification of, 303 f.; rationalization of, 303 f.; American aboard, 312 f. *See also* Industry, and specific industries
Fair, James, 163
Family, and city, 259
Far East, 13, 54, 207, 208 ff.
Farmers, *see* Agriculture
Farmers Trust Co., 320
Farragut, Admiral, David G., 112
Faulkner, Wm., 349
Federal Aid to Highways Act, 296
Federal Farm Loan Act, 225, 296
Federal Reserve Act, 286, 294 f.
Federal Reserve Board, 321
Federal Trade Commission, 295, 341, 346, 348
Felch, Isaac, quoted, 9
Feminists, 89
Field, Marshall, 153, 194, 250
Field, Justice S. J., 180

Filene, Edward, 247
Finance, *see* Banking; Banking, Investment; Capital; Securities
Finance Capitalism, *see* Banking, Investment
First National Bank of N. Y., 194
Fish, Hamilton, 98, 167
Fisk, Jim, 134, 148
Fiske, John, 125, 128, 204, 205
Fitzgerald, F. Scott, 349
Florida, 48, 80, 96
Flour mills, 11; new processes, 138; overexpanded, 139 f.; combination in, 146
Force Act, 50
Ford, Henry, 186, 187 ff., 200, 230, 307; Model T, 187; and Brazilian rubber, 314; and Prohibition, 346
Forest Reserve Act, 289 f.
Fort Sumter, 99, 101, 103, 104
Fortuny, Mariano, 257
Fourierists, 89
Fourteenth Amendment, 178, 180, 242
France, 182, 208, 298, 300, 313
Free enterprise, *see* Enterprise
Free-land, *see* Land
Freight rates, effect of Erie Canal on, 7; on turnpikes, 7; capitalization and, 133 ff.; farmers and, 220 f. *See also* Interstate Commerce Act, Interstate Commerce Commission
Frenzied Finance, 202
Freud, Sigmund, 328
Frick, H. C., 257
Frontier, and labor, 29; intensive, Ch. III; Turner thesis, 30-31; extensive, 31; and democracy, 36-37; women and, 259 f. *See also* Agriculture
Fry, Henry C., 239
Fugitive Slave Law, 96
Fuller, Henry B., quoted, 249
Fulton, Robert, 6, 15
Furs, 13; and Hawaiian sandalwood, 13

G

Gallatin, Albert, 4
Garfield, James, 160, 162, 179, 293
Garland, Hamlin, 236, 258
Garrett, John W., 70
Garrison, William Lloyd, 36, 87, 89, 94; quoted, 94 f.
Gasoline motor, 181, 303
Gates, John W., 194, 195
Gates, Paul Wallace, quoted, 109
General Electric Co., 246, 306
General Federation of Women's Clubs, 260, 277, 278
General Motors Corp., 186 f., 200; overseas investment, 314 f.
George, Henry, 267
Georgia, 80, 96, 98

Georgia Power Co., 316 f.
Germany, 182, 259, 260, 267, 298; cartels in, 141; and labor legislation, 242
Gershwin, George, 350
Gettysburg, 112
Giannini, Amadeo P., 315
Gibbons v. Ogden, 15
Giddings, Joshua R., 94
Gilpin, Joshua, quoted, 12
Glasgow, Ellen, 349
Goddard, Charlotte, 109
Goddard, Moses B. J., 109
Godey's Lady's Book, 29
Godkin, E. L., quoted, 161
Gold Standard, 173 f.
Goldmark, Josephine, 276
Gompers, Samuel, 246
Good Government leagues, 284
Gorman, Arthur P., 176
Gould, Jay, 134, 145, 153, 228; quoted, 134; and security manipulation, 147 ff., 151; and society, 147 f.
Government, aid to industry, 5, 11, 15, 154 f., 301 f.; and internal improvements, 15, 41 ff., 50, 51, 55, 77-81, 296; and western lands, 38 f., 84, 107 ff., 224; and panic of 1837, 41 ff.; ownership, 70; expansion of, 156 ff., 298, 302, 355 ff.; city, 265-268; enterprise, 298 f., 301 f., 355 ff. See also Labor, Railroads, Tariffs, U. S. Government separate divisions
Grady, Henry, quoted, 162
Graduation Act, 84
Grain elevators, 220, 221
Granger Movement, 165, 168, 219 ff.
Grant, Ulysses S., 124, 157, 163, 293
Gray, Horace, 179, 180
Great Britain, 1, 122, 259, 267, 298, 300, 313; competition from, 8, 11, 12; business connections with, 8 ff., 33 ff., 41, 45 ff., 76; Parliament, 11, 14; and panic of 1837, 41, 45-49; investments in U. S., 41, 48, 137; railroad rails from, 79; stock frauds, 83; and panic of 1857, 84 f.; pools in, 141; common law of, 176
Great Lakes, 6, 32. See also Individual names of lakes
Great Plains, 211, 212, 218
Greeley, Horace, 89, 99, 101
Green, Duff, 48 f.
Greenback Party, 161, 164, 166 f.
Greenbacks, 105, 161, 164 ff., 166 f.; and commodity prices, 112
Gregg, Wm., quoted, 33
Grinnell, Moses H., 98
Guam, 207
Guggenheim family, 182, 194, 195, 290, 314
Gulf of Mexico, 6

H

Haiti, 208
Hallgarten & Co., 319
Hamilton, Alexander, 4, 10, 87
Hammond, Governor, 95; quoted, 95 f.
Hampton County Cotton Spinners Assoc., 61
Hanna, Mark, 287
Hannibal & St. Joseph R. R., 83
Harding, Warren G., 345, 348; quoted, 342
Harlan, Justice J. M., 176
Harlem R. R., 75, 114
Harmon, Arthur L., 351
Harper, Robert G., 95
Harper's, 204
Harper's Weekly, 292
Harriman, Edward H., 194, 202, 210, 284
Harris, Frank, 236
Harris, W. T., quoted, 127 f.
Harrisburg, 6; tariff convention, 17
Harrison, Benjamin, 161, 163, 175, 289
Harrison, Carter, 266
Harvard University, 36, 126, 128, 260; Graduate School of Business Administration, 243, 357
Harvey, George, 292
Hatch, Rufus, 109
Havemeyer, H. O., 146, 181
Havemeyer, W. F., 159
Hawaii, 13, 207
Hay, John, 203, 205, 209, 287; quoted, 206
Hayes, John L., 79
Hayes, Rutherford B., 162
Haywood, "Big Bill," 237
Hearst, George, 164; quoted, 164
Hearst, Wm. Randolph, 205, 206, 269 f., 270
Hemingway, Ernest, 349
Hendry and Noyes, 110
Hepburn Act, 287
Hepburn Committee, 144
Hewitt, Abram, 73, 79, 98; quoted, 125 f.
Highways, 187, 296, 298
Hill, David B., quoted, 167
Hill, James J., 131, 202; on pools, 141; aids Democrats, 162; on "trusts," 189
Hillquit, Morris, 237
Hoar, George F., 171
Hofer, E. & Sons, 343
Holding Companies, 150, 300; New Jersey law, 190; and boom of 1920's, 315, 318; Insull system, 316 ff.; motives for, 317 f.; in utilities, 316 ff., 348; and courts, 348
Holland, 313
Holmes, Oliver Wendell, quoted, 87 f.
Holmes, Justice Oliver W., 242

Holt, Henry, quoted, 124 f., 127
Holyoke, Mass., 63, 64, 71, 231, 264
Holyoke Transcript, 231
Homesteads, free, 77, 96, 224; Republican Party and, 105, 108–111
Homestead Steel Works, 146
Hone, Phillip, 266; Mattewan Company, 13
Hood, Raymond, 351
Hoover, Herbert, 304, 345 f., 348
Hours of Labor, early factory, 20, 65; ten hour movement, 20 f., 25 f., 65 f., 77, 241 f.; regulation of, 241 f., 279 f., 282 f.
House, Edward M., 293
Household Manufacturing, 3; competes with factories, 9 f.; to 1837, 10; decline, 58
Housing, industrial, 18, 28, 63, 64, 235, 262, 327; in New York City, 64; and city planning, 253 ff. See also Construction, Regulation
Howe, Timothy O., 109
Howells, William D., 236
Hudson river, 6, 15, 211
Hudson River R. R., 73, 114
Hull-House, 279
Humphreys, Colonel David, quoted, 11
Hunt, Richard M., 252, 260
Hunter, Robert, 263, 276, 278 f.
Hunter, Robert M. T., quoted, 99
Huntington, Collis P., 131, 145, 153, 157, 181; quoted, 158
Hunt's Merchants' Magazine, quoted, 83
Hurlburt, Gen. S. A., 118

I

Idaho, 131
Illinois, 213; internal improvements, 42, 72; growth of, 42; defaults, 48; banking privileges banned, 80; in politics, 92, 157, 159; railroad consolidations, 115; and Wabash Case, 169; Grange in, 220; dairying in, 222; tenancy, 224; Progressivism in, 277, 279; "American Plan" in, 334; education in, 339 f.
Illinois Central R. R., 67, 83; fails, 85
Illinois Public Utility Information Committee, 339
Illinois State Journal, 100
Illinois Steel Co., 146
Illinois & Wisconsin Dairymen's Assoc., 222
Immigrants, enterprise in settling U. S., 2; and markets, 4, 139; and agriculture, 4, 215, 217, 225; after 1820, 13; and labor, 13, 24, 64 ff., 77, 83, 152, 230 ff., 280, 346 f.; and West, 30, 36, 39, 109 ff., 215, 217, 225; and South,

32; Catholic, 52, 64 ff.; and cities, 63 ff., 152, 231, 280; Irish and German, 64 f.; and politics, 64 ff., 105, 156, 159, 323 f., 346 f.; decline of, 66; restriction of, 77, 323 f., 346 f.; societies for, 84, 107, 109, 346 f.; Republican Party and, 105; and Contract Labor Law, 106 f.; and homesteads, 109 ff.; and American legend, 130, 215; and railroads, 131, 215, 346 f.; and city government, 159, 268; number of, 217, 230, 346 f.
Imperialism, 202–210, 299, 312 ff.
Imports, 32, 33, 34; railroad rails, 79; during Civil War, 113. See also Commerce, Foreign
Income, national per capita, 39, 261; distribution in 20th century, 289, 312, 326; dividends, 84, 196 ff. See also Profits, Wages
Income Tax Amendment, 288
Independent, 100, 114
Independent Treasury, 77
Indiana, early settlement, 13; defaults, 48; in politics, 92, 157, 159, 162; dairying in, 222
Indians, 30, 31; land, 108–109, 110; and railroads, 131
Individualism, curtailed, 9, 87, 130, 141 ff., 150 ff., 188 ff., 193 f., 324 f., 326–331, 356; versus cooperation, 28, 144, 271 f., 326; and cities, 28, 249 f., 271 f., 323 f.; western influence on, 41; and courts, 180, 304; farmers and, 212, 217; and art, 350
Industrial Commissions, 282 f.
Industrial Conference, 1919, 333
Industrial Democracy, see Company Unions, Labor, Welfare Capitalism
Industrial design, 351 ff.
Industrial Workers of the World, 237
Industry, local, 3, 27; little interest in manufacturing, 4; and War of 1812, 5, 11, 15 f.; early difficulties, 8–12; feared by agrarians, 10, 49 f.; in West, 11, 40, 49, 55; conditions for success, 12–18; expansion and mechanization, 14, 59 ff., 181, 183 ff., 298 f., 303 ff.; and labor, 18–27, 63 f., 106 f., 230 f., 346 f.; profits of, 49, 59 f.; value of products, 52, 59, 136, 303; expositions, 58, 138; competition, 59 ff., 135 f., 140–146; oligopoly in, 61 f., 305; morale in, 65, 184, 197 ff., 238, 244 ff., 307 f., 336 f.; and railroads, 67 ff., 135 f., 152 f.; and Civil War, 91 f., 100, 111–117; after Civil War, 135–145; world leadership of, 136, 138; electric power, 181, 183 ff., 303 f.; and "biguess," 145 f., 189 f., 230; consumers' goods, 189, 229, 299, 309 ff.; accident rate in,

200 f., 231, 242; and cost accounting, 247, 327; and First World War, 298, 301 f., 355; scientific management of, 304, 326 f.; and prohibition, 346. *See also* Absentee owners; Banking; Banking, Investment; Booms; Business; Competition; Combination; Labor; Panics; Tariffs; Technology; Trade associations; and Individual industries
Industry, 334
Ingalls, Melville E., quoted, 135
Inland Press Assoc., 270
Inland Waterways Commission, 290
Inness, George, 257
Insecurity, and mechanization, 231; and labor turnover, 231 f., 261 f.; and unskilled labor, 235; in 1920's, 325, 326 ff.
Installment selling, *see* Credit
Insull, Samuel, 319, 343; quoted, 311; system, 316 ff.; and education, 339 f.
Insull Utility Investments, Inc., 317
Insurance, agents in St. Louis, 56; and "Boston Associates," 71; speculation in, 73; and savings, 73, 189; and "money trust," 191 f.; cooperative, 220; compensation, 231, 232, 241 ff., 279 f., 282 f.
Internal Improvements, government aid to, 15, 41 ff., 50, 51, 55, 77–81, 296; and debt repudiation, 48; and South, 92 f., 96; Republican Party and, 105; and railroad competition, 132; and highways, 187, 296, 298. *See also* Canals, Railroads, Turnpikes
International Mercantile Marine Co., 196
Interstate Commerce, *see* Commerce, Interstate
Interstate Commerce Act, 169 ff.
Interstate Commerce Commission, 169 ff.; and Hepburn Act, 287; and Mann Elkins Act, 288 f.; and "rule of reason," 348
Inventions, *see* Mechanization, Patents, Technology
Inventor's Guild, 199
Investment Banking, *see* Banking, Investment
Investment trusts, 315
Investments, *see* Capital
Iowa, 213; and Boston capital, 72; land grant, 132; Grange in, 169, 220
Iron industry, and tariff, 16, 18, 79, 105; early organization and labor policy, 19; trade association in, 61; combination in, 62; and railroad rails, 79; and Civil War, 99; overexpanded, 139. *See also,* Steel
Irving Trust Co., 320

Isolation, 182, 299, 313
Ives, Robert H., 109

J

Jackson, Andrew, 25; pet banks, 43; Specie Circular, 43, 43 n.; agrarian leader, 50 f.
Jackson family, 21, 74
James river, 6
Japan, 208
Jarves, James J., quoted, 352
Jefferson, Thomas, 10, 11, 54, 121, 293
Jervis, John B., 67
Johns Hopkins University, 260
Johnson, Andrew, 157
Johnson, Tom, 266
Jones, John P., 163
Journalism, *see* Magazines, Newspapers, and individual publications
Journeymen, union leadership, 24; loss of status, 24
Juilliard v. Greenman, 179 f.

K

Kansas, 6, 109, 213, 218, 224; banking privileges banned, 80; population, 84; border war, 97; land prices, 110; State Agricultural College, 110; land grants, 132; sues "trusts," 171; mortgages in, 217
Kansas-Nebraska Act, 84
Kansas & Neosho Valley R. R., 110
Kansas Pacific R. R., 110, 149
Kelley, Florence, 276, 279
Kentucky, 11, 65, 333
Keystone Bridge Co., 146
Kidder, Peabody, 191
Kidder Press Co., 238
Kirby, John, Jr., quoted, 240
Kiwanis, 328
Knickerbocker Club, 273
Knight, Jonathan, 67
Knights of Labor, 233, 236, 239
Know-Nothing Party, 65
Knox, Philander C., 208, 209
Kroger Grocery Co., 306
Ku Klux Klan, in politics, 166, 330; in 1920's, 330 f.
Kuhler, Otto, 352
Kuhn, Loeb & Co., 191, 194, 319
Kyle, Alexander, 75

L

Labor, in early manufacturing, 8; and population changes, 13; industrial, 18–23, 63 ff., Ch. XI, 261, 326 ff.; women in factories, 19, 21, 279; and railroads, 19, 66, 131, 135, 200; education and, 19, 25, 247; wages, 19 f., 22 f., 228 f.,

261, 234 f., 245 f., 279 f., 282 f., 298 f.,
304; hours, 20 f., 25 f., 65 f., 77, 241 f.,
279 f., 282 f.; contract, 21, 106 f.;
blacklist, 21, 66; and the courts, 22,
24, 180, 241 ff.; handicraft, 23–27, 66,
117; division of, 24, 274 f., 327 f.;
and depressions, 24 ff., 228, 322, 356 f.;
and radicalism, 25 f., 236 ff., 332 ff.;
and politics, 25, 65 f., 117, 241 f.,
275 ff., 282 ff.; and mechanization, 27,
112 f., 231 ff., 238, 242, 299; and the
West, 29; and cities, 63–66, 261 ff.;
and immigration, 64 ff., 77, 83, 152,
228, 230 ff., 280, 346; and morale, 65,
238, 245 ff.; and employer associations,
66, 229, 238 ff.; Republican Party and,
105; and Civil War, 106 f., 117, 118;
and Sherman Act, 172, 281; and scientific management, 184, 229, 243 ff.,
274 ff., 299, 304, 326 f.; accidents,
200 f., 231, 242 f.; bankers and conditions of, 200 f.; in agriculture, 214;
and expansion, 228, 238; and welfare
capitalism, 229, 232, 242 f., 243–248,
306, 336 f.; turnover, 229, 231 f.; speed
up and stretch out, 229, 244; and "personal relation," 230; and race, 231;
and insurance, 231, 241 ff., 282; K. of
L., 233; A. F. of L., 233 ff., 238,
239 ff.; I. W. W., 237; and N. A. M.,
239 ff., 334 f.; profit sharing, 245 ff.,
312; and company unions, 246; violence, 246, 333; and cost accounting,
247, 327; and city planning, 253 ff.;
and "bigness," 274; child, 275, 277 ff.;
Progressives and, 275 ff., 282 f.; industrial commissions and, 282 ff.; and
Clayton Act, 295; and Industrial Conference of 1919, 333; and "American
Plan," 333 ff.; "employee magazines,"
336 f.; unemployed in 1930's, 357. See
also Hours of Labor, Trade Unions,
Strikes, Wages

La Crosse & Milwaukee R. R., 81
Ladies' Home Journal, 269
LaFollette, Robert, 287, 291 ff., 296
LaFollette Seamen's Act, 296
Laissez-faire, 41, 119–128, 139, 140, 172,
213, 228, 243, 263, 280, 345, 356
Lake Erie, 36, 55, 114
Lake Michigan, 115
Lake Shore & Michigan Southern R. R.,
114; Rockefeller and, 143
Lamarck, Jean B., 122
Lancaster road, 6
Land, exhaustion in South, 32; prices,
38 f., 42 f., 84, 107, 109 f., 217, 226,
319; auctions, 38 f.; preemption, 38 f.;
sales, 39, 84, 108 ff.; urban values,
42 f., 250, 253 f., 319 f.; Graduation
Act, 84; conservation, 289 f. See also

Homesteads, Railroads, Speculation,
West
Land speculation, see Speculation, land
Lane, Wheaton, J., quoted, 80
Larson, Henrietta, 358; quoted, 357 f.
Lasalle, Ferdinand, 236
Lathrop, Julia, 288
Latin America, see America, Latin
Lawrence, Amos, quoted, 37 f.; and land
speculation, 109
The Laws of Etiquette, 37
Lawson, Thomas W., 202
Lead Trust (National Lead Co.), 142
League for Industrial Rights, 239, 241,
281
Leather Trust (The United States
Leather Co.), 142
Le Corbusier, C. E., 351
Lee, Higginson & Co., 76, 191; and Gen-
eral Motors, 187, 200
Leggett, William, 89
Lehigh Coal & Navigation Co. canal, 7
Leitch, John, 246
Lerner, Max, quoted, 350
Lewis, Sinclair, 349
Liberty bonds, 302
Lien laws, 25
Lincoln, Abraham, 94, 102, 103, 104; on
labor and capital, 117
Lindsay, Samuel M., 278
Lindsey, Ben, 276
Linseed Oil Trust (National Linseed Oil
Co.), 142
Lions, 325, 328
Literature, business influence on, 1, 71,
88 f., 251, 348–350; Spencerian, 125 ff.;
and "frenzied finance," 202; and So-
cialism, 236; on management, 243,
245; cities and, 251, 258 f.; in 1920's,
348–350
Little, Jacob, 74
Liverpool, 216, 220
Livingston, Edward, 266
Livingston-Fulton monopoly, 15
Lloyd, Henry Demarest, quoted, 142, 163
Loans, see Capital
Lobbying, see Pressure Groups
Lodge, Henry Cabot, 205, 209, 287;
quoted, 126
Loewy, Raymond, 352
Logan, George, 10
Logan, John A., 159, 160
London, 48, 137. See also Great Britain
London, Jack, 258
Los Angeles, 132, 254, 334
Lotteries, 11
Louisiana, internal improvements, 42;
banking, 42; defaults, 48; and seces-
sion, 96; land grant, 132; sues
"trusts," 170
Louisville, 6, 26, 80, 334

Low, Seth, 266
Lowell, Mrs. Charles Russell, 276
Lowell family, 21, 71
Lowell, James Russell, 96
Lowell, Mass., 18, 71–72; condition 1835, 20; condition 1846, 21; strike 1834, 22; health, 23
Lucy Furnaces, 146
Lumber, world leadership, 136; combination in, 146
Lyman, George, quoted, 99
Lyman family, 71
Lynd, Helen M., 262
Lynd, Robt. S., 262
Lynn, 113, 152
Lynn Reporter, quoted, 113

M

Maberley's Art of Conversation, 37
Machine shops, 11
Machinery, see Mechanization
Madison, James, 11
Magazines, 269; Godey's Lady's Book, 29; and "money trust," 202; national slick-paper, 269; and advertising, 310, 311. See also Individual Magazines.
Mahan, Alfred T., 204, 205
Mail order catalogues, 268
Maine, 206
Malthus, Thomas R., 120, 122
The Man Nobody Knows, 342
Man versus the State, 126
Management, problems of, 198 f., 230, 273 ff., 307 f., 326 f.; literature on, 243, 245; and "employee magazine," 336 f. See also Bureaucracy, Business, Labor, Scientific Management.
Manayunk, Pa., 22, 63
Manchester, N. H., 72
"Manifest destiny," 68, 204 ff.
Mann Elkins Act, 288
Manning, Daniel, 162
A Manual of Good Manners, 37
A Manual of Politeness for Both Sexes, 37
Manufacturing, see Industry
Maple Flooring Mfrs. Assoc. et. al. v. U. S., 304 f.
Markets, transportation builds, 6–8, 57 f., 135; auction, 8, 38; for foreign goods, 8, 13, 32 ff.; and Supreme Court, 15, 304; and internal improvements, 15; in South, 32 f., 98; and communication, 33, 59; and overhead costs, 59–62; centralized, 63, 151 ff.; and imperialism, 203 ff.; agriculture, 215 ff.; cooperation and, 220; and consumers' goods, 229, 299, 309 ff.; in 1920's, 304. See also Competition, Distribution, Merchandising, Transportation

Marshall, John, 15, 178, 179
Marshall Field store, 255, 256
Martin, Fredrick T., 285
Marx, Karl, 236
Marxism, 236. See also Communism, Socialism
Maryland, 15, 48
Mason, Roswell B., 67
Mason, Thomas F., 109
Mass Production, 13 ff., 63, 112 f., 130, 187, 200, 303 f.; and overhead costs, 59–61, 236; and labor, 22 ff., 63, 112 f., 231, 238, 242
Massachusetts, 179; factories, 20, 21, 71 f.; courts and labor, 24; immigrant labor, 65; nativism in, 65; and "Boston Associates," 71 ff.; Abolitionists' Riots, 97; railroad consolidations, 115; political machine, 159, 161. See also New England, North
Massachusetts Hospital Life Ins. Co., 71
Master workers, 9, 24
Masters, Edgar Lee, 349
Maxwell, William H., quoted, 271
Mayo, Rev. A. D., 271
Maysville bill, 50
McClelian, Gen. George B., 112
McClure, A. K., 175
McClure, S. S., 269
McClures, 202, 269
McCormick, Cyrus H., 153, 230, 307
McCormick, Leander, 230
McCormick, Medill, 291
McGuffey Readers, 55
McKay, Charles, 113
McKim, Charles F., 252, 257
McKim, Meade and White, 257
McKinley, William, 173, 175, 290, 293; on Spanish War, 207
McMillan, James, 163
Meat, 152; world leadership, 136; Armour, 137, 146; Morris, 137; "trusts," 142 f.; Swift, 146; cattle raising, 212, 218, 222; and So. America, 314
Mechanization, 14, 56–59; and labor, 27, 112 f., 231, 233 f., 238, 242; in agriculture, 56 ff., 111, 113, 213 f., 225 f.; and overhead costs, 59–61, 236, 304 f.; and cities, 63, 151 ff.; and Civil War, 111, 112 ff.; and philosophy, 128; and the international exchange of ideas, 138. See also Industry, Technology, Science
Medbery, James, quoted, 74
Medicine, cooperation in, 329
Meisel, Francis, quoted, 238
Mellon, Andrew, 343, 344
Melville, Herman, 53; quoted, 54
Memphis, 262, 265
Mencken, H. L., 349
Mercantilism, 2, 354

Merchandising, auction, 8; southern, 33 f.; and growth of cities, 63, 151 f.; through commodity exchanges, 151 f., 221; cooperative, 220; and consumers' goods, 229, 299, 310 ff.; mail order, 268; installment, 310, 328; security, 318 f.; chain store, 327. *See also* Advertising, Distribution, Income

Merchant capitalists, 9, 24

Merchants, retail, village, 3, 268; in West, 37 f., 55; mail order, 268; chain store, 327

Mergers, *see* Combinations

Merrimack River, 71

Metals, *see* Aluminum, Iron, Mining, Steel

Metropolitan Club, 273

Mexico, war with, 54, 82; land from, 55; investment in, 209

Meyers, B. H., quoted, 66

Miami canal, 7

Michigan, internal improvements, 42; defaults, 48; banking privileges banned, 80; ores, 115; political machine, 159, 163; "American Plan" in, 334

Michigan Central R. R., 73, 83

Middle Border, 218

Middle West Utilities Co., 316 f., 340

"Middletown," 329, 330

Midvale Steel Co., 184

Migration, 5 ff., 30 f., 36 ff., 55 f., 84, 107 ff., 131, 152 f., 215 ff., 224, 228, 230, 253 ff.

Mill, John Stuart, 120, 125

Millerites, 89

"Millionaire's Club," 164, 176

Mills Bill, 174, 175

Milwaukee, 115, 237

Milwaukee & St. Paul Railway case, *see* Chicago, Milwaukee & St. Paul Railway Co. v. Minnesota

Mining, 1, 82 f., 115, 136, 189; in Latin America, 209, 314. *See also* Aluminum, Iron, Metals, Steel

Minneapolis, 152, 216

Minnesota, 6, 72, 109, 131; railroad debt, 81; land grants, 81, 132; Grange in, 169, 220; mortgages in, 217

Mississippi, internal improvements, 42; defaults, 48; banking, 80; and secession, 96

Mississippi river, 3, 6, 15, 33, 93, 100

Missouri, internal improvements, 41 f., 72; railroad debt, 81; political machines, 157; Grange in, 220

Missouri Compromise, 96

Missouri Pacific Railroad, 147

Mitchell, Chas. E., 318

Mitchell, Sidney Z., 316, 318

Mohawk & Hudson R. R., 7 f., 74

Money, *see* Currency

"Money Trust," 192–202, 294; and panics, 195 ff.; World War and, 302. *See also* Banking, Investment

Monopolies and Trusts, 202

Monopoly, village, 3, 27, 216 f.; steamboat, 15; and overhead costs, 59, 61 f.; and technology, 61 f., 183 ff., 193, 236, 304 f.; and prices, 61 ff., 133, 305, 321; trend toward, 61 f., 71′ ff., 114 ff., 122 f., 138, 188 ff., 304 ff.; and railroads, 77 ff., 132 f., 152 f., 188, 191, 193; successful resistance to, 114; in refining, 143 f.; in steel, 145 f., 305; and politics, 164 ff., 170 ff., 286, 289, 295, 342, 345 f.; and bankers, 190 ff., 315 ff.; Grange and, 220; managerial problems of, 274, 307 f.; and courts, 286, 289, 304 f., 342; World War and, 302; and price leadership, 305; commercial, 354. *See also* Big Business, Combination, Corporations, Management, Oligopoly, Pools, Regulation, "Trusts"

Montana, 131, 132, 216, 334

Montgomery, Ala., 101

Moody, John, 190 f.

Moore, James, 194

Moore, Wm., 194

Morale, in industry, 65, 184, 197 ff., 238, 244 ff., 307 f., 336 f.; during Civil War, 118; "booster" clubs and, 328 f.; "employee magazines" and, 336 f.

Morgan, J. P., 147, 164, 190, 191, 202, 273, 284, 290; and reorganizations, 150, 196 ff., 201 f.; dominant, 182, 194 ff.; and General Motors, 186, 199 f.; and railroads, 191; and social welfare, 196, 284; and voting trusts, 201 f.; and foreign investments, 210; and art, 257. *See also* Banking, Investment

Mormons, 89

Morrill Act (land), 108–109

Morrill, Justin S., 105, 106; quoted, 106, 174

Morris, I. Nelson, 137

Morris canal, 7

Mortgages, farm, 40, 55, 217 f., 224 f., 226, 319; urban, 300, 327

Morton, Oliver P., 159, 160

Morton, Levi, 163, 164

Most, Johann, 236

Moving pictures, 225, 302, 303, 324, 351

Muckrakers, 282, 290, 335

Mullaney, Bernard J., 339

Muller v. Oregon, 279

Mumford, Lewis, quoted, 253

Munsey, Frank, 270, 291

Munsey's, 269

Murphy, Rev. E. G., 276, 277
Muscle Shoals, 346
Music, 350. *See also* Art, Patronage

N

National Assoc. of Manufacturers, 239 ff., 281, 331; and "American Plan," 334 f.
Nashua, N. H., 18, 72
Nast, Thomas, 267
Nation (New York), 161; quoted, 166
National Assoc. of Stove Manufacturers, 139
National Assoc. of Wool Manufacturers, 114
National Biscuit Co., 311
National Broadcasting Co., 338 f.
National Child Labor Committee, 278, 341
National City Bank of N. Y., 194, 318
National Consumers' League, 278, 282, 341
National Electric Light Assoc., 339, 341
National Electric Power Co., 316
National Erectors Assoc., 281
National Founders Assoc., 281
National Glass Co., 239
National Industrial Recovery Act, 325
National Institution for the Promotion of Industry, 17
National Labor Relations Board, 325, 357
National Lead Co., 142, 314. *See also* Lead Trust
National Metal Trades Assoc., 281
National Millers Assoc., 139 f.
National Progressive Republican League, 291
National Service Corp., 316
National Wool Growers Assoc., 114
Nationalism, Supreme Court and, 15, 178 ff.; and transportation, 57 f., 129 ff., 150 ff., 203; and imperialism, 203 ff.; and cities, 272; in 1920's, 323; Ku Klux Klan and, 330 f. *See also* Provincialism
Nativism, 65, 330 f.
Natural Law, *see Laissez-faire*
Navy, 208; in World War, 302
Nebraska, 109; banking privileges banned, 80; population, 84; border war, 97; land grant, 132; sues "trusts," 170; mortgages in, 217
Negroes, 36; and race, 103; and Republican party, 160; in factories, 230; and unionism, 233, 240; and Klan, 330. *See also* Slavery
Nepotism, 71, 273, 325. *See also* Bureaucracy
Nevada, 131, 163

Nevins, Allan, quoted, 79
New Deal, 120, 128, 226 f., 229, 325 f., 355 ff.
New England, 121; manufacturing in, 11, 18 ff., 71 f., 136, 230 f.; and West, 13, 72, 93; and tariff, 16 f., 105; labor in, 18–23, 63 ff., 230 f., 239; new business interests, in, 29, 71 f., 137; and "Boston Associates," 71 ff.; Brahmins, 71; radicals, 88 f., 119; and abolition, 94 f.; and Secession and Civil War, 98 f.; and homesteads, 107; telegraph in, 115; new power in, 185. *See also* Boston, Massachusetts, North
New England Assoc. of Railway Superintendents, Convention of, 66, 141
"New Freedom," 291–295
The New Freedom, 126
New Hampshire, 65
New Jersey, 98; labor in, 21–22; iron industry, 79; and Camden & Amboy, 79 f.; Gould and, 148; and corporation charters, 190 f.; Progressivism in, 278, 292
New Orleans, 6, 33, 93, 101, 262, 265; railroad debt, 80; victory at, 112
N. Y. Assoc. for the Improvement of the Condition of the Poor, 64
N. Y. Central R. R., 162; to West, 55; formed, 61; cost, 68; stockholders, 69; merger fails, 114; Rockefeller and, 144
N. Y. Chamber of Commerce, 28
N. Y. Child Labor Act, 278
N. Y. Child Labor Committee, 278
N. Y. Citizen's Committee, 159
New York City, 6, 7, 121, 151, 254, 268; and tariff, 16; labor party, 25 f.; and Tammany in, 26, 85 f.; panics, 26, 85 f.; 65, 157, 159, 161, 266, 267; fire of 1835, 28; southern trade, 33–35; foreign trade, 33–35; and West, 33, 93, 109, 151; banks, 34, 35, 85–86, 194; land values, 43, 250; as railroad terminal, 55; distribution center, 63, 216, 220; slums, 64, 264 ff.; condition of poor, 64, 264 ff., 280; stock exchange, 74 ff., 85, 147 ff.; private bankers in, 76, 191, 194 ff.; in election of 1860, 94; clothing industry in, 113; millionaires in, 114; oil refiners in, 144; rapid transit, 153; Tweed Ring, 157, 159, 266 f.; Conkling organization, 158 f.; reform in, 159, 266; and income tax, 167; architecture, 252, 255, 320; building regulations, 254 f., 264; infant mortality in, 262; schools, 270 ff.; World's Fair, 353
N. Y. Commercial Advertiser, quoted, 34
N. Y. Elevated Rway., 149
N. Y. Herald, quoted, 99
N. Y. Journal of Commerce, 99

N. Y. and New Haven R. R., 75
N. Y., New Haven & Hartford R. R., 193
N. Y. Observer, 99
N. Y. Public Ledger, quoted, 26
New York State, internal improvements, 7, 33, 42; early manufacturing, 11; early western settlement, 13; courts and labor, 24; constitutional convention, 1821, 28; manhood suffrage, 28; exports, 32; and tariff, 79; in election of 1860, 94; railroad consolidations, 115; telegraph in, 115; Supreme Court of, 159; Democratic Party, 161, 167; sues "trusts," 170; Progressivism in, 277; child labor in, 278 f.
N. Y. Sun, 28, 167
N. Y. Times, quoted, 207
N. Y. Tribune, 99, 100, 101; quoted, 112, 159
N. Y. Typographical Society, 24
N. Y. World, quoted, 107; Gould's, 148
N. Y. World's Fair, 353
N. Y. Yacht Club, 147
Newspapers, to promote manufacturing, 10; and tariff, 17; penny press, 28–29; and Abolition, 93–94; and Civil War, 99–104, 118; and science, 138; and securities speculation, 148; national services, 203, 343; farmers' lack of, 216; cities and, 251, 269 ff.; combination in (chains), 269 f., 338; advertising and, 269 f., 310, 311, 332, 337 f.; in World War, 302; "canned" editorials, 338, 343. See also Propaganda, and individual papers
Niagara Falls, electricity, 185
Nicaragua, 208
Ninth Ave. Elevated Rway., 153
Non-intercourse acts, 5
Norfolk, Va., 7, 32
"Normalcy," 345 f.
Norris, Frank, 236, 258
Norris, Geo. W., 346
Norristown, 252
North, early staples in, 3; and southern trade, 32 ff., 90, 91, 92 f.; and southern education, 36; and Kansas-Nebraska Act, 84; in 1860, 86 ff., 104 f.; and Secession and Civil War, 90–117; tenancy in, 224. See also New England, South, West, and individual states and cities
North American Review, 127
North Carolina, 96
North Dakota, 216; land grant, 132; mortgages in, 217
Northern Pacific R. R., 108, 132, 158
Northwest Territory, and Slavery, 92
Notes on Virginia, quoted, 10
Nye, Bill, quoted, 252

O

Ohio, early manufacturing, 11; early settlement, 13; politics, 92, 163; Abolitionists' Riot, 97; railroad consolidations, 115; and income tax, 167; sues "trusts," 170; "American Plan" in, 334
Ohio canal, 7
Ohio Life Ins. & Trust Co., 85
Ohio River, 6, 7, 33
Ohio Valley, 32, 36; and Civil War, 102
Oil, 1, 137; early consolidations in, 116; world leadership, 132; "trust," 142, 170. See also Standard Oil Co., Rockefeller
Oklahoma, 213, 224
Oligopoly, 61 f., 305
Olney, Richard S., 172; on I.C.C., 172 f.
Ommer, Will I., quoted, 244, 245
Open Shop, see "American Plan"
Open Shop Assoc., 334
Ore, see Metals, Mining
Oregon, 131
Origin of Species, 121
Other People's Money, 202
Our Country, 204
Outlook, quoted, 127
Overhead costs, see Costs
Owen, Robert Dale, 26, 89
Owen-Glass Act, 294
Owenites, 89

P

Pacific Railroad of Missouri, 83
Painting, see Arts
Panama, 207
Panama Canal, 208, 210
Panics, of 1819, 12; of 1837, 7, 10, 24, 26 f., 35, 41–49, 54; of 1854, 75, 83; of 1857, 81–86; after Civil War, 136 f.; of 1873, 143, 145; of 1893, 149, 181, 218 f.; and "Money Trust," 195 ff.; of 1903, 195, 196; of 1907, 182, 195, 196, 198; of 1929, 319, 321, 325, 355. See also Business Cycles
Paris Exhibition of 1856, 58
Paris International Exposition, 1867, 138
Parker, Theodore, 87; quoted, 88 f., 94
Parker Vein Coal Co., 75
Parry, David M., 239
Parties, see Politics
The Passing of the Idle Rich, 285
Patents, early laws, 14; number of, 14; after 1836, 14, 58; and monopoly, 71, 183 f., 193; royalties on shoe stitching machine, 113; international exchange of, 138; and new technology, 181, 183 ff.; bankers and, 199 f.; World War and, 301. See also Technology

Paterson, N. J., 22, 252
Paterson Assoc. for the Protection of the Labouring Classes . . . , 22
Patron of Industry, 17
Patronage, in arts, 55, 71 f., 249, 252, 256 ff., 350 ff.
Patronage, political, 154, 156 ff.; president and, 291
Patten, Simon, 260
Payne, H. B., 163
Payne, Sereno, 289
Pendleton Civil Service Act, 162
Peninsular R. R. Co., 115
Pennsylvania, early manufacturing, 11, 19; early western settlement, 13; and tariff, 18, 79, 105, 175; iron industry, 19, 79, 105; labor in, 21–22, 333; labor and courts, 22, 24; exports, 32; internal improvements, 42; defaults, 48; corporations in, 70; banking privileges banned, 80; and West, 93; in election of 1860, 94; political machine, 159, 163, 164; child labor law, 279
Pennsylvania R. R., 83; to West, 55; stockholders, 69, 319; combined, 115; and oil, 144
Pennsylvania Society for the Encouragement of Manufactures and Useful Arts, 10
Pennsylvania Society for the Promotion of Manufactures and Mechanic Arts, 17
Pennsylvania system (roads and canals), 7
Peoples Gas, Light & Coke Co., 317
Perkins, George W., 291, 296; quoted, 186
Perkins & Co., 13
Perkins, Charles C., 172
Personnel management, *see* Scientific management
Peru, 314
Phelps, Anson G., 153
Philadelphia, 6, 7, 22, 24, 33, 254, 268, 271; and tariff, 16 f.; labor party, 25 f.; general strike, 26; 10-hour movement, 26; new business interests, 29; land values, 43; as railroad terminal, 55; distribution center, 63; and stock exchanges, 74; private bankers in, 76; railroad debt, 80; bank failures, 86; in election of 1860, 94; clothing industry in, 113; Centennial, 138; oil refiners in, 144; Gas Ring, 157, 160; and income tax, 167; architecture in, 252
Philanthropy, 72, 257, 280
Philippines, 207, 208
Phillips, Wendell, 87, 89, 94
Photography, 351

Picasso, Pablo, 353
Pierce, Franklin, 94
Pillsbury, Charles A., 138, 146
Pinchot, Amos, 291
Pinchot, Gifford, 289 f., 291
Pinckney, Maria, quoted, 35
Pittsburgh, 6, 7, 8, 152, 268; and railroad rails, 79, 145; railroad debt, 80; telegraph in, 115; oil refiners in, 144; "American Plan" in, 334
Pittsburgh, Fort Wayne & Chicago R. R., 115
Pittsburgh Morning Post, quoted, 61 f.
Platt, Orville, quoted, 172
Platt, Tom, 161 f., 287
Politics, and business, 28, 49 ff., 53, 77 ff., 105 ff., 129, Ch. VIII, 201, 266 ff., 275 ff., 291 ff., 342 ff.; and labor, 25 f., 237 f., 275 f.; and nativism, 65 f., 330 f.; and secession, 96 ff.; and party organizations, 154, 156 ff., 160 ff., 291 ff.; issues in, 155, 164 ff., 173 ff.; and bureaucracy, 157, 282 f., 357; and social legislation, 164 ff.; bankers and, 201; Socialist, 237 f.; city, 266; volatility of, 343. *See also* Agrarians, Progressivism, Radicals, Regulation, and Parties by name
Pools, industrial, 61 ff., 140 ff., 355; and common law, 141; and I.C.C. Act, 170. *See also* Combination, "trusts"
Population, growth after 1820, 5, 13; in South, 32; movement West, 36–43; transient, 41; growth of western, 42 f., 56, 212, 223; urban, and agriculture, 212. *See also* Immigrants
Populists, 164 f. *See also* Agrarians, Agriculture
Porto Rico, 207
Post roads, 6
Postal Service, 151; in 1800, 3; uniform rates, 59
Potomac River, 6
Poverty, in cities, 63–65, 231, 263, 280; and "progress," 153, 263
Poverty, 263
Power, steam, 6, 185; early water, 18, 71; electric, 181, 183 ff., 303 f.; Muscle Shoals and, 346
Prague, 264
Preemption Acts, 38 f.
Pressure Groups, and tariff, 16 ff., 79, 106, 174 f., 303; industrial, 17 f., 79, 114, 281 ff., 324, 331 f., railroad lobby, 78 ff., 110 f.; agricultural, 114, 220 f.; and regulation, 140, 169; and income tax, 167; progressive, 275 ff.; and wide stockholding, 319; utility, 331 f. *See also* Propaganda, Individual Associations

Price agreements, 61 f., 114, 140 ff., 355; oligopoly and, 305

Prices, in 1820's, 13; agricultural, 16, 35, 216, 219, 222, 223, 225 f.; land, 38 f., 40, 42 f., 84, 107 ff., 217, 226, 253 f., 319; and trade associations, 61 f., 114; commodity, 85, 112, 228, 321; and greenbacks, 112; and limited competition, 140 ff., 305, 321; automobile, 187; art works, 257. *See also* Price agreements, Trade associations, Oligopoly, Monopoly

Prime, Nat, 74

Prince, Fred. H., 305

Princeton University, 36

Prison Reformers, 89

Private Bankers, *see* Banking, Investment

Proctor, Redfield, 163

Production, *see* Agriculture, Industry

Production goods, and business cycles, 44 f., 321; American leadership, 136; declining rate of expansion, 188 f., 229, 298 f. *See also* Capital, Railroads

Profits, in 1820's, 5, 14; cotton, 32–33; industrial, 49, 299 f.; and security manipulation, 52, 133–134; and railroad building, 133–135; Ford's 187; tenement, 264; corporate, 314

"Progress," 111, 129; philosophy of 119–128, 136; and business politics, 161; in South, 162; and poverty, 263

Progressivism, and imperialism, 203; and industrial accidents, 231, 279 f.; aims of, 274 ff.; organization of, 276 ff., 291 f.; legislation of, 278 ff.; and corruption, 280; wanes, 281 f., 296; height of, 282 ff.; and democracy, 283 f., 295; and Big Business, 284 f., 292 f.; Roosevelt and, 285 ff.; and railroads, 286, 287, 288; and "trusts," 286, 289; Taft and, 288 ff.; and tariff, 289; and election of 1912, 291 ff.; in 1920's, 348

Prohibition, 89, 325, 346

Prohibitionists, 89

Propaganda, for manufacturing, 4, 10; agrarian, 10; tariff, 15–17; reform, 89; abolition, 93–97; and business reorganizations, 201; and imperialism, 204; and labor, 240 ff., 333 ff.; Progressive, 276 ff., 281 ff.; in World War, 302; and business leadership, 331 ff., 337 ff. *See also* Pressure groups

"Pro-Slavery Argument," 95

Protection, *see* Tariffs

"Protestant Crusade," 65

Protestants, 52, 65, 330

Providence, R. I., 109

Provincialism, in 1800, 3; and standardization, 28 f., 225, 268 ff., 324; reduced by railroad, 57 f., 129 ff., 150 ff.; and cities, 249 f., 268 ff. *See also* Nationalism

Public lands, *see* Land

Public ownership, *see* Government

Public Service Co. of Northern Illinois, 317

Pulitzer, Joseph, 205, 206, 269 f.

Pullman, George, 145, 153

Public utilities, *see* Utilities, Public

Pujo Committee (U. S., H. of R.), 202, 294

Purchasing power, 28 f., 39, 118, 229, 299; and consumers' goods, 229, 299, 309 ff., 355; advertising and, 299, 311 f.; and employee stock ownership, 312; and farm prices, 347 f. *See also* Income, Profits, Wages

Pure Food and Drugs Act, 287

Puritans, 21

Q

Quay, Matt, 175, 287; quoted, 175

R

"Rackets," 325

Radicals, in early politics, 25 f.; in New England, 88 f., 119; and labor, 236 ff.; and city politics, 267; business and, 332 ff.

Radio, 225, 303, 324; in 1920, 309; and advertising, 310, 311; and Big Business, 338 f.

Radio City, 320

Radio Corp. of America, 339

Railroads, earliest, 7 f.; construction, 7 f., 45, 55, 82 f., 85, 110 f., 131 ff., 182, 188; in East by 1850, 8, 55; and labor, 19, 66, 131, 135, 237; eastern investment, 29, 45, 52 ff., 72, 83, 131 f.; government aid to, 42, 77 ff., 80 f., 107 ff., 132 f.; in panics, 46, 84 f., 148 ff.; cross Mississippi, 52; western, 54 f., 92, 130–135; transcontinentals, 54 f., 108, 131 ff.; and agriculture, 56 f., 131, 215 ff.; and nationalization, 57, 129, 151 ff.; combination in, 61 f., 114 f., 191, 196 f.; and rate agreements, 62 f., 135 f., 143 f., 170, 200, 220; corruption, 67 ff., 81, 132 ff., 148 f., 158; securities, 67 ff., 84 f., 146 f.; investment in, 68, 83, 131, 133, 181, 191, 197; stockholders, 69, 83, 134; free passes, 69; and "Boston Associates," 71; and politics, 77 ff., 108, 110, 132 ff., 157 f., 168 ff., 220 f.; imported rails, 79; and cities, 80, 129, 132 f., 151 ff., 251; and Civil War, 91, 111, 114 f., Republican Party and, 105, 108–

111; construction companies, 110 f., 131, 134 f.; monopoly, 132, 152 f., 191, 200; and competition, 132, 133, 135 f., 143 f., 152, 164, 169 ff.; need for rebuilding, 134 f.; Cullom Committee on, 136; Gould and, 147 ff.; reorganization, 148, 150; refrigerator cars, 153; and Supreme Court, 169, 180; and I.C.C., 169 ff., 286, 287, 288 f.; after 1893, 181, 191, 200; and automobiles, 185, 187 f.; "community of interest" in, 196; fatalities on, 200 f.; voting trusts in, 201 f.; Grange and, 220 ff.; Elkins Act, 286; Roosevelt and, 286; Hepburn Act, 287; Mann Elkins Act, 288; World War and, 302; and institutional advertising, 338; Esch-Cummins Act, 344. See also Corporations, J. P. Morgan, individual roads

Randall, Samuel J., 175
Randolph, John, on tariff, 16
Rappahannock River, 6
Raritan River, 6
Raskob, John J., 320
Rationalization, of production, 184, 303 f., 326; and labor, 244 ff., 326 f.
Raw materials, see Agriculture, Metals, and individual materials
Reading R. R., 85, 197
Rebates, etc., 135 f., 170; Rockefeller and, 143 f.; Grange and, 220
Reclamation Act, 290
Reconstruction, and business, 157; over, 160
Reed, Quincy, quoted, 9
Reed, Thomas B., 161 f.
Reed brothers, 9
Refining industry, see Oil, Rockefeller, Standard Oil Co.
Reform Movements, Spencer and, 125 ff.; after Civil War, 154 f., 169 ff.; in cities, 159 f., 266 f.; Progressive, Ch. XIII; and democracy, 233 f.
Regulation, Spencer and, 125 ff.; fear of, 140; and parties, 165; railroad, 169, 275, 286, 287, 288, 302, 348; "trusts," 170, 286, 287, 289, 295, 302, 348; factory, 200, 241, 275 f.; construction, 254, 264 f., 279 f.; World War and, 302
Religion, lack of churches, 18; and employment, 20; conflicts, 52, 65 f.; awakening of, 89; and socialism, 236; and Progressivism, 275; and business, 325, 342; and Klan, 330
Reorganizations, Morgan and, 150, 196 f.; in automobiles, 187; procedure, 196 f.
Republican Party, and election of 1860, 94, 105; and the West, 107–111; and nationalism, 110; party of Big Business, 118, 154, 156 ff., 162, 342 ff.; and issues, 155, 165 ff.; after Civil War, 156 f., 160 f.; National Convention, 1880, 157; Gas Ring, 157; liberal wing, 159, 161; stalwarts out, 160 f.; and Grange, 164; and election 1888, 175; and Supreme Court, 178; and N. A. M., 241; Roosevelt and, 288, 296; and election of 1912, 291 ff. See also Progressivism

Retailing, see Merchandising
Reynolds, George, 286
Reynolds, R. J., Corp., 305, 311
Rhett, Robert B., 95
Rhode Island, 21, 65, 164
Ricardo, David, 120
Rice, A. H., quoted, 105
Richardson, Henry H., 252, 260
Richmond, Va., 32
Ripley, Wm. Z., quoted, 197
River ports, 6
River traffic, 6
Rivers, navigable, 6. See also Names of rivers
Rives, W. C.; quoted, 103
Roads, see Communication, Turnpikes
Robinson, Lucius, 161
Rochester, 6, 152
Rockefeller Foundation, 246
Rockefeller, John D., 137, 153, 181, 273, 284, 307; on combinations, 116, 142, 143, 144; and depressions, 137; aids Republicans, 162; and banking, 182, 194; and railroads, 191; and philanthropy, 257; and Radio City, 320. See also Oil, Rockefeller Foundation, Standard Oil Co.
Rocky Mountains, 54
Roosevelt, Franklin D., 120
Roosevelt, Theodore, 38, 126, 276, 356; and imperialism, 182, 202, 205; on "Money Trust," 198, 284, 287; and Spanish War, 205 f.; and "emotional classes," 285; as Progressive, 285 ff., 296; and railroads, 286; and "trusts," 286; and coal strike, 287; and conservation, 289 f.; and election of 1912, 292
Root, Elihu, 208, 287
Ross, E. A., 200
Rotary, 325, 328
Rothschilds, 48 f., 76, 86
Rubber, 314
Rush, Richard, quoted, 39 f.
Russia, 200, 237, 291, 300, 332
Ryan, Thomas F., 182, 194, 195

S

Saarinen, Eliel, 351
Sac and Fox Indians, 110

Saco, Me., 72
Sage, Russell, 153
St. Lawrence Valley, 3
St. Louis, 6, 7, 36, 93, 117, 151; distribution center, 63, 152; immigrants, 65; private bankers in, 76; railroad debt, 80; telegraph in, 115; bosses in, 157, 158; city planning in, 253
St. Louis Post-Dispatch, quoted, 176
St. Mary's Ship Canal Co., 73
Sakier, George, 352
Salt Trust (Michigan Salt Association, later National Salt Co.), 142
San Francisco, 151, 157
Santo Domingo, 208
Satterlee, George B., 109
Saturday Evening Post, 269
Savannah Georgian, quoted, 96
Savannah river, 6
Savings, and art, 55, 257 f., 350 f.; drawn to railroads, 68, 181; and speculation, 74, 146 ff., 181, 188 ff., 300; concentration of, 150, 191 f., 298 ff., 355; expansion of, 181, 298 f., 323 ff. *See also* Capital; Banking; Banking, Investment; Insurance; Thrift
Sawyer, Philetus, 163
Schenk, P. H., 17
Schiff, Jacob, 182, 194
Schuyler, Robert, 67, 75
Schwab, Charles M., 196; on expansion, 305
Science, 58, 119, 122 ff., 138, 181, 183 ff., 260 f., 301, 306. *See also* Education, Patents, Technology
Scientific Management; Taylor and, 184; labor and, 229, 243 ff., 326 f.; in 1920's, 304, 307 f., 326 f., 336 f. *See also* Management
Scott, Tom, 144, 158
Scripps, E. W., 269 f., 270
Sculpture, *see* Arts
Seaboard Public Service Corp., 316
Sears family, 71
Secession, 90–91, 96, 100–104
Securities, speculation, 10, 53, 71 ff., 82, 146–150, 188 ff., 195 ff., 300, 302 f., 315 ff.; foreign holders of, 48, 137, 300 f.; manipulation, 52, 67, 133 ff., 300, 315 ff.; railroad, 67 ff., 84 f., 133, 134 f., 196 f.; non-voting, 67; and stock exchange, 74 ff., 82–86, 147 ff., 196, 321; government, and business credit, 112; and "trusts," 142, 149 f., 197 f. *See also* Banking, Investment; Capital; Corporations; Savings
Securities and Exchange Commission, 357
Seidel, Emil, 237
Seligman, Edwin, 260
Seligman, J. & W. Co., 187

Senior, Nassau, 120
Seventeenth Amendment, 295
Seward, William H., 94, 102; on parties, 157
Sewing machines, 59, 113
Seymour, Horatio, quoted, 159 f.
Sheridan, J. B., quoted, 308
Sherman, John, 166, 167, 171; on "trusts," 171
Sherman anti-trust act, 171 ff.; and labor, 172, 281; Roosevelt and, 286; Taft and, 289; and Clayton Act, 295; in 1920's, 348
Sherman Silver Purchase Act, 173, 176
Shipbuilding Trust (U. S. Shipbuilding Co.), 196
Shipping, threatened by new industry, 29; decline in South, 32–35; New York supremacy in, 33–34; magnates, 73, 196; after World War, 345; and immigration, 346 f.
Shoe Industry, *see* Boot and Shoe Industry
Silver, 163, 164, 166 f., 173 f., 176
Sinclair, Upton, 282
Sixteenth Amendment, 295
Skyscraper, 254 ff., 320, 350 f.
Slavery, and labor, 23; trade, 32; and West, 36, 92; and abolition, 93–97; Fugitive Slave Law, 96; and race, 103. *See also* Negroes
Slaves, *see* Slavery
Slichter, Sumner, 232
Sloan, Alfred P., Jr., quoted, 314
Sloan, John, 350
Sloane, W. and J., 159
Slums, 63, 64, 235, 253 ff., 263 ff., 275, 280
Smith, Adam, 120
Smith, Alfred E., 330
Smith, Sydney, quoted, 48
Smith-Lever Act, 225
Smythe v. Ames, 180
Socialism, 236 ff.; Christian, 236; Progressives and, 275 f., 291, 295 f.; in 1920's, 332. *See also* Communism
Sociology, and Spencer, 122, 128
Somersworth, N. H., 72
South, early staples in, 3; and northern business, 6, 8, 32 ff., 90, 91, 92 f.; early railroads, 8; and tariff, 16 ff., 35, 49 ff., 92, 96; economic changes in, 32 f., 35, 185, 221 f., 224; dependence of, 33; education in, 36, 271; and panic of 1837, 45 f.; opposed to transcontinentals, 55; resists change, 58; and Kansas-Nebraska, 84; and panic of 1857, 86; Secession and Civil War, 90–104; and West, 92 ff.; friends in North, 93–94; and abolition, 93–97; as sovereign nation, 101, 103; "solid,"

154, 160; reconstruction, 157; industrial enterprise, 162; new power in, 185; tenancy, 221 f., 224; Progressivism in, 277 f. *See also* Individual States and Cities

South America, American investments in, 314

South Carolina, and tariff, 18, 50; exports, 32; nullification, 35; and Bank of U. S., 49; banking privileges banned, 80; and secession, 90–91, 96, 97, 98; and Civil War, 101

South Dakota, mortgages in, 217; land prices in, 226; tenancy in, 226

Southern Pacific R. R., 132, 157 f., 162

Southern Railway Co., 197

Spahr, C. B., 261

Spain, War with, 203 ff.

Specialization, sectional, 13, 90, 130; in farming, 57 f., 211; in industry, 130, 137

Specie Circular, 43, 43 n., 45

Speculation, Land, 29, 38 ff., 84, 107–111; profits in 1790's, 4; user of investment capital, 10; "Boston Associates" in, 72; and agriculture, 215 ff., 226; in twenties, 300, 319 f. *See also* Land, Prices

Speculation, securities, *see* Securities

Speicher, Eugene, 350

Spencer, Herbert, 119–128, 136, 141, 161, 179, 180, 236, 280

Speyer & Co., 191

Spoilsmen, and business, 154 ff.; machines of, 156–160; decline of, 160 ff.

Spoon River Anthology, 349

Sports, 262, 329

Spring-Rice, Cecil, 205

Squatters, 38–40

Stalwarts, *see* Spoilsmen

Standard of living, and westward movement, 39 f.; in industrial cities, 63 ff., 72, 228, 256–265; during Civil War, 117–118; bankers and, 200 f.; specialization and, 211 f.; on farms, 211 f., 225 f., 325; and unionism, 234 f., 325; after World War, 299; in 1920, 309

Standard Oil Company, as "trust," 142, 170; and monopoly, 143 f.; and politics, 162, 163, 174; and Supreme Court, 286. *See also* Oil, Rockefeller

Standard Oil Co. of N. J., 318

Standardization, in production, 13, 112 f., 130, 187, 200, 301 f., 304; and cities, 28 f., 53, 153, 249 ff., 268 ff., 324; and Civil War, 112 f.; and nationalism, 203, 324; World War and, 301 f.

Stanford, Leland, 131, 153, 162

State Charities Aid Association (N. J.), 278

State Federation of Women's Clubs (Calif.), 279

State Federation of Women's Clubs (Illinois), 277

State Street, 74

Steam, *see* Power

Steamboats, 6; monopoly, 15, 196. *See also* Shipping

Steel, world leadership, 136; Bessemer process, 138, 185; combination in, 142 f., 145 f., 190; structural, 153, 255; alloys, 181, 184; and expansion, 181, 188; open-hearth, 184 f.; World War and, 301. *See also* U. S. Steel Co., American Iron & Steel Assoc.

Steffens, Lincoln, 2, 265, 282; quoted, 266, 272

Stein, Gertrude, 349

Stephens, Alexander H., 95, 121

Stevens, Frank W., quoted, 69

Stevens, Thaddeus, 106

Stevenson, Job E., quoted, 158

Stewart, A. T., 153

Stewart, J. B., 110

Stillman, James, 182, 194, 196

Stock exchanges, development, 53, 73 ff.; and panic of 1857, 82–86; and railroad construction, 134–135; and securities, 74 ff., 82–86, 147 ff., 196 f., 321. *See also* Securities

Stockbridge, Francis B., 163

Stowe, Harriet Beecher, 94

Strikes, early factory, 19, 22; and the courts, 22; general, 26; and Contract Labor Law, 107; during Civil War, 117; Colorado Coal & Iron Co., 246; coal, 287

"Streamlining," 353

Strong, Josiah, 204, 205; quoted, 204, 250

Stuyvesant, Peter G., 68

Suffrage, 28, 284

Sugar Trust (American Sugar Refining Co.), 142, 146, 170

Sullivan, Louis, 255 f., 351

Sumner, Charles, 94, 97

Sumner, William Graham, 128; quoted, 263

Susquehanna river, 6, 211

Superior, Minn., 132

Supreme Court, *see* U. S. Govt. Supreme Court

Swank, James M., 174; quoted, 174 f.

Swift, Gustavus, 146

Sylvis, William, quoted, 117

Syracuse & Utica R. R., 69

T

Tacoma Building, 255

Taft, William H., 182, 209, 296, 356; as president, 288 ff.

Tammany Hall, 26, 65, 157, 159, 161, 266, 267

Taney, Roger B., 121

Tanners, village, 3

Tarbell, Ida, 282

Tariff, of 1816, 15 f.; agitation for, 15 ff.; and textiles, 16, 18, 105; and iron industry, 16, 18, 79, 105; and home market, 16; and sections, 16 ff., 34, 49 ff., 92, 96, 121; bills defeated, 16 f.; of 1824, 16; of 1828, 17 f.; of 1832, 18; of 1833, 18, 50; nullification, 35; of 1842, 50; of 1846, 50; and railroads, 78 f.; Republican Party and, 105, 165; New England and, 105; Pennsylvania and, 105; Act of 1860–61, 105; "Compensation" Act, 1862, 106; of 1864, 106; and fraud, 156 f.; and parties after Civil War, 165 ff.; of 1890, 173, 175; Standard Oil Co. and, 174; Commission, 174; of 1883, 1888, 174, 175; of 1894, 176; of 1909, 289; Progressives and, 289; reciprocity, 289; of 1913, 294; of 1922, 303, 345; of 1897, 310; and consumer, 310; of 1930, 345; and war debts, 345. See also Pressure groups, Propaganda, Corruption

Taussig, F. W., quoted, 106

Taxation, and Civil War, 106; and industrial combinations, 113; and laissez-faire, 121, 125; for railroads, 132, 134 f.; and patronage, 154, 156; income, 165, 167, 176, 288 f., 295, 344; farm, 225; in 1920's, 344. See also Tariff

Taylor, Frederick W., 184, 244 ff., 307 f.; quoted, 307

Taylor, J. B., quoted, 271

Taylor, John, 121

Taylor and White, 184

Teague, Walter D., 352

Technology, 14, 58, 181, 183 ff.; inferior to British, 8; rewards for improvement, 11; and combination, 61, 63, 183 ff., 236, 304 f.; and cities, 63, 153; and education, 183, 306; research in, 183 ff., 306; bankers and, 199 f.; World War and, 298 f., 303 ff.; and employment, 298 f., 304; and art, 350 ff. See also Electricity, Mechanization, Patents, Science

Telegraph, speeds communication, 56, 59, 116, 151; and labor organization, 66; combination in, 115; construction, 115–116, 136; profits, 115; government operation of, 302. See also Individual companies, Communication

Telephones, 136, 137, 151, 303; in World War, 302; in 1920, 309. See also American Telephone & Telegraph Co.

Tenancy, agricultural, 221 f., 224, 226, 327; urban, 327

Tennessee Coal & Iron Co., 146, 195

Tennessee Valley Authority, 325

Texas, 96, 224

Texas & Pacific R. R., 158

Textiles, and tariff, 16, 18, 105; capital in, 61; value of products, 61; spindles in, 61; number of factories, 61; and "Boston Associates," 71 f.; and Civil War, 105, 111, 113

Thayer, H. B., quoted, 340

Thoreau, Henry D., 53

Thrift, 123, 229, 298, 355. See also Savings

Ticknor, George, quoted, 104

Tidewater Pipeline Co., 144

Tilden, Samuel J., 159 ff.

Times (of London), quoted, 48

Tobacco, 3, 219, 305, 311

Toombs, Robert, quoted, 97

Townshend, John, quoted, 96

Trade, see Commerce, Merchandising, Shipping

Trade Associations, 61 f., 122, 227, 303; and prices, 61, 114; and labor, 66; and Civil War, 111, 114; on competition, 139 f.; agricultural, 222; newspaper, 270; World War and, 302; and Supreme Court, 304; in 1920's, 304 f., 331 ff., 346; and science, 306; and "American Plan," 334 f. See also Individual names of associations

Trade conventions, 35

Trade Unions, early committees, 19; before Civil War, 21 ff., 65 f., 233; appearance in New Jersey and Pennsylvania, 21 f.; in handicrafts, 24, 65; 117 f.; and law, 24; and Workers Parties, 25 f., 164; growth, 1834–1837, 26; and panic of 1837, 26 f.; and Civil War, 117 f.; and Sherman Act, 172, 281; and employers associations, 229, 238 f., 334 ff.; and turnover, 229; and accidents, 231, 232; after Civil War, 233 ff.; and wages, 234 f.; as social organizations, 235; and company unions, 246; N. A. M. and, 281, 334 ff.; and Clayton Act, 295; and radicalism, 332 ff.; and "American Plan," 333 ff.; and New Deal, 357. See also Labor, and individual organizations

The Trade Unions of Pennsylvania, 22

Transportation, builds markets, 6 ff., 40; steamboat monopoly, 15; ocean packets, 33 f.; and panic of 1837, 41 ff.; increasing speed, 56 f.; and the corporation, 67 ff.; "Boston Associates," in 71 f.; and cities, 80, 129, 151; consolidations, 114 f., 188 ff.; and oil refining, 144; electric, 185; and bankers,

196 ff.; farmers' cost, 216 f.; Grange and, 220 ff. *See also* Canals, Commerce, Railroads, Turnpikes
Trenton, 252
Trust companies, 189; number and resources, 192
"Trusts," industrial, 142, 355; overcapitalization of, 149 f., 197 f.; attacked, 170 ff.; and Sherman Act, 171 ff., 286, 289, 295, 348; Hill on, 189; giant, 190 ff.; and labor, 239; Roosevelt and, 286; Taft and, 289; and Courts, 286, 289, 348; and Clayton Act, 295, 348
Tulsa, 334
Tumulty, Joseph, 293
Turner, Frederick Jackson, 31
Turnpikes, in 1800, 3; early boom, 6; government, 42
Tweed Ring, 157, 159, 266, 267

U

Union Carbide Co., 303
Union League Club, 273
Union Mills, 146
Union Pacific R. R., 54; land grants, 108, 110; Federal Charter, 110; Crédit Mobilier, 110, 111; corruption, 110, 111, 132; loans, 133; Gould and, 148 f.
United Copper Co., 196
U. S. v. U. S. Steel Co., 286, 348
U. S. Chamber of Commerce, 306, 331
U. S. Forest Service, 290
U. S. Govt., Congress of, and internal improvements, 15, 50; and western lands, 38 f., 84, 107 ff., 132 f.; and excise laws, 105 f.; and labor, 106 f.; and railroads, 110 f., 132 f., 157 f., 169 f.; business men in, 162 ff.; and "trusts," 170 ff., 295; and money, 173 f.; and social problems, 275 f., 287, 288 f., 296, 357; Progressivism in, 288 ff.; speakership of House, 288; and "money trust," 202, 294; relief, 325 f., 357. *See also* Tariffs; Corruption; U. S. Govt., Senate
U. S. Govt., Dept. of Agriculture, 225; U. S. Forest Service in, 290
U. S. Govt., Dept. of Commerce, 345 f., 348; Bureau of Corporations in, 287
U. S. Govt., Dept. of Commerce and Labor, 287; Bureau of Corporations in, 287; separated, 288
U. S. Govt., Dept. of Justice, and "trusts," 286, 289, 348
U. S. Govt., Dept. of Labor, 288
U. S. Govt., Dept. of State, 182; and economic imperialism, 208 f.; Bureau of Foreign Commerce, 209
U. S. Govt., Federal Courts, and labor, 164, 241 ff., 279 f., 281; and I. C. C., 170, 286; and "trusts," 286, 289, 295,

348. *See also* U. S. Govt., Supreme Court
U. S. Govt., Senate of, and tariff, 17, 174 f., 176, 289; on railroads, 136, 169; businessmen in, 162 ff.; "millionaire's club," 164, 176; committee on education and labor, 335. *See also* U. S. Govt., Congress of; Parties
U. S. Govt., Supreme Court of, 177–180; John Marshall and, 15, 178, 179; and nationalism, 15, 178 ff.; *Trustees of Dartmouth College v. Woodward*, 15, 15 n.; *Gibbons v. Ogden*, 15; *Brown v. Maryland*, 15; *Wabash, St. Louis & Pacific Rwy. Co. v. Illinois*, 169, 179; and I. C. C., 170, 286; and income tax, 176, 288 f.; and Fourteenth Amendment, 178, 242; *Juilliard v. Greenman*, 179 f.; *Chicago, Milwaukee & St. Paul Rwy. Co. v. Minnesota*, 180; *Smythe v. Ames*, 180; and labor, 180, 241 ff.; *Bunting v. Oregon*, 242; Progressivism and, 279; *Muller v. Oregon*, 279; and "trusts," 286, 289, 348; and "rule of reason," 286, 348; and trade associations, 304 f.; *Maple Flooring Mfrs. Assoc. v. U. S.*, 304; *U. S. v. U. S. Steel Co.*, 286, 348; and holding companies, 348
U. S. Govt., Treasury Dept., 77; refused loans, 48 f.; and Civil War, 112; surplus, 175
U. S. Industrial Commission, 197
U. S. Steel Corp., 190, 242, 244; skips dividend, 198; and Supreme Court, 286, 348; and price leadership, 305; in So. America, 314
U. S. Telegraph Co., 115
University Settlement, 278
Utah, 334
Utilities, public, holding companies, 316 ff., 348; pressure groups, 331 f., 339 ff.; and institutional advertising, 338; and education, 339 f.; and politics, 340, 342 ff.; commissions, 348. *See also* Railroads, Electricity, Holding Companies
Utopianism, 27

V

Vail, Theodore, quoted, 183
Van Alen, John H., quoted, 163
Van Alen, Wm., 351
Vanderbilt, Cornelius, 68, 69, 94, 147, 148, 307
Vanderbilt, William H., 145; quoted, 144 f., 311
Van Doren and Havens, 110
Van Ness, Judge, quoted, 28
Van Sweringen brothers, 315 f.

Vauclain, Samuel M., quoted, 306
Veblen, Thorstein, 2, 128, 177
Venezuela, 314; "affair," 206
Vermont Central R. R., 75
Vicksburg, 112
Virginia, exports, 32; economic decline, 32; and secession, 96; John Brown's Raid, 97; Peace Convention, 101, 103
Voting Trusts, 187, 201 f.

W

Wabash Canal, 7
Wabash, St. Louis & Pacific Railway v. Illinois, 169, 180
Wade, Benjamin F., 94
Wages, before factory system, 9–10; in early factories, 19–20, 22–23; after Civil War, 228 f., 261; and unionism, 234 f.; and profit sharing, 245 f.; regulation of, 279 f., 282 f.; in twenties, 298 f., 304
Wake, 207
Wald, Lillian, 276
Walker, Robert J., quoted, 103
Walker, T. H., 110
Wall Street, 73 ff., 134, 293, 294; Klan and, 330
Waltham, Mass., 18
Wanamaker, John, 153, 163
War Industries Board, 301 f.
War of 1812, effects on manufacturing, 5, 11, 15 f.
Warburg, Paul M., 182, 194
Ward, John, 74
Washington (state), 131, 132
Washington, D. C., 334; bosses, 157
Weaver, James B., 167
Webster, Daniel, 87; and tariff, 16, 18; and "Boston Associates," 71
Weed, Thurlow, 96
Weld, Isaac, 94
Welfare Capitalism, 229, 232, 242–248, 306, 336 f.
West, 36–47; grain from, 13; and tariff, 16–17, 92; expansion, 30 f., 53 ff., 82–84, 130 ff., 211; businessmen in, 30 f., 55 f.; and Erie Canal, 33; and slavery, 36, 84; and democracy, 36–37; political demands of, 38, 92 ff., 173 f.; pioneers, 38; squatters, 38 ff.; speculators, 38 f., 82, 107–111; banking, 40, 43, 82, 85 f.; factories, 40; and foreign capital, 41 ff.; and eastern capital, 39 ff., 53 ff., 72, 93, 108–111, 131; and panic of 1837, 41 ff.; state debts, 48, 81; and optimism, 53 f., 82 f., 112; railroads, 54 f., 80 f., 93, 108–111, 112, 130–135; and art, 55; and panic of 1857, 81–86; and Demo-

cratic Party, 93; and Civil War, 92–93, 100, 102, 107 ff.; and Republican Party, 107–111; and Homesteads, 108, 111; and silver, 173 ff.; drought in, 218 f.; and employers associations, 239 f.; women and, 259 f. *See also* Agriculture, Land, North, Railroads, and individual states and cities
West Virginia, 333
Western & Atlantic R. R., 8
Western Electric Co., 340
Western R. R. (Mass.), 8, 114; stockholders, 69
Western Union, curtails competition, 115 f.; Gould's, 148 f.
Westinghouse, George, 153
Westinghouse Electric and Manufacturing Co., 183
Weston, George, quoted, 96
Weyerhaeuser, Frederick, 146
Weyler, "Butcher," 206
Whaling, 26
Wharton, Edith, 258
Wheat, 213, 214; early western, 13; machinery for, 58, 214; boom in, 218, 224 f.; problems of, 219 ff.; prices, 219
Wheeling, 80
Whisky industry, overexpanded, 139; pools, 141 f.; "trusts," 142 f., 170
White, Andrew D., 265
White, Wm. Allen, quoted, 163
Whitlock, Brand, quoted, 291 f.
Whitman, Walt, 53
Whitney, Asa, 54, 55
Whitney, Eli, 304
Whitney, George, 194
Wickersham, George W., 289
Wiggin, Timothy, 45
Wilde, George, 45
Wilkinson, H. H., 291
Wilkinson, John, 69
Wilson, Thomas, 45
Wilson, William L., 176
Wilson, Woodrow, 126, 276, 333, 356; on credit monopoly, 193 f.; on stifling of invention, 199; quoted, 203, 308; as candidate, 292; as president, 293 ff.
Wisconsin, 109; banking privileges banned, 80; railroad corruption in, 81; land grant, 132; political machines, 157, 163; Grange in, 169, 220; dairying in, 222; socialism in, 237; industrial commission, 282
Women, in factories, 19 ff., 279 f.; and arts, 258 ff.; and frontier, 259 f.; and reform, 260, 274 ff.; clubs, 260
Women's Christian Temperance Union, 346
Woodbridge, Alice, 276
Woodruff Sleeping Car Co. (Central Transportation Co.), 145

Wool, manufacturers, 14; and tariff, 16, 105. *See also* Textiles

Work, John C., 109

Workingman's Advocate, quoted, 14 f.

World War (First), 183; and agriculture, 224; and Progressives, 282, 296 f.; and private enterprise, 298; and technology, 298 f., 303 ff.; and America's economy, 300–303, 355; cost, 301; propaganda, 302; and civil liberties, 302; Army and Navy, 302; and politics of 1920's, 344 f.; debts, 345; bonus problem, 347; and art in 1920's, 349 f.

Wright, Fanny, 26

Wright, Frank L., 256, 351, 352

Wrigley, Wm., Jr., 341

Y

Y. M. C. A., 329

Y. W. C. A., 329

Yale University, 36, 128

Yancey, William L., 95

Yates, Governor, quoted, 100

Youmans, E. L., 125; quoted, 125

Young, Owen D., quoted, 316

Young Man's Own Book, 37

hARPER ⚜ TORChBOOKS

American Studies: General

HENRY STEELE COMMAGER, Ed.: The Struggle for Racial Equality TB/1300
CARL N. DEGLER: Out of Our Past: *The Forces that Shaped Modern America* CN/2
CARL N. DEGLER, Ed.: Pivotal Interpretations of American History
Vol. I TB/1240; Vol. II TB/1241
A. S. EISENSTADT, Ed.: The Craft of American History: *Selected Essays*
Vol. I TB/1255; Vol. II TB/1256
ROBERT L. HEILBRONER: The Limits of American Capitalism TB/1305
JOHN HIGHAM, Ed.: The Reconstruction of American History TB/1068
ROBERT H. JACKSON: The Supreme Court in the American System of Government TB/1106
JOHN F. KENNEDY: A Nation of Immigrants. *Illus. Revised and Enlarged. Introduction by Robert F. Kennedy* TB/1118
RICHARD B. MORRIS: Fair Trial: *Fourteen Who Stood Accused, from Anne Hutchinson to Alger Hiss* TB/1335
GUNNAR MYRDAL: An American Dilemma: *The Negro Problem and Modern Democracy. Introduction by the Author.*
Vol. I TB/1443; Vol. II TB/1444
GILBERT OSOFSKY, Ed.: The Burden of Race: *A Documentary History of Negro-White Relations in America* TB/1405
ARNOLD ROSE: The Negro in America: *The Condensed Version of Gunnar Myrdal's* An American Dilemma. *Second Edition* TB/3048
JOHN E. SMITH: Themes in American Philosophy: *Purpose, Experience and Community* TB/1466
WILLIAM R. TAYLOR: Cavalier and Yankee: *The Old South and American National Character* TB/1474

American Studies: Colonial

BERNARD BAILYN: The New England Merchants in the Seventeenth Century TB/1149
ROBERT E. BROWN: Middle-Class Democracy and Revolution in Massachusetts, 1691-1780. *New Introduction by Author* TB/1413
JOSEPH CHARLES: The Origins of the American Party System TB/1049
WESLEY FRANK CRAVEN: The Colonies in Transition: 1660-1712† TB/3084

CHARLES GIBSON: Spain in America † TB/3077
CHARLES GIBSON, Ed.: The Spanish Tradition in America + HR/1351
LAWRENCE HENRY GIPSON: The Coming of the Revolution: 1763-1775. † *Illus.* TB/3007
PERRY MILLER: Errand Into the Wilderness TB/1139
PERRY MILLER & T. H. JOHNSON, Eds.: The Puritans: *A Sourcebook of Their Writings*
Vol. I TB/1093; Vol. II TB/1094
EDMUND S. MORGAN: The Puritan Family: *Religion and Domestic Relations in Seventeenth Century New England* TB/1227
WALLACE NOTESTEIN: The English People on the Eve of Colonization: 1603-1630. † *Illus.* TB/3006
LOUIS B. WRIGHT: The Cultural Life of the American Colonies: 1607-1763. † *Illus.* TB/3005

American Studies: The Revolution to 1860

JOHN R. ALDEN: The American Revolution: 1775-1783. † *Illus.* TB/3011
RAY A. BILLINGTON: The Far Western Frontier: 1830-1860. † *Illus.* TB/3012
GEORGE DANGERFIELD: The Awakening of American Nationalism, 1815-1828. † *Illus.* TB/3061
CLEMENT EATON: The Growth of Southern Civilization, 1790-1860. † *Illus.* TB/3040
LOUIS FILLER: The Crusade against Slavery: 1830-1860. † *Illus.* TB/3029
WILLIM W. FREEHLING: Prelude to Civil War: *The Nullification Controversy in South Carolina, 1816-1836* TB/1359
THOMAS JEFFERSON: Notes on the State of Virginia. ‡ *Edited by Thomas P. Abernethy* TB/3052
JOHN C. MILLER: The Federalist Era: 1789-1801. † *Illus.* TB/3027
RICHARD B. MORRIS: The American Revolution Reconsidered TB/1363
GILBERT OSOFSKY, Ed.: Puttin' On Ole Massa: *The Slave Narratives of Henry Bibb, William Wells Brown, and Solomon Northup* ‡ TB/1432
FRANCIS S. PHILBRICK: The Rise of the West, 1754-1830. † *Illus.* TB/3067
MARSHALL SMELSER: The Democratic Republic, 1801-1815 † TB/1406

---

† The New American Nation Series, edited by Henry Steele Commager and Richard B. Morris.
‡ American Perspectives series, edited by Bernard Wishy and William E. Leuchtenburg.
a History of Europe series, edited by J. H. Plumb.
§ The Library of Religion and Culture, edited by Benjamin Nelson.
‖ Researches in the Social, Cultural, and Behavioral Sciences, edited by Benjamin Nelson.
Σ Harper Modern Science Series, edited by James A. Newman.
° Not for sale in Canada.
+ Documentary History of the United States series, edited by Richard B. Morris.
# Documentary History of Western Civilization series, edited by Eugene C. Black and Leonard W. Levy.
Λ The Economic History of the United States series, edited by Henry David et al.
¶ European Perspectives series, edited by Eugene C. Black.
** Contemporary Essays series, edited by Leonard W. Levy.
* The Stratum Series, edited by John Hale.

LOUIS B. WRIGHT: Culture on the Moving Frontier TB/1053

American Studies: The Civil War to 1900

T. C. COCHRAN & WILLIAM MILLER: The Age of Enterprise: *A Social History of Industrial America* TB/1054
W. A. DUNNING: Reconstruction, Political and Economic: 1865-1877 TB/1073
HAROLD U. FAULKNER: Politics, Reform and Expansion: 1890-1900. † *Illus.* TB/3020
GEORGE M. FREDRICKSON: The Inner Civil War: *Northern Intellectuals and the Crisis of the Union* TB/1358
JOHN A. GARRATY: The New Commonwealth, 1877-1890 † TB/1410
HELEN HUNT JACKSON: A Century of Dishonor: *The Early Crusade for Indian Reform.* † *Edited by Andrew F. Rolle* TB/3063
WILLIAM G. MCLOUGHLIN, Ed.: The American Evangelicals, 1800-1900: An Anthology ‡ TB/1382
JAMES S. PIKE: The Prostrate State: *South Carolina under Negro Government.* ‡ *Intro. by Robert F. Durden* TB/3085
VERNON LANE WHARTON: The Negro in Mississippi, 1865-1890 TB/1178

American Studies: The Twentieth Century

RAY STANNARD BAKER: Following the Color Line: *American Negro Citizenship in Progressive Era.* ‡ *Edited by Dewey W. Grantham, Jr. Illus.* TB/3053
RANDOLPH S. BOURNE: War and the Intellectuals: *Collected Essays, 1915-1919.* ‡ *Edited by Carl Resek* TB/3043
A. RUSSELL BUCHANAN: The United States and World War II. † *Illus.*
Vol. I TB/3044; Vol. II TB/3045
THOMAS C. COCHRAN: The American Business System: *A Historical Perspective, 1900-1955* TB/1080
FOSTER RHEA DULLES: America's Rise to World Power: 1898-1954. † *Illus.* TB/3021
HAROLD U. FAULKNER: The Decline of Laissez Faire, 1897-1917 TB/1397
JOHN D. HICKS: Republican Ascendancy: 1921-1933. † *Illus.* TB/3041
WILLIAM E. LEUCHTENBURG: Franklin D. Roosevelt and the New Deal: 1932-1940. † *Illus.* TB/3025
WILLIAM E. LEUCHTENBURG, Ed.: The New Deal: *A Documentary History* + HR/1354
ARTHUR S. LINK: Woodrow Wilson and the Progressive Era: 1910-1917. † *Illus.* TB/3023
BROADUS MITCHELL: Depression Decade: *From New Era through New Deal, 1929-1941* ∧ TB/1439
GEORGE E. MOWRY: The Era of Theodore Roosevelt and the Birth of Modern America: 1900-1912. † *Illus.* TB/3022
WILLIAM PRESTON, JR.: Aliens and Dissenters:
TWELVE SOUTHERNERS: I'll Take My Stand: *The South and the Agrarian Tradition. Intro. by Louis D. Rubin, Jr.; Biographical Essays by Virginia Rock* TB/1072

Art, Art History, Aesthetics

ERWIN PANOFSKY: Renaissance and Renascences in Western Art. *Illus.* TB/1447
ERWIN PANOFSKY: Studies in Iconology: *Humanistic Themes in the Art of the Renaissance. 180 illus.* TB/1077
HEINRICH ZIMMER: Myths and Symbols in Indian Art and Civilization. *70 illus.* TB/2005

Asian Studies

WOLFGANG FRANKE: China and the West: *The Cultural Encounter, 13th to 20th Centuries. Trans. by R. A. Wilson* TB/1326
L. CARRINGTON GOODRICH: A Short History of the Chinese People. *Illus.* TB/3015

Economics & Economic History

C. E. BLACK: The Dynamics of Modernization: *A Study in Comparative History* TB/1321
GILBERT BURCK & EDITORS OF *Fortune:* The Computer Age: *And its Potential for Management* TB/1179
ROBERT L. HEILBRONER: The Future as History: *The Historic Currents of Our Time and the Direction in Which They Are Taking America* TB/1386
ROBERT L. HEILBRONER: The Great Ascent: *The Struggle for Economic Development in Our Time* TB/3030
FRANK H. KNIGHT: The Economic Organization TB/1214
DAVID S. LANDES: Bankers and Pashas: *International Finance and Economic Imperialism in Egypt. New Preface by the Author* TB/1412
ROBERT LATOUCHE: The Birth of Western Economy: *Economic Aspects of the Dark Ages* TB/1290
W. ARTHUR LEWIS: The Principles of Economic Planning. *New Introduction by the Author*° TB/1436
WILLIAM MILLER, Ed.: Men in Business: *Essays on the Historical Role of the Entrepreneur* TB/1081
HERBERT A. SIMON: The Shape of Automation: *For Men and Management* TB/1245

Historiography and History of Ideas

J. BRONOWSKI & BRUCE MAZLISH: The Western Intellectual Tradition: *From Leonardo to Hegel* TB/3001
WILHELM DILTHEY: Pattern and Meaning in History: *Thoughts on History and Society.*° *Edited with an Intro. by H. P. Rickman* TB/1075
J. H. HEXTER: More's Utopia: *The Biography of an Idea. Epilogue by the Author* TB/1195
H. STUART HUGHES: History as Art and as Science: *Twin Vistas on the Past* TB/1207
ARTHUR O. LOVEJOY: The Great Chain of Being: *A Study of the History of an Idea* TB/1009
RICHARD H. POPKIN: The History of Scepticism from Erasmus to Descartes. *Revised Edition* TB/1391
BRUNO SNELL: The Discovery of the Mind: *The Greek Origins of European Thought* TB/1018

History: General

HANS KOHN: The Age of Nationalism: *The First Era of Global History* TB/1380
BERNARD LEWIS: The Arabs in History TB/1029
BERNARD LEWIS: The Middle East and the West ° TB/1274

History: Ancient

A. ANDREWS: The Greek Tyrants TB/1103
THEODOR H. GASTER: Thespis: *Ritual Myth and Drama in the Ancient Near East* TB/1281

A. H. M. JONES, Ed.: A History of Rome through the Fifth Century # *Vol. I: The Republic* HR/1364
Vol. II The Empire: HR/1460
SAMUEL NOAH KRAMER: Sumerian Mythology TB/1055
NAPHTALI LEWIS & MEYER REINHOLD, Eds.: Roman Civilization *Vol. I: The Republic* TB/1231
Vol. II: The Empire TB/1232

History: Medieval

NORMAN COHN: The Pursuit of the Millennium: *Revolutionary Messianism in Medieval and Reformation Europe* TB/1037
F. L. GANSHOF: Feudalism TB/1058
F. L. GANSHOF: The Middle Ages: *A History of International Relations. Translated by Rémy Hall* TB/1411
HENRY CHARLES LEA: The Inquisition of the Middle Ages. || *Introduction by Walter Ullmann* TB/1456

History: Renaissance & Reformation

JACOB BURCKHARDT: The Civilization of the Renaissance in Italy. *Introduction by Benjamin Nelson and Charles Trinkaus. Illus.* Vol. I TB/40; Vol. II TB/41
JOHN CALVIN & JACOPO SADOLETO: A Reformation Debate. *Edited by John C. Olin* TB/1239
J. H. ELLIOTT: Europe Divided, 1559-1598 *a* ° TB/1414
G. R. ELTON: Reformation Europe, 1517-1559 ° *a* TB/1270
HANS J. HILLERBRAND, Ed., The Protestant Reformation # HR/1342
JOHAN HUIZINGA: Erasmus and the Age of Reformation. *Illus.* TB/19
JOEL HURSTFIELD: The Elizabethan Nation TB/1312
JOEL HURSTFIELD, Ed.: The Reformation Crisis TB/1267
PAUL OSKAR KRISTELLER: Renaissance Thought: *The Classic, Scholastic, and Humanist Strains* TB/1048
DAVID LITTLE: Religion, Order and Law: *A Study in Pre-Revolutionary England.* § *Preface by R. Bellah* TB/1418
PAOLO ROSSI: Philosophy, Technology, and the Arts, in the Early Modern Era 1400-1700. || *Edited by Benjamin Nelson. Translated by Salvator Attanasio* TB/1458
H. R. TREVOR-ROPER: The European Witch-craze of the Sixteenth and Seventeenth Centuries and Other Essays ° TB/1416

History: Modern European

ALAN BULLOCK: Hitler, A Study in Tyranny ° *Revised Edition. Illus.* TB/1123
JOHANN GOTTLIEB FICHTE: Addresses to the German Nation. *Ed. with Intro. by George A. Kelly* ¶ TB/1366
ALBERT GOODWIN: The French Revolution TB/1064
STANLEY HOFFMANN et al.: In Search of France: *The Economy, Society and Political System In the Twentieth Century* TB/1219
H. STUART HUGHES: The Obstructed Path: *French Social Thought in the Years of Desperation* TB/1451
JOHAN HUIZINGA: Dutch Civilisation in the 17th Century and Other Essays TB/1453

JOHN MCMANNERS: European History, 1789-1914: *Men, Machines and Freedom* TB/1419
HUGH SETON-WATSON: Eastern Europe Between the Wars, 1918-1941 TB/1330
ALBERT SOREL: Europe Under the Old Regime. *Translated by Francis H. Herrick* TB/1121
A. J. P. TAYLOR: From Napoleon to Lenin: *Historical Essays* ° TB/1268
A. J. P. TAYLOR: The Habsburg Monarchy, 1809-1918: *A History of the Austrian Empire and Austria-Hungary* ° TB/1187
J. M. THOMPSON: European History, 1494-1789 TB/1431
H. R. TREVOR-ROPER: Historical Essays TB/1269

Literature & Literary Criticism

W. J. BATE: From Classic to Romantic: *Premises of Taste in Eighteenth Century England* TB/1036
VAN WYCK BROOKS: Van Wyck Brooks: The Early Years: *A Selection from his Works, 1908-1921 Ed. with Intro. by Claire Sprague* TB/3082
RICHMOND LATTIMORE, Translator: The Odyssey of Homer TB/1389
ROBERT PREYER, Ed.: Victorian Literature ** TB/1302

Philosophy

HENRI BERGSON: Time and Free Will: *An Essay on the Immediate Data of Consciousness* ° TB/1021
H. J. BLACKHAM: Six Existentialist Thinkers: *Kierkegaard, Nietzsche, Jaspers, Marcel, Heidegger, Sartre* ° TB/1002
J. M. BOCHENSKI: The Methods of Contemporary Thought. *Trans. by Peter Caws* TB/1377
ERNST CASSIRER: Rousseau, Kant and Goethe. *Intro. by Peter Gay* TB/1092
MICHAEL GELVEN: A Commentary on Heidegger's "Being and Time" TB/1464
J. GLENN GRAY: Hegel and Greek Thought TB/1409
W. K. C. GUTHRIE: The Greek Philosophers: *From Thales to Aristotle* ° TB/1008
G. W. F. HEGEL: Phenomenology of Mind. ° || *Introduction by George Lichtheim* TB/1303
MARTIN HEIDEGGER: Discourse on Thinking. *Translated with a Preface by John M. Anderson and E. Hans Freund. Introduction by John M. Anderson* TB/1459
F. H. HEINEMANN: Existentialism and the Modern Predicament TB/28
WERER HEISENBERG: Physics and Philosophy: *The Revolution in Modern Science. Intro. by F. S. C. Northrop* TB/549
EDMUND HUSSERL: Phenomenology and the Crisis of Philosophy. § *Translated with an Introduction by Quentin Lauer* TB/1170
IMMANUEL KANT: Groundwork of the Metaphysic of Morals. *Translated and Analyzed by H. J. Paton* TB/1159
WALTER KAUFMANN, Ed.: Religion From Tolstoy to Camus: *Basic Writings on Religious Truth and Morals* TB/123
QUENTIN LAUER: Phenomenology: *Its Genesis and Prospect. Preface by Aron Gurwitsch* TB/1169
MICHAEL POLANYI: Personal Knowledge: *Towards a Post-Critical Philosophy* TB/1158
WILLARD VAN ORMAN QUINE: Elementary Logic *Revised Edition* TB/577
WILHELM WINDELBAND: A History of Philosophy *Vol. I: Greek, Roman, Medieval* TB/38

3

Vol. II: Renaissance, Enlightenment, Modern
TB/39
LUDWIG WITTGENSTEIN: The Blue and Brown
Books °   TB/1211
LUDWIG WITTGENSTEIN: Notebooks, 1914-1916
TB/1441

Political Science & Government

C. E. BLACK: The Dynamics of Modernization:
A Study in Comparative History TB/1321
DENIS W. BROGAN: Politics in America. *New
Introduction by the Author* TB/1469
ROBERT CONQUEST: Power and Policy in the
USSR: *The Study of Soviet Dynastics* °
TB/1307
JOHN B. MORRALL: Political Thought in Medieval
Times   TB/1076
KARL R. POPPER: The Open Society and Its
Enemies *Vol. I: The Spell of Plato* TB/1101
*Vol. II: The High Tide of Prophecy: Hegel,
Marx, and the Aftermath* TB/1102
HENRI DE SAINT-SIMON: Social Organization, The
Science of Man, and Other Writings. ||
*Edited and Translated with an Introduction
by Felix Markham* TB/1152
CHARLES SCHOTTLAND, Ed.: The Welfare State **
TB/1323
JOSEPH A. SCHUMPETER: Capitalism, Socialism
and Democracy TB/3008

Psychology

LUDWIG BINSWANGER: Being-in-the-World: *Se-
lected Papers.* || *Trans. with Intro. by Jacob
Needleman* TB/1365
MIRCEA ELIADE: Cosmos and History: *The Myth
of the Eternal Return* § TB/2050
MIRCEA ELIADE: Myth and Reality TB/1369
SIGMUND FREUD: On Creativity and the Uncon-
scious: *Papers on the Psychology of Art,
Literature, Love, Religion.* § *Intro. by Ben-
jamin Nelson* TB/45
J. GLENN GRAY: The Warriors: *Reflections on
Men in Battle. Introduction by Hannah
Arendt* TB/1294
WILLIAM JAMES: Psychology: *The Briefer
Course. Edited with an Intro. by Gordon
Allport* TB/1034

Religion: Ancient and Classical, Biblical and
Judaic Traditions

MARTIN BUBER: Eclipse of God: *Studies in the
Relation Between Religion and Philosophy*
TB/12
MARTIN BUBER: Hasidism and Modern Man.
Edited and Translated by Maurice Friedman
TB/839
MARTIN BUBER: The Knowledge of Man. *Edited
with an Introduction by Maurice Friedman.
Translated by Maurice Friedman and Ronald
Gregor Smith* TB/135
MARTIN BUBER: Moses. *The Revelation and the
Covenant* TB/837
MARTIN BUBER: The Origin and Meaning of
Hasidism. *Edited and Translated by Maurice
Friedman* TB/835
MARTIN BUBER: The Prophetic Faith TB/73
MARTIN BUBER: Two Types of Faith: *Interpene-
tration of Judaism and Christianity* ° TB/75
M. S. ENSLIN: Christian Beginnings TB/5
M. S. ENSLIN: The Literature of the Christian
Movement TB/6
HENRI FRANKFORT: Ancient Egyptian Religion:
An Interpretation TB/77

Religion: Early Christianity Through
Reformation

ANSELM OF CANTERBURY: Truth, Freedom, and
Evil: *Three Philosophical Dialogues. Edited
and Translated by Jasper Hopkins and Herbert Richardson* TB/317
EDGAR J. GOODSPEED: A Life of Jesus TB/1
ROBERT M. GRANT: Gnosticism and Early Christianity TB/136

Religion: Oriental Religions

TOR ANDRAE: Mohammed: *The Man and His
Faith* § TB/62
EDWARD CONZE: Buddhism: *Its Essence and De-
velopment.* ° *Foreword by Arthur Waley*
TB/58
H. G. CREEL: Confucius and the Chinese Way
TB/63
FRANKLIN EDGERTON, Trans. & Ed.: The Bhaga-
vad Gita TB/115
SWAMI NIKHILANANDA, Trans. & Ed.: The
Upanishads TB/114
D. T. SUZUKI: On Indian Mahayana Buddhism.
° *Ed. with Intro. by Edward Conze.* TB/1403

Science and Mathematics

W. E. LE GROS CLARK: The Antecedents of
Man: *An Introduction to the Evolution of
the Primates.* ° *Illus.* TB/559
ROBERT E. COKER: Streams, Lakes, Ponds. *Illus.*
TB/586
ROBERT E. COKER: This Great and Wide Sea: *An
Introduction to Oceanography and Marine
Biology. Illus.* TB/551
WILLARD VAN ORMAN QUINE: Mathematical Logic
TB/558

Sociology and Anthropology

REINHARD BENDIX: Work and Authority in In-
dustry: *Ideologies of Management in the
Course of Industrialization* TB/3035
KENNETH B. CLARK: Dark Ghetto: *Dilemmas of
Social Power. Foreword by Gunnar Myrdal*
TB/1317
KENNETH CLARK & JEANNETTE HOPKINS: A Rele-
vant War Against Poverty: *A Study of Com-
munity Action Programs and Observable So-
cial Change* TB/1480
LEWIS COSER, Ed.: Political Sociology TB/1293
GARY T. MARX: Protest and Prejudice: *A Study
of Belief in the Black Community* TB/1435
ROBERT K. MERTON, LEONARD BROOM, LEONARD S.
COTTRELL, JR., Editors: Sociology Today:
Problems and Prospects ||
Vol. I TB/1173; Vol. II TB/1174
GILBERT OSOFSKY, Ed.: The Burden of Race: *A
Documentary History of Negro-White Rela-
tions in America* TB/1405
GILBERT OSOFSKY: Harlem: The Making of a
Ghetto: *Negro New York 1890-1930* ° TB/1381
PHILIP RIEFF: The Triumph of the Therapeutic:
Uses of Faith After Freud TB/1360
ARNOLD ROSE: The Negro in America: *The Con-
densed Version of Gunnar Myrdal's* An
American Dilemma. *Second Edition* TB/3048
GEORGE ROSEN: Madness in Society: *Chapters in
the Historical Sociology of Mental Illness.* ||
Preface by Benjamin Nelson TB/1337
PITIRIM A. SOROKIN: Contemporary Sociological
Theories: *Through the First Quarter of the
Twentieth Century* TB/3046
FLORIAN ZNANIECKI: The Social Role of the
Man of Knowledge. *Introduction by Lewis
A. Coser* TB/1372